Sports Illustrated

PRO FOOTBALL '90-91

Sports Illustrated

PRO FOOTBALL '90-91

By Peter King

WITH JILL LIEBER AND RICK REILLY

Copyright 1991 The Time Inc. Magazine Company

Published by Oxmoor House, Inc.
1271 Avenue of the Americas
New York, New York 10020

ISBN: O-8487-1040-1
ISSN: 1049-3670

Manufactured in The United States of America
First Printing 1991

Senior Editor: **Morin Bishop**
Director of Manufacturing: **Jerry Higdon**
      Production Manager: **Rick Litton**
      Associate Production Manager: **Terri Beste**

PRO FOOTBALL '90–91
Editor: **Jay Jennings**
      Editorial Assistants: **Stacey Harmis, Roxana Lonergan**
      Copyreader: **Pamela Roberts**
      Reporter: **Stefanie Krasnow**
Director of Photography & Research: **Geraldine Howard**
      Photography Editor: **Robert Mitchell**
      Research Assistants: **Jan Baxter, Norma Mandt**
Designer: **Steven Hoffman**
      Design Assistant: **Magdalena Deskur**
Artist: **Victor Juhász**

Original work by the following SPORTS ILLUSTRATED senior writers
and staff writers provided the basis for portions of PRO FOOTBALL '90–91:
Jay Greenberg: feature on Anthony Munoz.
Richard Hoffer: story on the L.A. Raiders–Cincinnati playoff game.
Peter King: stories on the Cincinnati-Houston,
Buffalo-Miami and Buffalo–L.A. Raiders playoff games.
Jill Lieber: features on the Matthews brothers,
Andre Rison and Herschel Walker.
Bruce Newman: feature on Burt Grossman.
Rick Reilly: stories on the Miami–Kansas City, Washington–San Francisco
and N.Y. Giants–San Francisco playoff games.
Rick Telander: feature on Paul Tagliabue and story on the
Chicago–New Orleans playoff game.
Paul Zimmerman: feature on Warren Moon and stories on
the Washington-Philadelphia and N.Y. Giants–Chicago playoff game
and the Super Bowl.

To order SPORTS ILLUSTRATED magazine, write to:
      SPORTS ILLUSTRATED Subscription Service Department
      P.O. Box 60001
      Tampa, Florida 33660-0001

C O N T E N T S

GENIUS OF THE YEAR

We now have a new genius—Bill Parcells, the coach of the Giants. To be a genius in the National Football League, a coach has to win a Super Bowl or two and have an accepted handle. Like Vince Lombardi: genius disciplinarian. Don Shula: offensive genius. Bill Walsh: passing-game and organizational genius. Bill Parcells: motivational genius.

How does Parcells do it? Oh, he'll make the occasional stirring speech, but generally his approach is more personal. Parcells begins his man-to-man prodding in the locker room at 8 in the morning, when the players begin to appear for the day's work. "It's early," he says, "and that's when you can get their attention." He might hit seven or eight stools over the next hour, telling Everson Walls he had better not let Art Monk make that quick first step by him that week, reminding Leonard Marshall he

had better get to Mark Rypien or he would soon find a warm spot on the bench, coaxing Bart Oates to master the Washington stunts so he'll be able to open holes for the running game.

Many of these pointed tips are accompanied by one of his trademark Parcellsisms, a collection of no-nonsense aphorisms that usually cut right to the heart of the matter. And so it is in honor of Parcells that we bring you the 1990 story of the NFL as seen through the quips and quotes of Mister Motivation.

"It's not a sprint. It's a marathon."
          —PARCELLS on the football season.

The Giants and the 49ers severely tested this one. For two months, they were Ben Johnson and Carl Lewis dashing neck-and-neck, 10 meters ahead of the field. They both started 10–0. They both lost to arch-rivals in Week 12, the Giants to the Eagles and the 49ers to the Rams. Then they fought an even defensive struggle in December at Candlestick Park, with Phil Simms leading a drive for the winning score in San Francisco territory, wriggling out of the pocket to pass as the clock wound down to :00, then getting wrapped up by 49er Kevin Fagan for the game-ending sack. The 49ers won, 7–3. Now the marathon was on. "There's no question in my mind that we'll meet again in the playoffs," Giants defensive end Leonard Marshall crystal-balled. Nice hunch, big fella. Meanwhile, over in the other conference, the Bills, led by Jim Kelly and Thurman Thomas, the league's best all-purpose back, were showing that they had some staying power too. In fact, as the season turned for home, the Bills exhibited the NFL's most potent kick, pulling away from the rest of the field in winning four

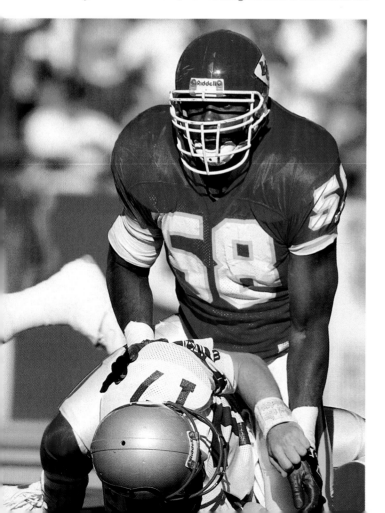

◀ Thomas's seven sacks against Seattle was one of the season's greatest individual performances. Unfortunately, the one sack he didn't make cost Kansas City the game.

out of their last five regular season games, with the loss coming in a meaningless finale with Washington.

The league's other sprinters all fell back as winter descended on the sport. Cincinnati, its vintage offense churning through September, burst out 3–0 but couldn't stay on track, finishing at a disappointing 9–7. The Raiders began 4–0 and won the AFC West, at 12–4, for the first time since 1985. But just as coach Art Shell was proclaiming the Raiders' seemingly sturdy defense "probably the best in Raider history," the walls came tumbling down in Buffalo. AFC Championship Game: Bills 51, Raiders 3. In the NFC, the Bears, at 9–1, had their best start under Mike Ditka since the Super Bowl season of 1985. But they lost five of their final eight as their aging offensive and defensive lines and lack of quarterback depth cost them dearly.

▲ Though Parcells sometimes delivers a pointed barb during the game, his usual motivational tools are early morning one-on-one sessions and trademark Parcellsisms.

"My players know where they stand at all times. I just tell 'em: 'I go by what I see.' "
—PARCELLS, on picking his starters.

What we saw, first of all, was some of the game's most impressive individual performances ever. In Week 6, a running back for the Chiefs named Barry Word, who had been working for a long-distance phone company a year earlier, rushed for 200 yards against Detroit. No warning. It just happened. Four Sundays later, Chiefs linebacker Derrick Thomas sacked Seattle QB Dave Krieg a league-record seven times. Seven times! Then Krieg slipped through Thomas's grasp on the last play of the game to throw the winning TD pass. In Week 15, the Chiefs were in

▲ The Patriots' sorry season got even sadder in the aftermath of the Lisa Olson incident as Kiam made matters worse with his bumbling response and callous comments.

on another great day, but this time on the receiving end. Warren Moon of the Oilers threw for 527 yards, the second-most in history, in a 27–10 win. In the playoffs, one lineman above all did himself proud. Giants left tackle Jumbo Elliott in successive weeks snuffed out three of the best right ends in football—Richard Dent, Kevin Fagan and Bruce Smith—as the Giants made their Super Bowl run.

Unfortunately what we saw wasn't always graceful. In fact, it was often downright shameful. New England owner Victor Kiam led the league in shame in 1990. When *Boston Herald* reporter Lisa Olson was sexually harassed by several Patriots while conducting a locker room interview, Kiam tried to dismiss the incident, calling it "a flyspeck in the ocean." Then he spent the rest of the season apologizing all over himself when the league disciplined him and the club. Buffoon that he is, Kiam couldn't leave it alone. After the season, at an all-male sports dinner in Connecticut, he told a lewd joke involving Olson. Get a job, Victor. And go back to the Dark Ages while you're at it.

"It ain't how. It's how many."

—PARCELLS, on winning, and wins.

Or, in the case of the NFL's new television contract: It ain't how; it's how much. In 1987, '88 and '89, the 28 league teams each earned $17 million per year from their network and cable-TV contracts. In March 1990, the NFL finalized a deal with the three networks and cable outlets ESPN and TNT that would bring each team an average of $32 million annually from '90 through '93. In belt-tightening times, it was an amazing deal. Why did the TV moguls agree to it? Simple. Cable maverick Ted Turner offered the NFL a blank check to win half of the Sunday-night cable package, thereby forcing the networks and ESPN to follow suit. Ain't that America?

Of course such hard-won riches need protecting. So the NFL teams were busy shoring up the World League of American Football, which was scheduled to begin play in spring 1991. Great idea, this WLAF. It means the NFL won't have to worry about new leagues popping up and inflating its salary structure. The WLAF, with franchises in London, Frankfurt and Barcelona as well as seven North American sites, would be a nice Triple A league, developing players and bringing a full slate of pro football to Europe for the first time.

Did all this make Al Davis feel financially comfortable? Apparently not. The Raiders played a cruel guessing game with their fans, dickering with Sacramento, abandoning Irwindale, planning to move from L.A. to Oakland, abandoning Oakland again and finally coming back to L.A.

But is that the last word on Davis's well-traveled franchise? Here are the Vegas odds on where the Raiders will open their 1992 home season:

1. Oakland, 4–1.
2. Sacramento, 7–1.
3. Kalamazoo, Michigan, 10–1.
4. Beaver Crossing, Nebraska, 25–1.
5. Los Angeles, 500–1.

"He doesn't know if it's blown up or stuffed with feathers."

—PARCELLS on football neophytes.

In 1990, the off-field news often became as big as the games. The Lisa Olson story was reported in September almost as avidly as the American troop buildup in the Middle East. Each network and cable outlet had its own well-paid inside information guy. And a half-hour before kickoff, America sat back to hear the latest gossip. After Cleveland's 1–3 start, the media speculated endlessly about how long embattled coach Bud Carson would last and who his replacement would be. He was fired eventually, but only after the Browns fell to 2–7.

Storms swirled around other teams too. We sighed when Eagle owner Norman Braman finally fired the coach he always hated, Buddy Ryan. It was like a Ford management type canning the union leader from the assembly line. "The owner is a moron," Eagle tight end Keith Jackson said succinctly. Elsewhere, the Bucs were their usual lousy selves at 6–10, and owner Hugh Culverhouse chose, as owners often do, to fire the coach, Ray Perkins. Culverhouse offered Bill Walsh $2 million a year and 10% of the team to take the coach and G.M. job. But Walsh decided to stay with NBC and live in his beloved San Francisco Bay Area, so Culverhouse handed the job to interim coach Richard Williamson. Some ringing endorsement, Hugh. Williamson got a two-year contract, and his coaching staff was handpicked for him. He's sure to last until at least October.

"God is playing in some of these games."

—PARCELLS on fate.

Look at the last two games of the year.

NFC Championship Game, Jan. 20, at San Francisco. The 49ers, with 2:36 left, trying to run out the clock on a 13–12 win, send running back Roger Craig into the line at the New York 40. The Giants swarm Craig, and nosetackle Erik Howard's helmet hits the ball, which falls into Lawrence Taylor's hands at the 43. Hostetler drives the Giants to the San Francisco 25, and with no time left, Matt Bahr's 42-yard field goal drifts just inside the left upright. Giants win 15–13.

Super Bowl XXV, Jan. 27, at Tampa. Bahr's 21-yarder midway through the fourth quarter puts the Giants ahead 20–19. With eight seconds left and the Bills at the Giants 30, kicker Scott Norwood trots onto the field. The kick will be from 47 yards away. According to the Elias Sports Bureau, which keeps stats for the NFL, the yard line where kickers begin to miss more than they make is the 47. And Norwood is excited. The adrenaline flows, and he moves toward the ball. The adrenaline flows too much. His plant foot is three inches ahead of where it should be. He pushes the kick wide right, by about five feet. Giants win again.

"Like I've told you guys before," a sweaty and hoarse Parcells said later, "God is playing in some of these games."

1990. Good year for Parcells, and for Parcellsisms too, wasn't it?

▼ The Giants defense took a vicious toll on Montana in the NFC Championship Game, denying him a chance to become the first QB to win three straight Super Bowls.

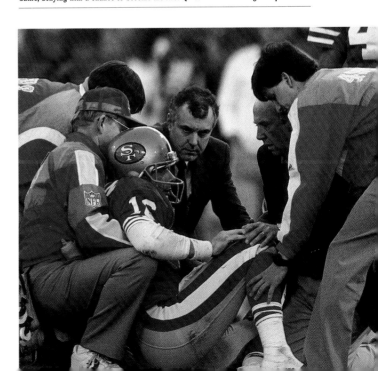

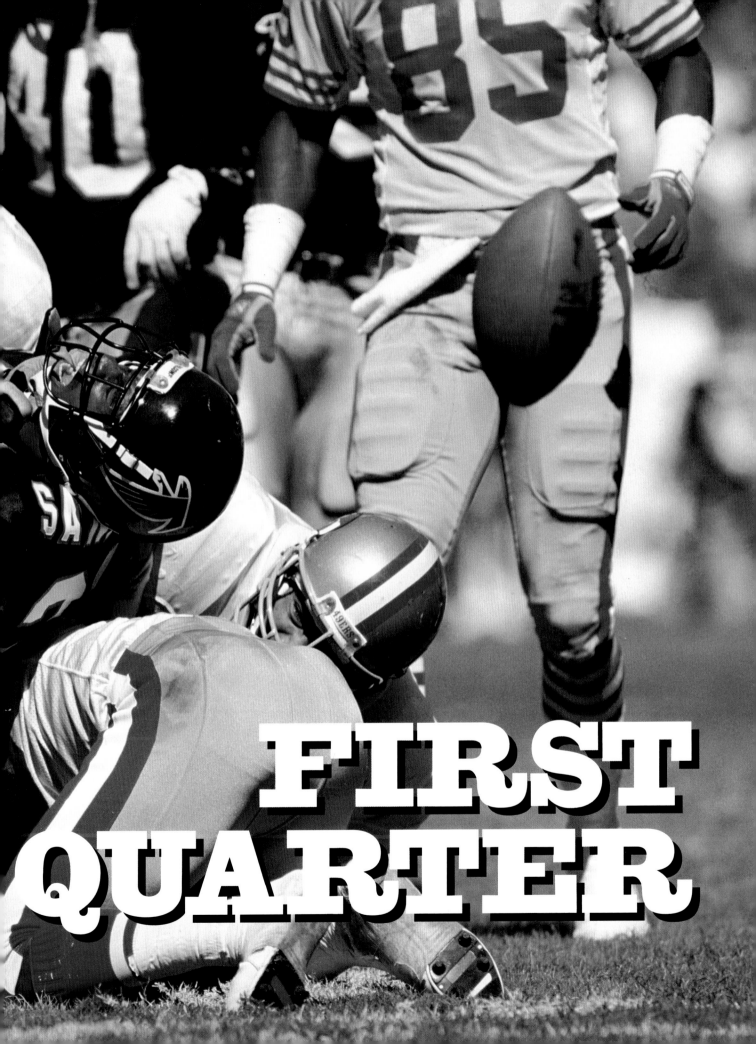

FIRST QUARTER

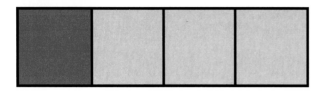

OVERVIEW

BACK TO THE FUTURE

After the fourth week of the 1990 season, commissioner Paul Tagliabue sent a letter to each of the league's 28 teams. Attendance was on course to be the second-highest in the 71-year history of the league. Scores were close. Though games were shorter by 11 minutes, offensive production was not suffering. Great year so far, Tagliabue wrote.

But the letter contained more than greetings and congratulations. Tagliabue also had to address two off-field incidents that occurred in the first month of the season and clouded this happy picture, forcing the new commissioner to tell his

owners in the letter not to let these things mar such a nice beginning. First, of course, there was the Olson affair, a nasty piece of business involving the claim by *Boston Herald* reporter Lisa Olson that she was sexually harassed by several New England Patriots in their locker room on Sept. 17. The ensuing fire storm consumed the media and the public, spurring Tagliabue to name Harvard law professor and former Watergate special prosecutor Philip Heymann to investigate the incident.

On Oct. 1, Tagliabue was on the spot again when Cincinnati coach Sam Wyche barred *USA Today* reporter Denise Tom from the Bengal locker room after a Monday night loss in Seattle. Tagliabue, incensed that Wyche would so blatantly disobey a league rule (not to mention the law of the land), fined Wyche an unprecedented amount for a coach: one-seventeenth of Wyche's $475,000 salary (about $28,000) for the indiscretion. Wyche eventually paid the fine and allowed equal access for female reporters at subsequent games, but he remained steadfastly unrepentant, choosing to outfit the Bengal shower area with curtains to protect the modesty of his players. "I will not allow women to walk in on 50 naked men," said Wyche.

Though a federal court decided in 1978 that female reporters must be granted equal access to the athletes covered by male colleagues, the Olson and Wyche incidents resurrected the debate. The issue was hotly discussed not only in sports sections but also on op-ed pages and national news programs like *Nightline* and *Prime Time Live*. Victor Kiam, the owner of the Patriots, offered his opinion to the *Herald*: "Freedom of speech is fine, but letting a woman in the locker room goes beyond that." A SPORTS ILLUSTRATED poll of 143 NFL players found that 47.6% were against allowing female reporters in the locker room. By opening the debate once again, the league, off the field at least, seemed to be traveling backward into the future.

Regression was the order of the day on the field as well. Experts had forecast wide-open football for 1990 and the rest of the decade, but through the first six weeks of the season, that prediction just didn't pan out. Atlanta, Houston and Detroit were playing the wide-open run-and-shoot offense full-time, and there were other teams using consistent four-wide-receiver sets on passing downs. But the really dominant teams—all but one—were running to success.

After six weeks, the 49ers and the Giants were undefeated, and the Bears, the Bills, the Dolphins and the Raiders had only one loss apiece. San Francisco, with its controlled air attack, ranked No. 1 in the league in passing, but the others were moving the ball by the rush. The Giants were 13th in the league in passing. Buffalo was 22th. Chicago was 26th. The Raiders were 23rd. Even with the golden arm of Dan Marino, Miami was 12th. Those teams won because they were able to control the ball on the ground and because they played solid defense. "It's almost like football has gotten back to being a pride thing," says Dallas director of pro personnel John Wooten. "They come out and say, 'We're going to kick your butt.' They're playing hard-nosed, in-your-face football and trying to dominate games physically, beat teams down physically. It's like the football Vince Lombardi taught. Teams have turned back the clock."

"Football doesn't change," Giants coach Bill Parcells said. "The way to win doesn't change. You try to control the ball, so you can control the clock. And you try to play tough defense. Those are the important things to winning."

The run-and-shoot? It was coming along. Warren Moon was on his way to a record year in Houston, and the Oilers had four receivers in the NFL's top 15 at the six-week point. But wide-open offense still wasn't the way to win. Smash-mouth football was.

WINNING ON THE RUN

After the first six weeks of the season, the teams with one loss or less—except for the pass-happy 49ers—had all improved by relying on the rush more heavily than in 1989. Even the Dolphins, usually dependent upon the throwing of QB Dan Marino, put the weight of their offense on the strong legs of second-year man Sammie Smith (above).

1990			
Team	W-L	% Rush	Time of Possession
N.Y. Giants	5-0	58.9	33:41
San Francisco	5-0	37.1	33:30
Chicago	5-1	59.3	34:53
L.A. Raiders	5-1	58.8	31:01
Miami	4-1	46.0	30:28
Buffalo	4-1	43.2	26:17

1989			
Team	W-L	% Rush	Time of Possession
N.Y. Giants	5-1	55.2	32:11
San Francisco	5-1	46.3	30:58
Chicago	4-2	53.2	32:50
L.A. Raiders	3-3	50.9	28:42
Miami	3-3	40.1	28:16
Buffalo	4-2	39.1	26:04

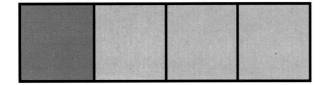

KEY GAMES

BEARS 31
PACKERS 13

▼ Bears veterans like Richard Dent (95) and Dan Hampton (99) are no longer the Monsters of the Midway, but they proved they can still deliver the knockout punch.

Week 2, at Green Bay. It seemed so strange to hear a nice, polite Bear. The Bears of the mid-'80s made their living barking off the field and biting people on it. But on the night before the 1–0 Bears were to face the 1–0 Packers, Chicago linebacker Ron Rivera spent a couple of hours talking about unselfishness.

"We're not trying to feature one defensive player or a group of a few defensive players," Rivera said. "We're featuring a defense now."

The next day, the teamwork-minded Bears played like the vicious Bears of old, punishing the Packers with six sacks, six forced fumbles and two interceptions. The final score was 31–13, and in truth, it wasn't much of a game. Nineteen players see time in defensive coordinator Vince Tobin's scheme. The emphasis is on avoiding mistakes, preventing the game breaker. Read. React. Pressure the quarterback into making quick decisions, but don't throw Buddy Ryan's kitchen sink at the guy. "I don't think they're as big or as bad as they were," said Packer guard Billy Ard. "But they're smart. They're good. And they still have that knockout punch."

The Pack took an early 7–3 lead, but then Chicago began flexing its shoulders. Suddenly the big plays started coming like rain. Bears rookie safety Mark Carrier forced a fumble, leading to a Neal Anderson one-yard TD run. On the Pack's next play from scrimmage, not even a holding call could stop William Perry from sacking Green Bay QB Anthony Dilweg and forcing another fumble. Six plays later, Bears quarterback Jim Harbaugh rolled right, found no one open and sneaked into the corner of the end zone. Bears, 17–7. Early in the third quarter a Trace Armstrong sack forced another turnover, and the Bears scored again on a Harbaugh-to–Ron Morris 40-yard go pattern.

"We're not the Monsters of the Midway anymore," Bears safety Shaun Gayle said afterward. "But we're going to play every down hard and see what happens."

▲ Harbaugh ran the conservative offense to perfection, scoring on a two-yard rollout and throwing two TD passes, a 40-yarder to Morris and a 16-yarder to Anderson.

▼ Anderson has taken Walter Payton's place: Against the Packers he led the team in rushing yards and receptions, totaling more than one-third of the Bears' 303 yards.

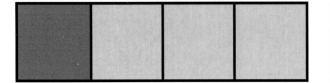

BILLS 29
BRONCOS 28

▼ Kept away from Elway for more than a half, Bills' sack artist Bruce Smith broke through in the third quarter and caused the fumble that set up Buffalo's first TD.

Week 4, at Buffalo. Four weeks after it happened, Bronco coach Dan Reeves still found it hard to get over his loss to the Bills. "That," he said, sounding like a grandfather telling a story about the big war to his grandchildren, "was just a devastating one. You just don't forget about that." This is how you feel when an automatic win turns into a ridiculous loss.

How automatic was it? Denver's offense was chugging along nicely, with running back Bobby Humphrey slashing his way toward the best day of his career (177 yards on 34 carries). David Treadwell was about to kick a 24-yard chip shot with just under 11 minutes to play, which would have made the score Denver 24, Buffalo 9. For the Bills to get three scores in 11 minutes on a day when they had played terrible offensive football seemed highly unlikely.

So they got three scores in 77 seconds.

Cornerback Nate Odomes blocked Treadwell's field goal try, and linebacker Cornelius Bennett ran 80 yards with the ball for a touchdown. Broncos, 21–16. Two plays later, with Rich Stadium so loud you would have thought they had domed the place at halftime, Buffalo strong safety Leonard Smith picked off a John Elway pass and returned it 39 yards for a touchdown. The PAT failed. Bills, 22–21. Then Elway fumbled a snap from center and Bennett recovered. Bills ball on the Denver two-yard line. Kenneth Davis plunged into the end zone on the next play. Bills, 29–21. Seventy-seven seconds, 20 points. The Broncos were able to score a touchdown on a seven-yard pass from Elway to Ricky Nattiel with 1:25 left, but Buffalo recovered the ensuing onside kick and ran out the clock. The final: Buffalo 29, Denver 28.

"If you don't quit," Bills coach Marv Levy said, "sometimes you get lucky. We had some breaks, yeah. But I feel our players made some of those breaks. You have to work hard to block a kick."

True. But none of this salved Reeves's feelings. "If you're around long enough, you'll see everything," he said. "We did today."

▲ Humphrey's career-best rushing day helped the Broncos outgain the Bills on the ground 208–64, but in the fourth quarter Buffalo's opportunistic defense took over.

▼ When Bennett flashed a victory sign after his TD run, the Broncos still led by five points; little more than a minute and two Bills TDs later, his gesture proved prophetic.

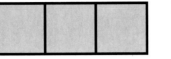

WEEK 1

STANDINGS

AFC EAST	W	L	T	Pct	PF	PA
Buffalo	1	0	0	1.000	26	10
Miami	1	0	0	1.000	27	24
Indianapolis	0	1	0	.000	10	26
New England	0	1	0	.000	24	27
N.Y. Jets	0	1	0	.000	20	25
AFC CENTRAL	W	L	T	Pct	PF	PA
Cincinnati	1	0	0	1.000	25	20
Cleveland	1	0	0	1.000	13	3
Houston	0	1	0	.000	27	47
Pittsburgh	0	1	0	.000	3	13
AFC WEST	W	L	T	Pct	PF	PA
Kansas City	1	0	0	1.000	24	21
L.A. Raiders	1	0	0	1.000	14	9
Denver	0	1	0	.000	9	14
San Diego	0	1	0	.000	14	17
Seattle	0	1	0	.000	0	17
NFC EAST	W	L	T	Pct	PF	PA
Dallas	1	0	0	1.000	17	14
N.Y. Giants	1	0	0	1.000	27	20
Washington	1	0	0	1.000	31	0
Philadelphia	0	1	0	.000	20	27
Phoenix	0	1	0	.000	0	31
NFC CENTRAL	W	L	T	Pct	PF	PA
Chicago	1	0	0	1.000	17	0
Green Bay	1	0	0	1.000	36	24
Tampa Bay	1	0	0	1.000	38	21
Detroit	0	1	0	.000	21	38
Minnesota	0	1	0	.000	21	24
NFC WEST	W	L	T	Pct	PF	PA
Atlanta	1	0	0	1.000	47	27
San Francisco	1	0	0	1.000	13	12
L.A. Rams	0	1	0	.000	24	36
New Orleans	0	1	0	.000	12	13

RESULTS

N.Y. Giants 27, Philadelphia 20
Chicago 17, Seattle 0
Green Bay 36, L.A. Rams 24
Kansas City 24, Minnesota 21
Cincinnati 25, N.Y. Jets 20
Buffalo 26, Indianapolis 10
Cleveland 13, Pittsburgh 3
Dallas 17, San Diego 14
Tampa Bay 38, Detroit 21
Miami 27, New England 24
Washington 31, Phoenix 0
Atlanta 47, Houston 27
L.A. Raiders 14, Denver 9
San Francisco 13, New Orleans 12 (Monday night)

SUDDEN STAR

▼ In Jerry Glanville's debut as Atlanta's coach, his new charges faced his old, the Oilers, in a black-and-blue affair: The teams totaled 209 penalty yards, and the Falcon defense—converging on Lorenzo White below—scored three TDs in a 47–27 win.

ANTHONY DILWEG, QUARTERBACK, GREEN BAY

Dilweg's childhood in Bethesda, Md., was a sheltered one. His mother considered football too dangerous, pushing him instead to learn the violin and piano and to take dancing lessons. "The rhumba, the fox trot, everything," he says. The sport, however, was in his blood: His grandfather Lavvie Dilweg played for the Packers from 1927 to '34.

As a high school sophomore, Dilweg finally overcame his mother's objections and began playing football, although he didn't start until his senior year. At Duke, Dilweg again played a backup role until his final season. "My life doesn't exactly fit the NFL profile," he says. But as a double major in drama and psychology, he impressed the pros with his intelligence.

The holdout of Don Majkowski, Green Bay's marquee quarterback, thrust Dilweg into the starting job where his smarts prepared him well for coach Lindy Infante's complex offense. Against the Rams, Dilweg completed 20 of 32 passes for three TDs, leading the Pack to a 36–24 upset win. He picked at the corners of the secondary, setting it up for the big play, a 47-yard TD toss to wideout Jeff Query. "Don's winning back the job sometime is inevitable. My challenge is to keep it for as long as I can," Dilweg said. That proved to be just one more game, until Majkowski suffered an injury in Week 11.

HIGHLIGHTS

▶ The Dolphins' Sammie Smith gained a career-high 159 yards rushing as Miami beat the Patriots.
▶ Warren Moon passed for 397 yards and four touchdowns in the Oilers' loss to the Falcons.
▶ Running back Neal Anderson of the Bears rushed 20 times for 101 yards and two touchdowns in Chicago's win over the Seahawks.
▶ Raider defensive end Greg Townsend had six solo tackles and three sacks in L.A.'s victory over the Broncos.
▶ Ervin Randle, a linebacker for the Buccaneers, had five tackles and three sacks in a win over the Lions.

19

WEEK 2

STANDINGS

AFC EAST	W	L	T	Pct	PF	PA
Miami	2	0	0	1.000	57	31
Buffalo	1	1	0	.500	33	40
New England	1	1	0	.500	40	41
N.Y. Jets	1	1	0	.500	44	46
Indianapolis	0	2	0	.000	24	42

AFC CENTRAL	W	L	T	Pct	PF	PA
Cincinnati	2	0	0	1.000	46	36
Cleveland	1	1	0	.500	34	27
Pittsburgh	1	1	0	.500	23	22
Houston	0	2	0	.000	36	67

AFC WEST	W	L	T	Pct	PF	PA
L.A. Raiders	2	0	0	1.000	31	22
Denver	1	1	0	.500	33	37
Kansas City	1	1	0	.500	47	45
San Diego	0	2	0	.000	30	38
Seattle	0	2	0	.000	13	34

NFC EAST	W	L	T	Pct	PF	PA
N.Y. Giants	2	0	0	1.000	55	27
Dallas	1	1	0	.500	24	42
Phoenix	1	1	0	.500	23	52
Washington	1	1	0	.500	44	26
Philadelphia	0	2	0	.000	41	50

NFC CENTRAL	W	L	T	Pct	PF	PA
Chicago	2	0	0	1.000	48	13
Detroit	1	1	0	.500	42	52
Green Bay	1	1	0	.500	49	55
Minnesota	1	1	0	.500	53	27
Tampa Bay	1	1	0	.500	52	56

NFC WEST	W	L	T	Pct	PF	PA
San Francisco	2	0	0	1.000	39	25
Atlanta	1	1	0	.500	61	48
L.A. Rams	1	1	0	.500	59	50
New Orleans	0	2	0	.000	15	45

RESULTS

N.Y. Giants 28, Dallas 7
Phoenix 23, Philadelphia 21
San Francisco 26, Washington 13
Chicago 31, Green Bay 13
Pittsburgh 20, Houston 9
Miami 30, Buffalo 7
N.Y. Jets 24, Cleveland 21
L.A. Raiders 17, Seattle 13
Detroit 21, Atlanta 14
New England 16, Indianapolis 14
Cincinnati 21, San Diego 16
L.A. Rams 35, Tampa Bay 14
Minnesota 32, New Orleans 3
Denver 24, Kansas City 23 (Monday night)

HIGHLIGHTS

▶ In Denver's win over Kansas City, Chiefs QB Steve DeBerg passed for 395 yards, 206 of them to Stephone Paige, and Bronco running back Bobby Humphrey rushed for 132 yards.

▶ In Cincinnati's victory over San Diego, Charger running back Marion Butts gained 103 yards on 18 carries.

▶ Cardinals kicker Al Del Greco made three fourth-quarter field goals, including the game-winner with 25 seconds remaining, to give coach Joe Bugel his first NFL win.

◀ Redskins coach Joe Gibbs watched from the sidelines as 49er wide receiver John Taylor dashed past him during San Francisco's 26–13 win. Taylor caught eight passes for 160 yards on the day, and Joe Montana threw for 390 yards to give him a career total of 31,654, surpassing John Brodie as the 49ers' alltime passing yardage leader.

▲ Dennis Byrd dumped Browns QB Bernie Kosar for one of New York's three sacks as the Jets built a 24–7 halftime lead, then held on to win 24–21, giving coach Bruce Coslet his first NFL victory. Kosar suffered 10 sacks in his first two games.

SUDDEN STAR

JOHNNY JOHNSON, RUNNING BACK, PHOENIX

Someone like Johnson comes along every year just to tell this computerized league: You don't know everything. He is a classic case of a great player falling through the cracks in the scouting system.

A seventh-round pick in the 1990 draft, Johnson dominated the NFC East in the first six weeks. His 88-yard rushing day helped the Cards stun the Eagles in Week 2. He followed with 100-yard games against Dallas and the Giants. How was he overlooked? After Johnson starred at tailback as a junior at San Jose State, the next season coach Claude Gilbert switched him to fullback, which reduced his carries. Five games into the year, an unhappy Johnson left the team without permission for three days, allegedly to help his mother dig out from the San Francisco earthquake. Unconvinced by the explanation, Gilbert kicked him off the team. Johnson subsequently chose to skip many NFL workouts rather than answer questions about the incident. Lacking approval from the scouts, Johnson saw 25 running backs drafted ahead of him. "Now," says Phoenix coach Joe Bugel, "he's the rookie of the year."

WEEK 3

STANDINGS

AFC EAST	W	L	T	Pct	PF	PA
Buffalo	2	1	0	.667	63	47
Miami	2	1	0	.667	60	51
New England	1	2	0	.333	47	82
N.Y. Jets	1	2	0	.333	51	76
Indianapolis	0	3	0	.000	34	66

AFC CENTRAL	W	L	T	Pct	PF	PA
Cincinnati	3	0	0	1.000	87	43
Cleveland	1	2	0	.333	48	51
Houston	1	2	0	.333	60	77
Pittsburgh	1	2	0	.333	26	42

AFC WEST	W	L	T	Pct	PF	PA
L.A. Raiders	3	0	0	1.000	51	25
Denver	2	1	0	.667	67	68
Kansas City	2	1	0	.667	64	48
San Diego	1	2	0	.333	54	52
Seattle	0	3	0	.000	44	68

NFC EAST	W	L	T	Pct	PF	PA
N.Y. Giants	3	0	0	1.000	75	30
Washington	2	1	0	.667	63	41
Dallas	1	2	0	.333	39	61
Philadelphia	1	2	0	.333	68	71
Phoenix	1	2	0	.333	30	80

NFC CENTRAL	W	L	T	Pct	PF	PA
Chicago	3	0	0	1.000	67	29
Tampa Bay	2	1	0	.667	75	76
Detroit	1	2	0	.333	62	75
Green Bay	1	2	0	.333	52	72
Minnesota	1	2	0	.333	69	46

NFC WEST	W	L	T	Pct	PF	PA
San Francisco	3	0	0	1.000	58	38
Atlanta	1	2	0	.333	74	67
L.A. Rams	1	2	0	.333	80	77
New Orleans	1	2	0	.333	43	52

RESULTS

Chicago 19, Minnesota 16
Philadelphia 27, L.A. Rams 21
L.A. Raiders 20, Pittsburgh 3
N.Y. Giants 20, Miami 3
San Diego 24, Cleveland 14
Kansas City 17, Green Bay 3
Denver 34, Seattle 31 (OT)
San Francisco 19, Atlanta 13
New Orleans 28, Phoenix 7
Washington 19, Dallas 15
Cincinnati 41, New England 7
Houston 24, Indianapolis 10
Tampa Bay 23, Detroit 20
Buffalo 30, N.Y. Jets 7 (Monday night)

SUDDEN STAR

DERRICK FENNER, RUNNING BACK, SEATTLE

This is how good (and bad) Fenner was in college: At North Carolina, he began a 1986 game against Virginia on the sidelines after he had been late that week for practice. He finished the game with 328 rushing yards. At season's end, he lost his scholarship because of bad grades.

The following June, Fenner was in jail, accused of murdering a man in Hyattsville, Md. In November 1987 the murder charges were dropped owing to conflicting evidence, but his football career seemed over. Because of his troubled history, Fenner, a first-round talent, lasted until the 10th round of the 1989 draft when Seattle chose him. Fenner emerged this year when the Seahawks went to a power backfield pairing the 229-pound Fenner and 228-pound John L. Williams. Though the Seahawks lost to Denver 34–31, Fenner rushed for 144 yards and three TDs. On four TD drives, he accounted for 115 of 197 yards.

"Time will tell whether he's arrived or not," says running back coach Chick Harris. Says Fenner, "Adversity has been something that's been part of my life for a while. I pretty much know how to handle it."

◀ While the Raiders waited for Bo Jackson to finish the baseball season, another Heisman Trophy winner, Marcus Allen, carried the rushing load. Against the Steelers, he gained 44 yards on 11 carries, including a one-yard TD plunge in the fourth quarter that broke open a defensive battle and helped the Raiders to a 20–3 victory.

▼ After two weeks of sputtering in close, come-from-behind victories, the Bengal offense, led by Boomer Esiason, shifted into high gear against the Patriots, scoring the game's first 31 points and cruising to a 41–7 win. Esiason threw for 271 yards and two TDs, including a 52-yarder to Tim McGee, who caught six passes for 163 yards.

HIGHLIGHTS

▶ Buffalo running back Thurman Thomas gained 214 yards on 18 carries—an average of 11.89 yards per carry—as the Bills defeated the Jets.

▶ Playing little more than one and one-half quarters, Saints running back Rueben Mayes gained 99 yards rushing and scored three touchdowns in a win over Phoenix.

▶ Kicker Jim Breech of the Bengals set an NFL record by scoring in his 152nd straight game, breaking the record of 151 set by Fred Cox of the Vikings from 1963 to '73.

▶ Running back Anthony Toney of the Eagles rushed for 103 yards on 24 carries as Philadelphia beat the Rams.

WEEK 4

STANDINGS

AFC EAST	W	L	T	Pct	PF	PA
Buffalo	3	1	0	.750	88	57
Miami	3	1	0	.750	92	75
N.Y. Jets	2	2	0	.500	88	89
New England	1	3	0	.250	60	119
Indianapolis	1	3	0	.250	58	89
AFC CENTRAL	W	L	T	Pct	PF	PA
Cincinnati	3	1	0	.750	103	74
Houston	2	2	0	.500	77	84
Cleveland	1	3	0	.250	48	85
Pittsburgh	1	3	0	.250	32	70
AFC WEST	W	L	T	Pct	PF	PA
L.A. Raiders	4	0	0	1.000	75	35
Kansas City	3	1	0	.750	98	48
Denver	2	2	0	.500	95	97
San Diego	1	3	0	.250	61	69
Seattle	1	3	0	.250	75	84
NFC EAST	W	L	T	Pct	PF	PA
N.Y. Giants	4	0	0	1.000	106	47
Washington	3	1	0	.750	101	51
Phoenix	1	3	0	.250	40	118
Dallas	1	3	0	.250	56	92
Philadelphia	1	3	0	.250	91	95
NFC CENTRAL	W	L	T	Pct	PF	PA
Chicago	3	1	0	.750	77	53
Tampa Bay	3	1	0	.750	98	96
Green Bay	2	2	0	.500	76	93
Detroit	1	3	0	.250	83	99
Minnesota	1	3	0	.250	89	69
NFC WEST	W	L	T	Pct	PF	PA
San Francisco	3	0	0	1.000	58	38
Atlanta	1	2	0	.333	74	67
L.A. Rams	1	2	0	.333	80	77
New Orleans	1	2	0	.333	43	52

RESULTS

L.A. Raiders 24, Chicago 10
Buffalo 29, Denver 28
Indianapolis 24, Philadelphia 23
N.Y. Giants 31, Dallas 17
Houston 17, San Diego 7
Miami 28, Pittsburgh 6
N.Y. Jets 37, New England 13
Tampa Bay 23, Minnesota 20 (OT)
Green Bay 24, Detroit 21
Kansas City 34, Cleveland 0
Washington 38, Phoenix 10
Seattle 31, Cincinnati 16 (Monday night)
Open dates: San Francisco, Atlanta, New Orleans,
L.A. Rams

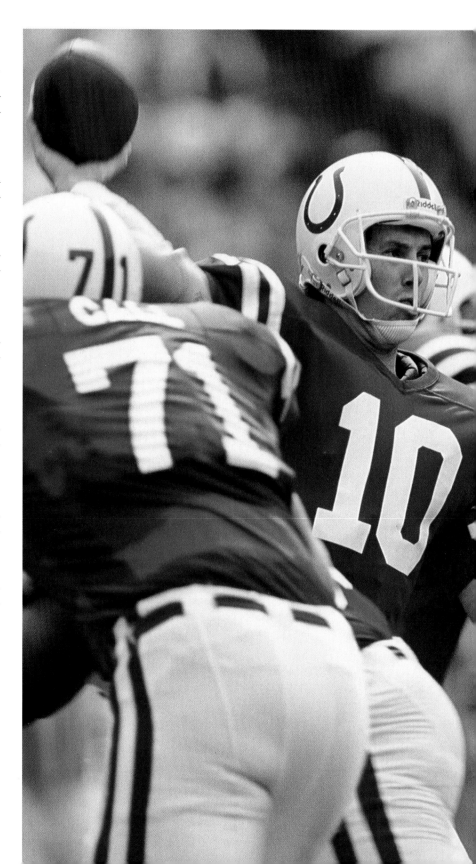

▼ With no time remaining, Jack Trudeau, starting in place of injured rookie Jeff George, fired a six-yard TD pass to wideout Bill Brooks to give the Colts a 24–23 upset win over the Eagles. The play finished a 14-play, 82-yard drive in the final 2:56.

LISA OLSON, REPORTER, "BOSTON HERALD"

"I'm so mad at myself," Olson said from Cincinnati. "I let them get to me today. They made me cry." Olson, 26, was talking about the bullying of the New England Patriots, the team she covered for the "Boston Herald." That day, after the Patriots' loss to the Bengals in Week 3, she was interviewing a player whose locker was near the showers, and she heard someone say how coincidental it was that she wanted to talk to a player in that area. That's when she broke down.

Six days earlier, Olson claimed, she was interviewing a Patriot in the locker room when some players shouted, "Make her look!" Tight end Zeke Mowatt allegedly approached her with no clothes on and said, "Is this what you want?" Commissioner Paul Tagliabue ordered an investigation, and the league assessed fines of $50,000 against the team, $12,500 against Mowatt and $5,000 against two others.

The paper moved Olson to other beats, but the incidents left scars on her and on the league. "They dare say that I'm in the locker room to do something other than my job," she said. "How dare they! My dream since I was nine years old was to be a sportswriter."

HIGHLIGHTS

▶ Don Majkowski, the Packers' quarterback, ran for 88 yards and completed 28 of 46 passes for 289 yards and three touchdowns, including a 26-yarder to wide receiver Jeff Query with :55 left to cap a comeback win over the Lions.

▶ Rookie wide receiver Rob Moore of the Jets caught nine passes for 175 yards and one TD as New York beat the Patriots.

▶ Bronco running back Bobby Humphrey gained 177 yards on 34 carries and scored a touchdown in a loss to the Bills.

▶ Dolphin defensive end Jeff Cross sacked Steeler quarterbacks three times and had four solo tackles in Miami's victory.

▶ Buccaneer running back Gary Anderson rushed for 108 yards on 22 carries and scored a touchdown in a win over the Vikings.

▶ Four games into the season, the Steeler offense, under new coordinator Joe Walton, had not scored a touchdown.

WEEK 5

STANDINGS

AFC EAST	W	L	T	Pct	PF	PA
Buffalo	4	1	0	.800	130	99
Miami	4	1	0	.800	108	73
Indianapolis	2	3	0	.400	81	108
N.Y. Jets	2	3	0	.400	104	109
New England	1	4	0	.200	80	152

AFC CENTRAL	W	L	T	Pct	PF	PA
Cincinnati	4	1	0	.800	137	105
Cleveland	2	3	0	.400	78	114
Houston	2	3	0	.400	98	108
Pittsburgh	2	3	0	.400	68	84

AFC WEST	W	L	T	Pct	PF	PA
L.A. Raiders	4	1	0	.800	99	73
Kansas City	3	2	0	.600	117	71
Denver	2	3	0	.400	124	127
Seattle	2	3	0	.400	108	104
San Diego	1	4	0	.200	75	105

NFC EAST	W	L	T	Pct	PF	PA
N.Y. Giants	4	0	0	1.000	106	47
Washington	3	1	0	.750	101	51
Dallas	2	3	0	.400	70	102
Philadelphia	1	3	0	.250	91	95
Phoenix	1	3	0	.250	40	118

NFC CENTRAL	W	L	T	Pct	PF	PA
Chicago	4	1	0	.800	104	66
Tampa Bay	3	2	0	.600	108	110
Detroit	2	3	0	.400	117	126
Green Bay	2	3	0	.400	89	120
Minnesota	1	4	0	.200	116	103

NFC WEST	W	L	T	Pct	PF	PA
San Francisco	4	0	0	1.000	82	59
Atlanta	2	2	0	.500	102	94
L.A. Rams	1	3	0	.250	111	111
New Orleans	1	3	0	.250	70	80

RESULTS

Chicago 27, Green Bay 13
Buffalo 38, L.A. Raiders 24
Miami 20, N.Y. Jets 16
Atlanta 28, New Orleans 27
Cincinnati 34, L.A. Rams 31 (OT)
Detroit 34, Minnesota 27
Pittsburgh 36, San Diego 14
San Francisco 24, Houston 21
Dallas 14, Tampa Bay 10
Seattle 33, New England 20
Indianapolis 23, Kansas City 19
Cleveland 30, Denver 29 (Monday night)
Open dates: N.Y. Giants, Philadelphia, Phoenix, Washington

HIGHLIGHTS

▶ Falcon QB Chris Miller threw for 366 yards and three TDs in a win over the Saints.
▶ Running back Neal Anderson of the Bears rushed for 141 yards on 21 carries in a victory over the Packers.
▶ In a win over the Buccaneers, Cowboy rookie running back Emmitt Smith rushed for 121 yards and one touchdown.
▶ Lion backup QB Bob Gagliano threw three TD passes as the Lions defeated the Vikings.

▲ Dan Marino punched the air in celebration after throwing a 69-yard TD pass to Mark Duper. A 13-yard TD pass to Duper with 1:03 left gave Miami the 20–16 win.

◀ With two TDs in the Seahawks' 33–20 win over the Patriots, Seattle running back Derrick Fenner took the league touchdown lead with a total of eight. The Seahawks scored on their first four possessions and, after New England answered with 17 points to go up 20–19, converted two Patriots turnovers into touchdowns in the final 2:37.

▼ Bengal coach Sam Wyche found his back against the wall while addressing the media after a win over the Rams. The week before, he had barred a female reporter from the locker room, an action that drew a fine of almost $28,000 from the league.

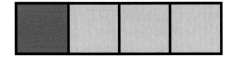

WEEK 6

STANDINGS

AFC EAST	W	L	T	Pct	PF	PA
Buffalo	4	1	0	.800	130	99
Miami	4	1	0	.800	108	73
Indianapolis	2	3	0	.400	81	108
N.Y. Jets	2	4	0	.333	107	148
New England	1	4	0	.200	80	152

AFC CENTRAL	W	L	T	Pct	PF	PA
Cincinnati	4	2	0	.667	154	153
Houston	3	3	0	.500	146	125
Pittsburgh	3	3	0	.500	102	101
Cleveland	2	4	0	.333	98	139

AFC WEST	W	L	T	Pct	PF	PA
L.A. Raiders	5	1	0	.833	123	90
Kansas City	4	2	0	.667	160	95
Denver	2	4	0	.333	141	161
San Diego	2	4	0	.333	114	108
Seattle	2	4	0	.333	125	128

NFC EAST	W	L	T	Pct	PF	PA
N.Y. Giants	5	0	0	1.000	130	67
Washington	3	2	0	.600	121	75
Philadelphia	2	3	0	.400	123	119
Phoenix	2	3	0	.400	60	121
Dallas	2	4	0	.333	73	122

NFC CENTRAL	W	L	T	Pct	PF	PA
Chicago	5	1	0	.833	142	75
Tampa Bay	4	2	0	.667	134	124
Detroit	2	4	0	.333	141	169
Green Bay	2	4	0	.333	103	146
Minnesota	1	5	0	.167	140	135

NFC WEST	W	L	T	Pct	PF	PA
San Francisco	5	0	0	1.000	127	94
Atlanta	2	3	0	.400	137	139
New Orleans	2	3	0	.400	95	100
L.A. Rams	1	4	0	.200	120	149

RESULTS

N.Y. Giants 24, Washington 20
Chicago 38, L.A. Rams 9
New Orleans 25, Cleveland 20
L.A. Raiders 24, Seattle 17
Tampa Bay 26, Green Bay 14
Houston 48, Cincinnati 17
Kansas City 43, Detroit 24
Pittsburgh 34, Denver 17
San Francisco 45, Atlanta 35
San Diego 39, N.Y. Jets 3
Phoenix 20, Dallas 3
Philadelphia 32, Minnesota 24 (Monday night)
Open dates: Buffalo, Indianapolis, Miami, New England

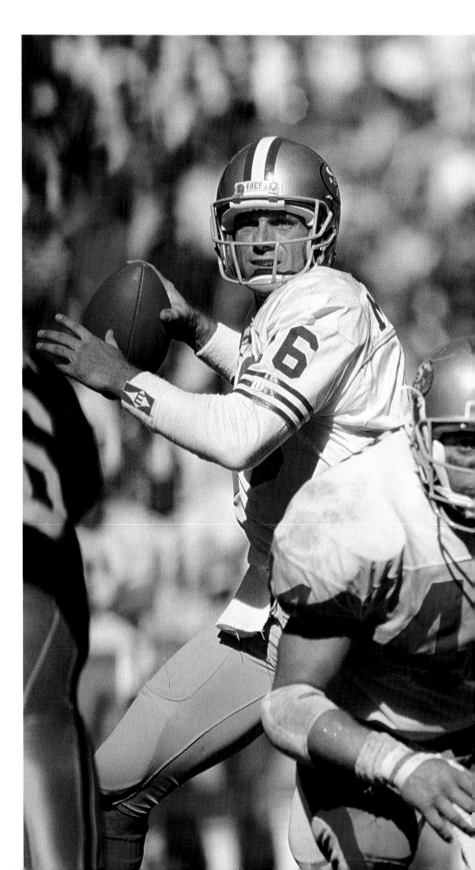

SUDDEN STAR

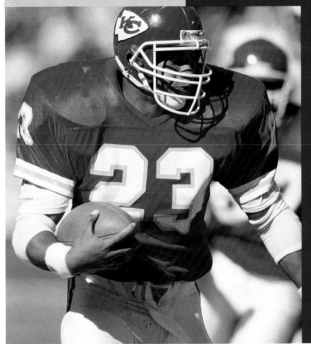

In football, a 100-yard rushing day is the gold standard by which backs are measured. When the Chiefs and the Lions met in Week 6, the unheralded Barry—Word, not Sanders—hit the mother lode, running for 200 yards on 18 carries in Kansas City's 43–24 rout of the Lions.

Four years before, life wasn't glittering so brightly for Word. After his senior season at Virginia in 1986, he was convicted of conspiracy to distribute cocaine. So the third-round draft pick of the Saints spent four and a half months in federal prison in West Virginia. He vowed to come back, not only to football but also to a productive life. In prison, he lifted weights and taught English to inmates with low reading levels.

Joining the Saints in 1987, Word played little before being released in 1989. He spent that season working for a long-distance phone company. "I wanted to get back in football, but no one would give me the chance," he says. Kansas City did this season, inviting the 6'2", 240-pound Word to training camp, where he performed well enough to earn a spot as Christian Okoye's backup. Spelling Okoye against the Lions, Word had runs of 34, 45 and 53 yards and scored two TDs.

◄ In the 49ers' 45–35 win over the Falcons, Joe Montana completed 32 of 49 passes for 476 yards—the 10th-best total in league history—and six TDs, including an NFL-record-tying five TDs to Jerry Rice. San Francisco wasn't the only team playing catch: Atlanta's Andre Rison hauled in nine passes for 172 yards and two touchdowns.

▼ The Steelers' early-season offensive woes ended when QB Bubby Brister began throwing to rookie tight end Eric Green. In Pittsburgh's 34–17 victory over Denver, Green caught three TD passes, giving him five of the Steelers' nine offensive TDs.

HIGHLIGHTS

▶ Warren Moon of the Oilers threw for 369 yards and five TDs in a win over the Bengals.

▶ In his first game for the Saints after being traded by the Cowboys, Steve Walsh threw for 243 yards and three touchdowns as New Orleans defeated the Browns.

▶ Marion Butts of the Chargers rushed for 121 yards and two touchdowns on 26 carries in a win over the Jets.

▶ Placekicker Mike Cofer of the 49ers booted a club-record 56-yard field goal in a victory over the Falcons.

▶ Phil Simms threw two TD passes—one an 80-yarder to Stephen Baker—as the Giants beat the Redskins for the fifth straight time.

SECOND QUARTER

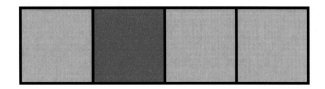

OVERVIEW

WHO'S FIRST AMONG EQUALS?

In late November, about seven in the morning, New York Giants coach Bill Parcells sat in his office at Giants Stadium. His team was 10–0, but you have to understand one thing about Parcells: The more he wins, the grimmer he gets. Here's a guy fond of telling anyone who will listen: "The longer you're in this game … you enjoy the wins much less and you feel the losses much more." That's why, three days after winning 20–0 over Detroit, Parcells was somber and determined, not light and chipper.

And he certainly wasn't all bouncy-stepped over the prospect of facing the also-undefeated 10–0 San Francisco 49ers in a week and a half. "I'm telling you," Parcells said earnestly, "I'm down in our locker room every day, and none of my players are talking about the 49ers. Everybody else is promoting it. Not us. Everybody thinks we sit around and talk about that game, but we don't." Across the continent, San Francisco coach George Seifert was also tired of hearing about the game. "We think about our next opponent, not the Giants," he said in early November.

The rest of the nation, though, found it hard to be as oblivious to the mounting drama as the teams and coaches were. Since Oct. 7, there had been two unbeaten teams in the NFL. For six weeks the Giants and the 49ers had won in stereo. The Giants slug out a victory in a boxing match at Washington; the 49ers shoot down the Falcons in Atlanta. The Giants squeak by Phoenix with a late field goal; the 49ers rout Pittsburgh. The Giants pound the Redskins; the 49ers luck out against Cleveland.

Back and forth.

Week 9: The Niners nip the Packers, the Giants grind up the Colts in prime time. Week 10: The Giants rip the Rams, the 49ers grind up Dallas in prime time. Week 11: Both call off the dogs as the Giants win by 20 over Detroit and the 49ers by 24 over Tampa.

Forth and back.

And so the topic in the barber chairs of Bismarck and the gas stations of Grand Rapids and the diners of Danbury was this: Who's better—the Giants or the 49ers? And the real answer was: Nobody knew.

Which made the guessing more fun. With each succeeding week, the Giants' trip to San Francisco for their Monday night game on Dec. 3 loomed larger. The only time in league history two teams had started a season with records as good as 10–0 was in 1934. America seemed to catch the wave of anticipation and ride it. John Madden said he liked the Giants to win, maybe by about 20–10. Wow. Somebody holding the 49ers to 10 points. Well, he said, hold on a minute. If Montana got hot and the 49ers could run a little, well, then he liked the 49ers, maybe by about 20–10.

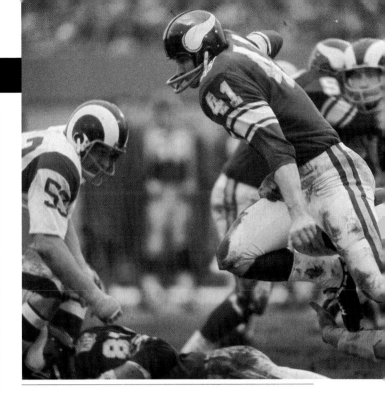

See? No one knew. Joe Montana was the league's premier quarterback. Everybody agreed on that. So why was Phil Simms—efficient, mistake-free, a foot soldier in Parcells' plodding offensive army—at the top of the NFL quarterback ratings for eight weeks? Lawrence Taylor was the premier linebacker of his time. Everybody knew that. So what was Charles Haley—like Taylor a quick, brutal and relentless pass rusher—doing out-Tayloring Taylor so far this year? Both teams had Hall of Fame defensive players in decline—Ronnie Lott in San Francisco, Taylor in East Rutherford—and so had turned to team defense to smother the opposition. Both teams had flaws in formerly dominant areas. The 49ers were the NFL's worst rushing team, by the numbers. The Giants had a diminished pass rush. Both teams possessed great equalizers. The 49ers had Montana. The Giants had the best special teams in football.

Commissioner Tagliabue and the league brass must have been thankful for all the on-field drama. Off the field, the Lisa Olson case (see page 25) was still hanging over the league. Pressure was mounting on the NFL to move Super Bowl XXVII away from Phoenix after Arizona voters failed to ratify a Martin Luther King Jr. holiday. The league was quietly checking its telex wires every day to see if the Supreme Court was going to hear the appeal of the players' three-year-old free-agency lawsuit. This may sound funny, but the streaks of the Giants and the 49ers became an opiate for the football masses. Yes, even the NFL needs to forget sometimes, to throw its fist in the air and root for the action on the field. That's why, in the gut of the 1990 season, it was so good to have a great story line to follow. And even when the game was marred on Nov. 25 by the Eagles' victory over the Giants in Philadelphia, fate provided a favor. Across the continent, the 49ers lost to the Rams. Now it wouldn't be 10-1 versus 11-0. It would be equal. The Giants and the 49ers. The 49ers and the Giants. Who's better? Who knows? Week 13 would decide it.

RECORD MATCHUPS

When Dave Osborn (above) and the 10-1 Vikings met the 11-0 Rams in 1969, the matchup was as eagerly awaited as this season's battle between the Giants and the 49ers, both at 10-1. The chart below shows the outcome of the other dramatic showdowns between teams with records of 10-2 or better after at least 11 games.

YEAR	HOME TEAM RECORD	VISITING TEAM RECORD
1987	*San Francisco 10-2*	*Chicago 10-2*
	OUTCOME: SAN FRANCISCO 41-0	
1986	*Washington 11-2*	*N.Y. Giants 11-2*
	OUTCOME: N.Y. GIANTS 24-14	
1983	*Dallas 12-2*	*Washington 12-2*
	OUTCOME: WASHINGTON 31-10	
1977	*Dallas 11-2*	*Denver 12-1*
	OUTCOME: DALLAS 14-6	
1975	*L.A. Rams 11-2*	*Pittsburgh 12-1*
	OUTCOME: LOS ANGELES 10-3	
1969	*Oakland 11-1-1*	*Kansas City 11-2*
	OUTCOME: OAKLAND 10-6	
1969	*L.A. Rams 11-0*	*Minnesota 10-1*
	OUTCOME: MINNESOTA 20-13	
1968	*L.A. Rams 10-2-1*	*Baltimore 12-1*
	OUTCOME: BALTIMORE 28-24	
1967	*L.A. Rams 10-1-2*	*Baltimore 11-0-2*
	OUTCOME: LOS ANGELES 34-10	
1948	*Chicago 10-1*	*Chicago Cards 10-1*
	OUTCOME: CHICAGO CARDS 24-21	
1934	*Detroit 10-1*	*Chicago 11-0*
	OUTCOME: CHICAGO 19-16	
1934	*Chicago 12-0*	*Detroit 10-2*
	OUTCOME: CHICAGO 10-7	

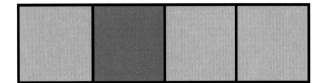

GIANTS 21
REDSKINS 10

▼ The Giants defense stifled Washington's offense, harassing the inexperienced Humphries with three sacks and three interceptions; Jackson came up with one of each.

Week 8, at East Rutherford. When it was over, Earnest Byner went out and cried. A metropolis did, too. Watching the Redskins, you get the feeling that even a District of Columbia motorcade couldn't give them quite enough horsepower to get by the Giants. In their last five meetings, New York had beaten Washington by seven, one, three, three and four points. This time it was 11, but it may as well have been one. That's how close it was. The efficient Giants sprinted out to a 14–0 lead on two TD throws from NFL passing leader Phil Simms—a four-yarder to Stephen Baker and 16-yarder to tight end Mark Bavaro. But Washington, behind inexperienced backup quarterback Stan Humphries, answered with two scores, the latter a five-yard TD scramble by Humphries midway through the third quarter cut the Giants' lead to 14–10.

Then it was time for one of the calamities that always seem to sabotage the Redskins when they play New York. After driving to the Giants three with 6:51 left, Humphries spotted Byner all alone in the end zone and rifled a perfect spiral right to him. A sure touchdown, right? Wrong. The ball bounced off Byner's shoulder and into the hands of diving safety Greg Jackson, who landed in his own end zone for the touchback. Then on Washington's last-gasp drive, Everson Walls, the cagey old cornerback whom the Giants culled from Dallas' waiver list, returned an intercepted pass for a 28-yard touchdown with 4:34 left to clinch it. Byner, who fumbled away the touchdown that would have put Cleveland into Super Bowl XXII, was so overcome afterward that he walked the parking lot at Giants Stadium, crying.

The win made it six in a row for New York over Washington, all hinging on fourth-quarter plays. "Losses like this can destroy a team," DE Charles Mann said after this one. "The key is to be able to bounce back." Said Giants QB Phil Simms: "We always seem to be able to make the plays when we need to." A tale of two seasons, this game.

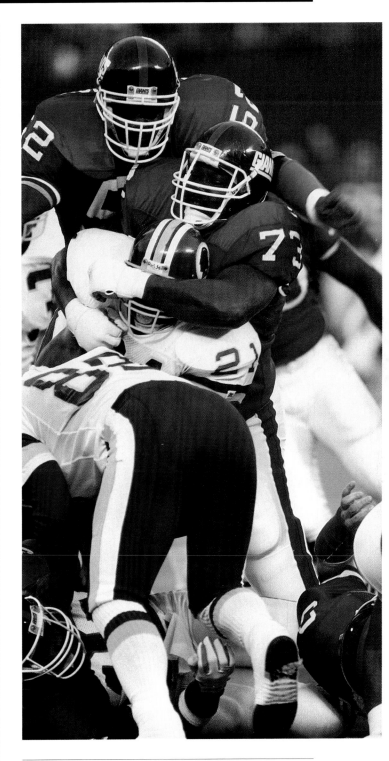

▲ John Washington played a nasty game of Guess who? with Byner as the Giants defense held Redskins running backs to only 37 yards rushing on 16 attempts.

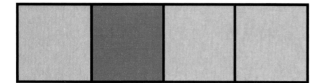

DOLPHINS 23
CARDINALS 3

▼ Miami's new "hands-off" policy: Marino hands off more often to his backs, making it easier for the young line to keep the defense's hands off him when he passes.

Week 9, at Miami. A perfect game to illustrate the new Dolphins. What makes them so different this season? Consider the following: They run now, they play defense, they feature a bunch of guys no one had heard of at the start of the season and—most amazing of all—they have converted Dan Marino from the centerpiece of their offense into just one of their many role players.

The Cardinals came in looking strong, just two weeks removed from an impressive one-point loss to the powerful Giants and featuring the leading NFC rusher in rookie Johnny Johnson.

None of which impressed the pesky Dolphins, who ran the ball 38 times, passed only 25 times and controlled the clock for 35 minutes with scoring drives of 79, 65, 21, 69 and 84 yards. (Last season, the Dolphins' airy offense passed 60.4% of the time.) Marc Logan and Sammie Smith ran for more than 50 yards apiece behind blocker *extraordinaire* Tony Paige. No-names abounded on defense. Former free-agent Kerry Glenn and young draftees Rodney Thomas (fifth round, 1988), Rick Graf (second round, 1987) and Jeff Cross (ninth round, 1988) combined for the Dolphins' five sacks and held Johnson to 27 yards.

Kicker Pete Stoyanovich contributed three field goals, and the new Marino had a typical 1990 day: 18 of 25, 205 yards, two touchdowns and no interceptions. Those aren't the kind of big numbers that he used to produce, but his 17-yard touchdown pass to Paige through a hole between the Cardinals safeties made it 10–0 early in the second quarter, and his quick seven-yard pass out of the shotgun to Mark Clayton made it 20–3 early in the third. Ball game.

"Sure I'd like to throw the ball more," Marino said, "but the most satisfying thing is that we're winning." And winning Don Shula's way: with a running game, the threat of a great passer and tough defense. "We're 7–1 halfway through the season," Shula said after the game. "But we need to build on that to make it meaningful."

▲ Linemen Keith Sims and Harry Galbreath flattened Phoenix's defense, springing Smith for 55 yards on 14 carries. Overall, the Dolphins ran 38 times for 145 yards.

▼ New "no-names" Liffort Hobley (foreground) and Louis Oliver punished Roy Green after a reception as the top-ranked Dolphin defense didn't allow a touchdown.

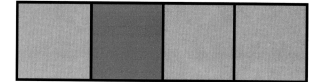

COLTS 34
BENGALS 20

▼ Albert Bentley and the lowly Colt offense kept the Bengal defense lunging and missing all day. Bentley finished with 40 yards rushing and 53 yards receiving.

Week 12, at Cincinnati. If the word *gimme* was in Webster's sporting dictionary, this game would be the perfect definition. The AFC Central–leading Bengals were at home against the Colts, who were 4–6 and struggling. Cincinnati was coming off a 27–3 stomping of the Steelers, and its steamroller of a running game was just warming up. Indianapolis's offensive and defensive lines were weak, and an inconsistent rookie quarterback (Jeff George) and a divisive running back (Eric Dickerson) had put the offense badly out of synch. Entering this game, the Colts had led games for only 25 minutes and 25 seconds out of 600 minutes played.

But from the start, this gimme was anything but a given. The Bengals trailed early in the second quarter 7–6 and were driving for the go-ahead touchdown behind the power and quickness of fullback Ickey Woods, who broke a 32-yard run to the Indianapolis one-yard line. Two plays later, when Woods tried to smash through the right side for the score, Colts Jeff Herrod and Mike Prior punched the ball loose and Indianapolis recovered in the end zone. A quarter later, the Colts led 31–6. "It was my fault we lost the game," a disconsolate Woods said afterward. Not so fast, Ickey. The defense must take some of the blame. Dickerson, in five games since returning from a season-opening suspension, had accumulated 183 rushing yards. Against Cincinnati, he ran 22 times for 143 yards, illustrating perfectly why the Bengals are July's Team, not January's.

Before the season, people always look at the Bengals' offensive explosiveness and classify them as a Super Bowl contender. But the rosy predictions are invariably undermined by the Bengals' leaky defense. Indianapolis, last in the league in offense, exploded for 419 yards against Cincinnati. "You know what I'm most satisfied with?" asked a rejuvenated Dickerson after the game. "People say, 'Has he lost a step?' It's hilarious to hear people say that." But nobody in Cincinnati was laughing.

▲ George teamed up with Bill Brooks for a five-yard TD pass that put the Colts up 24–6. The rookie quarterback burned the Bengals for three touchdowns and 251 yards.

▼ Dickerson fired back at his critics after the 59th 100-yard rushing day of his career. He should have thanked the Bengal defense for providing the ammunition.

MEMORABLE MOMENTS
WEEK 7

STANDINGS

AFC EAST	W	L	T	Pct	PF	PA
Buffalo	5	1	0	.833	160	126
Miami	5	1	0	.833	125	83
Indianapolis	2	4	0	.333	98	135
N.Y. Jets	2	5	0	.286	134	178
New England	1	5	0	.167	90	169
AFC CENTRAL	**W**	**L**	**T**	**Pct**	**PF**	**PA**
Cincinnati	5	2	0	.714	188	166
Houston	4	3	0	.571	169	135
Pittsburgh	3	4	0	.429	109	128
Cleveland	2	5	0	.286	111	173
AFC WEST	**W**	**L**	**T**	**Pct**	**PF**	**PA**
L.A. Raiders	6	1	0	.857	147	99
Kansas City	4	3	0	.571	167	114
Denver	3	4	0	.429	168	178
Seattle	3	4	0	.429	144	135
San Diego	2	5	0	.286	123	132
NFC EAST	**W**	**L**	**T**	**Pct**	**PF**	**PA**
N.Y. Giants	6	0	0	1.000	150	86
Washington	4	2	0	.667	134	82
Dallas	3	4	0	.429	90	135
Philadelphia	2	4	0	.333	130	132
Phoenix	2	4	0	.333	79	141
NFC CENTRAL	**W**	**L**	**T**	**Pct**	**PF**	**PA**
Chicago	5	1	0	.833	142	75
Tampa Bay	4	3	0	.571	147	141
Detroit	2	4	0	.333	141	169
Green Bay	2	4	0	.333	103	146
Minnesota	1	5	0	.167	140	135
NFC WEST	**W**	**L**	**T**	**Pct**	**PF**	**PA**
San Francisco	6	0	0	1.000	154	101
Atlanta	2	4	0	.333	161	183
L.A. Rams	2	4	0	.333	164	173
New Orleans	2	4	0	.333	105	123

RESULTS

Miami 17, New England 10 (Thursday night)
Dallas 17, Tampa Bay 13
Washington 13, Philadelphia 7
Houston 23, New Orleans 10
San Francisco 27, Pittsburgh 7
Buffalo 30, N.Y. Jets 27
Denver 27, Indianapolis 17
N.Y. Giants 20, Phoenix 19
L.A. Raiders 24, San Diego 9
Seattle 19, Kansas City 7
L.A. Rams 44, Atlanta 24
Cincinnati 34, Cleveland 13 (Monday night)
Open dates: Chicago, Detroit, Green Bay, Minnesota

40

▼ Redskins safety Alvin Walton upended Eagle receiver Fred Barnett in a 13-7 Washington win that left Philadelphia winless in the NFC East. Walton's eight tackles tied for the team lead as the Redskins held the Eagles to 270 total yards.

KEN NORTON JR., LINEBACKER, DALLAS

Ken Norton Sr. was not always fighting for million-dollar purses, so life was not always pleasant for Ken Norton Jr. Raised in Watts, the young Norton was so scared of strangers that he sometimes slept in a closet with a baseball bat by his side. While his father was out boxing for $900 purses, neighbors would come over to stay with him. "Some people think I had a silver spoon," Norton Jr. told "The Dallas Times Herald." "They don't know the other part of my life."

Norton Jr. believes that the early hardship drove him to football excellence at UCLA, where his sterling play resulted in his selection by the Cowboys in the second round of the 1988 draft. Now, in his third NFL season, Norton has begun to shine, in part because of coach Jimmy Johnson's decision to shift him from inside to outside linebacker. His brightest moment: 10 unassisted tackles, a sack and a forced fumble in a 17–13 upset win at Tampa Bay. Finally, the son of the fighter who took the title from Muhammad Ali has emerged from his father's shadow. "It seems that now he has discovered his own identity," defensive coordinator Dave Wannstedt says. That identity? "You want to be the man your teammates depend on," Norton says.

HIGHLIGHTS

▶ Wide receiver Michael Irvin caught a touchdown pass with 23 seconds remaining to give the Cowboys a win over the Buccaneers.
▶ In the Rams' victory over the Falcons, Los Angeles running back Cleveland Gary gained 102 yards and scored two touchdowns.
▶ The Giants' Matt Bahr kicked a 40-yard field goal with no time remaining to beat the Cardinals, overcoming the efforts of Ken Harvey, who had nine tackles, three sacks and a fumble recovery, and of Johnny Johnson, who rushed 30 times for 108 yards.
▶ Quarterback Jim Kelly of the Bills threw four touchdown passes, including the winning TD to Jamie Mueller with 19 seconds remaining, to lead Buffalo to a victory over the Jets.
▶ The Colts' Eric Dickerson made his 1990 debut in a loss to the Broncos, gaining 55 yards to become the NFL's sixth alltime rusher.

WEEK 8

STANDINGS

AFC EAST	W	L	T	Pct	PF	PA
Buffalo	6	1	0	.857	187	136
Miami	6	1	0	.857	152	90
N.Y. Jets	3	5	0	.375	151	190
Indianapolis	2	5	0	.286	105	162
New England	1	6	0	.143	100	196

AFC CENTRAL	W	L	T	Pct	PF	PA
Cincinnati	5	3	0	.625	205	204
Houston	4	4	0	.500	181	152
Pittsburgh	4	4	0	.500	150	138
Cleveland	2	6	0	.250	128	193

AFC WEST	W	L	T	Pct	PF	PA
L.A. Raiders	6	1	0	.857	147	99
Kansas City	4	3	0	.571	167	114
Denver	3	4	0	.429	168	178
Seattle	3	4	0	.429	144	135
San Diego	3	5	0	.375	164	142

NFC EAST	W	L	T	Pct	PF	PA
N.Y. Giants	7	0	0	1.000	171	96
Washington	4	3	0	.571	144	103
Philadelphia	3	4	0	.429	151	152
Dallas	3	5	0	.375	110	156
Phoenix	2	5	0	.286	100	172

NFC CENTRAL	W	L	T	Pct	PF	PA
Chicago	6	1	0	.857	173	96
Tampa Bay	4	4	0	.500	157	182
Detroit	3	4	0	.429	168	179
Green Bay	3	4	0	.429	127	156
Minnesota	1	6	0	.143	150	159

NFC WEST	W	L	T	Pct	PF	PA
San Francisco	7	0	0	1.000	174	118
Atlanta	3	4	0	.429	199	200
L.A. Rams	2	5	0	.286	174	214
New Orleans	2	5	0	.286	115	150

RESULTS

Philadelphia 21, Dallas 20
San Francisco 20, Cleveland 17
Chicago 31, Phoenix 21
Atlanta 38, Cincinnati 17
San Diego 41, Tampa Bay 10
Detroit 27, New Orleans 10
N.Y. Jets 17, Houston 12
Buffalo 27, New England 10
Miami 27, Indianapolis 7
N.Y. Giants 21, Washington 10
Green Bay 24, Minnesota 10
Pittsburgh 41, L.A. Rams 10 (Monday night)
Open dates: Denver, L.A. Raiders, Kansas City, Seattle

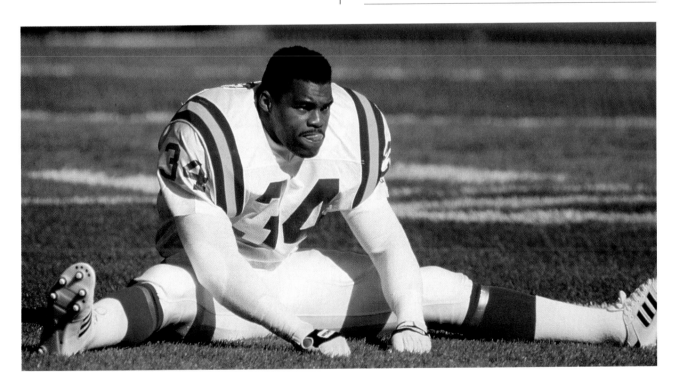

HIGHLIGHTS

▶ Bills running back Thurman Thomas rushed for 136 yards and one TD on 22 carries in a win over the Patriots.

▶ In the Jets' win over the Oilers, New York defensive end Darrell Davis had one sack and recovered a fumble in the end zone for a TD, and Houston QB Warren Moon completed 30 of 43 passes for 381 yards and a TD.

▶ Randall Cunningham of the Eagles tossed a 10-yard TD pass to Calvin Williams with 44 seconds left to beat the Cowboys 21–20.

▶ Kicker Mike Cofer booted a 45-yard field goal with five seconds remaining to give the 49ers a victory over the Browns.

▶ Pittsburgh QB Bubby Brister threw four touchdown passes in a win over the Rams.

◀ Jim Harbaugh connected on all six of his first-half passes, including a 67-yarder for a touchdown to Ron Morris, as the Bears bolted to a 28–0 lead and held on for a 31–21 win over the Cardinals. Chicago's backfield ground out 223 yards rushing.

▲ Safety Lester Lyles of San Diego headed upfield—literally—after one of the Chargers' four interceptions of Chris Chandler in a 41–10 victory over Tampa Bay.

▼ Herschel Walker stuck out his tongue at critics who blamed him for the Vikings' woes, but in a 24–10 loss to the Packers, he rushed for six yards and lost a fumble.

WEEK 9

STANDINGS

AFC EAST	W	L	T	Pct	PF	PA
Buffalo	7	1	0	.875	229	136
Miami	7	1	0	.875	175	93
N.Y. Jets	4	5	0	.444	175	199
Indianapolis	2	6	0	.250	112	186
New England	1	7	0	.125	120	244
AFC CENTRAL	W	L	T	Pct	PF	PA
Cincinnati	5	4	0	.556	212	225
Pittsburgh	5	4	0	.556	171	147
Houston	4	5	0	.444	194	169
Cleveland	2	7	0	.222	128	235
AFC WEST	W	L	T	Pct	PF	PA
L.A. Raiders	6	2	0	.750	154	108
Kansas City	5	3	0	.625	176	121
San Diego	4	5	0	.444	195	156
Denver	3	5	0	.375	190	205
Seattle	3	5	0	.375	158	166
NFC EAST	W	L	T	Pct	PF	PA
N.Y. Giants	8	0	0	1.000	195	103
Washington	5	3	0	.625	185	141
Philadelphia	4	4	0	.500	199	172
Dallas	3	6	0	.333	119	180
Phoenix	2	6	0	.250	103	195
NFC CENTRAL	W	L	T	Pct	PF	PA
Chicago	7	1	0	.875	199	102
Tampa Bay	4	5	0	.444	163	208
Detroit	3	5	0	.375	206	220
Green Bay	3	5	0	.375	147	180
Minnesota	2	6	0	.250	177	181
NFC WEST	W	L	T	Pct	PF	PA
San Francisco	8	0	0	1.000	198	138
Atlanta	3	5	0	.375	208	221
L.A. Rams	3	5	0	.375	191	227
New Orleans	3	5	0	.375	136	157

RESULTS

Kansas City 9, L.A. Raiders 7
N.Y. Jets 24, Dallas 9
New Orleans 21, Cincinnati 7
Buffalo 42, Cleveland 0
San Francisco 24, Green Bay 20
Chicago 26, Tampa Bay 6
Washington 41, Detroit 38 (OT)
L.A. Rams 17, Houston 13
Miami 23, Phoenix 3
Philadelphia 48, New England 20
Pittsburgh 21, Atlanta 9
San Diego 31, Seattle 14
Minnesota 27, Denver 22
N.Y. Giants 24, Indianapolis 7 (Monday night)

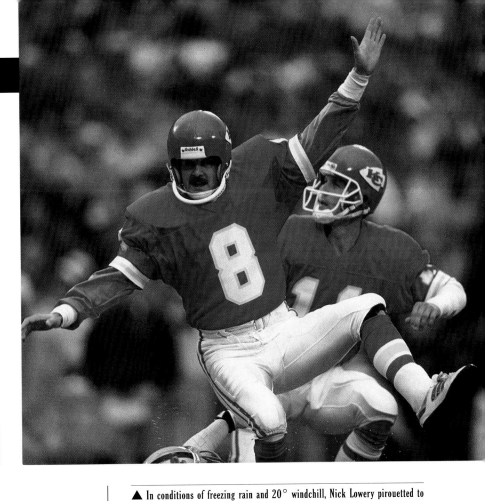

▶ For the first time since 1976, two Saints running backs rushed for more than 100 yards in the same game: Craig Heyward gained 122 yards, and Rueben Mayes ran for 115 in New Orleans's win over the Bengals.

▶ Joe Montana completed 25 of 40 passes for 411 yards—187 to Jerry Rice—and three TDs in a 49er victory over the Packers.

▶ The Broncos sacked Minnesota QB Rich Gannon seven times, but the Vikings rallied for 20 second-half points to pull out the win.

▶ In a win over the Buccaneers, Bears safety Mark Carrier had four tackles, a forced fumble and two interceptions.

▶ Jet rookie Terance Mathis tied an NFL record with a 98-yard punt return for a touchdown in a victory over the Cowboys.

◀ Running back Heath Sherman of the Eagles galloped for 113 yards on 24 carries in a 48–20 whipping of the Patriots, but he couldn't top his own quarterback, Randall Cunningham, who ran for 124 yards and a TD and threw four touchdown passes.

▲ In conditions of freezing rain and 20° windchill, Nick Lowery pirouetted to recover his balance after booting the winning 41-yard field goal–his third of the game–with 11:57 left, as Kansas City pulled out a 9–7 victory over the Raiders.

SUDDEN STAR

JEFF RUTLEDGE, QUARTERBACK, WASHINGTON

For 12 seasons, Jeff Rutledge was a caddy. He caddied for Vince Ferragamo in L.A., for Phil Simms in New York, and in Washington this season, he was caddying for Mark Rypien and Stan Humphries.

In Week 9 at the Silverdome, the caddy finally got his invitation to play in the Open. The Redskins trailed Detroit by 21 with 10:23 left in the third quarter when coach Joe Gibbs yanked an ineffective Humphries and replaced him with Rutledge. Rutledge completed his first eight passes. Quickly, he had the team moving, directing scoring drives of 63, 58 and 80 yards to pull to 38–31. With 24 seconds left, Washington was at the Detroit 12. The day before, the Redskins had inserted a quarterback draw into the game plan—but not for the plodding Rutledge. "Jeff's probably the last guy in the world to run that play," Gibbs said. "Sometimes that's why things work." Rutledge ran the draw and scored. The Redskins won in OT, 41–38, and Rutledge had a career day: 30 of 42, 363 yards, one TD, no interceptions. "I may never play another down," Rutledge said, "but this is something they can never take away from me."

WEEK 10

STANDINGS

AFC EAST	W	L	T	Pct	PF	PA
Buffalo	8	1	0	.889	274	150
Miami	8	1	0	.889	192	96
N.Y. Jets	4	6	0	.400	178	216
Indianapolis	3	6	0	.333	125	196
New England	1	8	0	.111	130	257
AFC CENTRAL	**W**	**L**	**T**	**Pct**	**PF**	**PA**
Cincinnati	5	4	0	.556	212	225
Pittsburgh	5	4	0	.556	171	147
Houston	4	5	0	.444	194	169
Cleveland	2	7	0	.222	128	235
AFC WEST	**W**	**L**	**T**	**Pct**	**PF**	**PA**
L.A. Raiders	6	3	0	.667	170	137
Kansas City	5	4	0	.556	192	138
San Diego	5	5	0	.500	214	163
Seattle	4	5	0	.444	175	182
Denver	3	6	0	.333	197	224
NFC EAST	**W**	**L**	**T**	**Pct**	**PF**	**PA**
N.Y. Giants	9	0	0	1.000	226	110
Philadelphia	5	4	0	.556	227	186
Washington	5	4	0	.556	199	169
Dallas	3	7	0	.300	125	204
Phoenix	2	7	0	.222	117	240
NFC CENTRAL	**W**	**L**	**T**	**Pct**	**PF**	**PA**
Chicago	8	1	0	.889	229	126
Green Bay	4	5	0	.444	176	196
Tampa Bay	4	6	0	.400	170	243
Detroit	3	6	0	.333	213	237
Minnesota	3	6	0	.333	194	188
NFC WEST	**W**	**L**	**T**	**Pct**	**PF**	**PA**
San Francisco	9	0	0	1.000	222	144
New Orleans	4	5	0	.444	171	164
Atlanta	3	6	0	.333	232	251
L.A. Rams	3	6	0	.333	198	258

RESULTS

Chicago 30, Atlanta 24
Indianapolis 13, New England 10
Miami 17, N.Y. Jets 3
Minnesota 17, Detroit 7
Buffalo 45, Phoenix 14
Seattle 17, Kansas City 16
New Orleans 35, Tampa Bay 7
San Diego 19, Denver 7
Green Bay 29, L.A. Raiders 16
N.Y. Giants 31, L.A. Rams 7
San Francisco 24, Dallas 6
Philadelphia 28, Washington 14 (Monday night)
Open dates: Cincinnati, Cleveland, Houston, Pittsburgh

▼ Giants linebacker Steve DeOssie rode Ram tight end Pete Holohan to the turf as Myron Guyton closed in. New York's 31–7 win featured the punting of Sean Landetta, who three times pinned L.A. on its own three, and the 73% passing of Phil Simms.

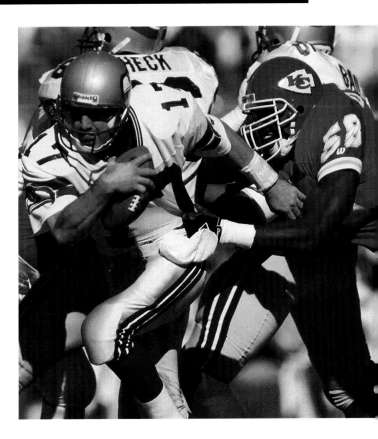

▲ Chiefs linebacker Derrick Thomas sacked Seahawk quarterback Dave Krieg an NFL-record seven times, but on the game's final play, Krieg shook off a potential eighth and fired a 25-yard touchdown pass to Paul Skansi for Seattle's 17–16 victory.

HIGHLIGHTS

▶ Craig Heyward of the Saints rushed for 155 yards and two TDs on 20 carries in New Orleans's win over Tampa Bay.

▶ In the Bears victory over the Falcons, defensive end Richard Dent had two sacks and a fumble recovery, cornerback Lemuel Stinson intercepted two passes and wide receiver Wendell Davis caught five passes for 105 yards and a TD.

▶ Four of quarterback Jim Kelly's 11 completions went for touchdowns as Buffalo overcame snow, cold weather and strong winds to defeat Phoenix.

▶ In the Chargers' win over the Broncos, running back Marion Butts rushed for 114 yards on 16 carries and defensive back Gill Byrd intercepted two passes.

▶ Jerry Rice of the 49ers caught 12 passes for 147 yards and a touchdown in a victory over Dallas.

WEEK 11

STANDINGS

AFC EAST	W	L	T	Pct	PF	PA
Buffalo	9	1	0	.900	288	150
Miami	8	2	0	.800	202	109
Indianapolis	4	6	0	.400	142	210
N.Y. Jets	4	7	0	.364	192	233
New England	1	9	0	.100	130	271
AFC CENTRAL	W	L	T	Pct	PF	PA
Cincinnati	6	4	0	.600	239	228
Houston	5	5	0	.500	229	192
Pittsburgh	5	5	0	.500	174	174
Cleveland	2	8	0	.200	151	270
AFC WEST	W	L	T	Pct	PF	PA
L.A. Raiders	7	3	0	.700	183	147
Kansas City	6	4	0	.600	219	148
San Diego	5	6	0	.455	224	190
Seattle	4	6	0	.400	196	206
Denver	3	7	0	.300	210	240
NFC EAST	W	L	T	Pct	PF	PA
N.Y. Giants	10	0	0	1.000	246	110
Philadelphia	6	4	0	.600	251	209
Washington	6	4	0	.600	230	186
Dallas	4	7	0	.364	149	225
Phoenix	2	8	0	.200	138	264
NFC CENTRAL	W	L	T	Pct	PF	PA
Chicago	9	1	0	.900	245	139
Green Bay	5	5	0	.500	200	217
Minnesota	4	6	0	.400	218	209
Tampa Bay	4	7	0	.364	177	274
Detroit	3	7	0	.300	213	257
NFC WEST	W	L	T	Pct	PF	PA
San Francisco	10	0	0	1.000	253	151
New Orleans	4	6	0	.400	188	195
Atlanta	3	7	0	.300	255	275
L.A. Rams	3	7	0	.300	219	282

RESULTS

N.Y. Giants 20, Detroit 0
Houston 35, Cleveland 23
Buffalo 14, New England 0
Washington 31, New Orleans 17
Philadelphia 24, Atlanta 23
Kansas City 27, San Diego 10
Chicago 16, Denver 13 OT
Dallas 24, L.A. Rams 21
Green Bay 24, Phoenix 21
Minnesota 24, Seattle 21
Indianapolis 17, N.Y. Jets 14
San Francisco 31, Tampa Bay 7
Cincinnati 27, Pittsburgh 3
L.A. Raiders 13, Miami 10 (Monday night)

SUDDEN STAR

CURTIS DUNCAN, WIDE RECEIVER, HOUSTON

Hill, Givins, Jeffires, Duncan. In Houston's run-and-shoot offense, receivers get rich. Four wideouts instead of the customary two play on every play, and because QB Warren Moon shares the wealth so well, anyone can emerge in any week. After eight weeks, four Houston receivers were the top four receivers in the AFC. It's not surprising when the star is Drew Hill, who has caught more than 400 passes in his career, or former high draft picks Ernest Givins or Haywood Jeffires. But when Curtis Duncan breaks out, that's news, if only because of his background. Duncan graduated on time from that football factory, Northwestern, with a business and prelaw degree. He was a 10th-round Oiler pick in 1987. "When Curtis first came here," Hill says, "he was basically a speed guy. But he's been one of the hardest workers on the team, and his work has paid off." Especially in Week 11 against the Browns, when Moon threw seven times to Duncan for 130 yards, including a 37-yard TD pass with 12 minutes left that put Houston in the lead for good in a 35–23 win. "I'm just trying to open the offense up a little more," Duncan said.

◀ Michael Irvin welcomed with open arms this 61-yard TD pass from Troy Aikman, one of two TDs to Irvin in the Cowboys' 24–21 win over the Rams. Aikman finished at 17 of 32 for 303 yards, and Ken Wills kicked the winning field goal with 4:24 left.

▼ The Pats hardly looked like patsies against the Bills, staying close until Thurman Thomas broke loose on an 80-yard TD jaunt with 1:38 remaining to ice the game at 14–0. Thomas rushed for 165 yards, but the defense keyed the win with a second-quarter stand that held New England scoreless after a first-and-goal from the one.

HIGHLIGHTS

▶ Redskins quarterback Mark Rypien, playing in his first game after missing six weeks with a knee injury, completed 26 of 38 passes for 311 yards and three touchdowns in a victory over the Saints.

▶ The Eagles rallied with 17 fourth-quarter points, including the winning 46-yard field goal by Roger Ruzek with 1:45 left, to defeat the Falcons 24–23.

▶ Herschel Walker broke out of a slump and gained 99 yards on 16 carries in the Vikings' win over the Seahawks.

▶ Kevin Butler kicked a 44-yard field goal in OT to give the Bears a win over the Broncos.

WEEK 12

STANDINGS

AFC EAST	W	L	T	Pct	PF	PA
Miami	9	2	0	.818	232	122
Buffalo	9	2	0	.818	312	177
Indianapolis	5	6	0	.455	176	230
N.Y. Jets	4	8	0	.333	199	257
New England	1	10	0	.091	144	305

AFC CENTRAL	W	L	T	Pct	PF	PA
Houston	6	5	0	.545	256	216
Cincinnati	6	5	0	.545	259	262
Pittsburgh	6	5	0	.545	198	181
Cleveland	2	9	0	.182	164	300

AFC WEST	W	L	T	Pct	PF	PA
Kansas City	7	4	0	.636	246	172
L.A. Raiders	7	4	0	.636	207	174
Seattle	5	6	0	.455	209	216
San Diego	5	7	0	.417	234	203
Denver	3	8	0	.273	237	280

NFC EAST	W	L	T	Pct	PF	PA
N.Y. Giants	10	1	0	.909	259	141
Philadelphia	7	4	0	.636	282	222
Washington	6	5	0	.545	247	213
Dallas	5	7	0	.417	176	242
Phoenix	3	8	0	.273	172	278

NFC CENTRAL	W	L	T	Pct	PF	PA
Chicago	9	2	0	.818	258	180
Green Bay	6	5	0	.545	220	227
Minnesota	5	6	0	.455	259	222
Detroit	4	7	0	.364	253	284
Tampa Bay	4	8	0	.333	187	294

NFC WEST	W	L	T	Pct	PF	PA
San Francisco	10	1	0	.909	270	179
New Orleans	5	6	0	.455	198	202
L.A. Rams	4	7	0	.364	247	299
Atlanta	3	8	0	.273	262	285

RESULTS

Detroit 40, Denver 27 (Thursday)
Dallas 27, Washington 17 (Thursday)
New Orleans 10, Atlanta 13
Indianapolis 34, Cincinnati 20
Miami 30, Cleveland 13
Philadelphia 31, N.Y. Giants 13
Green Bay 20, Tampa Bay 10
Kansas City 27, L.A. Raiders 24
L.A. Rams 28, San Francisco 17
Phoenix 34, New England 14
Pittsburgh 24, N.Y. Jets 7
Seattle 13, San Diego 10 (OT)
Minnesota 41, Chicago 13
Houston 27, Buffalo 24 (Monday night)

HIGHLIGHTS

▶ Backup rookie running back Anthony Thompson of the Cardinals, subbing for fellow rookie Johnny Johnson, gained 136 yards on 28 carries in a win over the Pats.

▶ Seahawk kicker Norm Johnson booted a 40-yard field goal with 3:01 gone in overtime to overcome a 128-yard rushing performance by the Chargers' Marion Butts and defeat San Diego 13–10.

▶ Lorenzo White of the Oilers rushed for 125 yards on 18 carries in a win over the Bills.

▶ In the Vikings' upset of the Bears, linebacker Mike Merriweather had 12 tackles, 1.5 sacks and a fumble return for a TD.

◀ Fall of the Undefeated, Part I: The Giants-Eagles game was up in the air until the fourth quarter when Calvin Williams outjumped Myron Guyton for a tipped pass and landed in the end zone to give Philadelphia a 24–13 lead. Seconds later the Eagles' Byron Evans intercepted a deflected Phil Simms pass for a TD and the 31–13 margin.

▲ In first quarter, Mike Harden broke up a pass intended for Robb Thomas as the Raiders battered the Chiefs in the stats but lost three fumbles and the game 27–24.

▼ Fall of the Undefeated, Part II: The Ram defense smothered Joe Montana with three interceptions and two sacks to end the 49ers' 18-game win streak 28–17.

51

LOCKER ROOM FOLLIES

The locker room, that aromatic sanctum of sport, is teeming with life, some of it even human.

BY RICK REILLY

For a place with the decor of a meat cellar, the luxurious smell of Gary, Indiana, and the charm of an airport restaurant employee, there sure are a lot of people in this country who want to enter the glorious world of locker rooms. Luckily, we are here to save you the trouble.

A locker room consists of a bunch of four-by-eight steel mesh cubicles lining the walls, a few plain tables in the middle, a trainers' room with some ice in it, some showers that double nicely as marine-life laboratories and a stereo that is turned to 11 on a scale of 10. Better to have died as a young boy than to try to touch this. We turned down the Atlanta Falcons'

stereo once and every eye looked at us like we had just nailed up the Iraqi flag. A Denver Bronco linebacker once pulled a gun on a teammate in a locker room, and our guess is that it had something to do with changing FM stations.

Still, the locker room is home to the athlete—a rank petrie dish of a home, but home nonetheless—and so has become sacred territory. Every December, Mark Lee of the Green Bay Packers adorns his locker with Christmas lights. Very festive. Bo Jackson hangs a deer head over his Kansas City Royals locker, just above a sign that reads: DON'T BE STUPID AND ASK A FOOTBALL QUESTION. Above his Los Angeles Raider football locker reads the vice versa.

Players do what they can to personalize their space. Willis Reed of the New York Knicks used to have a bull above his locker on account of he considered himself one. Dennis (Bucket Head) Harrah, ex-lineman for the Los Angeles

Rams known for his 8½ hat size, kept over his locker a large upturned bucket, sporting a face mask and painted in the Rams' colors. Some guys line their lockers with contact paper, the kind used for kitchen shelves. Bart Starr kept an exceedingly neat locker.

On the other hand, New York Knick Bill Bradley kept one of the sloppiest lockers in history, a morass of shoes, jocks, socks, sweat pants, talcum powder, books, mail and tape. Luckily there is a place for slobs like him—the U.S. Senate.

Almost anything you see in a professional athlete's locker came to him free: shoes, packages, paintings, plaques, putrid ashtrays and obscenely ugly personalized clocks. Fans cannot help themselves.

This stuff is not only unsolicited but also disdained. One day, standing in front of the locker of Oakland A's outfielder Jose Canseco, we noticed a large, unopened Federal Express box that had been delivered more than a week before. We were so curious about the box, we hounded Canseco until he opened it. It

turned out to be home-baked cookies, sent at great expense from an unknown fan in Tennessee.

"Does this kind of thing come often?" we asked.

"Just about every day," he said.

Finally the clubhouse boys ate them.

Do not send your heroes baked goods. It will only break your heart. When Wayne Gretzky turned 19, a fan baked him a gorgeous five-tier cake, with scenes from his hockey career illustrated in frosting at each level and lavish adornment all around. When it was delivered to the locker room for safekeeping after a pregame ceremony, a teammate sat in it.

The life-form that has settled in locker rooms is not high on the food chain. The Milwaukee Brewers

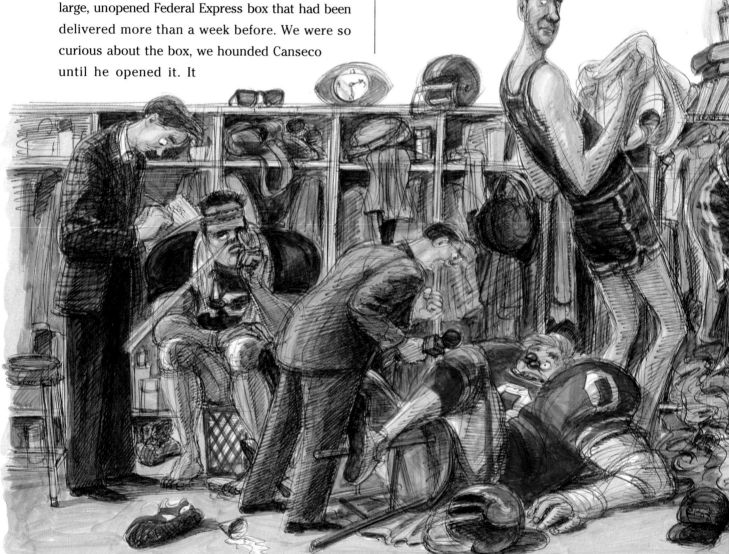

used to make birthday cakes the object of a quaint tribal ritual. A clubhouse boy would set the cake down in the middle of the room. Soon, the players would begin chanting and dancing around. When the chanting reached a frenzy, in would slink Pete Vuckovich, a crazed pitcher and sometime witch doctor with a huge moustache that, according to rumor, housed birds. Holding a bat, he would begin dancing slowly and carefully around the cake, gradually increasing his speed, faster and faster until ... SPLAT! ... he would cleave it in two with the bat, much to the satisfaction of his tribesmen.

No wonder people are clamoring to get into these dens of high society. And the lucky ones who *do* get in, like sportswriters, are usually hit with something gooey upon entering. One time, a reporter for the *San Diego Union* asked quarterback Jim McMahon a question that McMahon didn't much feel like answering. He did, however, feel like putting his finger to the right side of his nose, rearing his head back and blowing the entire contents of his left nostril on the reporter, who now goes by the name of Kleenex.

Athletes are ahead in this interprofessional rivalry with reporters, 1,286 to 1. The 1 came when Will McDonough, sportswriter for *The Boston Globe* and idol of his peers, punched Raymond Clayborn, New England Patriots defensive back, right in the nose. All sportswriters now get that day off.

Injuries are not a common hazard of the locker room, but in locker room parlance, players "die" all the time. That is, they get released. And when there is a death in the locker room, there is absolutely no talking about it. Bad luck. In fact, whenever the Denver Nuggets cut somebody, trainer Chopper Travaglini immediately clears out any sign that the player has ever been there. "It's best if you pretend the guy never existed,"

Chopper says. In 1990 so many guys from one locker in the Detroit Piston dressing room had been cut that the trainer refused to let anybody use it. Luckily, it was the one next to Bill Laimbeer.

One of the weirdest locker room superstitions belonged to a former NHL goalie named Dave Reece. Reece's habit was to stop talking, come hell or high stick, from one hour before the game until the final horn. This meant that even if Reece needed something special from the trainer or the coach, he had to go through an elaborate combination of charades, grunts and silent skits. There is no record, however, of a referee complaining.

Reece's reticence probably cost him some fun because that last hour in a locker room, any locker room, when the fans and the press and the hangers-on are not allowed in, is a period to be savored.

Gretzky once said it was his favorite time of all because last night's game is too far gone to worry about anymore and tonight's is too far away to begin fretting over. So what's left is just the players themselves—no coaches—sitting on the benches in front of their cubicles, getting their equipment ready, taping their sticks and forgetting how much money they make. "You could hear anything anybody said because it was just one big open room," Gretzky says. "I mean, sometimes you'd get laughing so hard your stomach would hurt."

Of course, some of the worst jokes are the locker rooms themselves. It is a long-standing tradition in sports to make the visitors' locker rooms just one Michelin star above your basic bus depot. They are usually spare, sterile places, without decorations, carpeting or, sometimes, soap. The locker room at Cleveland Stadium, for example, is done up in Early Bastille. It's so cramped that Atlanta Falcon coach

Jerry Glanville always brings a hammer and a nail. "So I have somewhere to hang my coat," he says.

Boston Garden is famously hospitable that way. When an opposing team arrives, the locker room is only slightly hotter than Belize. The opponents complain, and the management responds. By the time they come back at halftime, the locker room is freezing. Boston Garden is a great place if you happen to be a virus.

At Millersville (Pa.) University, they make the visiting team walk through a public restroom to get to their lockers. *Excuse me, sir, but do you mind not using that? That's our playbook.* At Iowa's Nile Kinnick Stadium, the visitors' locker room is painted pink, with kelly green carpeting. "All right, you guys, go out there and macrame!" Which, of course, is the idea. When Wisconsin coach Barry Alvarez went there the first time, he said, "I didn't know whether to throw up or fall asleep."

Well, as for that, the tradition of locker rooms is definitely to throw up. Bill Russell threw up before every game. Former Seattle Seahawk linebacker Brian Bosworth was once asked what head coach Chuck Knox's pregame speeches were like.

"I don't know," the Boz answered. "I'm always in the stalls throwing up."

Eventually, the coziness of these wonderful places must be left and the contest must be played. But first comes the essential pregame prayer. Florida State head coach Bill Peterson was about to lead his charges out on the field for his first game as a college head coach when a player stopped him. "Coach," he said, "you forgot the prayer."

Flustered, the coach stammered a bit. He had not thought of this. Finally, he said, "O.K., everybody take a knee." There was quiet in the room. The players looked at him. Solemnly, he began.

"Now I lay me down to sleep ...."

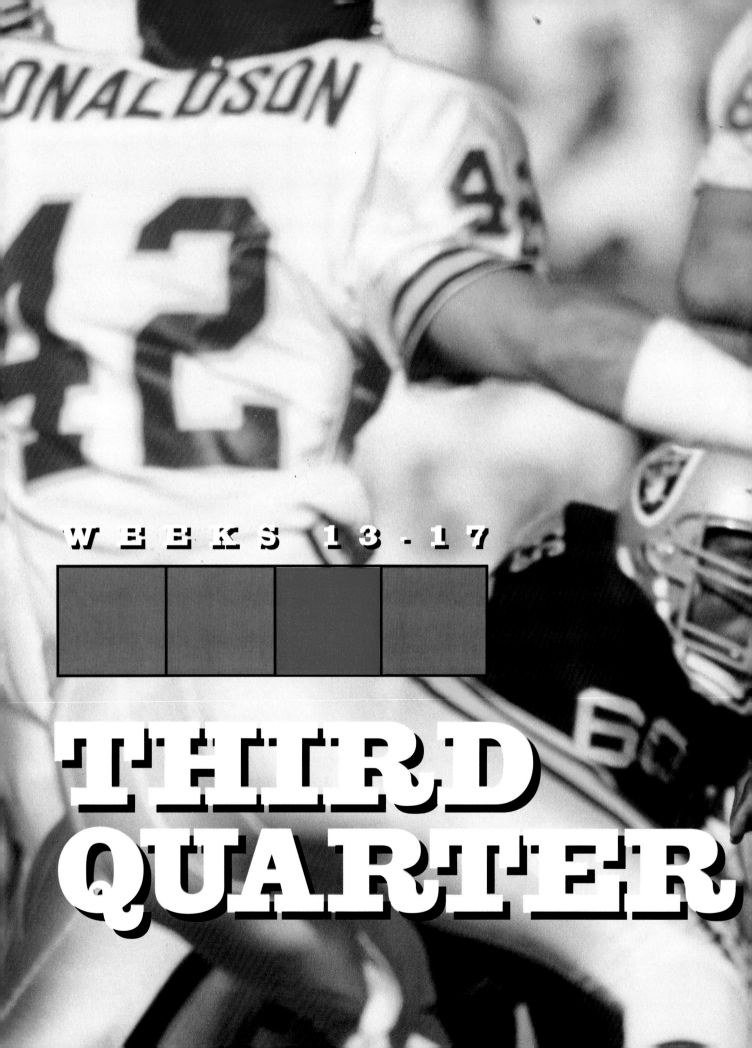

WEEKS 13-17

THIRD
QUARTER

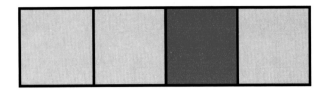

OVERVIEW

A PAIN IN THE BACK-FIELD

The biggest news as dusk fell on the NFL's 71st season was the spate of injuries to quarterbacks. The season-ending blows exploded with such force around the league, in fact, that a John Madden–narrated highlight film seems in order. BANG! Chris Miller goes down in Atlanta. WHAP! Phil Simms is grimacing in pain on the Giants Stadium turf. BOOM! Warren Moon is cradling his dislocated thumb in Houston. CRUNCH! There's Troy Aikman writhing on the carpet in Philadelphia. In the last five weeks of the regular season, an incredible seven starting quarterbacks were felled in battle (see chart).

"Entering the season," says former quarterback Gary Danielson, "it's like quarterbacks are going on a death march. Five or six will survive, but you never know who they'll be. Just look at these guys before the season. They aren't the bright, chipper guys you think they'd be. They look worried, nervous."

With good reason. Any quarterback with half a brain knows that he's going to get it. He just doesn't know when or how. He might pull a groin on an awkward scramble. A 280-pound defensive end might land on his ankle. A pop from the blind side might bruise his back. Something will happen, sometime. Only 11 of 28 quarterbacks who took the first snap in Week 1 started all 16 of their team's games. "It's the risk you take," Aikman said stoically after the Eagles' Clyde Simmons ended his season with a hard tackle. "It's not something you can think about a lot."

Can a quarterback do anything to reduce that risk? One remedy is for quarterbacks to "give their body an extra suit of armor in the off-season," as suggested by Giants strength and conditioning coach Johnny Parker. That's a polite way of saying that QBs must work out maniacally to have any chance of staying healthy. Which is exactly the prescription followed by the Giants' Simms.

In 1987, Simms added a weight room and sauna to his home. In 1989, he heard that javelin throwers work out with medicine balls to strengthen the front and back of their throwing shoulders, so he learned their exercises and spent $200 on different-sized balls to allow him to perform them. In 1990, he began his off-season workouts with 30 minutes of stretching instituted by former kick-boxing champion Steve Valencia. "If I had fighters in Simms's shape, I'd have world champions," Valencia says. So, after all that preparation, what happens? Simms goes down in Week 15 when a huge defensive lineman lands on his foot. How can you protect against that?

The fact of the matter is that quarterbacks today, unlike the pot-bellied Billy Kilmers of the past, are almost exclusively lean and trim all year round. So

what explains the rash of injuries? The answer lies in where football—not just pro football, but high school and college football, too—chooses to position its biggest and best athletes. With few exceptions, they are going to defense. Early and often.

When high school and college coaches see a big, quick-footed 18-year-old, they don't even briefly entertain the notion of making him, say, a left tackle. Instead, their eyes light up with manic glee at the prospect of how great he'll be at getting to the quarterback. So the kid plays outside linebacker or defensive end, develops into a 6'6", 260-pound juggernaut, becomes a first-round draft pick and spends his pro career flying around bulky, stodgy NFL tackles in pursuit of the quarterback sack. That is why the Giants spent their top two picks in 1988 and '89 on offensive linemen. They felt they had to get the best guys out there to block these defensive supermen.

The result of this season's carnage was that, as teams looked to the playoffs, their quarterback rosters began to resemble Red Cross reports. With Simms lost for the season, the NFC East champion Giants were forced to enter the Super Bowl tournament with a very green Jeff Hostetler. NFC Central champ Chicago would go with the shaky Mike Tomczak because of Jim Harbaugh's bum shoulder. In the AFC, Steve DeBerg would play for the Chiefs even with his left pinkie sporting a pin to hold together a shattered bone. But the Oilers would have to start Cody Carlson in place of MVP candidate Moon. Now we would see who drafted well and who had the steely and well-prepared backups.

Jack Lambert, the great Pittsburgh linebacker, once said that the league protected quarterbacks so much that the signal-callers ought to wear dresses. Maybe so, but no matter what the NFL does, the bottom line remains the same: There's a death march out there. It starts every September, and quarterbacks will continue to drop.

THE QUARTERBACK TOLL

The injuries to starting QBs gave backups a chance to shine. When Kelly was hurt against the Giants (above), Frank Reich, who also starred in relief last season, finished off New York and beat Miami before losing a meaningless game to Washington.

QB, TEAM INJURY	WEEK HURT	GAMES MISSED
WARREN MOON, *Houston* DISLOCATED THUMB	16	2
BACKUP: CODY CARLSON *Record 1-1*[*]		
TROY AIKMAN, *Dallas* SEPARATED SHOULDER	16	1
BACKUP: BABE LAUFENBERG *Record 0-1*		
JIM KELLY, *Buffalo* KNEE SPRAIN	15	2
BACKUP: FRANK REICH *Record 1-1*		
BERNIE KOSAR, *Cleveland* BONE CHIPS IN THUMB	15	2
BACKUP: MIKE PAGEL *Record 0-2*		
PHIL SIMMS, *N.Y. Giants* BONE AND LIGAMENT DAMAGE IN FOOT	15	5
BACKUP: JEFF HOSTETLER *Record 5-0*[*]		
JIM HARBAUGH, *Chicago* SEPARATED SHOULDER	15	4
BACKUP: MIKE TOMZCAK *Record 2-2*[*]		
CHRIS MILLER, *Atlanta* BROKEN COLLARBONE	13	4
BACKUPS: SCOTT CAMPBELL *Record 0-2* HUGH MILLEN *Record 2-0*		

including playoffs

49ERS 7
GIANTS 3

▼ Dave Waymer (left) and Keith DeLong wrestled Ottis Anderson to the ground for a loss in the first quarter as the 49ers held the Giants to a paltry 2.6 yards per rush.

Week 13, at San Francisco. The worst perception floating around America after the big showdown was that this was a bad game. Are you kidding? Great game! "This was the best defensive game with which I've been associated," 49er coach George Seifert said. A lot of viewers agreed: 41 million TV sets were tuned to the contest.

The Giants gained 221 yards, the 49ers 240, lousy totals for 10–1 teams. But the defense! There was Ronnie Lott lowering the boom on Mark Bavaro. There was Pepper Johnson laying a big hit on Roger Craig. In a year when the spotlight was on offense, this was the football equivalent of Dwight Gooden versus Orel Hershiser, 0–0 in the seventh, a one-hitter against a four-hitter. It was sweet to see.

With 1:30 left in the half, on the only drive of more than 60 yards, Joe Montana led John Taylor perfectly on a 23-yard pass into the end zone, and a sliding Taylor caught the ball right in his gut, maybe six or eight inches from the outstretched hand of Giants cornerback Mark Collins. It gave the 49ers a 7–3 lead. No one scored again.

The Giants came closest, failing on four Phil Simms throws from the San Francisco nine-yard line with four minutes left. Why did Giants coach Bill Parcells, with his defense playing superbly, choose to go for the TD on fourth-and-goal, instead of trying a field goal? "You can't expect to stop the 49ers every time they get the ball," a defensive Parcells said. "It was my decision, and I'll stand by it. We probably wouldn't have gotten the ball back into field goal position anyway." They did get the ball close again, to the San Francisco 16, but they needed a TD and more time. With the clock at :00, Simms ran around trying to find a receiver. For the fourth time that night, he was sacked. It was a fitting end.

For days in New York, Parcells was either brilliant or incompetent. People were impassioned. The game lingered. As it should have. These 60 minutes were among the finest of the NFL's 71st season.

▲ Charles Haley caught up with Simms on this play for a sack—one of four by the 49ers—as San Francisco's defense held the Giants 20 points below their average.

▼ Exhausted Giants linebacker Lawrence Taylor and his defensive teammates had no reason to hang their heads: They limited Montana to 12-of-29 passing for 152 yards.

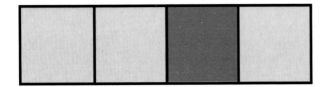
EAGLES 17 COWBOYS 3

▼ This second-quarter pass slipped away from Eagle receivers Fred Barnett and Keith Byars, but it didn't prevent their team from holding on for the victory.

Week 16, at Philadelphia. The night before this game, in the Cowboys' team hotel, Dallas wide receiver Michael Irvin's eyes got big in amazement. "A SPORTS ILLUSTRATED game?" he said when he learned the contest would be featured in the magazine the following week. "Really? Great! That's the whole reason I came to Dallas, to play in big games."

It was the biggest game for Dallas in Jimmy Johnson's two years as coach. The Cowboys were riding a four-game winning streak and, at 7–7, were one victory away from clinching a playoff spot. Lofty stuff, a year after going 1–15. How did they get this far this fast? In short: trades, defense and Emmitt Smith.

The two biggest deals—Herschel Walker to the Vikings and Steve Walsh to the Saints—have already paid huge dividends and will continue to do so in the future. From those trades, Dallas corralled eight draft picks in the first three rounds of 1990, '91 and '92 as well as getting three players who contributed on defense this season: starting corner Issiac Holt and reserve linebackers Jesse Solomon and David Howard. Along with linebacker Ken Norton Jr. and defensive linemen Dan Stubbs and Jimmie Jones, they have steadied last season's revolving-door defensive lineup. And in their rookie Smith, the Cowboys have a go-to back to add consistency to the offense.

Against the Eagles, even Smith's 61 yards rushing couldn't make up for the loss of QB Troy Aikman, who suffered a separated shoulder after a hit on the second series that put him out for the year. His replacement, Babe Laufenberg, completed only 13 of 36 passes against a ferocious Eagle pass rush, while Philadelphia, doing just enough offensively, made an early-second-half lead stand up. "The thing that disappoints me," said Laufenberg, "is I didn't give our team a chance to win." That's for sure.

Atlanta knocked Dallas out of the playoffs the next week, but the improvement in 1990 was encouraging. "They're obviously on the road to being much, much better," said Philadelphia kicker Roger Ruzek.

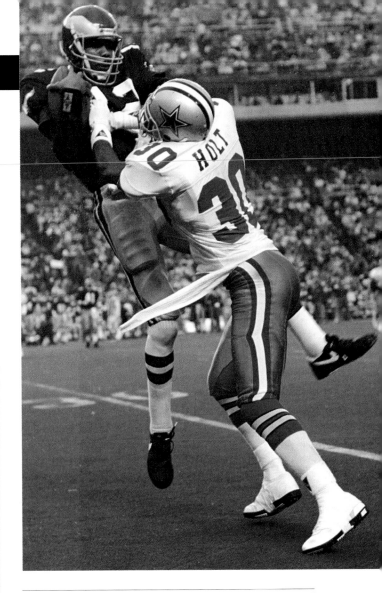

▲ Randall Cunningham's close encounters with the Dallas secondary: Holt popped him after this run, and Robert Williams and Manny Hendrix each picked off a pass.

▼ Despite the loss of Aikman on this sack early in the game, the Cowboys hung tough until midway through the final period, when Eric Allen returned an interception for a TD.

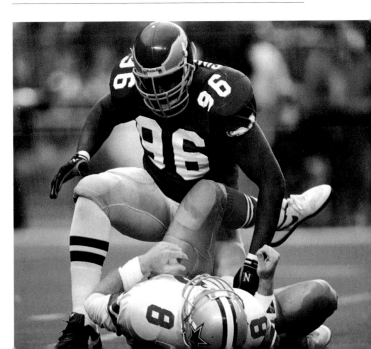

K E Y   G A M E S

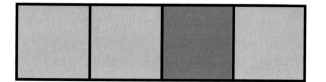

SAINTS 13
49ERS 10

▼ New Orleans quarterback Steve Walsh tossed two interceptions and completed only nine of 25 passes for 112 yards, but he did throw for the Saints' only touchdown.

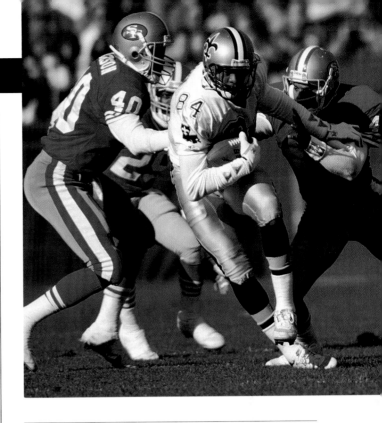

Week 16, at San Francisco. An upset seemed scripted from the start. The game was crucial for the Saints, who were fighting for their playoff lives; it meant nothing to the 49ers, who had already clinched a first-round bye. The Saints were healthy and at full-strength; the 49ers, looking toward the playoffs, were resting Joe Montana, Ronnie Lott and Roger Craig, the very heart of the team. Also in New Orleans's favor—ready for this?—was San Francisco's home-field *dis*advantage. Going into the game, the Niners had won 22 straight games on the road since a loss at Phoenix on Nov. 6, 1988. All five defeats since then have come at Candlestick. On this day, New Orleans would make it six. Barely.

It was an anybody's-game game, the final margin just a Morten Andersen 40-yard field goal with 4:43 left in the fourth quarter. While Montana stood on the sidelines in street clothes with a sore abdominal muscle, the Saints spent the afternoon chasing around Steve Young, his more mobile replacement, who outrushed the entire New Orleans team 102 to 84. Young moved the 49ers to a quick TD with a no-huddle offense on San Francisco's first series, and it looked like it might be a long day for New Orleans. But the Saints would hold the mighty 49ers to just a field goal thereafter as the defense always seemed to come up with the key play in crucial situations. The two biggest turnovers came in the fourth quarter, both as the Niners were driving for go-ahead scores. San Francisco tight end Brent Jones fumbled and linebacker Vaughn Johnson recovered to set up Andersen's winning kick. Then with 47 seconds remaining and New Orleans leading by three, Dexter Carter fumbled, and Saints linebacker Rickey Jackson recovered. Another loss at the Stick.

The Saints gladly took credit for the win. "When you come to play against the Saints' defense, it's going to be a battle," said safety Gene Atkins. San Francisco center Jesse Sapolu was more likely right. "Something was missing," he said.

▲ Dave Waymer (right) and Johnny Jackson (40) allowed Eric Martin to slip through their fingers as the Saints took advantage of a less fearsome secondary. A Lott less.

▼ New Orleans had trouble catching Young when he ran, but defensive end Renaldo Turnbull nailed him for two sacks in the backfield, half of the Saints' total.

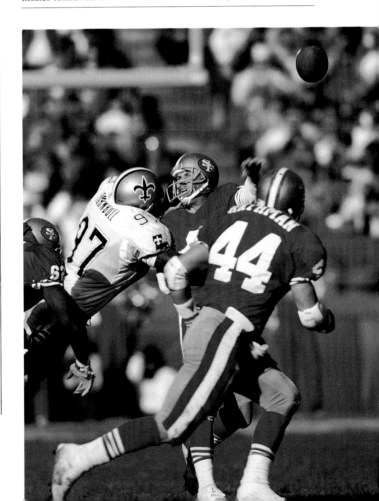

M E M O R A B L E   M O M E N T S

WEEK 13

S T A N D I N G S

AFC EAST	W	L	T	Pct	PF	PA
Buffalo	10	2	0	.833	342	200
Miami	9	3	0	.750	252	164
Indianapolis	5	7	0	.417	193	250
N.Y. Jets	4	9	0	.308	216	295
New England	1	11	0	.083	151	342

AFC CENTRAL	W	L	T	Pct	PF	PA
Cincinnati	7	5	0	.583	275	274
Houston	6	6	0	.500	266	229
Pittsburgh	6	6	0	.500	210	197
Cleveland	2	10	0	.167	187	338

AFC WEST	W	L	T	Pct	PF	PA
Kansas City	8	4	0	.667	283	179
L.A. Raiders	8	4	0	.667	230	194
Seattle	6	6	0	.500	222	226
San Diego	6	7	0	.462	272	220
Denver	3	9	0	.250	257	303

NFC EAST	W	L	T	Pct	PF	PA
N.Y. Giants	10	2	0	.909	262	148
Philadelphia	7	5	0	.583	305	252
Washington	7	5	0	.583	289	233
Dallas	6	7	0	.462	193	255
Phoenix	4	8	0	.333	192	295

NFC CENTRAL	W	L	T	Pct	PF	PA
Chicago	10	2	0	.833	281	197
Green Bay	6	6	0	.500	227	250
Minnesota	6	6	0	.500	282	229
Tampa Bay	5	8	0	.385	210	311
Detroit	4	8	0	.333	270	307

NFC WEST	W	L	T	Pct	PF	PA
San Francisco	11	1	0	.909	277	182
L.A. Rams	5	7	0	.417	285	322
New Orleans	5	7	0	.417	211	219
Atlanta	3	9	0	.250	279	308

RESULTS

Chicago 23, Detroit 17 (OT)
Tampa Bay 23, Atlanta 17
Cincinnati 16, Pittsburgh 12
Kansas City 37, New England 7
L.A. Rams 38, Cleveland 23
Buffalo 30, Philadelphia 23
Washington 42, Miami 20
Seattle 13, Houston 10 (OT)
San Diego 38, N.Y. Jets 17
Phoenix 20, Indianapolis 17
L.A. Raiders 23, Denver 20
Dallas 17, New Orleans 13
Minnesota 23, Green Bay 7
San Francisco 7, N.Y. Giants 3 (Monday night)

▼ Bruce Smith closed in on Eagle QB Randall Cunningham for one of his two sacks–the Bills had six total–as Buffalo jumped out to a 24–0 lead, then held on to win 30–23. Bills QB Jim Kelly threw for 334 yards, 174 of them to James Lofton.

▲ Cornerback Rod Jones upended Steeler tight end Mike Mularkey in Cincinnati's sixth straight win over Pittsburgh, a 16–13 victory that propelled the Bengals into the AFC Central lead. Pittsburgh had a third-and-goal from the seven with 2:25 remaining, but Cincinnati's defense held the Steelers scoreless to preserve the victory.

HIGHLIGHTS

▶ Chiefs quarterback Steve DeBerg completed 15 of 21 passes for 331 yards and two touchdowns, including an 86-yarder to Stephone Paige, and running back Barry Word rushed for 112 yards on 19 carries in a victory over the Patriots.

▶ In a rout over the Dolphins, the Redskins offense overwhelmed Miami's league-leading defense, scoring 42 points, rushing for 222 yards—157 by Earnest Byner—and controlling the ball for more than 40 minutes.

▶ Bears kicker Kevin Butler booted a 19-yard field goal with 33 seconds left to tie the Lions, and quarterback Jim Harbaugh found Neal Anderson open down the sideline for a 50-yard touchdown with 4:03 left in overtime to give Chicago the win.

▶ In the Chargers' win over the Jets, running back Marion Butts rushed for 159 yards on 26 carries.

▶ With seven seconds remaining, Raider defensive lineman Scott Davis blocked a game-tying 41-yard field goal attempt by the Broncos to preserve a Los Angeles victory.

WEEK 14

STANDINGS

AFC EAST	W	L	T	Pct	PF	PA
Buffalo	11	2	0	.846	373	207
Miami	10	3	0	.769	275	184
Indianapolis	5	8	0	.385	200	281
N.Y. Jets	4	9	0	.308	216	295
New England	1	12	0	.077	154	366
AFC CENTRAL	**W**	**L**	**T**	**Pct**	**PF**	**PA**
Cincinnati	7	6	0	.538	292	294
Houston	7	6	0	.538	324	243
Pittsburgh	7	6	0	.538	234	200
Cleveland	2	11	0	.154	201	396
AFC WEST	**W**	**L**	**T**	**Pct**	**PF**	**PA**
Kansas City	9	4	0	.692	314	199
L.A. Raiders	9	4	0	.692	268	225
Seattle	7	6	0	.538	242	240
San Diego	6	7	0	.462	272	220
Denver	3	10	0	.231	277	334
NFC EAST	**W**	**L**	**T**	**Pct**	**PF**	**PA**
N.Y. Giants	11	2	0	.846	285	163
Washington	8	5	0	.615	299	242
Philadelphia	7	6	0	.538	325	275
Dallas	6	7	0	.462	193	255
Phoenix	5	8	0	.385	206	308
NFC CENTRAL	**W**	**L**	**T**	**Pct**	**PF**	**PA**
Chicago	10	3	0	.769	290	207
Green Bay	6	7	0	.462	241	270
Minnesota	6	7	0	.462	297	252
Tampa Bay	5	8	0	.385	210	311
Detroit	4	9	0	.308	301	345
NFC WEST	**W**	**L**	**T**	**Pct**	**PF**	**PA**
San Francisco	12	1	0	.923	297	199
New Orleans	6	7	0	.462	235	239
L.A. Rams	5	8	0	.385	305	346
Atlanta	3	10	0	.231	292	332

RESULTS

Buffalo 31, Indianapolis 7
Houston 58, Cleveland 14
N.Y. Giants 23, Minnesota 15
Pittsburgh 24, New England 3
Phoenix 24, Atlanta 13
San Francisco 20, Cincinnati 17 (OT)
Seattle 20, Green Bay 14
Washington 10, Chicago 9
Kansas City 31, Denver 20
New Orleans 24, L.A. Rams 20
Miami 23, Philadelphia 20 (OT)
L.A. Raiders 38, Detroit 31 (Monday night)
Open dates: Dallas, N.Y. Jets, San Diego, Tampa Bay

HIGHLIGHTS

▶ Mike Cofer kicked a 23-yard field goal with 6:12 gone in overtime to give the 49ers a win over the Bengals, San Francisco's 17th consecutive victory on the road.

▶ Dan Marino completed 27 of 54 passes for 357 yards and two TDs as the Dolphins tied the Eagles with a last-second field goal, then won the game in OT when Pete Stoyanovich kicked a 39-yarder with 2:28 left.

▶ Oiler running back Lorenzo White rushed for 116 yards and scored four TDs in a win over the Browns.

▶ Former Heisman Trophy winners Bo Jackson and Barry Sanders put on a show in the Raiders' win over the Lions. Jackson rushed for 129 yards and a TD on 18 carries; Sanders ran for 176 yards and scored two TDs.

◀ Steve Walsh's four-yard touchdown pass to Eric Martin with 6:39 left gave New Orleans a 24–20 come-from-behind win over the Rams and kept the Saints' playoff hopes alive. The sloppy game produced four interceptions and seven fumbles, including one lost by Los Angeles running back Cleveland Gary at the New Orleans goal line.

▲ The Giants' Lawrence Taylor led a fourth-quarter defensive charge against Minnesota's Rich Gannon that produced two sacks, a fumble and an interception as New York pulled out a 23–15 win. Ottis Anderson gained 26 yards to lift his career total to 10,012 and become the eighth player to rush for more than 10,000 yards.

SUDDEN STAR

MARK CARRIER, SAFETY, CHICAGO

In Week 14 at Washington, Carrier picked off three Mark Rypien passes in a 10–9 Bears' loss. The groundwork for the interceptions, really, was laid eight months earlier when Carrier, an all-America at USC, made one of the smartest decisions in recent draft history. Sick of rookies holding out through training camp and contributing little in their first year, the Bears requested something unusual from three prospective draftees. "We wanted their agreement that they'd sign right away," said Bears personnel boss Bill Tobin. Two players refused. Carrier agreed, and when the Bears made him the sixth choice overall, he signed a five-year, $3.65 million deal. "For once, we wanted to get our money's worth with the first-rounder," Tobin said. And they did.

With the contract out of the way, Carrier spent all spring and summer learning the complexities of pro defenses. By the beginning of the season, he was firmly in place as a starter. By the end, his 10 interceptions led all NFL defenders. "Being signed right away is a huge factor in how I've done," Carrier says.

WEEK 15

STANDINGS

AFC EAST	W	L	T	Pct	PF	PA
Buffalo	12	2	0	.857	390	220
Miami	11	3	0	.786	299	201
Indianapolis	6	8	0	.429	229	302
N.Y. Jets	4	10	0	.286	237	324
New England	1	13	0	.071	164	391
AFC CENTRAL	W	L	T	Pct	PF	PA
Pittsburgh	8	6	0	.571	243	206
Houston	8	6	0	.571	351	253
Cincinnati	7	7	0	.500	299	318
Cleveland	3	11	0	.214	214	406
AFC WEST	W	L	T	Pct	PF	PA
L.A. Raiders	10	4	0	.714	292	232
Kansas City	9	5	0	.643	324	226
Seattle	7	7	0	.500	259	264
San Diego	6	8	0	.429	282	240
Denver	4	10	0	.286	297	344
NFC EAST	W	L	T	Pct	PF	PA
N.Y. Giants	11	3	0	.786	298	180
Washington	9	5	0	.643	324	252
Philadelphia	8	6	0	.571	356	275
Dallas	7	7	0	.500	234	265
Phoenix	5	9	0	.357	216	349
NFC CENTRAL	W	L	T	Pct	PF	PA
Chicago	10	4	0	.714	311	245
Tampa Bay	6	8	0	.429	236	324
Green Bay	6	8	0	.429	241	301
Minnesota	6	8	0	.429	310	278
Detroit	5	9	0	.357	339	366
NFC WEST	W	L	T	Pct	PF	PA
San Francisco	13	1	0	.929	323	209
New Orleans	6	8	0	.429	241	248
L.A. Rams	5	9	0	.357	315	372
Atlanta	3	11	0	.214	302	345

RESULTS

Buffalo 17, N.Y. Giants 13 (Saturday)
Washington 25, New England 10 (Saturday)
Cleveland 13, Atlanta 10
Philadelphia 31, Green Bay 0
Indianapolis 29, N.Y. Jets 21
Tampa Bay 26, Minnesota 13
Dallas 41, Phoenix 10
Miami 24, Seattle 17
Pittsburgh 9, New Orleans 6
L.A. Raiders 24, Cincinnati 7
Denver 20, San Diego 10
Detroit 38, Chicago 21
Houston 27, Kansas City 10
San Francisco 26, L.A. Rams 10 (Monday night)

◀ Bo Jackson (34) and cornerback Rod Jones met face-to-face on this play, then ran into each other again, much to Jackson's surprise, when Jones chased and caught him from behind at the one, preventing a TD after Bo broke clear on an 88-yard dash early in the third quarter. It was a hollow victory for Jones, a former NCAA 400-meter champion, as Jackson gained 117 yards and the Raiders beat the Bengals 24–7.

▲ When the Bills beat the Giants 17–13, the game took a greater toll on New York than a mark in the loss column: QB Phil Simms suffered a severe foot sprain that ended his season. Buffalo's Jim Kelly injured a knee but returned for the playoffs.

▼ In a 27–10 win over the Chiefs, Warren Moon passed for 527 yards, second only to Norm Van Brocklin's 554 in 1951. With the game already won, he showed class by throwing only twice on his final two series, thereby forfeiting a shot at the record.

HIGHLIGHTS

▶ The Eagles clinched a playoff spot by routing the Packers as running back Keith Byars caught one TD pass and threw another.
▶ Rookie running back Emmitt Smith rushed for 103 yards on 24 carries as the Cowboys kept their playoff hopes alive with a win over Phoenix.
▶ With 149 yards on 39 carries in a victory over the Patriots, Redskins running back Earnest Byner gained more than 1,000 yards for the second time in his career.
▶ Lion QB Rodney Peete threw for four TDs in Detroit's win over the Bears, who lost Jim Harbaugh for the year to a separated shoulder.

WEEK 16

STANDINGS

AFC EAST	W	L	T	Pct	PF	PA
Buffalo	13	2	0	.867	414	234
Miami	11	4	0	.733	313	225
Indianapolis	7	8	0	.467	264	330
N.Y. Jets	5	10	0	.333	279	331
New England	1	14	0	.067	171	433
AFC CENTRAL	W	L	T	Pct	PF	PA
Pittsburgh	9	6	0	.600	278	206
Cincinnati	8	7	0	.533	339	338
Houston	8	7	0	.533	371	293
Cleveland	3	12	0	.200	214	441
AFC WEST	W	L	T	Pct	PF	PA
L.A. Raiders	11	4	0	.733	320	256
Kansas City	10	5	0	.667	348	247
Seattle	8	7	0	.533	276	276
San Diego	6	9	0	.400	303	264
Denver	4	11	0	.267	309	361
NFC EAST	W	L	T	Pct	PF	PA
N.Y. Giants	12	3	0	.800	322	201
Philadelphia	9	6	0	.600	373	278
Washington	9	6	0	.600	352	287
Dallas	7	8	0	.467	237	282
Phoenix	5	10	0	.333	237	373
NFC CENTRAL	W	L	T	Pct	PF	PA
Chicago	11	4	0	.733	338	259
Tampa Bay	6	9	0	.400	250	351
Green Bay	6	9	0	.400	258	325
Detroit	6	9	0	.400	363	383
Minnesota	6	9	0	.400	334	306
NFC WEST	W	L	T	Pct	PF	PA
San Francisco	13	2	0	.867	333	222
New Orleans	7	8	0	.467	254	258
L.A. Rams	5	10	0	.333	328	393
Atlanta	4	11	0	.267	322	358

RESULTS

Detroit 24, Green Bay 17 (Saturday)
Indianapolis 35, Washington 28 (Saturday)
L.A. Raiders 28, Minnesota 24 (Saturday)
Kansas City 24, San Diego 21
Atlanta 20, L.A. Rams 13
Buffalo 24, Miami 14
Chicago 27, Tampa Bay 14
Cincinnati 40, Houston 20
New Orleans 13, San Francisco 10
N.Y. Giants 24, Phoenix 21
N.Y. Jets 42, New England 7
Philadelphia 17, Dallas 3
Pittsburgh 35, Cleveland 0
Seattle 17, Denver 12

▼ Quick-footed backup Jeff Hostetler, replacing the injured Phil Simms, eluded Ken Harvey and kept the Cardinals defense off-balance all day as he scrambled for 31 yards in the Giants' 24–21 win, which assured New York of a first-round playoff bye.

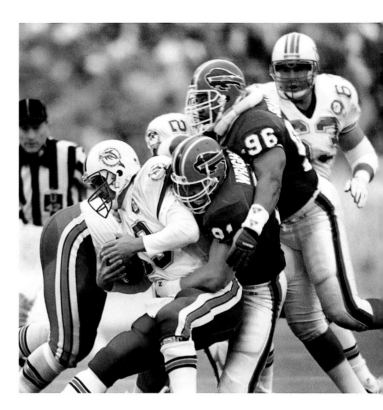

▲ Jeff Wright and Leon Seals (96) rode Dan Marino to the ground for one of Buffalo's three sacks in a 24–14 win that clinched a third straight AFC East title for the Bills and gave them the home-field advantage throughout the playoffs. Backup QB Frank Reich started for the injured Jim Kelly and threw for 234 yards and two TDs.

HIGHLIGHTS

▶ In the Bengals' win over the Oilers, Cincinnati running back James Brooks rushed for a club-record 201 yards on 20 carries as the Bengals took over the lead in the AFC Central. Houston quarterback Warren Moon suffered a dislocated right thumb, which sidelined him for the rest of the season.

▶ With the game between the Colts and the Redskins tied in the final minute, Indianapolis DB Alan Grant intercepted a Mark Rypien pass and returned it 25 yards for a TD to give the Colts a comeback win. Washington running back Earnest Byner rushed for 154 yards.

▶ The Seahawks kept their playoff hopes alive with a victory over the Broncos as Seattle cornerback Melvin Jenkins intercepted a John Elway pass in the closing moments to preserve the win.

▶ The Chiefs clinched a wild-card spot and remained in the race for the AFC West title with a win over the Chargers as Kansas City's Barry Word rushed for 106 yards and a touchdown on 28 carries.

▶ In a victory over the Vikings, Raider quarterback Jay Schroeder completed 10 of 15 passes for 234 yards and four touchdowns.

WEEK 17

STANDINGS

AFC EAST	W	L	T	Pct	PF	PA
Buffalo	13	3	0	.813	428	263
Miami	12	4	0	.750	336	242
Indianapolis	7	9	0	.438	281	353
N.Y. Jets	6	10	0	.375	295	345
New England	1	15	0	.063	181	446
AFC CENTRAL	**W**	**L**	**T**	**Pct**	**PF**	**PA**
Cincinnati	9	7	0	.563	360	352
Houston	9	7	0	.563	405	307
Pittsburgh	9	7	0	.563	292	240
Cleveland	3	13	0	.188	228	462
AFC WEST	**W**	**L**	**T**	**Pct**	**PF**	**PA**
L.A. Raiders	12	4	0	.750	337	268
Kansas City	11	5	0	.688	369	257
Seattle	9	7	0	.563	306	286
San Diego	6	10	0	.375	315	281
Denver	5	11	0	.313	331	374
NFC EAST	**W**	**L**	**T**	**Pct**	**PF**	**PA**
N.Y. Giants	13	3	0	.813	335	211
Philadelphia	10	6	0	.625	396	299
Washington	10	6	0	.625	381	301
Dallas	7	9	0	.438	244	308
Phoenix	5	11	0	.313	268	396
NFC CENTRAL	**W**	**L**	**T**	**Pct**	**PF**	**PA**
Chicago	11	5	0	.688	348	280
Tampa Bay	6	10	0	.375	264	367
Detroit	6	10	0	.375	373	413
Green Bay	6	10	0	.375	271	347
Minnesota	6	10	0	.375	351	326
NFC WEST	**W**	**L**	**T**	**Pct**	**PF**	**PA**
San Francisco	14	2	0	.875	353	239
New Orleans	8	8	0	.500	274	275
L.A. Rams	5	11	0	.313	345	412
Atlanta	5	11	0	.313	348	365

RESULTS

Kansas City 21, Chicago 10 (Saturday)
Philadelphia 23, Phoenix 21 (Saturday)
Washington 29, Buffalo 14
Cincinnati 21, Cleveland 14
Atlanta 26, Dallas 7
Miami 23, Indianapolis 17
N.Y. Giants 13, New England 10
San Francisco 20, Minnesota 17
Seattle 30, Detroit 10
Denver 22, Green Bay 13
N.Y. Jets 16, Tampa Bay 14
L.A. Raiders 17, San Diego 12
Houston 34, Pittsburgh 14
New Orleans 20, L.A. Rams 17 (Monday night)

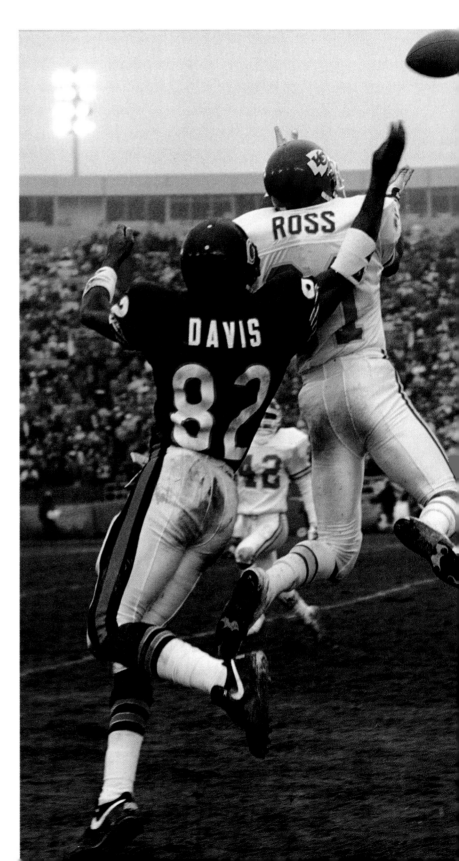

SUDDEN STAR

CODY CARLSON, QUARTERBACK, HOUSTON

When a dislocated thumb in Warren Moon's throwing hand sidelined him for the season in a Week 16 loss to the Bengals, the outlook for the Oilers seemed bleak. Needing a win over Pittsburgh in Week 17 to make the playoffs, Houston was forced to turn to Cody Carlson, a fourth-year player from Baylor with only five pro starts. To make matters worse, Carlson had held out of training camp until August, which was especially detrimental because the Oilers were installing the complicated run-and-shoot. Playing catch-up ball all season, Carlson appeared ill-prepared for the hero's role when Moon went down.

So much for appearances. Against the top-ranked defense in the NFL, all Carlson did was complete 22 of 29 passes for 247 yards and three TDs. After five Oiler possessions, Pittsburgh, which hadn't given up a touchdown in 14 quarters, trailed 24–0 en route to a 34–14 loss. "I'm just an ordinary Joe who happens to throw a football," Carlson said, but when the Oilers needed a big win in a big game, he looked more like an ordinary Joe Montana.

◀ Kevin Ross missed this interception but kept Wendell Davis from making the catch as the Chiefs ended the year with a 21–10 victory over Chicago. Bears QB Mike Tomczak had trouble connecting with anybody, completing only five of 23 passes.

▼ Washington's Tracy Rocker sacked Bills QB Frank Reich twice in the Redskins' 29–14 win. With playoff spots clinched, both teams rested their starters, costing Buffalo's Thurman Thomas the rushing title when he gained no yards on five carries.

HIGHLIGHTS

▶ The Cowboys lost a chance to make the playoffs when the Falcons beat them 26–7. That loss, combined with the Saints' win over the Rams on a 24-yard field goal by Morten Andersen with two seconds left, propelled New Orleans into the final NFC playoff spot.

▶ Bengal safety David Fulcher intercepted a pass from Browns QB Mike Pagel with 55 seconds left to seal a win, which, combined with the Oilers' victory over the Steelers, gave Cincinnati the AFC Central title.

▶ Barry Sanders finished the season with 1,304 yards to win the NFL rushing title by seven yards over the Bills' Thurman Thomas.

FOURTH QUARTER

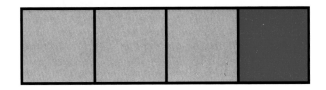

OVERVIEW

A GIANT GROUP EFFORT

You stare at the scores, and they seem unreal, like this was some other team, maybe the 1978 Steelers or the 1985 Bears or the 1989 49ers or even the 1986 Giants.

Giants 31, Chicago 3.

Giants 15, San Francisco 13.

Giants 20, Buffalo 19.

You peer into the locker room the moment Super Bowl XXV is over, and you know the New York Giants feel the same thing. A soaked-with-sweat Bill Parcells bursts through the door before anyone else and waits for his champions. Lawrence Taylor arrives. "They said we couldn't do it!" shrieks LT,

and he bear hugs Parcells, then kisses him flush on the lips. Then you see all the other Giants stream in with this little-kid-at-Christmas look. "We're the champions OF THE WORLD!" tight end Howard Cross sing-songs, loudly.

You look at the ABC podium, set up in front of the locker room to interview the winners, and there's Parcells again, holding the Super Bowl trophy, next to commissioner Paul Tagliabue, motioning to Super Bowl MVP Ottis Anderson to come up onto the podium, and Anderson does, and Parcells gives him a wet one on a sweaty left cheek.

You go outside, and some Giants are giving individual interviews on portable podiums in the bowels of Tampa Stadium. Center Bart Oates is holding the Super Bowl champion's trophy while talking to a knot of reporters. Twenty feet away, the man who kicked the winning field goals in the NFC Championship Game and in the Super Bowl, Matt Bahr, tells reporters: "Excuse me. Excuse me for a second. I'll be right back." And you see Bahr walk over to Oates's podium, nudge through the gaggle of reporters and step up alongside Oates. Then you see him lift his right hand to the silver football on the trophy, and you see him pet it. "I just wanted to touch it," he says, sheepishly and seriously at the same time.

You go back into the locker room, and linebacker Carl Banks is about the last player left, and you look into his eyes to see what he's feeling, and he says, "Team, baby. Team this time."

Which, you come to find out, is why we enter 1991 with the New York Giants on the NFL throne. They didn't have the best individual players. Buffalo had better. San Francisco had better. The Giants were a selfless, wonderfully motivated group, a just-win-baby group, a group of players with attitudes we thought had died a generation ago.

The day after the Super Bowl, you're still trying to figure the Giants out. You know about the motivation of Parcells, about how effectively he blunts the tendency of today's athletes to advance their own careers while neglecting their teams. You've heard during Super Bowl week, off the record, from one Buffalo player who said bluntly: "You know what this is about? This is about putting ourselves on the map. You drive around Tampa, and you see Bo Jackson and Randall Cunningham on billboards. We want to be up on billboards. We want our piece." Hmmm, you think. What about the win? And you listen to Parcells and Anderson bantering in the back of the limousine that is taking them to the day-after news conference, and you realize: For them, the win is still supreme. "What a great group this was," Parcells said in the car. "This sounds corny. But I wish the world, with all the problems we're having, was like this team. All they cared about was winning. They didn't care about the score or about the stats. Not once did I have any serious discipline problems. They policed themselves. What great guys."

Team, baby. Team this time. You think of how many important people there were to this team. You think of the assistant coaches, of Bill Belichick designing terrific game plans, blueprinting ways to hold Joe Montana to two touchdowns in eight quarters in their two meetings, of opening this Super Bowl with six defensive backs in the lineup, of Jim Kelly looking around and wondering, "Huh? On first down? On the first play of the game?" You think of Anderson, a nonperson in 1986, whom Parcells put in on a meaningless final drive in Super Bowl XXI to get a garbage-time touchdown because he might not ever play another NFL game, and you think how important he was down the stretch of this season, with 62 playoff carries and 249 playoff rushing yards. And you think of Mark Ingram, a forgotten wide receiver, Ping-Ponging and fighting for a crucial Super Bowl third-quarter first down, breaking three tackles to make a first down and set up a go-ahead touchdown. And you think of tackle John Elliott, who

▲ Running to the locker room after their second Super Bowl win, both Taylor and Parcells were dripping: one from sweat, the other from a Gatorade victory bath.

beat up Bills defensive end Bruce Smith so thoroughly that Smith touched quarterback Jeff Hostetler only twice all Super Bowl day. And you think of Hostetler, of course, the Phil Simms stand-in, who was supposed to hand off all day and put the ball up maybe 17 or 18 times in the Super Bowl, and instead threw 32 times and almost won the MVP. And you think of Bahr, whose range is questionable but whose heart isn't, and you think of Mark Bavaro and Leonard Marshall and Maurice Carthon, all Super Bowl XXI vets who came up big in Super Bowl XXV.

And you think of the odds against them. You think of Montana to Rice in Candlestick and Kelly to everyone in Tampa, and you think how everything was going to have to be just so for them to win.

Well, everything was just so. But it was just so because the Giants willed it to be just so and worked hard to make it just so, and in team sports, that counts for something.

PLAYOFFS

MIAMI 17
KANSAS CITY 16

Maybe the Kansas City Chiefs forgot that it was still Dan Marino standing over there. Yeah, it had been four years since Marino had even made the playoffs. And true, the K.C. guys had steamed up and down the field for three quarters, taking a 13–3 lead in the AFC wild-card game. And yes, Marino started out 9-for-20 passing, for piddling yardage. Even so—they should have remembered.

Certainly the Chiefs should have remembered when they smothered a Mark Duper fumble late in the third quarter at the Miami 29, giving them a chance to put the game away. But they didn't. In fact, the Chiefs turtled, choosing to give the ball to Christian Okoye, three times for eight yards. No passes, no play action. Just three clouds of Nigerian dust and a 38-yard field goal for a 16–3 lead. This is not exactly going for the jugular. This is going for the eyeliner.

"I couldn't *believe* when they did that," said Dolphin Tim McKyer. "That was a big lift." Now Miami could still win with two TDs, and the Dolphins knew it. So did Marino, who responded by going 8 for 8 in the fourth quarter for 101 yards. First he hit Tony Paige with a one-yard TD flip to make it 16–10 with 12:18 to go. Then, on a first-and-10 from the 12 with 3:28 left, he snaked the ball past the oustretched fingers of the Chiefs' Albert Lewis and into the waiting hands of Mark Clayton for the game-winning score.

"We've beaten nobody," Clayton said after the game. "Well, just let us keep on beating nobody, and we'll see you in Tampa, O.K.?"   —*RICK REILLY*

◀ Marino was a forgotten man in the early going, but by the end of the game his passing exploits made the conservative Chiefs wish that their memory hadn't faltered.

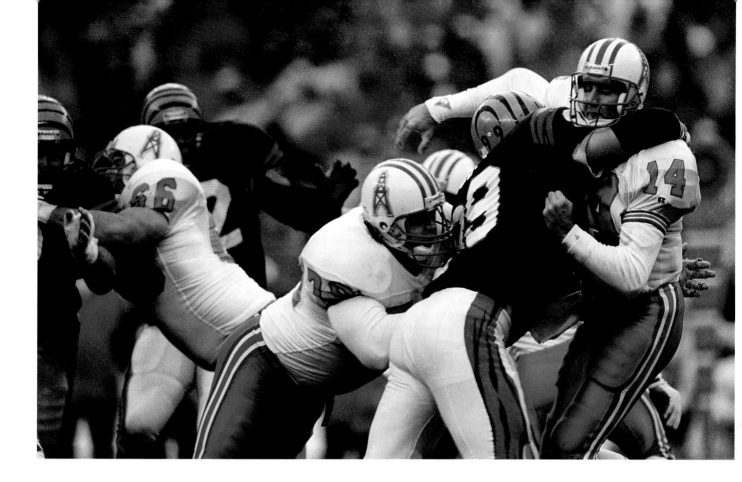

CINCINNATI 41
HOUSTON 14

Twenty-four hours before the Cincinnati Bengals played the Houston Oilers in an AFC wild-card game, coach Sam Wyche spent a relaxing afternoon riding through Cincinnati's poorest neighborhood, Over-the-Rhine, where he frequently does volunteer work. At a shelter for the homeless, one indigent soul urged Wyche to beat the Los Angeles Raiders. "Not this week," Wyche said. "We'll get them next week."

Back at the Bengals' practice complex, Wyche remained confident. He said, "I've never felt as good entering a game in my life as I feel about this one."

With good reason. The last three times the Oilers had met Cincinnati at Riverfront Stadium, the Bengals had won, by an average margin of 32.3 points. And this time, in rainy, near-freezing weather, the Bengals played their best game of the season and crushed Houston 41–14. As a result, Cincinnati would indeed face the Raiders.

After playing 34 minutes against the Oilers, the Bengals had 34 points, 265 yards of total offense and

▲ Lineman Jason Buck fashioned a human necklace for Carlson, and the rest of the Bengal defense hung around long enough to limit the Oiler offense to 226 total yards.

16 first downs. Houston had zero, 37 and one, respectively. To be sure, Houston quarterback Cody Carlson, who would finish with 16 completions in 33 attempts for 165 yards, was not going to be confused with Warren Moon again. Carlson was making his second start in place of Moon, who was sidelined with a dislocated thumb. Just a week earlier, Carlson had put up terrific stats against the Pittsburgh Steelers to help Houston clinch its wild-card spot.

For their part, the Bengals, who this season have been inconsistent on offense and among the worst teams in the league on defense, looked suspiciously like their 1989 Super Bowl selves. The offense ran like a clock (187 rushing yards, 162 passing yards, no turnovers), and the defense held Oiler back Lorenzo White to two yards on four carries and pushed Carlson's blockers back in his face. Basically, everything went right. To beat the Raiders, the Bengals would need another perfect day.

—*Peter King*

83

PLAYOFFS

CHICAGO 16
NEW ORLEANS 6

There was ammunition everywhere; the only question was how the crowd at Soldier Field would use it. Snow was heaped under every seat, and if the Chicago Bears stank up the joint one more time—the way they had in losing four of their last six games—the fans would bombard them with snowballs as surely as aldermen will stuff ballot boxes. The main target, of course, would be QB Mike Tomczak, the sensitive, streaky backup filling in for injured Jim Harbaugh.

But against the New Orleans Saints in the NFC wild-card game, Tomczak put together a nifty 5-of-6 passing display in the middle of the first half, highlighting it with an 18-yard scoring toss to tight end James Thornton, and Chicago went on to win 16–6.

The crowd deemed the Bears' one-TD, three-field-goal performance acceptable and spared the home team, pelting visiting fans instead.

For a while, it seemed that Tomczak might not have any numbers at all. He didn't throw a pass during the Bears' first series—which nonetheless produced a field goal for a 3–0 lead—and had only one attempt on their second. Then came Tomczak's flurry, producing the TD pass to Thornton and a 10–0 lead. Following the score, Tomczak, who would finish with 12 completions in 25 attempts for 166 yards, grinned, pumped his fists in the air, butted helmets with teammates and looked, basically, like a lost soul who had been saved. After the touchdown, the kickers traded two field goals each, and that was the game.

The offensive standout, as usual, was Neal Anderson, who rushed for 102 yards on 27 carries and even completed one pass for 22 yards. But most of the credit for the win had to go to Chicago's defense, particularly cornerback John Mangum, who had one pickoff and broke up several key passes. Added inspiration came from rickety and soon-to-be pastured defensive tackle Dan Hampton, who knocked down a pass and made one early tackle in which he grabbed the ballcarrier in one hand and Saints guard Steve Trapilo in the other.

But this frigid game produced little heat otherwise, except for a body slam of 270-pound Craig (Ironhead) Heyward by 320-pound William (the Refrigerator) Perry, which moved the frozen earth. "It looked like a Japanese monster movie," said Chicago's Steve McMichael. The next week, it would be the Bears versus Godzilla in New York. —*RICK TELANDER*

◀ Anderson was the key to the Bears' somewhat primitive, eat-up-the-clock attack; he rushed 32 times and caught four passes for 144 of Chicago's 365 total yards.

WASHINGTON 20 PHILADELPHIA 6

Whenever the Washington Redskins get ready to play the Philadelphia Eagles, Skins defensive coordinator Richie Petitbon puts the same message on the bulletin board: "Randall Cunningham is the greatest scrambler ever to play this game." He reminded his players again in preparing them for this one. "This time he put it in extra big letters," said defensive tackle Tim Johnson.

The Eagles had lived by the miracle play, but the Age of Miracles ended on a cold afternoon with a 20–6 loss to the Redskins. There was no remarkable Cunningham scramble ending in a TD pass, none of the wild plays that helped Philly all year.

What the fans at the Vet saw instead was a collection of things that weren't supposed to happen. Washington's front four got to Cunningham for five sacks. The banged-up Skins' offensive line, held Philadelphia's mighty pass rush to no sacks. "We just sort of swelled up," said guard Raleigh McKenzie. When the Eagles blitzed, Washington QB Mark Rypien beat them by dumping the ball to tailback Earnest Byner (seven catches, 77 yards).

▲ Buddy Ryan predicted a Byner fumble, but the replay judge clouded Ryan's crystal ball by ruling–correctly, as shown here–that Byner lost the ball after hitting the ground.

That was the pattern in the second quarter, when the Skins, leading 7–6, tried another short one to Byner. He rambled to the Philadelphia six, where Ben Smith made the tackle, and the ball popped free. Smith picked it up and was off—94 yards for a score, according to referee Gene Barth. After a review, the replay judge reversed the call, ruling that the ball had been knocked loose when Byner hit the ground, and therefore there was no fumble. The Skins got a field goal. It was a 10-point call.

The other controversial call came from the Eagles' bench. With 2:29 left in the third and the score 13–6, Ryan replaced Cunningham with 31-year-old Jim McMahon, who had thrown only nine passes all year. "I was getting ready to go in," Cunningham said, "and they just said, 'Jim's in.' I said, 'Thanks for letting me know.' " McMahon contributed three incomplete passes. The game was essentially over.

The Skins would next travel to San Francisco, where they would be heavy underdogs. But the unpredictable has been known to happen. Just ask Randall Cunningham.   —*PAUL ZIMMERMAN*

BUFFALO 44
MIAMI 34

We'll know soon enough whether it was a mirage. But through the freezing rain and driving snow at Rich Stadium last Saturday, the Buffalo Bills looked very much like a true Super Bowl team—not like the typical AFC representative of the 1980s, the one waving a white flag.

This is a fast-maturing Buffalo team that froze out the Miami Dolphins 44–34 in their AFC divisional playoff. This is a team playing with a new, Joe Montana–like efficiency on offense, running a sort of weatherproof run-and-shoot that an opponent is going to have to flat outscore if it hopes to win. This is an offense so potent that it nearly reduced Dolphin defensive coordinator Tom Olivadotti to tears.

This is a team with an all-star defense, featuring four Pro Bowl players—end Bruce Smith, outside linebacker Cornelius Bennett and inside linebacker Shane Conlan and outside linebacker Darryl Talley—among its front seven, plus two near All-Pros in cornerback Nate Odomes and strong safety Leonard Smith.

Bills quarterback Jim Kelly, who didn't return to practice until four days before the playoffs, was quite healthy by the kickoff, thank you. Operating out of a no-huddle offense, he completed 19 of 29 passes for 339 yards and three touchdowns, with one interception and very few mistakes. Instead of moving around gingerly on the tender knee, Kelly returned to action like a man coming off a four-week vacation; he looked rested and sharp. He even ran with the ball five times for 37 yards.

On this day, the Bills offense was near unstoppable, as the results of 10 of their first 12 possessions attested: touchdown, field goal, field goal, touchdown, touchdown, halftime, interception, field goal, touchdown, touchdown.

Olivadotti, who elevated the Dolphin defense from 24th in last year's NFL rankings to seventh this year, decided to use much more man-to-man pass coverage rather than rely on zone coverage, as Miami had most of the season. The benefit of the man-to-man, Olivadotti thought, would be to free his front seven to blitz more. The result: Kelly and his receivers embarrassed the Dolphin secondary.

Buffalo's X factor, as always, was Thurman Thomas, football's most versatile back. No offensive

◀ Back in action after missing four weeks with a knee injury, Kelly looked as frisky as a housebound kid let loose to play in the snow. One of his five runs covered 16 yards.

player in the game has more rushing-receiving yards over the past two years than Thomas. He touched the ball on the first play of nine of the Bills' 12 drives against Miami. His average gain: seven yards. "I love this offense," Kelly said after the Bills had won for the 14th time in 17 games this season. "We can do so many things, so many different ways."

Miami's Dan Marino had resuscitated the Dolphins with a brilliant two-yard TD run on a bootleg just before halftime, so Miami trailed by only 27–17 at the half. After the teams exchanged field goals in the third quarter, Marino dumped a two-yard touchdown pass to tackle-eligible Roy Foster on third-and-goal at the start of the fourth quarter. Buffalo's lead was 30–27, with 13:54 left to play.

Kelly didn't blink. He hit James Lofton for 42 yards, Keith McKeller on fourth-and-two for five and Al Edwards for 12 to move the Bills to the Miami 17. Four plays later, Thomas (32 carries for 117 yards)

▲ Lofton's 13-yard tochdown reception late in the second quarter gave the Bills a 27–10 lead. He finished as the game's leading receiver with seven grabs for 149 yards.

burst past center Kent Hull for a five-yard score. The lead was 10 again, 37–27. On the kick return, Buffalo's Hal Garner knocked the ball out of return man Marc Logan's grasp at the Dolphin 26-yard line. "I thought I was gone," Logan said. "I really didn't see him. He put his head right on the ball." Buffalo recovered, and 25 seconds later, Kelly hit Andre Reed with the 26-yard TD that clinched the victory.

"Kelly's like a Magic Johnson or Michael Jordan in this offense," said Bills offensive coordinator Ted Marchibroda. "The ball's in his hands. The game's in his hands. Jimmy calls the game all by himself, and we've got the personnel now to run the offense right."

Soon, the rest of the world may learn just how good this offense is. It's a new decade, and a new team is giving new hope to the AFC.   —*PETER KING*

PLAYOFFS

L. A. R A I D E R S 2 0
C I N C I N N A T I 1 0

Let us rephrase the cynic's retort as it applies to Cincinnati Bengal coach Sam Wyche: Just because he says his players are injured doesn't mean they're not. In fact, the Bengals were pretty well banged up as advertised, with possible airplane food poisoning thrown in as an AFC divisional playoff bonus malady. "I think it was the chicken," said Cincinnati quarterback Boomer Esiason, who by then believed he should have gone with the sirloin tips. Maybe it was just the stomach flu, as officially reported. Either way, the ailment occurred too late for Wyche to add it to his injury reports, which are always greeted with skeptical anticipation in the NFL.

But perennial All-Pro tackle Anthony Munoz, out with an injured rotator cuff, truly didn't play a down for the Bengals, guard Bruce Reimers, on crutches with a sprained ankle, indeed was inactive and the upshot was pretty much as Wyche would have had everyone believe. Esiason had neither the stomach nor the protection for the game, while the Raiders brought both a pass rush (four sacks) and their appetite. Indeed, their 20–10 win before a rare full house (92,045) at the L.A. Memorial Coliseum should lead some folks to think that maybe the Silver and Black *is* back.

If it's true, you'll have to hand it to owner Al Davis, who can smile smugly at a couple of his inventions—quarterback Jay Schroeder and tight end Ethan Horton. The two hooked up on a 41-yard pass that Horton carried in for a touchdown to make the score 17–10 with 8:52 to play. Of course, Davis's established talents were hardly idle. True, Bo Jackson was hampered by a hip injury, but the often-overlooked Marcus Allen was his usual brilliant self, slashing through the Cincinnati defense for 140 yards. That's hardly a surprise: Allen is one of the five veterans from the Raider Super Bowl team of seven seasons ago, and since then he has made lots of cornerbacks eat their game plans. What's new is Schroeder, an erratic performer who has benefited from Davis's and coach Art Shell's patience. With a simplified offense and wonder-backs Jackson and Allen behind him, Schroeder has settled into uncharacteristic efficiency. His performance against the Bengals was typical: 11 of 21 passes for 172 yards.

But Horton was more reminiscent of Davis's scrap-heap finds, the forgotten and the misunderstood that he turns into Raider institutions. Waived four times as a running back, Horton was out of the NFL for most of two seasons. "The phone didn't ring once," says Horton, until "Mr. Davis" phoned out of the blue after the '88 season and proposed that Horton play tight end. "He told me he had a gut feeling I could catch the ball. If Mr. Davis said that, it was enough for me." Horton proved Davis's salvage savvy yet again, leading the Raiders with four receptions and 77 yards against the Bengals.

It looks as if the Raiders are now a team that the NFL must worry about. Fair warning may be gathered from the Bengals' Leon White, the poor linebacker who was isolated one-on-one on Horton's big catch. "It was way over my head, so I thought it was way over his, too," he explained innocently. The Raiders may indeed be playing over their heads. Just like the old days.

—*RICHARD HOFFER*

▶ Allen bolted away from Skip McClendon on the way to his first 100-yard rushing day since 1988. On L.A.'s final clock-eating drive, Allen had two crucial first-down runs.

PLAYOFFS

SAN FRANCISCO 28 WASHINGTON 10

DIARY OF A WASHINGTON REDSKINS SPY:

Spylog, Tuesday, Jan. 8: I'm not so sure about this. Look, I've done the Kremlin, the Lebanese embassy, even Madonna's house, but this San Francisco 49er practice facility is the toughest nut to crack yet. I actually had to climb a eucalyptus tree just to get a look inside today. Unfortunately, 49er coach George Seifert had his security staff chase me out before I could get any good pictures. While I was able to slip away without being identified, it was embarrassing to read in all of the papers that I had been sighted. "Honest to God, there was somebody in that tree," Seifert told the media.

Spylog, Wednesday, Jan. 9: Seifert admits he's getting "very paranoid," and I like to think I'm part of

it. Today, I tried the Fuji blimp. Seifert and his guys glared at me, but what could they do? Rent a chase blimp? Unfortunately, from a circling blimp, it is difficult to tell a tight end from a Gatorade cooler.

Not that I think we Redskins will have any touble with the 49ers. The Niners? Get bent. They've been flat. Joe Montana, 34, has played 30 minutes in the last three weeks and a lousy 30 minutes at that. Ronnie Lott, 31, hasn't played in four weeks. They're about as In as eight-track tapes.

Spylog, Thursday, Jan. 10: Today I flew over the Niner practice field in a helicopter. Seifert got so flustered he told somebody to go get a starter's pistol to fire at the chopper, but nobody could find him one. You think I'm going to be scared by a starter's pistol? Who am I, Carl Lewis?

Spylog, Friday, Jan. 11: This baby is in the bag. Seifert even went up to Mark Purdy, columnist for the *San Jose Mercury News*, and said, "I read your story on how Joe Montana is better than Mark Rypien. Thanks a lot for motivating Washington." Uh-oh. Somebody call Reuters. NEWSFLASH: MONTANA SAID TO BE BETTER THAN RYPIEN!

Spylog, Saturday, Jan. 12: This is not the team I saw from the blimp. Somebody double-crossed me. I think the team I spied on was Stanford.

We scored a TD on our first drive, got a field goal the next time down and then never scored again. We got vaporized 28–10. Most of the problem was this damn Montana. He was running like Cunningham and gunning like Elway and cunning like, well, himself.

Maybe I wasn't seeing too well out of my seagull

◀ Even though he was snuffed by Kevin Fagan on this play and missed more than half the game with a shoulder injury, Byner led all rushers with 51 yards on 12 carries.

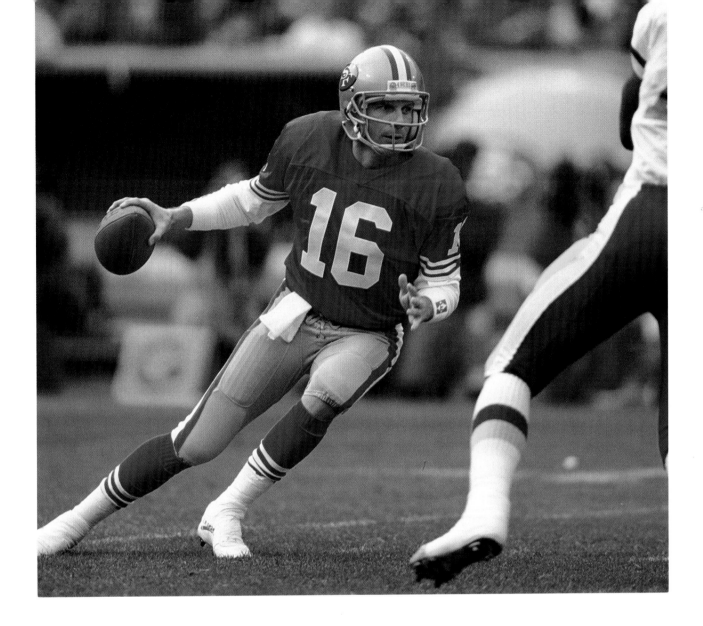

disguise, but I could've sworn we were in this game for a minute there. Rypien started off sizzling. He hit Art Monk for a 31-yard touchdown, and we were up 7–0. They answered with that running back who looks like a Russian professor, Tom Rathman, whose one-yard TD tied it. But we came right back with a field goal, and we led 10–7 in the first quarter. Who would ever think they would egg us from there?

I should've known we were in trouble, though, when Montana slipped a 10-yard touchdown pass just past the cuticles of our cornerback, Darrell Green, and right onto the fingertips of third-look receiver Jerry Rice. On the next drive he put a spiral through the crook of the elbow of our linebacker, Andre Collins, and into the disbelieving mitts of tight end Brent Jones, for 47 yards. Two plays later Mike

▲ Montana didn't look so hot from the spy blimp, but down on the field he was as limber as ever in dancing away from the Redskins' pass rush and firing two TD passes.

Sherrard, who was coming off a broken right ankle, gimped into the clear and caught the eight-yard TD pass that made it 21–10.

Oh, then there was the humiliating ending. San Francisco's 285-pound noseguard, Michael Carter, picked off a Rypien pass and ran it back 61 yards for a touchdown. Although, maybe *ran* isn't the right word. It was more the way a doughnut truck gets down Broadway with five pistons and three wheels.

All our locker room talk was about Montana, who completed 22 of 31 passes for 274 yards. Our defensive coordinator, Richie Petitbon, said it best: "We shoulda kidnapped the s.o.b." —*RICK REILLY*

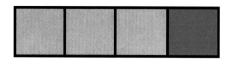

PLAYOFFS

N.Y. GIANTS 31 CHICAGO 3

Here's the biggest lie in playoff football: You dance with who brung ya ... you don't get away from your tendencies ... you do what you do best. The New York Giants danced with the other guy's wife. They lined up in a brand-new defensive formation. They squashed the Chicago Bears' running game, and they earned the right to meet the San Francisco 49ers for the NFC championship with their 31–3 victory at Giants Stadium.

New York's Lawrence Taylor called the new alignment "not really a true 4–3, more of a wide-tackle six-man line, because the outside linebackers, me and Carl Banks, were playing so close up."

Pepper Johnson, normally the weak inside linebacker in the 3–4, was the middle linebacker, a position he had never played before. "My responsibility was to look for Neal Anderson's cutbacks," he said of Chicago's leading rusher, "but our two tackles, Mike Fox and Erik Howard, were doing such a good job stuffing everything inside that I wasn't in on a whole lot of tackles." The overall result: 27 yards rushing for the Bears, their lowest total in 23 years.

The Giants' idea was to force the game into the hands of quarterback Mike Tomczak, who has been starting in place of injured Jim Harbaugh, and the Bears obliged by stubbornly running the ball on eight of their first nine downs (for a net of 16 yards), giving Tomczak a succession of third-and-long situations.

Early in the game, however, Tomczak did better than expected. He shocked the Giants with a neat 37-yard pass to wideout Wendell Davis on the game's second play. The Bears would have been in field goal range three plays later had Anderson not dropped a pass. Dennis Gentry mishandled Tomczak's next throw, and cornerback Mark Collins picked it off and returned it 11 yards to set up a Giants field goal.

New York's offensive philosophy was to throw early to take the edge off the Bears' defensive linemen and then come back and pound them with the run. The Giants' first touchdown drive featured the pass, the second was on the ground. O.J. Anderson, showing an amazingly fresh pair of legs for a 33-year-old back with 12 NFL seasons behind him, did most of the work as the Giant running game produced a thumping 194 yards on 48 carries.

The joker in the deck was Jeff Hostetler, who had done well in subbing for Phil Simms during the regular season but was an unknown commodity in the pressure-filled playoffs. It was Hostetler's running, not his throwing, that gave Chicago headaches. He converted two fourth-down plays on bootlegs, scored a touchdown on another keeper and ended with 43 yards on six carries. He gives New York another element, something the 49ers didn't have to worry about when they beat the Giants and Simms 7–3 in December.

"I'm sure Montana's eyes had to light up at the way we were throwing the ball," said Tomczak, who ended up 17 of 36 for 205 yards and was not sacked. "They could play a 10–9 game against the Giants, or it could be 30–3, either way. It's NFL championship football."

Where you dance with whoever's around.

—*PAUL ZIMMERMAN*

▶ Everson Walls left Bears receiver Ron Morris grasping at air when he broke up this pass; Walls later had an interception to set up the Giants final score in the fourth quarter.

AFC CHAMPIONSHIP
PLAYOFFS

▼ Lofton's 18-yard reception to the one-yard line set up Davis's third TD, which made the score 48–3. The recycled receiver caught five passes for 113 yards and two TDs.

BUFFALO 51
L.A. RAIDERS 3

Three years ago, before the NFL draft, the Buffalo Bills had to decide whether to use their second-round choice—and their first in that draft—on a running back from Oklahoma State named Thurman Thomas. Thomas had been a productive college player, but he had a tear in the anterior cruciate ligament in his left knee, which scared off most teams in the league. Still, Buffalo general manager Bill Polian thought Thomas was a tremendous talent, and Polian appealed to the Bills' owner, Ralph Wilson. "Boss, this is a first-round player," Polian said. "As the doctors will tell you, his knee's risky. He's a gamble. But we'd like to take him." "Well," Wilson said, "life's a gamble. Go ahead."

Fast-forward to the AFC Championship Game against the Los Angeles Raiders at Rich Stadium, and look at what happens on the first series of the day: Thomas bursts through the middle for 12 yards; Thomas takes a pass in the flat from quarterback Jim Kelly and bounces for 14; after Andre Reed pulls down a pass for 15, Thomas ricochets through traffic up the middle for five; Thomas takes another dump-off pass and burrows for nine. Less than two minutes into the game, the Raiders, reeling, take a time-out, like a basketball team trying to stop its opponent's momentum. "They weren't ready for this," Thomas would say later.

When play resumes, Kelly passes to Thomas for five, and then Thomas runs up the gut again for three more. The Bills' no-huddle attack is a fast-break offense, and Kelly and Thomas are Magic Johnson and James Worthy. This particular fast break ends with Kelly hitting wideout James Lofton for a 13-yard touchdown. It's hammer time.

By the end of the first half, Thomas had 170 rushing and receiving yards, and Buffalo led 41–3. The final score was 51–3, with Thomas responsible for

a total of 199 yards from scrimmage (138 rushing and 61 receiving). Thomas was that quick, that powerful, that elusive—that good. "It's like he runs with snow tires and everybody else on the field has on sneakers," Raider defensive coordinator Dave Adolph said.

The impact that Thomas has on the Bills' game plan is something just shy of Kelly's. It's best put this way: Kelly draws the blueprint and Thomas erects the building. The Raiders used six defensive backs against Buffalo, which meant conditions were ripe for Thomas to ram the ball up the middle, powering into the teeth of a run defense ranked second in the league. The Bills' pregame locker room blackboard message clearly stated their strategy: "6 DBs—Runs Football. 4–5 DBs—Basic Offense." And the L.A. defense, which coach Art Shell said before the game was probably the best in Raider history, had no clue.

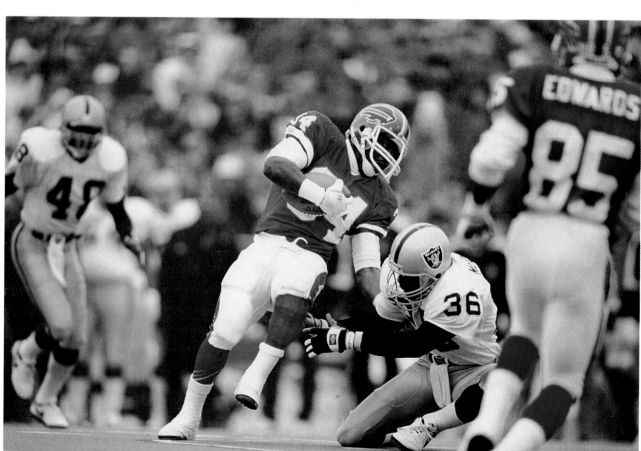

Los Angeles knew the game would come down to stopping Kelly and Thomas. The Raiders couldn't halt either one.

"I love having pressure on me," Thomas said before the game. "A lot of players don't have good games when the pressure's on. But I wish they could throw the whole load on my shoulders every week."

"Thurman's acceleration through the hole, his quickness through the hole and his cuts are un-matched," said Buffalo tackle Will Wolford. "He hits a hole as fast as anyone I've ever seen, and it makes the linemen's job a lot easier. You know if you have your man blocked well, Thurman's not going to make the bad cut."

Thomas is so versatile that the Bills now use him as a single setback most of the time, and he runs screen, intermediate and deep patterns from the backfield when he's not carrying the ball.

Of the rest of Kelly's Heroes, only Andre Reed had a subpar day, catching only two passes, but the Raider double coverage on him left easy pickings for other Kelly targets like Steve Tasker, tight end Keith McKeller and, especially, a rejuvenated James Lofton.

Lofton had his second straight 100-yard playoff game. In spite of the Bills' dictum to run against the six-DB alignment, Lofton and Kelly combined on a 41-yard completion out of the no-huddle just six minutes into the game. Kelly came up to the line, guessed that the Raiders weren't going to blitz, saw out of the corner of his eye that Lionel Washington was in single coverage on Lofton, took the snap, looked off safety Mike Harden so he wouldn't double on Lofton and waited for Lofton to beat Washington deep. "Then I just throw it," Kelly recalled after the game. Nothing to this no-huddle thing. Thomas finished off the drive with a beautiful 12-yard touchdown run on a draw from the shotgun. Bills 14, Raiders 3.

The Bills defense got into the fun on Buffalo's next score when linebacker Darryl Talley

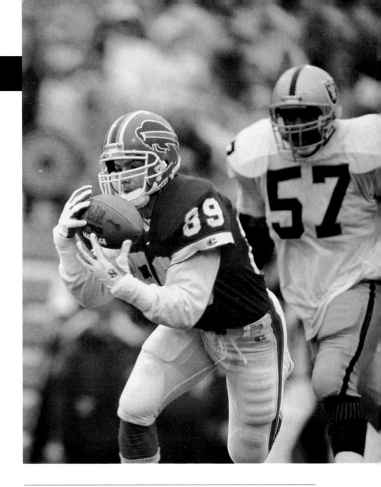

▲ Backup wide receiver Steve Tasker corralled this Kelly pass for a 44-yard second-quarter completion that set up yet another of Buffalo's six unanswered touchdowns.

intercepted Raider QB Jay Schroeder, who would throw five interceptions on the day, and returned the ball 27 yards into the end zone. For three of the next four TDs—all unanswered—Buffalo got it close, then gave it to Thomas backup Kenneth Davis, who busted through a vaunted Raider defense, which had allowed only four rushing TDs all season. And when Scott Norwood finished off the scoring with a 39-yard field goal 2:46 into the fourth quarter, the Bills' 48-point margin became the second-largest in a conference championship game, second only to the Bears' 73–0 win over the Redskins in 1940.

"Two years ago, it was Andre Reed," says Kelly, clicking off his list of offensive options. "Last year, it was Andre Reed and Thurman Thomas. This year, it's Andre Reed, Thurman Thomas, James Lofton and Keith McKeller. We can do a lot of things right now."

Good teams make the right decisions. The Bills made one when they drafted Thomas, and now they are a good team—Super good.   —*PETER KING*

PLAYOFFS

N.Y. GIANTS 15
SAN FRANCISCO 13

So what if Jeff Hostetler got straight A's his whole life, when his career as an NFL quarterback was one big Incomplete?

So what if he could run and throw and read defenses as though he had a photographic memory (which he does), when he spent his Sundays welded to a clipboard?

How did he find the patience to keep from publicly ripping the coach in an attempt to force his team to trade him? And what kept him from quitting?

Maybe Jason, that's what. Maybe he kept thinking that if his son Jason could go through four heart operations before his first birthday and never quit, then how could he?

So Jeff Hostetler didn't leave the New York Giants through seven long seasons, even though he wanted to. He held on. He held for kicks and he held his clipboard and, almost always, he held his tongue. And as he came into the 1990 season, the one that would be the most remarkable in his life, he held the world record for perseverance. Job should have tried a clipboard for seven years.

But Jason got better, and so did the football. When starter Phil Simms went down with an ankle injury in the middle of the 1989 season, Giants coach Bill Parcells finally gave Hostetler a shot. Once he found his helmet, he started twice and won twice, throwing a touchdown pass in each game. So when Simms suffered a sprained right arch in Week 15 of this season, Hoss, as his teammates call him, found his ship had finally docked. He beat the Phoenix Cardinals and the New England Patriots, then wiped out the Chicago Bears in New York's first playoff game, running two times to convert fourth downs. Yeah, but could he beat Joe God and the San Francisco 49ers in The Stick? He could. Somehow he forgot to wilt before the Niner legend. Damned if he wasn't still right in it with a quarter to play and San Francisco leading 13–9.

Then suddenly it looked as if his ship had sunk. As Hostetler dropped back to pass, 49er noseguard Jim Burt, a former Giant, dived at Hostetler's left knee and buckled it. "I figured I was out of the game," Hostetler said afterward. Beautiful. One quarter away from going to The Show and destiny blew by Hostetler as if he were a hitchhiker with pets.

The backup's backup, Matt Cavanaugh, looked catatonic, and New York punted. Defensive end Leonard Marshall of the Giants got a payback on Montana, creaming him from behind, breaking a bone in his right hand, severely bruising his sternum and generally testing his Tylenol supply.

The Niners punted. Destiny made a U-turn.

"Can you go?" Parcells had asked Hostetler minutes before.

"I think so," Hoss said.

"You think you can go?" Parcells asked him one play later.

"Yeah," Hoss said.

"Can you go?" Parcells asked again as the offense took the field.

"Bill, I'm going!" he barked.

Hostetler tested his knee on the second play, a six-yard scramble, and the Giants scratched out a field goal to close the deficit to 13–12 with 5:47 left.

▶ With 20 carries for 67 yards, the 33-year-old Anderson was the workhorse of New York's grind-it-out offense, which controlled the ball for nearly 39 minutes.

It's funny about dynasties. They roll along smooth as chiffon for three years, and then all of a sudden the warranty expires and the lug nuts fall off. First, Montana got the flu three days before the game. Then Marshall made him feel worse with that hit. Then Roger Craig decided to fumble at the worst possible moment, with less than three minutes to play. Taylor caught it in mid-drop. Giants' ball.

Here it was for Hoss: 57 yards and 2:36 to make a dream come around that he had waited for through seven years and 4,000 No. 2 pencils.

All he did was become bulletproof. Rolling right on what remained of his knee, he should have gone out of bounds but instead chose to pivot and fire a rope to tight end Mark Bavaro. Plus 19, first down. Two plays later, he rolled right and threw an NFL Films–type spiral to Stephen Baker. Plus 13, to the Niner 29. O.J. Anderson advanced the ball four more yards on two carries, then the Giants called timeout with :04 remaining. What's left for Hostetler to do but hold for Matt Bahr's kick?

Across the way, a group of about eight Giants knelt in a semicircle, praying to God for victory. So now God had to worry about a war *and* the Giants.

So they prayed and the snap came and Hostetler didn't bobble, as he hasn't in his entire career as a holder in New York, and Bahr's kick faded left but not left enough to hurt, and it went through just as the clock ticked down to zero.

Hostetler, who completed 15 of 27 pass attempts for 176 yards, was so rusty at being a hero that he actually said hello to his wife and kids on TV, just as a rookie might do. Then Bahr, an old friend from Penn State, came up and said, "I'm proud of you," and he wasn't the only one.

Not a bad story. Hostetler goes to Tampa not only unbeaten as a starter—6–0, read it and believe,

◀ Tackle Eric Moore and the Giants line didn't always give Hostetler this clear a view, but he saw and threw well enough to complete more than 50% of his passes.

Parcells—but also as the third scrub quarterback to take his team to the Super Bowl, preceded only by the Los Angeles Raiders' Jim Plunkett in 1981 and the Washington Redskins' Doug Williams in 1988.

"I don't want to just *take* a team to the Super Bowl," Hostetler says. "I want to *win* one."

Boy, some guys just don't know their place.

—*RICK REILLY*

▼ As time ran out, Bahr's fifth field goal, from yet another perfect hold by Hostetler, ignited a wild celebration that included a flip by Hoss and a blindside hug from Taylor.

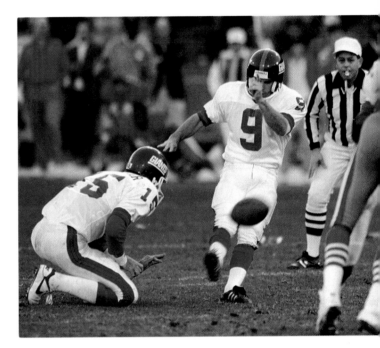

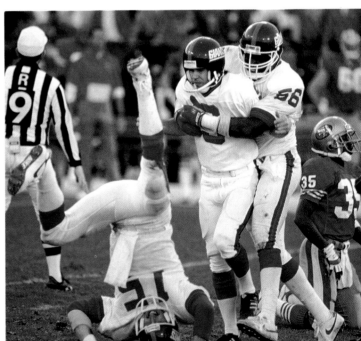

N.Y. GIANTS 20
BUFFALO 19

Win one Super Bowl and you're a winning Super Bowl coach. Win two and you're a genius, a man with a system, an approach to the game that must be studied and copied. So it is with Bill Parcells, whose New York Giants beat the Buffalo Bills 20–19 in a heart-stopping Super Bowl XXV, four years after New York had defeated the Denver Broncos 39–20 in Super Bowl XXI. "Power wins football games," Parcells repeated endlessly amidst the postgame locker room turmoil.

That philosophy has permeated his approach to the game: Big people attacking little people. It's a rather brutal concept, and it resulted in a whopping advantage in possession time—40:33 to 19:27—that left the Bills defenders groggy and rubber-legged in the Florida humidity of Tampa Stadium. Said Andre Reed, who caught seven balls but dropped several others, "No other team ever hit me this hard."

This is not meant to take anything away from the Bills, who played with courage and resiliency. As the game moved toward the two-minute warning, the Bills pulled themselves together and forced the Giants to punt from the Buffalo 48. The Bills took over on their own 10 with 2:16 left, and with eight seconds remaining they were on the New York 30, their Scott Norwood was lining up a 47-yard field goal attempt and prayers were being offered on both sidelines.

The kick never had a chance. It started right, but "it wasn't moving, it wasn't being drawn in," said a disconsolate Norwood afterward. The Giants' one-point lead was preserved, but if the kick had been

▼ Placed at the center of attention in Super Bowl XXV, Hostetler responded with a combination of toughness and savvy, completing 20 of 32 passes for 222 yards.

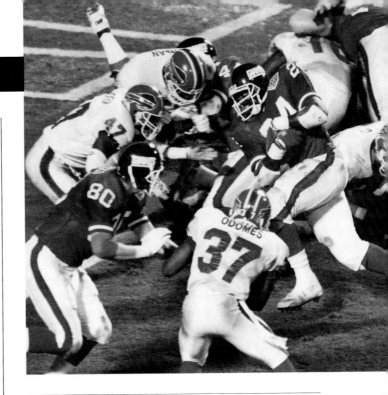

good, well, we would all be writing about Buffalo's no-huddle offense. It was that kind of game. "It came down to the last kick, and the Super Bowl is supposed to be played that way," said Bills QB Jim Kelly.

Super Bowl XXV had few penalties (66 yards all told) and no turnovers, despite all the vicious hitting. Only one play could be considered a slight fluke—Kelly's 61-yard first-quarter completion to wideout James Lofton, who caught the ball after cornerback Perry Williams tipped it. The game highlighted two power runners, New York's O.J. Anderson, who was voted MVP for his 102 yards rushing, and Buffalo's Thurman Thomas, who should have won for his 135 yards on the ground, plus five catches for 55 yards. If there had been an MVP for courage, it would have gone to the Giants' QB Jeff Hostetler, who was whacked unmercifully by Buffalo pass rushers in the first half.

In Parcells' power system, wideouts are almost an afterthought, but Mark Ingram made what was probably the pivotal play of the game. On a third-and-13 pass play, he faked out or ran over four Bills for a 14-yard gain to keep alive the third-quarter TD drive—14 plays, 75 yards, 9:29—that put the Giants in front 17–12.

Thomas kept the Bills in the game with his individual brilliance, answering Ingram's feat with a 31-yard fourth-quarter run in which he bounced free of safety Myron Guyton's head-on tackle. Buffalo 19, New York 17.

But the Giants responded yet again, this time with their game-winning drive—14 plays, 74 yards, 7:32—which ended with Matt Bahr's 21-yard field goal. Hostetler completed four of six passes against a rush that had lost its zip.

▲ MVP Anderson finished off the most time-consuming drive in Super Bowl history with a one-yard run that put the Giants up by five midway through the third quarter.

So a game played under the shadow of war in the Mideast, in a stadium fortified against terrorism, became a classic. It was Parcells' kind of football, Giants football, the fruition of a dream that began eight seasons ago when he became New York's coach. If a legacy is to be attached to this game, it will be that it was played the way Super Bowls are supposed to be played.
—*PAUL ZIMMERMAN*

▼ The scoreboard told the story as Norwood struck the ball for his 47-yard field goal try; the kick was long enough but sailed wide right to preserve the win for New York.

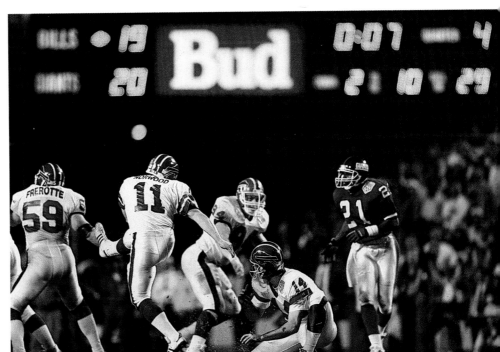

TALES FROM THE ROAD

Our intrepid reporter shares his recollections from another year on the NFL beat

BY PETER KING

Saturday, Sept. 8, 1990, Villa Hills, Kentucky: The U.S. Open semifinals drone on from the other room, and I realize I have something in common with John McEnroe: We're both getting whipped. Pete Sampras whomps McEnroe in tennis on center court; Cincinnati quarterback Boomer Esiason slams me in Ping-Pong in his rec room. "Best three out of five," says Esiason, still stinging from his 1989 loss to me on this very same table. Going into today's action, I'm 1–9 against him. Today, he adds to his winning percentage. I can't solve his forehand slams with my flimsy backhand returns, and he takes me 22–20, 19–21, 21–15, 21–14. "Great week for me," he announces. "I won at cards Thursday night, I won two friendly wagers today because Maryland beat West Virginia, and now I beat you. This is my week." Right, I say. Beating an overweight 33-year-old sportswriter in Ping-Pong is some feat.

Sunday, Sept. 9, Cincinnati: Esiason's winning week continues. The Bengals pull out a 25–20 Opening Day win over the Jets. Afterward, former Bengal offensive coordinator Bruce Coslet, who now coaches the Jets, walks to midfield. I'm just over his left shoulder. Esiason hugs his former mentor. "You've got a lot to be proud of," Esiason says into Coslet's ear. "I love you Bruce." This isn't fake. Coslet turns away, and there are tears rolling down his right cheek. He wipes them away quickly. A half-hour later, I ask Coslet if he was crying out there. He looks at the ground. "Damn right I was," he says.

Thursday, Sept. 27, Potter, Nebraska: I'm on the Madden Cruiser, the bus that CBS analyst John Madden uses to travel around the country for his various assignments. So here's Madden—sweatpants, sneakers, white socks, white polo shirt—sitting on this customized bus, looking out the picture window at miles and miles of tall grass and cornfields, when suddenly the landscape is interrupted by a wide and deep patch of beautiful red flowers, acres and acres of them. "What's that red stuff out there?" he says. His son, Joe, opens a

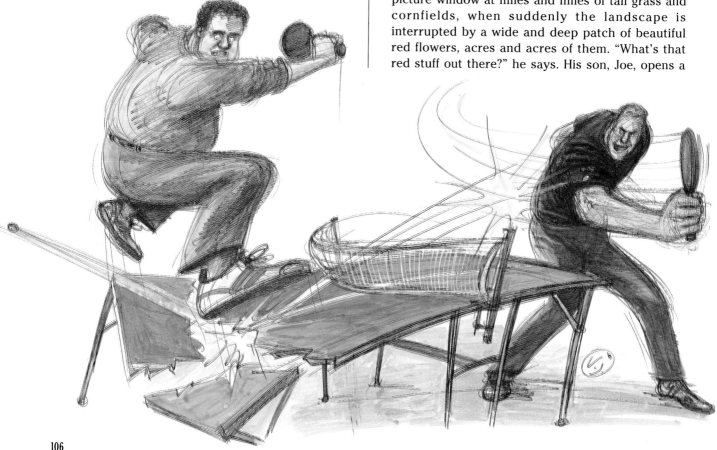

drawer and pulls out a thick, coffee-table-sized book called *Wildflowers Across America*.

"*Wildflowers Across America*?" I holler. "Come on! You keep that on the bus? I'm going to write about this, and your reputation will be ruined!"

Madden grins. Joe hands him the book, opened to the proper page. "There they are," Madden says. "Spotted knapweed. Sure look pretty to me."

Moral of the story: Things aren't always as they appear on TV.

Sunday, Dec. 9, Washington, D.C.: You probably hear that the players hate reporters. Well, that's not really true. In general, they're bemused and frustrated by us. They *do* wonder sometimes about where we get our questions. For a case in point, I take you to Mike Singletary's locker on a Sunday night in Washington, soon after the Bears have lost a close game to the Redskins 10–9. Chicago has the NFC Central clinched, so the loss is hardly devastating. Singletary is tired. But he's such a good guy, truly one of the nicest and most sincere players in the game, that he doesn't mind a Chicago TV guy sticking a mike in front of his eyes and asking: "Could this be described as one of those life-or-death losses or just one of those tough losses?"

If it's possible, Singletary does a triple take. Then he mutters something about how no one died so everything would be all right.

Sheeeesh.

Sunday, Jan. 27, 1991, Tampa: It is Super Bowl Sunday, but all I can do while standing in the hazy sun and midafternoon warmth of Florida's Gulf coast is think of Seoul, Korea, and the 1988 Summer Olympics, the only time I had been subjected to such strict security. To enter the stadium, your press credential is checked at a chain-link fence. Then you pass through another chain-link fence where security-force members in yellow coats give you the once-over. Then you pass through a concrete barrier, showing your credential again. Then there's a line and, for me, a 30-minute wait. Outside the press gate, I walk through an airport-like security system. When I get through, I have to turn on my computer and portable radio. I have to be frisked by a metal-detecting wand. I have to send my bag through the X-ray machine. I watch my bag being searched when the yellow-coats feel a strange lump. "Three bananas," I tell them.

Then I'm in the press box, and except for the paramilitary types standing with rifles on the rooftop, it's just another game. All I know is: I've never felt safer at an event.

Monday, Jan. 28, Tampa, About 1:00 a.m.: There is a hanging bag and an adidas gym bag on the king-sized bed in Room 502 at the Tampa Westshore Hyatt Regency. Wherever he can find space, Giants coach Bill Parcells is stuffing in sneakers and dirty shirts and socks.

Several items won't make it. The replica Super Bowl trophy—white-chocolate base, milk-chocolate football—is one of them. That's okay. Parcells will carry the real one on board the Giants' charter to New Jersey.

Parcells is talking as he stuffs. I've known Parcells since 1985, and I'm trying to figure out if he's happier today than the only other time I saw him like this—in a limo ride the day after the Giants' 1987 Super Bowl win. I decide he's happier right now. That's what an *unexpected* Super Bowl win does to a guy.

"This," he says, "is a high no one else can describe. It's a high I can only experience by winning this one game. You know what it's like?"

He stuffs some socks into the hanging bag.

"It's like a drug. It's a narcotic. It's an absolute narcotic. That's the only way I can describe it to someone who's not in football."

He zips the garment bag, and then the gym bag, and he walks toward the door of Room 502.

"And you know what? It's why you coach. You coach the sport to feel like I feel right now."

PROFILES

Personalities of the NFL

PAUL TAGLIABUE

If you saw Pete Rozelle at the end, you saw a man who needed out. He didn't so much look old as he looked annoyed. After 30 years as NFL commissioner, Rozelle looked as though he were sitting in an idling supercharged race car, waiting for his replacement driver, and nobody would come.

When Paul Tagliabue, a 6'5", 49-year-old former Georgetown basketball center and the NFL's chief outside legal counsel finally took the keys from his longtime pal in October of 1989, it came first as a relief that a replacement had arrived and then as a surprise that he immediately put the hammer down.

The following month he had NFL Charities contribute $1 million to San Francisco earthquake victims. In February 1990 he added a preseason date in West Germany to the American Bowl series of exhibition games that already had stops in Canada, England and Japan. Sensing imminent legal attack, he also declared college juniors eligible for the NFL's regular draft, amending a cozy seniors-only rule that had served the league nicely for 53 years.

That March he swung some biggies. He completed negotiations on four-year contracts with ABC, CBS, NBC, ESPN and TBS for a total of $3.643 billion, the largest deal of its kind in TV history. He pushed through a more stringent steroid-testing policy for players. He fought off a move to dump instant replay but agreed to a two-minute cap on reviews and unveiled minor rules changes to help shorten games to three hours or less.

After the Berlin Wall crumbled, Tagliabue extended the NFL's international visibility with a game in Germany.

Tagliabue's working motto seemed to be: Head off criticism before it occurs. A questioner recently brought up some small concerns about one of Tagliabue's big decisions, to which he replied, "*De minimis non curat lex.* The law doesn't worry about tiny details." Close the door, and let's burn rubber.

Once this season started, Tagliabue confidently rode over a major bump–the locker room access controversy. When the Lisa Olson incident threatened to overshadow the game (page 25), he quickly appointed an independent investigator, got the facts and meted out a fair-minded series of fines. When Cincinnati coach Sam Wyche illegally denied access to a woman reporter, Tagliabue responded forcefully by hitting Wyche with the largest fine an NFL coach had ever received. Finally, Tagliabue showed everyone that he was in charge by taking the 1993 Super Bowl away from Phoenix because the state failed to vote for a Martin Luther King Jr. holiday. So much for controversy.

After a year and a half as NFL commissioner, his report card showed straight A's–just as it had when he was an honor-roll student, state high-jump champion and star hoopster at St. Michael's High in Union City, N.J.–with a gold star for effort. His graders now, of course, are the 28 NFL owners, a tough, contentious, pushy, whiny lot, if there ever was one. "I think our commissioner has shown an instinctive ability to deliver," says Mike Lynn, the former Minnesota G.M. and the current president of the new World League of American Football.

In his brief tenure, Tagliabue–speaking to the Rams in Germany– has addressed concerns of both players and management.

The man is certainly no party animal. "A crazy period in my life?" says Tagliabue. "Nothing in particular." He grins. "Except when I fell in love with my wife." That would be the former Chandler Minter of Milledgeville, Ga., to whom he has been married for a quarter of a century. The pretty, slow-talking Protestant lass from the Deep South and the gangly Italian Catholic from New Jersey must have seemed an odd pair at first. However, time has shown that the union was built on nothing if not respect and good sense.

In June 1990 their daughter, Emily (the Tagliabues also have a son, Drew, 22), introduced her dad as the commencement speaker at her high school graduation by noting that when he was named NFL commissioner, his reviews ranged "from 'an intellectual lawyer–brilliant but uninspired' to 'extremely competent but humorless–perhaps a bit dull.'" Says Chicago Bears owner Mike McCaskey, "Charisma is the most overrated aspect of leadership. Vision is what matters. And Paul has it."

As the NFL's chief outside counsel from 1969 to '89, Tagliabue dealt with traumatic issues for the league, from the Joe Namath–Bachelor's III affair to the Al Davis–Oakland Raider antitrust suit to the USFL antitrust trial. His low-profile, hardworking role served him well in the acrimonious seven-month-long commissioner's derby, a race he didn't really enter. "I never thought about being commissioner," he says of the $800,000 a year position. "I took the job because people said it would be best for the league."

An attorney who started his legal career in 1966 by working for the Department of Defense and helping decide which way NATO aimed its nuclear missiles, Tagliabue can be excused if his demeanor is best described as wry, businesslike and sober. When he left the Defense Department, in 1969, to join the Washington, D.C., law firm of Covington & Burling (the NFL was one of the first clients assigned to him), Secretary of Defense Melvin Laird presented him with a meritorious service award. The citation noted that the kid who used to slam his elbows against the cement-block walls of his basement, to toughen them up for rebounding, "approached every problem with an intellectual curiosity, thoughtfulness and imagination, which won him the high respect of his colleagues and superiors."

The biggest pothole in the road ahead is the lack of a collective-bargaining agreement between the players' union and management. In that and other issues, he sticks to the same philosophy that served him so well in his first season: Head off criticism and *de minimis non curat lex.*
　　　　　　　　　　　　　　　　　　—RICK TELANDER

STEVE DeBERG

ansas City Chiefs quarterback Steve DeBerg writhed in pain on the cold, hard Arrowhead Stadium turf. Midway through the third quarter against Houston on Dec. 16, he was sandwiched between two Oilers on an all-out blitz. He hobbled off the field, holding his bloody left pinky, a bone protruding through the skin. That night, DeBerg underwent surgery to repair a compound fracture, and he gutted out the rest of the season and one playoff game, wearing a plastic case over the damaged finger. He refused all painkillers.

"I don't believe in pain medicine," says DeBerg, who completed 258 of 444 passes for 3,444 yards and 23 TDs during the regular season. "The mind gets used to the pain. It learns to block it out."

Right from the start, the Chiefs tried to minimize the injury, stating that DeBerg had broken just one bone and that only one pin had been inserted into the finger. DeBerg admits that there were actually two broken bones and three pins. "I almost had to have the tip amputated," he says. "The skin was torn badly, and it was barely hanging on. I was lucky."

DeBerg's adjustment to his compound fracture is symbolic of the resilience and determination he has demonstrated throughout his 14-year career. At 37, he is the NFL's premier never-say-die quarterback. In 1990, he quietly moved into 17th place on the alltime list for passing yards (28,490), surpassing illustrious names like Bradshaw, Stabler, Namath and Griese.

Since the Cowboys cut him in training camp after drafting him 10th in 1977, he has lost NFL starting jobs to Joe Montana in San Francisco, John Elway in Denver, and Steve Young and Vinny Testaverde in Tampa Bay. Before the 1988 season, the Bucs shipped DeBerg off to Kansas City.

"It amazes me how history repeated itself," DeBerg says. "Each time a 'franchise quarterback' would come in, I'd ask myself, Is it possible this could happen again?"

After being yanked from the starting lineup twice last year, DeBerg determined in the off-season to give himself the best chance to keep the starting job. He threw into a net for hours, perfecting his mechanics and visualizing pass coverages. The result of all this hard work? DeBerg was the third-rated quarterback in the NFL in 1990, and he was able to drastically reduce his interceptions, a longtime nemesis. In one stretch, he went 233 straight passes without being picked off—the NFL's second-longest streak ever—and his season total of four interceptions gave him the second-best interception avoidance mark in league history. His performance was a big reason the Chiefs made the playoffs for the first time since 1986.

Even with a broken pinkie, the veteran DeBerg pointed the Chiefs in the right direction in 1990.

Thorough mental and physical preparation has kept DeBerg in the NFL all these years. No quarterback has a more grueling schedule. Even on the Chiefs' days off, he is either lifting weights, running or watching videotapes. Before a game, he will memorize the responsibility of each of his offensive teammates on every play and quiz them. In his hotel room the night before and in his locker before kickoff, his portable VCR is whirring away. "Overlearning the material is my goal," DeBerg says.

Some day he hopes to take advantage of this obsession by publishing the ultimate playbook—his own greatest hits album—consisting of words of wisdom and successful plays from his career.

"I've never wished that my career would have gone differently," DeBerg says. "I've never said I got a raw deal. I wasn't supposed to make it one year, let alone 14." —*Jill Lieber*

ANTHONY MUNOZ

As skilled as he is at knocking down football players, Bengal offensive tackle Anthony Munoz is just as well known in Cincinnati for helping people get on their feet. Since coming to the NFL in 1980, Munoz has begrudged every inch of ground he has given up to the league's best pass rushers, yet he has given tirelessly of himself to God, family and community.

A 6'6", 285-pound man-mountain, he is considered the best in the business at an either-he-goes-on-his-backside-or-I-go-on-mine job. He is held in equally high regard for his compassion in working with handicapped and underprivileged children and speaking to teenagers on the dangers of drug and alcohol abuse. This all comes in one package.

"I don't see any contrast between what he does and the way he is," says DeDe Munoz, his wife of 12 years. "Ever watch him? It's an artistic way of playing the offensive line. He makes it look easy."

To appreciate an artist is to admire his work, so Bengal offensive line coach Jim McNally played a game tape recently to illustrate why Munoz, 32, is considered the premier tackle of the last decade. "Watch, here he's pushing the guy right past the quarterback. Now, watch. See the change of direction? The rusher changes and Anthony doesn't fall down. That's tremendous balance."

"He has the best feet of any tackle I've gone against," says Houston Oiler defensive end William Fuller. "Because he has such good hand-foot coordination, you never catch him out of position."

Some NFL talent evaluators will allow that Munoz, who has had shoulder surgery three times in the last four off-seasons, has slipped, if only slightly. That may mean that Munoz's blocks are less visually stimulating, but just as effective. "What really matters," Munoz says, "is that the block is successful and the play works."

Bengal quarterback Boomer Esiason may be biased, but he unabashedly stands up for the guy who keeps him standing. "If I were as good at my position as Anthony is at his," Esiason says, "then I'd be 10 times better than Joe Montana."

The flood of praise does not swell Munoz's head. He pursues excellence, not status. And he does it clean. "Anthony's commitment is to be the best at his position, not a bench-press goon," says Kim Wood, the Bengals' strength coach. "A lot of kids have had exposure to steroids in college and come to pro football believing you have to take them to be able to compete. But Anthony Munoz has been the best offensive lineman in football for a decade without ever taking a steroid."

Teammates, who watch their language in Munoz's company but never feel uncomfortable around him, say that when things get dirty in the pits, Munoz doesn't get angry. He gets better. "There is the drive to be great," says Cincinnati coach Sam Wyche, "and then there is a desire like Anthony's to be superlative. You won't know if you can get there, but you want to see how close you can come." Munoz has come close—both on and off the field. "If pro sports could point to one guy who would be the ideal to look up to, Anthony would be it," says Wyche.

When he was growing up in Ontario, California, Munoz had only his mother to look up to. "Anthony was very young when his father left," his mother, Esther, says. Her face clouds over and she shakes her head, preferring not to go into details. Munoz's father continued to live not far from the yellow stucco house on D Street, where Esther kept her three sons and two daughters fed, clothed and motivated. Munoz says that his father attempted to contact him only twice, when Anthony was five and 12. They never got together, and Munoz's mother says Anthony's father has since died.

"I probably have thought about him more in the last few years since I had children of my own," says Munoz. "See, I never had a father, so I never knew what I was missing. As I look back, I don't even know if I was poor. We were provided for, but we didn't have any extras. We didn't have a car, but we had relatives who drove. I got everywhere I wanted to go."

Esther worked packing eggs into cartons at a nearby farm. On weekends, when a new batch of chicks had to be vaccinated, Anthony and one of his brothers, Tom, could find work shooing them from coop to coop. Most other days of the week, Anthony could be found on the city's playing fields.

By the time he was five, Anthony looked nine, so he never had any trouble getting into a game. For years, baseball remained his first love, even after it was pointed out to him that he was too big not to play football. Munoz signed with Southern Cal with an agreement that he could skip spring football practice to play for the Trojans' baseball team, but the need to rehabilitate knee injuries that he incurred while playing football kept him from playing baseball except during his sophomore year.

Munoz's worst injury occurred in the opening game of his senior season when the helmet of a Texas Tech player struck his left knee, forcing him to undergo major reconstructive surgery. Desperate to fulfill every Trojan's dream of participating in at least one Rose Bowl, Munoz made it back for that game. He threw the key block that sprung tailback Charles White for the winning touchdown against Ohio State.

At the game were Paul Brown, founder and general manager of the Bengals, and his sons, Mike, the assistant general manager, and Pete, the player personnel director, who were facing a difficult decision: Whatever Munoz's potential, could they risk using a first-round draft pick on a player with a questionable knee? Munoz spent the day blowing away Buckeyes and the Brown family's fears. "The three of us sat there and laughed out loud," says Mike. "The guy was so big and so good it was a joke."

Munoz and his family are very much at home in Cincinnati. Anthony, DeDe and their children, Michael, 9, and Michelle, 7, live in a Tudor-style house on a one-acre lot in suburban Ellenwood. Munoz gives 30 to 40 talks a year on drug and alcohol abuse as a representative of Teen Challenge and Athletes in Action. He also makes appearances on behalf of the United Appeal, organizes and speaks at events that benefit Cystic Fibrosis, and fulfills other civic and charitable requests. Anthony and DeDe decided in 1982 to settle year-round in Cincinnati because they felt the city had a sense of community that was missing in Southern California.

Munoz made the Pro Bowl once again this season, the 10th straight time he has been selected, a record for offensive linemen. Even though a shoulder injury in the first round of the playoffs ended his season on a sour note, his prognosis for recovery is good, and he has no plans to retire. He retains the healthy fear of slipping a notch that drives superior men to superior deeds. When you come so far in life, it must be hard to stop. "I don't think Anthony thinks of himself as Superman," says Wyche.

Only everybody else does. —*Jay Greenberg*

A gentle giant, Munoz serves the community by appearing at benefits, like the one below for muscular dystrophy.

BURT GROSSMAN

Burt Grossman is lying in bed with large wads of toilet paper sticking out of his ears, but the din in the room is so loud that he is awakened over and over again—his head shooting straight off the pillow—only to find the room silent and dark. "It's a good thing for her my girlfriend doesn't snore," Grossman says. "I can't sleep if there's any noise whatsoever. If somebody breathes heavy, I have to put toilet paper in my ears."

But wait. It is Grossman who is waking Grossman! He is talking in his sleep, and not only that, talking so loud that the noise has startled him. Wakened him. The only way to stop these nocturnal outbursts would be to stuff the toilet paper in Grossman's mouth. Which might not be a bad idea. The prospect of a world with Burt Grossman always out there talking, night and day, day and night, is an extremely sobering one to those who know him.

If breeding counts for anything, the 24-year-old defensive end for the San Diego Chargers was born to play football and born to shoot off his mouth. He is a cousin of former Pittsburgh Steeler tight end Randy Grossman, and his half sister is noted baseball aficionada Margo Adams. "For my bloodlines, I'm very conservative," he says. He has never spoken to Adams, which stands to reason because Grossman has never actually seen in person the national pastime—baseball, not extramarital sex—and practically the only people in all the world Grossman doesn't talk to are members of his family.

Grossman's parents separated when he was in the third grade, while the family lived in Bala Cynwyd, on suburban Philadelphia's fashionable Main Line. "We had no idea my parents were getting a divorce," he recalls. "My sister and I came home from school one day and there were four moving trucks outside the house." His mother, Cathy, had decided to leave his father, Burt Sr., a construction superintendent, and she told her two children they were coming with her.

Cathy Grossman moved them about 50 miles outside Philadelphia, to Bucks County, and got a job as a waitress working nights. "When your mom works, you have a lot of time to do what you want," he says. "I had a little too much time. I was a troublemaker, always getting into fights, and I had bad grades—straight F's, as a matter of fact.

"When I was in the sixth grade my mother kicked me out of the house. She said, 'You're going to live with your father. I don't want you here.' He came and picked me up one day, and that was the last time I ever saw her."

After moving back to his father's house in Bala Cynwyd, Burt attended public schools until the 10th grade, when he transferred to Archbishop Carroll. "I had my usual all F's, and then it was time for Catholic guidance," he says. "If I hadn't gone to Catholic school, I'd probably be wrestling Ric Flair for the NWA title instead of playing pro football." As a senior in 1984, he was one of the top high school shot-putters in the country, even though he rarely trained for the event, and he was a highly recruited defensive lineman. "By my senior year I had more power than the school principal," he says modestly of his schoolyard stature.

In a typical snap decision, Grossman chose to

one of them got loose one day, so I had to get rid of them." To fill the terrible void in his heart, Grossman brought home a tankful of piranhas. To cheer himself up, he would drop live goldfish into the tank and dream about quarterbacks.

His dreams came true often enough on the field to make him a three-year starter at defensive end, where he collected 22.5 sacks and attracted the attention of the Chargers. "There was some question about him because of his physical stature," says San Diego coach Dan Henning. "He doesn't look the part of a defensive end with those thin spindly legs." The Chargers flew Grossman to San Diego before the '89 draft and were sufficiently impressed to make him the eighth player drafted. "The day he came for his interview," recalls defensive line coach Gunther Cunningham, "Burt held court. We watched film for four or five hours, and the things [knowledge of his position] he was talking about I haven't heard from most coaches' mouths."

Most of what Grossman has said since that day has been unlike anything heard from practically *anyone's* mouth in the normally buttoned-down NFL. He held the Steelers in such low regard that he threatened to hold out cryogenically if they chose him in the draft. "If the Steelers drafted me I would have gotten myself frozen for 20 years," Grossman says, "and had myself revived at a later time to reenter the draft."

Luckily for San Diego, Grossman decided to stay defrosted and play for the Chargers. He finished the '89 season with 10 sacks and added another 10 this season. "Burt's a very difficult guy to pass protect against," Henning says. "He's one of the quickest guys I've ever seen off the ball." Many of the Chargers feel Grossman's finest moment came in 1989 when he threw up on himself while chasing Philadelphia's scrambling quarterback, Randall Cunningham.

The soft center of Grossman's marshmallow macho is apparent when he is around kids the same age he was when his parents split up. When he went to a school to speak to a group of third-, fourth- and fifth-grade students, he told the little girls he would walk them home from school anytime they wanted. Then he told them they could call him at home. "They asked for my phone number; what was I going to do, lie to them?" Burt says. "There were a lot of messages on my answering machine the first two days. Mostly the little girls would call and say things like, 'Don't tell your girlfriend I called,' stupid stuff like that." Now when they call, Burt just stuffs more toilet paper in his ears, then goes right on talking. Soon, the only sound he can hear is his own voice.　　　　—BRUCE NEWMAN

attend Pitt, where the Panthers were coming off a 3–7–1 season. "I don't want to say that the place was corrupt, but they made you a lot of promises when you went there for a visit, and when

Grossman's earplugs may muffle the noise of the world, but they can't silence the sound of his own voice.

you got there the place wasn't as great as they said it was," he says. Grossman had several addresses at Pitt and he developed a love of animals that seemed to grow with each stop. "If you live on campus, everything's cockroach-infested and there are rats everywhere," says Grossman, who lived in a dorm as an underclassman. "Pitiful places, you can't even imagine." In any case, Grossman's affection for rodents grew enormously when he moved off campus and bought two baby alligators to go with a pet boa constrictor. "They eat mice, that's the big thrill," he says. "The alligators weren't that big, but

REYNA THOMPSON

hether New York Giants cornerback Reyna Thompson is sitting in an airplane seat or propped on the trainer's table, his teammates are likely to ask him the same question: What are you reading now? His most recent answer: Dante's *Inferno*.

He is as absorbed in books as he is in becoming the best special teams player in pro football, a distinction that many believe he already owns. He thrives on punishing collisions and has a knack for hurling himself through the air to down punts inside an opponent's five-yard line. His work on punt and kickoff coverage in 1990 earned him the spot as the special teams player on the NFC Pro Bowl squad.

Nine credits shy of a master's degree in English from Florida International University, Thompson has studied the writings of Edgar Allan Poe and

Christopher Marlowe and is a writer himself. He has already completed six short stories for a collection he hopes to publish. "I believe in what Poe said in his critique of short stories," says Thompson, 27. "He felt the reader should be engulfed in his fiction, that he should transfuse himself into the words, live through each of the characters, feel their emotions and experience their thoughts. Then, he should be able to jump out from the pages, close the book and get back into his normal day."

Thompson takes a similar approach to his special teams craft, and it's best illustrated on Wednesday nights in the living room of his apartment in Hackensack, N.J. There on a 13-inch color-television screen, he analyzes at least four games of his upcoming special teams opponents. "I wear out the remote control," he kids.

In the first viewing, Thompson pops in kickoff coverage tapes and focuses on the kickoff team's L3 man, Thompson's position, the player three slots to the left of the kicker. "I watch—just 'dummy up,' " he says. The second time through, he studies how the upcoming opponents block L3. Do they hit him square or do they come at an angle? Thompson also dissects the running style of the return man.

The third time through the tapes, Thompson visualizes himself as L3, projecting himself onto the field, in much the same way he and Poe read short stories. Thompson pictures himself neutralizing the strengths of opposing blockers. For example, if he feels a player is going to try to beat him with speed, Thompson will aggressively attack, push him around and run through him.

Thompson believes another key to his success is his background as a hurdler. Thompson attended Baylor on a track scholarship and was good enough to qualify for the 1984 Olympic trials, but an injury kept him from competing. He didn't join the football team until his sophomore year, when he walked on and played cornerback and on special teams.

Running hurdles taught Thompson to keep his speed and balance while hitting the hurdles and sometimes the opposing runners. He still conditions himself like a track athlete and, once a week, runs the 18 miles round-trip from his apartment to Giants Stadium. "Special teams will always be made up of crazies," he says, "guys who have one foot in the real world and the other in the insane asylum. That's me." Sounds like a Poe story. —*JILL LIEBER*

Whether he is reading books or covering kicks, Thompson is always ready to throw himself into the action.

MARION BUTTS

Marion Butts knows all about overcoming obstacles and crashing through barriers. The San Diego Chargers 6' 1", 248-pound bull of a running back has spent much of his life proving his critics wrong.

"Life has been an uphill battle," says Butts, 24, who in only his second season was the NFL's third-leading rusher, with 1,225 yards, eight touchdowns and only one fumble in 265 carries.

Butts, who grew up in Sylvester, Ga., faced one of his first obstacles as a junior at Worth County High School. Playing against Bainbridge High, he fractured his leg. Following surgery that night, doctors told Butts he would never play football again. "I refused to listen to them," he says.

Butts stayed at home for four months with his leg in a cast. A classmate, entrusted to deliver his homework, failed to follow through, and before Butts realized what was happening—so he says—he had flunked all of his classes. The following season, after rehabilitating the leg, he made All-State but his grades continued to be a problem. Florida State, Butts says, promised him a starting position if he would first enroll at Northeastern Oklahoma A&M Junior College to work on his academics.

However, when he showed up in Tallahassee two years later, Butts found himself as the third-string fullback on a team that included eventual first-round NFL draft picks Sammie Smith (Miami Dolphins) and Dexter Carter (San Francisco 49ers). In two years, Butts totaled only 64 carries. Head coach Bobby Bowden said of Butts: "I liked his running ability, but he was one of those guys who was too big. People always said he wasn't a land changer; he'd run over you, but he didn't have any moves."

To this day, Butts disagrees with Bowden's assessment. "I was bigger than the rest of the running backs, faster than the rest of the fullbacks," Butts says. "But I was from Georgia. And at a Florida school, the alumni would rather a kid from Florida play over a kid from Georgia."

During the hard times, Butts threatened to quit school or transfer, but his mother, Mary Jane, advised him to stay at Florida State. "Get an education," she counseled, "and I guarantee that good

After limited success in high school and college, the persistent Butts finds himself among the top rushers in the NFL.

things will happen to you." The good things finally materialized, thanks to Wayne McDuffie, the Florida State offensive coordinator, who recommended Butts to the Charger scouts. "Marion's a cold-blooded runner; he'll flatten people," McDuffie told them.

San Diego made Butts their seventh-round pick in 1989, the 183rd player and the 25th running back chosen overall. At the time of the draft, the San Diego offense was built around Gary Anderson, a finesse back who was a half-inch shorter and 67 pounds lighter than Butts. "I couldn't believe I was drafted by a team where my power running style didn't fit," Butts says. "Of all the luck."

Well, his luck finally changed. Anderson held out the entire 1989 season, and new head coach Dan Henning arrived from Washington with his favorite style of offense, one featuring a big power back. That suited Butts, who started five games and led the Chargers in rushing with 683 yards and nine TDs.

Butts doesn't feel he was owed this good fortune in payment for his years of struggle; rather, he is humbled by success. "The limelight comes with dedication and leaves with foolishness," Butts says. "I've learned a lot in a short period of time. Regardless of who you are, and what you do, you can be high and mighty one day and at rock bottom the next. I work hard, and I don't take anything for granted."

—*JILL LIEBER*

WARREN MOON

They have finally found an offense for Warren Moon in Houston, the run-and-shoot, and if ever a player was born for a system, that player is Moon. First they told him, You had better keep your arm healthy, because you're going to throw, maybe more than any quarterback has ever thrown in one year. Throwing? No problem. Whip it or dink it or gun it deep or throw the touch pass—Moon can do it all. Always has.

Wait, that's not all. You're going to have to run, too, because a lot of the stuff comes on rollouts and half rolls, throws on the move. You'll also have to be able to read defenses as well as your wide receivers. You'll have four of them on every play, with each having as many as four routes from which to choose. That's 16 reads every snap of the ball.

And you had better be tough because you're going to get hit. Oh, brother, are you going to be hit. All that running and throwing means all those pass rushers.

Moon qualifies—in all categories. As a runner he's right up there with the premier quarterback-athletes—Randall Cunningham, John Elway and Boomer Esiason—the guys who can make tacklers miss. He's smart. That's the first thing that University of Washington coach Don James noticed about him in 1975, when Moon arrived in Seattle from West Los Angeles Junior College. It's what people mentioned in Canada when Moon was leading the Edmonton Eskimos to five straight Grey Cup championships, from 1978 to '82, during his six seasons in the CFL. Tough? Beyond question. When he takes off on a scramble, the guy doesn't even like to slide when he's about to be tackled. "I'd rather dive headfirst," says Moon. "You get more yards that way."

This season, with flamboyant former coach Jerry Glanville departed for Atlanta, the Oilers gave Moon this nifty offense. The guy who installed it is new coach Jack Pardee, who had used the run-and-shoot for three years at the University of Houston, which set more than 100 NCAA and SWC passing and total-offense records in 1988 and '89. The assistant coach Pardee retained to work with Moon is Kevin Gilbride, who was once a run-and-shoot specialist in the CFL. Moon's four wide receivers—Drew Hill, Ernest Givins, Haywood Jeffires and Curtis Duncan—are mostly little guys who fly, able to run any route invented.

The result is that Moon sprinted away from the rest of the NFL in the numbers department. His 527 yards passing in a victory over Kansas City was the second-highest total in NFL history. He also led the league in yards passing (4,689) and TD passes (33). Unfortunately for Moon, he wasn't turned loose in the run-and-shoot until late in his career. "I'm 33," he said at midseason, "so I'm in the winding-down stage of my career. I can see things on the field I couldn't see when I was younger, but physically, I can see myself

slowing down. I still have pretty good escapability, but once I turn upfield, I don't move as quickly."

The toll of the run-and-shoot on Moon, including a dislocated thumb in Week 16 that knocked him out of the playoffs, hasn't dampened his enthusiasm. "I have faith in this offense. I know we can move the ball consistently. We just have to take that step upward."

The step upward. For Moon, it's the difference between being another good quarterback and a guy mentioned with the likes of Montana, Marino and Elway. "I'm used to it by now," says Moon, "but somehow I never seem to be spoken of in the same breath with the really top names in the game."

Recognition has never come easily for Moon. He spent a year in junior college because he wasn't heavily recruited out of Hamilton High in Los

A 13-year veteran, Moon was at the top of his game in 1990, leading the league in four different passing categories.

Angeles. At Washington he was under the microscope as a black quarterback at a school where the student body was only 3.5% black. As a senior in 1977, he was named Pac-8 Player of the Year, but when scouts projected him as no better than a fourth-round pick, he chose Canada. Black QBs were still on the exotic side in the late '70s, looked at first as "athletes," then as signal callers.

While with Edmonton he put up some stunning numbers—21,228 yards passing and 1,700 yards rushing. He had back-to-back 5,000-yard passing seasons, including 5,648 in 1983, an alltime high for a 16-game pro football season.

The time was right to make a move south. Seattle was interested, but the Oilers prevailed by offering a more appealing contract and the chance to rejoin his Edmonton coach, Hugh Campbell, whom Houston had hired a month earlier. The two joined the sorriest franchise in the NFL, a team that had won a total of three games the previous two seasons. After Houston went 3–13 in '84 and 5–9 with two games to go in '85, Campbell was fired, and Glanville, his defensive coordinator, took over.

Over the next four seasons, Glanville turned the Oilers into his personal freak show: House of Pain, the Man in Black, the tickets for Elvis. Moon kept his mouth shut. Everyone did. No one wanted to get into Glanville's doghouse. In private, though, Moon echoed what most of the other offensive players felt. All that smash-mouth House of Pain stuff was fine for the defense, but then the offense had to take the field against an enemy defense psyched to inflict some pain of its own.

A coolness developed between coach and quarterback. Glanville never criticized Moon publicly, knowing that the quickest way to turn the town against him would have been to rip Moon in print. Moon was among the most popular sports figures in Houston. The Jaycees named him one of the Five Outstanding Young Men of Texas. The Travelers insurance company honored him with its coveted NFL Man of the Year award. When Moon's church in Houston, Windsor Village Methodist, needed $200,000 to complete a community center, Moon donated the entire amount.

Moon is comfortable with the Oilers' new system. Pardee devotes most of his attention to the defense and leaves Gilbride and Moon alone to dream up wrinkles in the run-and-shoot. Everyone gets along fine. Now, with a full year of run-and-shoot behind him, perhaps Moon's 14th pro season will be the year that will vault him to the top. The guy has paid his dues. He deserves it. *—PAUL ZIMMERMAN*

ANDRE RISON

Atlanta Falcon wide receiver Andre Previn Rison slips a headphone over his ears, pumps up the volume on the stereo and starts gyrating to one of his soon-to-be hit songs. Shoulders dip and hips swivel. Closing his eyes, he sings into a mike.

Rison's stage for this gig is the empty back bedroom of his rented suburban Atlanta condominium. Rison and his friend Ray (Stingray) Potter, a singer-songwriter from Lansing, Michigan, are collaborating on an album they plan to record.

"A few months ago, he sounded like James Brown, shrieking and screaming into the microphone," Stingray says. "He'll only get better. What Andre has going for him is a passion for music."

Polished or not, Rison has grandiose plans. "You just wait," he boasts. "When we go into the studio, I'll blow everybody away. I'm such a cocky and arrogant guy. I'm determined to make it. I'll be a star someday. M.C. Hammer—you can't touch me."

Those who have watched Rison develop into one of the NFL's best receivers in only his second year have learned not to underestimate his determination. As the seam man in Atlanta's four-receiver Red Gun offensive set, the job of the 5'11", 185-pound Rison is to race along the hash marks, sprint across no-man's-land—the middle of the field—catch the ball in heavy traffic, then run like mad.

Rison's uninhibited receiving style produced 100 catches in his first 24 games; only one other wide receiver in NFL history has done it quicker, the New York Jets' Al Toon, who reached the milestone in 23. Rison finished the '90 season with 82 receptions, second in the league and 18 catches behind league-leader Jerry Rice of the 49ers. "What I like is his concentration," Rice says of his rival. "He can be stuck in a crowd over the middle, with people all around him, and he still puts his hand on the ball."

And, sometimes, his foot in his mouth. Rison has coined his own term for taunting opponents. He calls it "trappin'" or "talkin' smack." If you believe Rison, he sounds off only after being provoked. His most publicized smack-talkin' outburst occurred before Atlanta's game with the Bears in Week 10. Chicago cornerback Lemuel Stinson started the hostilities by proclaiming Falcon cornerback Deion (Prime Time) Sanders "a nobody" when it came to playing cornerback. After Rison read Stinson's comments about his closest friend on the team, he proceeded to lay some serious smack on Stinson. "If he has to play me man-to-man the whole game," he said, "I'll be in the Hall of Fame by Monday. I've got my [induction] speech ready."

As it turned out, Stinson intercepted two passes, and the Bears defeated the Falcons 30–24. Rison, who caught six passes, was at fault on one of the pickoffs when he ran an outside pattern rather than an inside route. Still, he refuses to retract any of his smack.

"It's like you've got a no trespassing sign in your yard, and somebody walks up anyway," Rison says. "I don't throw my achievements in anybody's face. The comments I make are always funny. Ask my friends. They'll tell you I'm a comedian." That's hardly an assessment shared by Rison's opponents, who are forced to endure his post-TD victory celebration, a duck-walk dance that he calls "The Highlight Zone." But the Falcon faithful love it; he is often asked to re-create the routine in parking lots, grocery stores, shopping malls and public restrooms around Atlanta.

Instant celebrity. Toast of the town. One of the best receivers in the NFL. Not so long ago those were just wild and ridiculous aspirations for a kid whose childhood in depressed Flint, Michigan, was full of upheaval and tragedy. Money was always a problem, forcing the family to move some 15 times during Andre's childhood. When Andre was 11, his natural father, who had been wounded in Vietnam, left for California, and his stepfather, Reggie Brown, was shot and killed as a bystander during a robbery in Morgantown, West Virginia. About Brown's death Rison says, "My brother [Reggie] and sister [Raquel] were too young to understand. I used to tell them Dad was on the moon, that he could see us wherever we were going. We were on our way home to Flint after his death, just us four, and I remember looking up at the moon and saying, 'There goes daddy.'"

Growing up in such turmoil, Rison took strength from his mother, Merdice Brown, 42, a fiery, 5'11", 150-pound bundle of energy with whom Andre is extremely close. He refers to her as "Roseanne," after the wise-cracking, blue-collar, sitcom housewife. Says Andre: "She runs her house like Roseanne. She can hold her own."

After starring in football and basketball at Flint Northwestern High, Rison became a record-setting receiver at Michigan State. But personal problems continued to dog him. The summer before his junior season, he eloped with his high school sweetheart, Tonja Harden, who was pregnant. When Merdice heard the news from a friend, she confronted Andre.

He initially denied the wedding had taken place. "I didn't want him to get married," she says. "He was too young." Andre Jr. was born just before the 1988 Rose Bowl.

While his personal life may have been troubled, Rison showed no evidence of it on the field. He finished his collegiate career with a sensational performance in the 1989 Gator Bowl, catching nine passes for 252 yards and three TDs. But NFL scouts were hearing rumors that he was spoiled, moody and immature. What most of them failed to uncover was that Rison was going through a stressful time that spring, trying to hold on to a rapidly disintegrating marriage. "I was a 21-year-old kid, wondering how I was going to support everybody—my mother, brother, sister, wife and son," Rison says.

In the 1989 NFL draft, the Colts made him the 22nd pick overall, far lower than Rison thought he deserved. Tonja and Andre Jr. joined him in Indianapolis, but the friction between husband and wife intensified. "The prestige of being an NFL player put pressure on the marriage," Rison says. The couple filed for divorce within a year of the draft.

Rison's latest trauma occurred in the spring of 1990, when he discovered that he had been traded, along with offensive tackle Chris Hinton, a fifth-round draft pick in 1990 and a first-round pick in '91 to the Falcons in exchange for Atlanta's first- and fourth-round picks in '90. The trade left Rison confused and feeling underappreciated. "Everywhere I've gone, I feel like I've disappointed people," he says. "I feel I have so much to prove. I want to show Michigan State I should have caught more passes. I want to show the NFL I should have been drafted higher. I need to show the Colts they made a big mistake trading me."

And so Rison perseveres. Growing up poor in Flint made him tough. Being Merdice's son taught him to be his own man. And as a gifted athlete, he learned never to give up. "My arrogance and cockiness have always been a cover-up for the disappointments in my life," Rison says. "I realized at a young age if I didn't stick up for myself, then I'd fall through the cracks with everybody else. I wouldn't get noticed. I had to talk myself up to believe I could achieve something in life. Somebody had to believe in me. Somebody had to say it out loud." —JILL LIEBER

CHARLES HALEY

Charles Haley, the San Francisco 49er pass rusher *extraordinaire*, may be the most misunderstood man in the NFL. His mood swings are legendary. Even his coaches and teammates aren't sure which Haley to expect each day. Will it be the one who inspires the 49ers with stirring pregame speeches? The one who provokes fights in the locker room and on the practice field with childish pranks and harsh, ill-timed words? Or the one who apologizes to opponents he inadvertently injures?

Whoever he is, there's no mistaking that Haley, 27, is one of the best defensive players in pro football. Many of San Francisco's defenses revolve around trying to free Haley, who is used either as a down lineman or as an outside linebacker, for one of his trademark sacks. This season, Haley ranked third in the NFL—and first in the NFC—in sacks, with 16, had the team's only blocked field goal and made the Pro Bowl for the second time in his five-year career.

Haley's unpredictability may be the result of a rough childhood. The second youngest of George and Virginia Haley's five sons, Charles grew up in Gladys, Virginia (pop. 350). Until Charles was 13, the family lived in a small, three-bedroom house with no electricity, indoor plumbing or telephone. His father drove tractor-trailers during the day, worked the night shift at a textile factory and, in spare moments on weekends, cut timber. His mother worked at a furniture store. To help make ends meet, Charles bagged groceries and, during the summers, was paid $20 a day to do chores on local farms. He pulled tobacco, hauled corn, baled hay and chased cows.

Haley was a chubby child, in part because he loved to devour his mother's fried chicken, freshly baked bread and sweet-potato pie. To burn off some of the extra pounds, he began playing football when he was eight. "I used to like to hurt people," Haley says. "It was the only way I could get back at the kids who made fun of me for being fat. I didn't feel good about myself."

Nor did he feel good about football. Haley despised lifting weights and often showed up late for practice, if he showed up at all. Because of his lackadaisical attitude, Haley was benched as a sophomore by his junior varsity coach and was repeatedly disciplined. He says he's still trying to understand his erratic behavior. "I was labeled the problem child," Haley says. "I did a lot of bad things. Stealing. Vandalism. It seemed like I'd get expelled three times a week. One of my high school teachers said, 'You'd be the last person to go to college and play professional football.' That hit me hard."

Mrs. Haley begged the JV coach to be patient.

"Why isn't he playing?" she asked after one game.

"All he does is joke," the coach replied. "He won't work."

"Put him in and he'll play," she said. "He'll work."

Mother knew best. In his senior season, Haley was named the county's defensive player of the year. "I turned it around," Charles says. "I didn't want to disappoint her."

James Madison University, a Division I-AA school in Harrisonburg, Virginia, was the only college that actively recruited Haley. As it turned out, the small-school setting was a blessing. Haley thrived under coach Challace McMillin and didn't miss a single game in four years. He recorded at least 130 tackles in each of his last three seasons, and as a senior was named to the Division I-AA All-America team. Uninvited to the NFL scouting combine, Haley came to the 49ers' attention only through some fuzzy, black-and-white game films sent to San Francisco by the coaches at James Madison. In spite of their technical quality, the films were impressive enough to persuade the 49ers to take a risk and draft Haley in the fourth round in 1986.

"The teachers at James Madison helped me one-on-one," Haley says. "It was a religious school. Nobody yelled or cursed. Everything was positive reinforcement. They cared about me."

Haley received similar nurturing from the 49ers in 1990. During the off-season, All-Pro safety Ronnie Lott took Haley under his wing, challenging the 6'5", 240-pounder to rigorous workouts consisting of running hills, lifting weights, aqua-aerobics, aerobic dance classes, karate and kick boxing. Owner Eddie DeBartolo rewarded Haley with a brand new four-year contract valued at a reported $4 million.

"I'm trying to control my emotions," Haley says. "I tried different techniques to keep my cool. When I get upset, I count to 10 and breathe deep. And I forget what I'm mad about. Now I try not to let people bother me. I tell myself, You're the best at what you do. The heck with everybody else." —*JILL LIEBER*

Striking a Sphinx-like pose on the 49er bench, Haley remains inscrutable to both himself and his teammates.

HERSCHEL WALKER

Minnesota Viking running back Herschel Walker and his 3-year-old Rottweiler named Al Capone wound their way through the rolling hills and tiny duck ponds in this plush northwestern Minneapolis suburb of Edina. It was an early Tuesday morning, a day off for the Vikings but not for Walker, who was on the first of two four-mile conditioning runs. Walker, who stands 6'2", 212 pounds, glided effortlessly, prancing on his toes as if he were a track runner warming up for a race. He barely broke a sweat. Capone, loping alongside his owner, is an awkward, beefy 120 pounds, his big butt swishing from side to side, his long tongue dangling out of his mouth.

"Come on, Blockhead," Walker yelled to the panting pup. "You can keep up with me."

Most pro football players relish their days off, taking the few hours to rest their battered and bruised bodies. But Walker has always been different. He needs just four hours of sleep a night and exists on only one meal a day. Instead of lifting weights, he keeps fit with a daily regimen of 3,500 situps and 1,500 pushups. He has never taken an aspirin and had his wisdom teeth pulled without a painkiller. He has never tasted beer or liquor.

"When I'm running, I feel at ease. I'm in my domain," Walker said. "I don't even feel my footsteps touching the ground. It's like I'm running on clouds. When I'm running, I'm at peace."

But Walker did not run very much on game days this season, and he was not at peace with the Vikings. For the first time in his illustrious and ballyhooed career—from his Heisman Trophy days at Georgia to his brief romp through the now-defunct USFL to his stint as a one-man offense with the Dallas Cowboys—Walker was caught in the middle of a football controversy. As the result of an extended period of weak performances, his football skills and his desire to play were questioned in Minneapolis and around the league. Blame was first assigned to the Vikings for failing to use Walker properly in the team's offense. But soon the critics had shifted their focus to Walker himself.

"Jumping on the anti-Herschel bandwagon is chic right now," he said at midseason. "It's the cool thing to do. I am not a dog. Al Capone is."

Walker's woes began with the blockbuster trade on Oct. 12, 1989, that shipped him from the Dallas Cowboys to the Vikings in exchange for five players and seven draft choices, including Minnesota's No. 1 and 2 picks from 1990 through 1992. Walker was heralded by former Viking president Mike Lynn, the mastermind of the deal, as "the last spoke in the wheel," the savior who would lead the Vikings to the promised land of the Super Bowl. There were high hopes for the team, and the expectations for Walker were off-the-map. In his first game, he met them, rushing for 148 yards.

Then the deal went sour. Walker failed to gain more than 90 yards in a game for the rest of the 1989 season and seemed lost without the I-back set that makes the best use of his abilities. He seemed even more out of place this season, finishing with 770 yards rushing, acceptable perhaps for an ordinary back but not for a would-be franchise-maker earning $2.25 million per year. His season's average of 22.0 yards per kickoff return was seventh in the league, but hardly justification enough for the future talent that the Vikings lost in the trade.

"I feel like I'm more of a burden than a help to this team," Walker admitted. Added his wife, Cindy, "This is a nightmare."

Some Vikings believed that Walker had completely lost his confidence. "He's not playing with the same reckless abandon as last year," said Rich Gannon, the Viking quarterback. Added offensive lineman David Huffman: "Herschel has never been in a slump before, and he is folding under the pressure."

Suggestions that he had lost his confidence angered Walker, who is a great believer in the power of positive thinking. "I don't think my play is affecting my confidence. I'm not saying it. Everyone else is. What affects me is what my family and closest friends are saying. Those are the people I care about."

Through much of the season, Herschel and Cindy hid their insecurity and anger from the public. But after the torrent of midseason criticism and after listening to Cindy talk about his problems for several hours, Herschel finally let down his guard.

"I don't know, Cindy, maybe I am running the ball differently," he said. "I don't know.... I do know if you tell a kid long enough that he's worthless, sooner or later he'll start believing it. I don't feel like I fit in here. I've never been given a chance to fit in. I don't feel like I was ever meant to fit in here. Who's fault is that? I didn't ask for the trade."

More than a year after the trade, the Walkers still feel out of place. During the season, Cindy received her fine china in the mail from her brother, but she was afraid to unpack the box because she worried that the Vikings would not sign her husband after the 1990 season, when his contract expired.

Even if Walker gets a new contract, it doesn't appear that he will ever be the focal point of the offense as long as Jerry Burns is coach. "In my optimum offense," Burns says, "I'd like my receivers and tight end to catch five or six passes. I'd like each back to carry the ball six to eight times and get 50 yards. If you do that, everybody will be fresh and everybody will be happy."

So why did the Vikings trade for Walker in the first place? Sources say Lynn, now head of the World League of American Football, did not consult with Burns before making the deal. Several Viking players believe Lynn used Walker to mend his public image. Before the trade, a handful of black players charged that Lynn was a racist in his contract dealings with players. By obtaining Walker, a positive black role model with a large contract, Lynn could wipe away the racist label.

Whatever the reason, until Walker starts to produce big, the Herschel bashing will not end. Meanwhile, Cindy and Herschel try to keep things in perspective. Says Cindy, "Let's get down to reality. This is football. So they're saying he's not a good football player. Is that going to kill us? His career is important, but it's no more important than being a good person, having your health or your family. In that respect, whatever happens, we'll make the best of it."

In the midst of controversy since his trade to the Vikings, Walker has tried not to wear his troubles on his sleeve.

—*JILL LIEBER*

CLAY & BRUCE MATTHEWS

When Clay and Bruce Matthews get together for a little brotherly competition, it's best to have an ambulance on standby. Boxing matches can turn into knock-down-and-drag-out fistfights; in Bruce's wedding pictures, you can see a scratch on his forehead that came from roughhousing with his brother. When they go knee-boarding on Castaic Lake in Southern California, pulled side by side behind a speedboat at 40 mph, they jump the wake and try to land on one another. A simple game of one-on-one basketball on Clay's backyard court usually turns into a shouting match or escalates into so much banging and shoving that one of them gets a black eye, bloody nose or cut lip.

Their sport of choice, naturally, is football. And while they may sound like a pair of teenagers, Clay, 35, is the Cleveland Browns' left linebacker and Bruce, 29, is the Houston Oilers' right guard.

Of the 140-plus brother combinations who have played pro football since the 1920s, none can match the Matthewses' overall achievements. Both received All-America honors in high school (Clay at New Trier East in suburban Chicago, Bruce in Arcadia, Calif.) and in college (while seniors at USC). Both were first round draft choices, the Browns picking Clay 12th overall in the '78 draft and the Oilers choosing Bruce ninth in '83. And they are the only brothers ever voted to the same Pro Bowl team, having both been chosen for the AFC squad in '88 and '89.

Clay and Bruce admit, however, that their intensity on the football field has wavered 16 times in the past eight years. On those occasions they lined up across from each other as the Browns and the Oilers, members of the highly competitive AFC Central, squared off. One brother does not enjoy seeing the other made to look foolish in front of a screaming, sell-out crowd and millions of TV viewers.

The brothers' competitive spirit originated with their father, William Clay Sr., now 62, tan and fit at 6'3" and 240 pounds. President of a Los Angeles air-pollution-control business, Clay Sr. lettered in football, wrestling and swimming at Georgia Tech (1944–49) and started at offensive tackle, defensive end and linebacker for the 49ers in the '50s. Clay Sr. has always taken pride in being tough. He tells a story

about a game against the Bears when he ran into the goalpost and knocked himself out but remained in the game to call the defensive signals.

When they were youngsters, Clay and Bruce developed a close relationship while the family crisscrossed the country. Their father worked in 27 different locations for seven companies, and their mother, Daisy, supervised the moves. Besides Bruce, the Matthews children are all in their thirties, with Kristy the eldest, followed by Clay, and twins Bradley and Raymond, who are educationally handicapped.

Although Clay Sr. worked long hours, he tried to be an involved father, both as a disciplinarian and a philosopher. Every six months or so, Clay Sr. would gather the children at the kitchen table and hand each of them a piece of paper and a pencil. He would

Like Clay Sr., Clay (left) and Bruce try to raise their children with high ideals.

Clay Sr. says, "They achieved, thanks to being pushed by their brothers. I just refused to do anything different from what I would do for a normal kid."

For the past nine years, Raymond has worked as a maintenance man at the data-tape division of Kodak, and until Friday, Sept. 30, 1988, Brad was an assembler for an electrical firm. That evening, after work, he was walking to a nearby high school track for his regular three-mile run, when he stepped into a crosswalk and was struck by a pickup truck. Brad was thrown 40 feet and suffered injuries that left him paralyzed from the shoulders down.

Three weeks later, Clay visited Brad in the hospital, composing himself just enough to offer some words of consolation. Recently, Brad, sitting in his motorized wheelchair, recounted the moment for Clay for the first time. "You told me to keep fighting," Brad says. "You said, 'Do the best you can. Keep pushing. Keep going with life. You're just like anybody else, you just had a bad break.' That gave me strength."

Clay is stunned and moved. "I didn't know that I made you feel strong," he says softly.

Brad smiles. "You told me how life goes on, that not everything can be perfect," he says. "It helped me. I wanted to be stronger because of you."

"What Brad lost physically, he has gained mentally," Bruce says. "His personality and mental skills have expanded so much. He has no bitterness about not being able to walk. He's glad to be alive."

Clay and Bruce share the same philosophies on life and about raising children, and they possess a similar offbeat sense of humor. Both are devoted family men who own sprawling two-story homes a few blocks apart in Agoura Hills, Calif. They met their wives as freshmen at Southern Cal. Clay and Leslie have been married 12 years and have five children. Bruce and Carrie, married seven years, have three kids and plan to have three more.

Clay and Bruce agree that they owe much of their success in football to the inspiration provided by the twins, whose presence is a constant reminder to Clay and Bruce that talent is a blessing and playing football should always be kept in its proper perspective. Says Bruce, "In their own way, Brad and Ray are as fortunate as Clay and I are. Because what's important in life isn't being a football star. It's doing the best with what God has given you." —*JILL LIEBER*

pose serious questions: What is God? What does marriage mean? What are brothers and sisters for? He would tuck away the answers in his dresser, then pull them out a few months later and call the children together for a review. "When we'd look at the slips of paper, I'd tell them, 'Until somebody convinces you that this is not true or that there are better answers, this is who you are. To thine own self be true.'"

Clay Sr. insisted that Raymond and Bradley be treated exactly the same as the other members of the family. "They aren't mentally handicapped," Clay Sr. likes to say. "They just don't have the horsepower." He had them compete in all of the backyard and playground sports against Clay and Bruce. And they did. "They hit hard, and so did we," Brad remembers. "We never backed down. No pain, no gain."

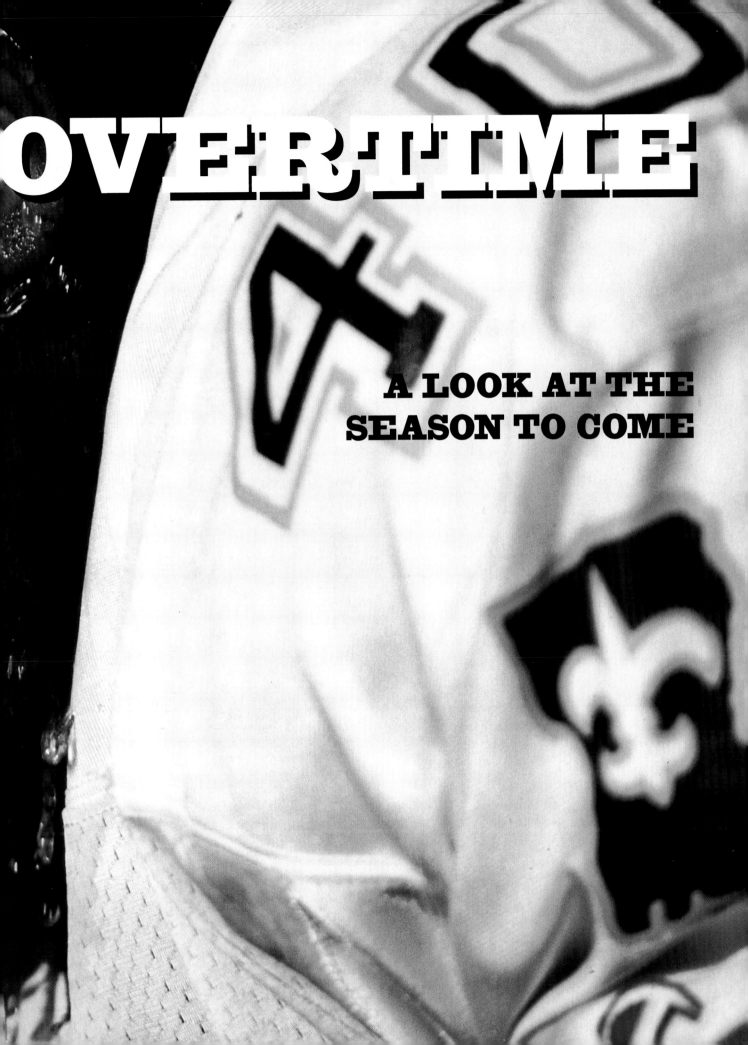

OVERTIME

A LOOK AT THE SEASON TO COME

OVERVIEW

THIS TIME, IT'S GOOD!

T his is how it will happen. There will be eight seconds left in Super Bowl XXVI in Minneapolis next January, and the Buffalo Bills will use their final timeout. The 49ers will be ahead 19–17. The Bills will be on the San Francisco 30.

The MVP vote will be a lock by this time, because Joe Montana will have completed 22 of 27 passes for 369 yards, including a 96-yard TD toss to John Taylor. Already, the Disney camera people will have Montana sequestered near the side of the field, ready for a five-second "I'm going to Disney World!" spot.

Then Scott Norwood will trot onto the field.

"HEY NORWOOD!" 49er linebacker Bill Romanowski will scream, struggling to be heard above the din in the Metrodome. "REMEMBER TAMPA!"

Buffalo general manager Bill Polian, up in the owners' box, will ask for a cigarette. He hasn't smoked in four years, but he will have to have one now. Thirty-two of the Bills will turn their back to the field, because they won't want to watch this and because they'll be in a fervent prayer huddle. Jim Kelly will hug Ted Marchibroda, his offensive coordinator, and mutter over and over again, "Please, Scott, please."

"HEY NORWOOD!" San Francisco fullback Tom Rathman will yell, as the television timeout winds down. "JUST LIKE LAST YEAR! JUST LIKE LAST YEAR!"

This time, there will be no field to tend to, no divots to replace, no wet spots to watch out for. This is the Homerdome. This is artificial turf. Norwood will step to the right hashmark at the San Francisco 37-yard line and point his right toes to the exact spot where he wants his holder, Frank Reich, to put the ball down. "No problem, Scotty," Reich will say, nodding to him. Nobody else will say a word to Norwood. He'll get six pats on the rump. No words. No one will know what to say. What do you say in a situation like this? Make it? Good luck? Nope. It's no time for words. Except from the San Francisco side of the ball.

"HEY NORWOOD!" 49er defensive end Pierce Holt will holler. "WIDE RIGHT! WIDE RIGHT! REMEMBER? WIDE RIGHT!"

"#@!$&*%+!&*@@," a couple of Bills will say back to him.

And now referee Jerry Markbreit's arm will rev up, and the Bills will break their huddle. Nine men will come to the line for the biggest play of their lives. Oh, they had had some big ones along the way in this 13–3 season. A huge Thurman Thomas touchdown gallop to break open the second-round playoff win over the tough San Diego Chargers. Four touchdown passes by Kelly to whip the Kansas City Chiefs in the AFC Championship Game. And, of

course, they had had the big play a year earlier, the missed Norwood 47-yarder that lost them Super Bowl XXV. But this was the current biggest. A Norwood 47-yarder. From the right hash. For the championship of the world.

And Norwood will say to himself: "Not again."

The ball will come back to Reich from the center. Reich will put it down, laces pointing straight toward the goalpost as he had been taught, at the 37, on exactly the spot where Norwood told him to place it. And Norwood will stride perfectly into the kick, planting his left foot four feet southwest of the ball, throwing his right leg into the ball, his right foot slamming into it three inches above the AstroTurf. It will sail above 19 men clawing at each other at the line of scrimmage. It will hook from just outside the right upright to just inside the right upright over the last 15 yards. It will pass to the left of the right upright, about four feet to the left, and about eight feet above the crossbar.

Dick Enberg will yell: "OH, MY! IT'S GOOOOOOOOOD!"

Jim Kelly will yell: "AHHHHHHHHHH!"

One thousand miles directly due east, the city of Buffalo will yell: "YEAAAAAAAAAAAAAA!"

And on the field, the Disney cameras will abandon Montana and, along with the rest of the stadium, scurry over to Norwood. The Bills will be lifting Norwood on their shoulders, and all the paparazzi will be snapping away at Norwood, and his helmet will get ripped off somehow, and he'll be bouncing up and down because the Bills by this time will be like one huge conga line. And the Disney cameras will point up at Norwood, with great expectations.

Norwood will say: "   "

Because he won't be able to speak. He will be crying. And words won't be able to come out of his mouth. Words won't be necessary.

We can dream, can't we?

THE WAY IT WILL BE

The NFC East is once again the toughest division, boasting four of the top eight slots in our team rankings, with the young Cardinals providing a surprising challenge or two. In the AFC it's everybody chasing Buffalo, all the way to the Super Bowl.

1.	**BUFFALO**	*"Norwood kicks ... on the way ... GOOD! BILLS WIN!*
2.	**SAN FRANCISCO**	*Montana finds a way. Always does. Even at 35.*
3.	**WASHINGTON**	*Finally, they get over the Giant Jinx.*
4.	**KANSAS CITY**	*But DeBerg has to last the year, and that's no gimme.*
5.	**N.Y. GIANTS**	*Pencil them in for 11 wins. But they'll struggle.*
6.	**DALLAS**	*Johnson's not afraid to play his rookies. It pays off.*
7.	**L.A. RAIDERS**	*It'd be nice if they learned how to play on the road.*
8.	**PHILADELPHIA**	*Hey, Buddy: Just watch. They can win without you.*
9.	**SAN DIEGO**	*Gosh, there's talent here. They've got to win soon.*
10.	**NEW ORLEANS**	*Will everyone please stop knocking the Walsh trade?*
11.	**HOUSTON**	*Key question: Will they ever play good D again?*
12.	**CINCINNATI**	*See No. 11, Houston.*
13.	**MIAMI**	*They move up if Marino plays DE, LB, or CB.*
14.	**TAMPA BAY**	*They don't need Parcells's coaching to go 9–7.*
15.	**CHICAGO**	*Mike, we just know you'll pull nine wins out of 'em.*
16.	**ATLANTA**	*Glanville would suit up Hell's Angels to go .500.*
17.	**GREEN BAY**	*Mandarich waived, becomes roadie for Guns 'n Roses.*
18.	**SEATTLE**	*Someday this QB situation will catch up to them.*
19.	**L.A. RAMS**	*Marcus Dupree's final totals: 178 carries, 926 yards.*
20.	**N.Y. JETS**	*Troy Taylor starts at QB by Oct. 1.*
21.	**INDIANAPOLIS**	*Jeff George wins four by himself.*
22.	**PITTSBURGH**	*Joe—Walton, that is—must go.*
23.	**MINNESOTA**	*Vike job would be big demotion for Lou Holtz now.*
24.	**DETROIT**	*Poor Chris Spielman. He deserves so much better.*
25.	**PHOENIX**	*The Cards are better, but the division's a knockout.*
26.	**DENVER**	*Can things be this bad? Yup.*
27.	**CLEVELAND**	*Big Belichick task in year one: Stop the bleeding.*
28.	**NEW ENGLAND**	*Actually, can we make them No. 29?*

AFC SCOUTING REPORT

By now, the Bills are sick of bromides. They're sick of hearing how good defense stops good offense, every time. They're sick of hearing how power football beats finesse football. They're sick of hearing how the game's too complicated now for a quarterback to call his own plays. Well, take heart, Buffalo faithful—your team won't have to listen to that stuff much longer, because 1991 is their year to own the NFL.

Look what they have going for them. They have the best offensive plan and the best people to execute it. Working behind a leakproof offensive line of nobodies, Jim Kelly has an almost limitless array of options. First, he has the greatness of Thurman Thomas behind him. What security. For two years, Thomas has led all NFL backs in yards from scrimmage, and in the playoffs, he was unstoppable, averaging 181.3 rushing-receiving yards per game.

Turning to the pass, Kelly can choose between the guile of James Lofton or the speed and productivity of Andre Reed. At tight end, Keith McKeller is *almost* a wideout, too, with the speed, hands and build of a basketball power forward, which is exactly what he was five years ago at Jacksonville (Ala.) State.

Point to offensive deficiencies that showed up in the Super Bowl, and we'll nod. But the Bills defense really lost that game. They have to play the run better, because the key to beating them, as the Giants showed, is simply keeping Kelly off the field. And they have to pressure the quarterback more consistently. Bruce Smith had 19 sacks, and he's probably the best defensive player in the sport right now. But he went five late-season games without a sack. "They could build a house with the guys they

had blocking me on every play," he groused after the Bills' playoff win over Miami. Hey, big guy, get used to it. You're the best, and they all know it.

Even with those warts, the Bills should win the AFC handily. Houston and Kansas City will win their divisions, but the Central and West races will go down to Week 18. Jack Pardee is building himself a swell team in Houston, an unbeatable team at home in the 'Dome. But the Oilers have to learn to win big games on the road. You do that with defense. "It's like *Nightmare on Elm Street* for us when we leave home," wideout Ernest Givins says. The Chiefs are a big-back, ball-control team, a team as comfortable in the midwestern heat of September as in the northeastern chill of December. They're a lot like the Giants, which makes them the team with the best chance of beating Buffalo in Rich Stadium in January. But in 1991 their chances will be slim—something akin to kick-boxing on ESPN out-rating "The Cosby Show."

The wild cards—the Raiders, the Chargers, the Bengals—won't be big playoff factors, although San Diego will set itself up for a nice 1992 run. General manager Bobby Beathard had better build an offensive line before making any big plans, though.

Elsewhere, Miami and Pittsburgh will disappoint after making recent runs toward renewed respectability. The Dolphins can outscore anyone because they have the best quarterback on the planet, Dan Marino. But they've got to get a pass rusher to take some pressure off up-and-coming defensive end Jeff Cross, and they've got to get some lasting stability at linebacker, where defensive coordinator Tom Olivadotti has had to start a Linebacker of the Month Club because of Miami's weakness there. The Steelers—well, we just can't tell you how they do it, sitting at 7–7 every December and challenging for the division title. Bubby Brister ain't the reason. The no-name defense probably is. The offensive woes of early 1990 will return in 1991. They play four strong NFC East foes, and Houston and Cincinnati should both sweep them.

The view here: Thomas and Kelly split the various MVP and Player of the Year awards, and Thomas has a 200-yard rushing-receiving day in the AFC Championship Game, a 31–10 rout of Kansas City. In Buffalo, of course. In minus-19 windchill.

▶ **Best Offense: Buffalo.** Don't punch out Kelly's Heroes because of one Super Bowl. This is the offense of the future.

▶ **Best Defense: Kansas City.** The secondary's graying, but young rushing studs Neil Smith and Derrick Thomas combined for 29.5 sacks in 1990.

▶ **Best Special Teams: Buffalo.** News flash: NFL bans Steve Tasker! Says he's too quick, too dangerous chasing down punts. Film at 11.

▶ **Breakthrough Player: Billy Brooks, Wide Receiver, Indianapolis.** This year, with Jeff George's maturation, he becomes great ... 90-catch great.

▶ **Surprise Team: San Diego.** We keep saying the Chargers are coming. If Billy Joe Tolliver is even competent, these guys win 10.

▶ **Most Disappointing Team: Denver.** Defensive coordinator Wade Phillips can flat coach, but not with flat players. Head for the basement, Broncos.

▶ With power backs Barry Word—here flattening safety Martin Bayless of the Chargers—and Christian Okoye, the Chiefs have the best chance of dethroning the Bills.

NFC SCOUTING REPORT

This is going to sound very weird, but we're going to say it anyway.

The Giants can afford to lose Lawrence Taylor. Basically, they've lost him already, because teams now know they can single-block him most of the time and he'll respond like an ordinary mortal, instead of like his former super self. The guy they couldn't afford to lose, they've lost. Bill Belichick.

We're not saying the Browns snagged the next Chuck Noll in Belichick, the Giants' bookish, quiet former defensive coordinator, but every week in last season he found a way to neutralize the opposition's best weapon. Against Detroit, the Giants switched to a five-linebacker defense and held Barry Sanders to 11 carries in a 20–0 win. The Giants held Eric Dickerson to 26 yards by smothering his rush lanes in a 24–7 victory. Most impressively, facing Joe Montana twice, the Giants nickelbacked him to distraction, and the 49ers scored two TDs in eight quarters. Okay,

▼ The Cowboys won't go down without a fight in '91, especially if their draft choices, and young players like tight end Rob Awalt, can make a contribution right away.

Belichick couldn't stop Thurman Thomas. Give the guy one mulligan. The point is, Belichick was the Giants' key to making their malleable defense work.

His loss helps put the NFC in a strange situation. In every recent season, a potentially dominant team was chasing a dominant team. After 1985, the Giants shadowed the Bears. Following '86, the Redskins were ready to take on the Giants. Then came the 49ers, with the Vikings a big threat after '87 and the Rams the big wheels after '88 and '89. Now the Giants are the champs, but they're not very scary and neither is anybody else. The 49ers are getting old. The Bears are in transition.

Given those observations, we hold these NFC truths to be self-evident:

1. George Seifert and Joe Gibbs will get every ounce out of their clubs. Isn't Gibbs something? In the last eight years, Washington has won at least 10 games seven times. What a scotch-taper this guy is. And all Seifert's done in two years is take over an aging great team and go 32–5. Now he'll have to get his offensive line rebuilt.

2. Bill Parcells probably got the most he could

out of his club in 1990. Taylor and Phil Simms, Parcells's cornerstones, reach the end of the line ... and if they don't leave the Giants, they can at least see the end from here.

3. The Cowboys will continue to surprise. Unless they've drafted a bunch of Marv Throneberrys, we're watching greatness waiting to happen.

4. The NFC Central is one large scrambled egg. The teams in second through fifth place in 1990 finished 6–10, and the only moves we think possible are the ascent of Tampa Bay and descent of Chicago. But hey, we've thought Vinny Testaverde was ready before, and we've thought the Bears were done.

5. Don't bet on anything we've just written.

So where does this leave us? We'll go with the surest thing: Joe Montana survives another battered year, and Seifert patches another defense together, and the Niners win with a passing game and a front seven. And we'll have the Giants and the Red-skins—surprise!—giving the 49ers their toughest tests. And we'll have Dallas winning a home wild-card game before falling at Candlestick next January.

San Francisco, Tampa Bay and Washington win the divisions. The Giants, Dallas and Philadelphia win the wild cards. With Steve Walsh finally finding his comfort zone, New Orleans will begin to reassert

▶ **Best Offense:** San Francisco. Okay, Montana and Craig are old, and the line's leaky. But just try holding them under 28 some Sunday this fall.
▶ **Best Defense:** Dallas. By November, the boy wonder in NFL coaching will be Cowboy defensive coordinator Dave Wannstedt.
▶ **Best Special Teams:** New York. Punt, Sean, punt. Cover, Reyna, cover. Scoot, Dave, scoot. Landeta, Thompson and Meggett, that is.
▶ **Breakthrough Player:** Steve Walsh, Quarterback, New Orleans. In 1990 he played in John Fourcade's league. In 1991 he graduates to Dan Marino's.
▶ **Surprise Team:** Dallas. They'll win 10 or 11 games and a wild-card spot. Troy Aikman, Emmitt Smith and a very big D will see to that.
▶ **Most Disappointing Team:** Minnesota. No quarterback. No great back. No defensive spine. And maybe no Millard. Might be a five-win season.

itself as a 49er threat. And what of the traditionally good teams? Chicago is always a valiant crew, but they now need help on both lines; Dan Hampton's understudy, Fred Washington, died in a car wreck last year. The Rams have imported defensive coordinator Jeff Fisher from Philadelphia, and he'll need at least a year to instill toughness and upgrade the front-seven talent. Green Bay and Minnesota won't escape the NFC Central pack, but the Packers, if Don Majkowski is right after rotator-cuff surgery, will be a threat every Sunday. Just not enough of one.

The view here: San Francisco gets fat in its division, wins the playoff home-field advantage by playing so well on the road, and beats the Skins 27–16 for the NFC Championship. It'll be Montana's last great NFL moment ... before flying to Canton for enshrinement in August 1998.

PLAYER RANKINGS

A high-profile image and a load of hype don't produce winning football—performance on the field is all that really counts. So who are the guys who get it done, week in and week out? Peter King offers his opinionated answer to that question, with his rankings of the best in the league at every position.

Quarterbacks

1. DAN MARINO, *Miami* *Genius at work, as we saw in the playoffs.*

2. JIM KELLY, *Buffalo* *Burst into top echelon with great late '90.*

3. JOE MONTANA, *San Francisco.* *Why not No. 1? Career-high 16 INTs.*

4. RANDALL CUNNINGHAM, *Philadelphia.* *Can he coach, too?*

5. WARREN MOON, *Houston* *In his run-and-shoot prime at 35.*

6. TROY AIKMAN, *Dallas* *1991 is his impact year.*

7. BOOMER ESIASON, *Cincinnati* *Smartest field general in the AFC.*

8. JEFF GEORGE, *Indianapolis* *If Bruce Smith doesn't kill him, he'll be great.*

9. JOHN ELWAY, *Denver* *Still the AFC West's most dangerous player.*

10. BERNIE KOSAR *Cleveland* *Give him another chance. Really.*

Running Backs

1. THURMAN THOMAS, *Buffalo* *Only guy the Giants just couldn't stop.*

2. BARRY SANDERS, *Detroit* *Best pure runner since Sayers or Simpson.*

3. NEAL ANDERSON, *Chicago* *Carries his team more than any back in NFL.*

4. MARION BUTTS, *San Diego* *Big backs are in; Butts, at 248, is classic.*

5. ERIC DICKERSON, *Indianapolis* *If he only had a line....*

6. BOBBY HUMPHREY, *Denver* *Classic workhorse guy, with a juke or two.*

7. JAMES BROOKS, *Cincinnati* *Bengals don't give it to him enough.*

8. EMMITT SMITH, *Dallas* *The new Tony Dorsett, with some muscles.*

9. STEVE BROUSSARD, *Atlanta* *If injury-free, he'll explode this year.*

10. BO JACKSON, *L.A. Raiders* *Can he play hurt, and play a full year?*

▼ As the primary receiver in Jerry Glanville's Red Gun run-and-shoot offense, the fearless Rison catches most of his balls over the middle where the linebackers roam.

Offensive Linemen

1. RICHMOND WEBB, *T, Miami* *In one year, he skyrocketed to the top.*

2. ANTHONY MUNOZ, *T, Cincinnati* *Cliché, but he allowed one sack in '90.*

3. PAUL GRUBER, *T, Tampa Bay* *Almost two years without a holding call.*

4. MARK BORTZ, *G, Chicago* *Neal Anderson's personal Bear escort.*

5. JUMBO ELLIOTT, *T, N.Y. Giants* *Stopped Dent, Bruce Smith in playoffs.*

6. JIM LACHEY, *T, Washington* *In the great tradition of Redskins linemen.*

7. KENT HULL, *C, Buffalo* *Anchor of football's most underrated line.*

8. STEVE WISNIEWSKI, *G, L.A. Raiders* *Brute force in Upshaw mold.*

9. LUIS SHARPE, *T, Phoenix* *It's about time he got some credit.*

10. HOWARD BALLARD, *T, Buffalo* *Great story: Kelly vilified him in '89.*

Wide Receivers

1. JERRY RICE, *San Francisco* *Wow. What a surprise.*

2. STERLING SHARPE, *Green Bay* *Grace, power and hands.*

3. ANDRE RISON, *Atlanta* *He's a 100-catch season waiting to happen.*

4. ANTHONY MILLER, *San Diego* *Ninety catches if Tolliver has good aim.*

5. GARY CLARK, *Washington* *Don't let stats fool you: He's tough and quick.*

6. ANDRE REED, *Buffalo* *Hurt by Super Bowl miscues in big spots.*

7. ERNEST GIVINS, *Houston* *You've got to love this guy over the middle.*

8. JOHN TAYLOR, *San Francisco* *One missed tackle, and he's gone.*

9. AL TOON, *N.Y. Jets* *Great hands, great target and fearless.*

10. ROB MOORE, *N.Y. Jets* *Why not? He's Toon's absolute double.*

Tight Ends

1. KEITH JACKSON, *Philadelphia* *Great hands and a psyche for blocking.*

2. RON HALL, *Tampa Bay* *If Vinny throws right, Hall's an All-Pro.*

3. KEITH McKELLER, *Buffalo* *Turned down '87 NBA trial for the NFL.*

4. RODNEY HOLMAN, *Cincinnati* *Selfless blocker, terrific hands.*

5. FERRELL EDMUNDS, *Miami* *Marino loves this Bavaro clone.*

6. MARV COOK, *New England* *What? A Patriot?! We're not kidding.*

7. PETE HOLOHAN, *L.A. Rams* *How could they have put him on Plan B?*

8. JAY NOVACEK, *Dallas* *But don't ask him to block.*

9. DON WARREN, *Washington* *Pure, classic tight end in the Ditka mold.*

10. STEVE JORDAN, *Minnesota* *30 and bruised; it's amazing he's lasted.*

Pass Rushers

1. BRUCE SMITH, *Buffalo* *Cocky? Sure. Somebody's got to crow.*

2. PAT SWILLING, *New Orleans* *Give him a healthy season, and watch out.*

3. REGGIE WHITE, *Philadelphia* *Preacher shows no mercy on the field.*

4. DERRICK THOMAS, *Kansas City* *At 23, he had league-high 20 sacks.*

5. CHARLES HALEY, *San Francisco* *Likes to rip heads off, in LT mold.*

6. LESLIE O'NEAL, *San Diego* *Comeback from '87 knee reconstruction.*

7. GREG TOWNSEND, *L.A. Raiders* *Led the Raiders with 12.5 sacks.*

8. LEE WILLIAMS, *San Diego* *Took 1990 off.*

9. MIKE COFER, *Detroit* *"Toughest guy I face," Phil Simms says.*

10. KEVIN GREENE, *L.A. Rams* *Memo to Greene: Stop talking and play.*

Defensive Linemen against the Run

1. **MICHAEL DEAN PERRY**, *Cleveland* To move him, bring two guys.
2. **KEVIN FAGAN**, *San Francisco* What a joke he wasn't in the Pro Bowl.
3. **ALVIN WRIGHT**, *L.A. Rams* Who? Just play him and find out, foes say.
4. **JERRY BALL**, *Detroit* Ankle sprain and sulking hampered him in '90.
5. **ERIK HOWARD**, *N.Y. Giants* Ties up every center he sees.
6. **HENRY THOMAS**, *Minnesota* Sack-happy Vikes' rock against the run.
7. **JEFF WRIGHT**, *Buffalo* Made a city forget about Fred Smerlas.
8. **HOWIE LONG**, *L.A. Raiders* Back to the top after a two-year absence.
9. **MICHAEL CARTER**, *San Francisco* When he isn't hurt, he's great.
10. **CORTEZ KENNEDY**, *Seattle* Next great one, if he wants it.

All-around Linebackers

1. **CHRIS SPIELMAN**, *Detroit* No player in football wants it more. Period.
2. **DARRYL TALLEY**, *Buffalo* Playoffs catapulted him to recognition.
3. **PEPPER JOHNSON**, *N.Y. Giants* The Giants' answer to LT in the '90s.
4. **CARL BANKS**, *N.Y. Giants* Great, great two-way player.
5. **SETH JOYNER**, *Philadelphia* Blossomed under Buddy, now one of best.
6. **BYRON EVANS**, *Philadelphia* See No. 5.
7. **HUGH GREEN**, *Miami* LT's '80 classmate is now better.
8. **KEN HARVEY**, *Phoenix* Once thought a bust, he's now busting heads.
9. **JAMES FRANCIS**, *Cincinnati* Best front-seven player among '90 rookies.
10. **MIKE SINGLETARY**, *Chicago* No charity pick, though '91 is his finale.

Defensive Backs

1. **ROD WOODSON**, *Pittsburgh* What coverage, and what return ability.
2. **ALBERT LEWIS**, *Kansas City* Might be the most feared cornerback.
3. **MARK CARRIER**, *Chicago* Signed early in '90, and the profits roll in.
4. **JOEY BROWNER**, *Minnesota* He'll be better without Mike Lynn around.
5. **MARK COLLINS**, *N.Y. Giants* Please send this guy to the Pro Bowl.
6. **LEMUEL STINSON**, *Chicago* Great man-to-man cover guy.
7. **DARRYL POLLARD**, *San Francisco* Surprising Weber State free agent.
8. **TIM MCDONALD**, *Phoenix* If there is a "next Ronnie Lott," this is he.
9. **DAVID FULCHER**, *Cincinnati* But will his knees hold up much longer?
10. **GILL BYRD**, *San Diego* He's 30, but boy, can he cover.

Punter

SEAN LANDETA, *N.Y. Giants* A master at dumping it inside the 10.

Kicker

GARY ANDERSON, *Pittsburgh* Even in bad weather, third-most accurate ever.

Special Teams

REYNA THOMPSON, *N.Y. Giants* Madden: "Best special-teams player ever."

Coaches

1. **GEORGE SEIFERT**, *San Francisco* Perfect temperament to lead team.
2. **DON SHULA**, *Miami* Brought a bad team all the way back.
3. **BILL PARCELLS**, *N.Y. Giants* Won another title with above-average talent.
4. **JOE GIBBS**, *Washington* Just look at the staying power of his team.
5. **BILL WALSH**, *NBC* Give him time. He'll be back. Trust us.
6. **MIKE DITKA**, *Chicago* What a loss for the game when he goes to TV.
7. **CHUCK NOLL**, *Pittsburgh* Canton, here he comes.
8. **ART SHELL**, *L.A. Raiders* Has as much respect from players as any coach.
9. **BILL BELICHICK**, *Cleveland* We know. He's new. But just wait.
10. **MARTY SCHOTTENHEIMER**, *Kansas City* His teams contend. Period.

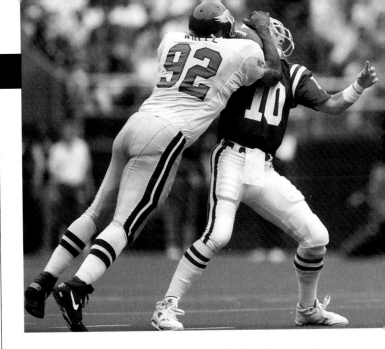

▲ When White gets airborne, quarterbacks like Jack Trudeau get grounded.

▼ Webb, collaring Lawrence Taylor, gave Marino time to take Miami to the playoffs.

▼ Fagan (75) and Haley make the 49ers tough against both the pass and the run.

APPENDIX

WEEK 1 STANDINGS

AFC EAST	W	L	T	Pct.	PF	PA
Buffalo	1	0	0	1.000	26	10
Miami	1	0	0	1.000	27	24
Indianapolis	0	1	0	.000	10	26
New England	0	1	0	.000	24	27
N.Y. Jets	0	1	0	.000	20	25

AFC CENTRAL	W	L	T	Pct.	PF	PA
Cincinnati	1	0	0	1.000	25	20
Cleveland	1	0	0	1.000	13	3
Houston	0	1	0	.000	27	47
Pittsburgh	0	1	0	.000	3	13

AFC WEST	W	L	T	Pct.	PF	PA
Kansas City	1	0	0	1.000	24	21
L.A. Raiders	1	0	0	1.000	14	9
Denver	0	1	0	1.000	9	14
San Diego	0	1	0	.000	14	17
Seattle	0	1	0	.000	0	17

NFC EAST	W	L	T	Pct.	PF	PA
Dallas	1	0	0	1.000	17	14
N.Y. Giants	1	0	0	1.000	27	20
Washington	1	0	0	1.000	31	0
Philadelphia	0	1	0	.000	20	27
Phoenix	0	1	0	.000	0	31

NFC CENTRAL	W	L	T	Pct.	PF	PA
Chicago	1	0	0	1.000	17	0
Green Bay	1	0	0	1.000	36	24
Tampa Bay	1	0	0	1.000	38	21
Detroit	0	1	0	.000	21	38
Minnesota	0	1	0	.000	21	24

NFC WEST	W	L	T	Pct.	PF	PA
Atlanta	1	0	0	1.000	47	27
San Francisco	1	0	0	1.000	13	12
L.A. Rams	0	1	0	.000	24	36
New Orleans	0	1	0	.000	12	13

RESULTS
N.Y. Giants 27, Philadelphia 20
Chicago 17, Seattle 0
Green Bay 36, L.A. Rams 24
Kansas City 24, Minnesota 21
Cincinnati 25, N.Y. Jets 20
Buffalo 26, Indianapolis 10
Cleveland 13, Pittsburgh 3
Dallas 17, San Diego 14
Tampa Bay 38, Detroit 21
Miami 27, New England 24
Washington 31, Phoenix 0
Atlanta 47, Houston 27
L.A. Raiders 14, Denver 9
San Francisco 13, New Orleans 12 (Monday night)

SUNDAY, SEPTEMBER 9

N.Y. GIANTS 27, PHILADELPHIA 20—At Giants Stadium. Just four days after ending his preseason holdout, Giants linebacker Lawrence Taylor forced a fumble and sacked Eagle quarterback Randall Cunningham three times as New York broke a four-game losing streak against Philadelphia. The Giants failed to convert on seven third-down attempts in the first half but took the second-half kickoff and went 70 yards for the score that put them ahead to stay.

Philadelphia	3	7	0	10	—	20
New York	6	0	14	7	—	27

N.Y. — FG Allegre 38
N.Y. — FG Allegre 46
Phi — FG Ruzek 37
Phi — Toney 18 pass from Byars (Ruzek kick)
N.Y. — Hampton 12 pass from Simms (Allegre kick)
N.Y. — Meggett 68 punt return (Allegre kick)
N.Y. — Ingram 41 pass from Simms (Allegre kick)
Phi — Cunningham 1 run (Ruzek kick)
Phi — FG Ruzek 29
A: 76,202 T: 2:59

CHICAGO 17, SEATTLE 0—At Soldier Field. The Bears defense dominated, sacking Seahawk quarterback Dave Krieg three times and intercepting three of his passes in limiting Seattle to 132 total yards. The Seahawks ran only five plays in Chicago territory. The game remained close, however, until the fourth quarter when the Bears drove 96 yards in nine plays to make the score 17-0. Bears running back Neal Anderson rushed for 101 yards, caught five passes for 42 yards and scored Chicago's two touchdowns.

Seattle	0	0	0	0	—	0
Chicago	3	7	0	7	—	17

Chi — FG Butler 47
Chi — Anderson 17 run (Butler kick)
Chi — Anderson 4 run (Butler kick)
A: 64,400 T: 2:54

GREEN BAY 36, L.A. RAMS 24—At Lambeau Field. A lengthy holdout by Packer quarterback Don Majkowski pushed backup Anthony Dilweg into the starter's role. He responded by completing 20 of 32 passes for 248 yards and three touchdowns. Green Bay took advantage of five Ram turnovers, the last a fourth-quarter fumble after a pass completion that Packer cornerback Jerry Holmes returned to the Ram four-yard line in the fourth quarter. The subsequent Packer touchdown made the score 33-17 to put the game away.

Los Angeles	7	7	3	7	—	24
Green Bay	0	17	3	16	—	36

L.A. — Warner 6 run (Lansford kick)
G.B. — West 4 pass from Dilweg (Jacke kick)
G.B. — FG Jacke 26
L.A. — Anderson 40 pass from Everett (Lansford kick)
G.B. — Query 47 pass from Dilweg (Jacke kick)
G.B. — FG Jacke 53
L.A. — FG Lansford 41
G.B. — West 7 pass from Dilweg (Jacke kick)
G.B. — Fullwood 2 run (kick failed)
L.A. — Holohan 2 pass from Everett (Lansford kick)
G.B. — FG Jacke 40
A: 57,685 T: 3:20

KANSAS CITY 24, MINNESOTA 21—At Arrowhead Stadium. Trailing 21-17 with only seconds left in the third quarter, the Chiefs stopped Viking running back Allen Rice on fourth-and-one, then drove 78 yards in 12 plays for the winning score. On a sweltering day, Kansas City running back Christian Okoye, last season's NFL rushing leader, carried 28 times for 92 yards. Viking quarterback Wade Wilson threw for 248 yards and three touchdowns but was sacked three times.

Minnesota	7	7	7	0	—	21
Kansas City	14	3	0	7	—	24

K.C. — Jones 4 pass from DeBerg (Lowery kick)
K.C. — McNair 22 pass from DeBerg (Lowery kick)
Minn — Walker 6 pass from Wilson (Igwebuike kick)
Minn — Jordan 26 pass from Wilson (Igwebuike kick)
K.C. — FG Lowery 43
Minn — Walker 8 pass from Wilson (Igwebuike kick)
K.C. — Okoye 2 run (Lowery kick)
A: 68,363 T: 3:06

CINCINNATI 25, N.Y. JETS 20—At Riverfront Stadium. The Bengals spoiled the coaching debut of Bruce Coslet—their former offensive coordinator—by coming back from a 20-10 deficit in the fourth quarter. The Jets had one last chance to win, but Cincinnati safety David Fulcher intercepted Ken O'Brien's fourth-down pass in the end zone with 30 seconds left. Fulcher also sacked O'Brien for a safety in the fourth quarter and had 10 tackles for the day. Jet wide receiver Al Toon caught eight passes for 118 yards and two touchdowns.

New York	0	10	7	3	—	20
Cincinnati	0	3	7	15	—	25

Cin — FG Breech 43
N.Y. — Toon 46 pass from O'Brien (Leahy kick)
N.Y. — FG Leahy 33
Cin — Brown 10 pass from Esiason (Breech kick)
N.Y. — Toon 9 pass from O'Brien (Leahy kick)
N.Y. — FG Leahy 26
Cin — Brooks 3 pass from Esiason (Breech kick)
Cin — Safety, O'Brien tackled in the end zone
Cin — FG Breech 44
Cin — FG Breech 27
A: 66,467 T: 3:10

BUFFALO 26, INDIANAPOLIS 10—At Rich Stadium. With Buffalo holding a 16-10 lead, blitzing Bills linebacker Cornelius Bennett blindsided Colt rookie quarterback Jeff George and knocked him out of the game with 11:48 remaining. The Colts could not move the ball under backup quarterback Jack Trudeau, and the Bills scored twice more to put the game out of reach. Buffalo quarterback Jim Kelly completed his first 14 passes and finished the day with 28 completions in 37 attempts for 283 yards and a touchdown.

Indianapolis	3	0	7	0	—	10
Buffalo	3	13	0	10	—	26

Buff — FG Norwood 29
Ind — FG Biasucci 24
Buff — Rolle 3 pass from Kelly (Norwood kick)
Buff — FG Norwood 31
Buff — FG Norwood 37
Ind — Morgan 25 pass from George (Biasucci kick)
Buff — FG Norwood 47
Buff — Thomas 6 run (Norwood kick)
A: 78,899 T: 2:53

CLEVELAND 13, PITTSBURGH 3—At Cleveland Stadium. Browns cornerback Tony Blaylock picked up a fumble in the third quarter and dashed into the end zone from 30 yards out for the game's only touchdown. The entire game was a defensive battle, with the two teams gaining only 368 total yards between them. Browns middle linebacker Mike Johnson had nine solo tackles and caused two fumbles. The Steeler defense sacked Browns quarterback Bernie Kosar seven times, the most in his six-year career.

Pittsburgh	0	3	0	0	—	3
Cleveland	0	0	10	3	—	13

Pitt — FG Anderson 19
Cle — Blaylock 30 fumble return
Cle — FG Kauric 28
Cle — FG Kauric 47
A: 78,298 T: 3:12

DALLAS 17, SAN DIEGO 14—At Texas Stadium. With a little more than five minutes left in the game and San Diego leading by four, Cowboy safety Bill Bates sniffed out a fake punt near midfield and dropped Charger upback Gary Plummer short of a first down. Facing a fourth-and-two on its first series after taking over, Dallas fullback Tommie Agee broke loose for a 16-yard gain. Soon after, quarterback Troy Aikman sneaked over from the one with 1:58 remaining as the Cowboys equaled last season's win total and Aikman got his first win as a starter.

San Diego	7	7	0	0	—	14
Dallas	7	0	0	10	—	17

Dall — McKinnon 28 pass from Aikman (Willis kick)
S.D. — McEwen 14 pass from Vlasic (Reveiz kick)
S.D. — Butts 1 run (Reveiz kick)
Dall — FG Willis 31
Dall — Aikman 1 run (Willis kick)
A: 48,063 T: 3:04

TAMPA BAY 38, DETROIT 21—At the Silverdome. After a string of nine wins (five at the end of last season and four in preseason), the Lions' run-and-shoot offense misfired, and the Bucs used a ball control offense to dominate the matchup between the two up-and-coming NFC Central teams. Detroit running back Barry Sanders, last season's rookie sensation, carried the ball only five times for 25 yards in the first half. Tampa Bay quarterback Vinny Testaverde threw for 237 yards, and running back Gary Anderson, who held out all last season with San Diego, rushed for 74 yards and caught six passes for 79 more.

Tampa Bay	7	14	7	10	—	38
Detroit	14	0	0	7	—	21

T.B. — Hall 54 pass from Testaverde (Christie kick)
Det — Clark 26 pass from Peete (Murray kick)
Det — Sanders 1 run (Murray kick)
T.B. — Perkins 8 pass from Testaverde (Christie kick)
T.B. — Anderson 19 pass from Testaverde (Christie kick)
T.B. — Cobb 2 run (Christie kick)
T.B. — FG Christie 22
Det — Clark 16 pass from Gagliano (Murray kick)
T.B. — Haddix 62 interception return (Christie kick)
A: 54,728 T: 2:50

MIAMI 27, NEW ENGLAND 24—At Foxboro Stadium. Dolphin quarterback Dan Marino had an up-and-down day, throwing three interceptions but connecting with a diving Tony Paige for the winning score with 1:46 remaining. Miami running back Sammie Smith pumped some lifeblood into the formerly anemic Dolphin running game, gaining 159 yards on 23 carries. With two touchdown passes, 37-year-old Patriots quarterback Steve Grogan led New England to a 21-6 lead in the second quarter before Miami mounted its second-half comeback. It was the first time in six seasons that the Dolphins had won a season opener.

Miami	3	10	7	7	—	27
New England	7	14	3	0	—	24

Mia — FG Stoyanovich 31
N.E. — Fryar 22 pass from Grogan (Staurovsky kick)
Mia — FG Stoyanovich 37
N.E. — Stephens 1 run (Staurovsky kick)
N.E. — Cook 35 pass from Grogan (Staurovsky kick)
Mia — Martin 35 pass from Marino (Stoyanovich kick)
Mia — Smith 3 run (Stoyanovich kick)
N.E. — FG Staurovsky 42
Mia — Paige 7 pass from Marino (Stoyanovich kick)
A: 45,305 T:2:58

WASHINGTON 31, PHOENIX 0—At RFK Stadium. The Redskins defense controlled the game from start to finish, picking off four passes by Cardinals quarterback Timm Rosenbach and sacking him three times. Longtime Redskins offensive coordinator Joe Bugel was making his debut as Phoenix's head coach, but his new charges were no match for his old. The Washington line allowed quarterback Mark Rypien ample time to find his receivers, and he finished 17 for 31 with three touchdowns. Rookie running back Johnny Johnson accounted for 153 yards of the Cardinals' offense.

Phoenix	0	0	0	0	—	0
Washington	7	7	14	3	—	31

Wash — Sanders 37 pass from Rypien (Lohmiller kick)
Wash — Byner 4 pass from Rypien (Lohmiller kick)
Wash — Clark 43 pass from Rypien (Lohmiller kick)
Wash — Walton 57 interception return (Lohmiller kick)
Wash — FG Lohmiller 29
A: 52,649 T: 2:53

ATLANTA 47, HOUSTON 27—At Atlanta-Fulton County Stadium. With new black jerseys and a new black-and-blue style of play instilled in them by their coach, the Falcons entered the Jerry Glanville era with a bang, routing Glanville's former team and punishing Oiler quarterback Warren Moon in the process. Atlanta scored three times in the space of 1:50 in the first quarter, twice off Moon fumbles. Moon still threw four touchdown passes, but the Oilers never got closer than 37-27. With only 13 seconds remaining, cornerback Deion Sanders punctuated the game with an 82-yard interception return for a touchdown.

Houston	0	7	0	20	—	27
Atlanta	21	6	7	13	—	47

Atl — Broussard 6 run (Davis kick)
Atl — Butler recovery of Moon fumble in end zone (Davis kick)
Atl — Tuggle 65 fumble return (Davis kick)
Atl — FG Davis 39
Atl — FG Davis 39
Hou — Jones 15 pass from Moon (Zendejas kick)
Atl — Rison 26 pass from Miller (Davis kick)
Atl — FG Davis 36
Hou — Givins 80 pass from Moon (Zendejas kick)
Hou — Givins 6 pass from Moon (Zendejas kick)
Hou — Ford 3 pass from Moon (kick failed)
Atl — FG Davis 51
Atl — Sanders 82 interception return (Davis kick)
A: 56,222 T: 3:49

L.A. RAIDERS 14, DENVER 9—At Memorial Coliseum. The Raiders, the original men in black, recalled their glory days with a defense-led victory over the Broncos as defensive ends Greg Townsend and Howie Long sacked Denver quarterback John Elway five times between them. L.A. took the lead for good in the third quarter when linebacker Jerry Robinson ran for a touchdown after an ill-advised screen pass on third-and-21 from the Denver five-yard line. The Bronco defense did some sacking of its own, dropping Raider quarterback Jay Schroeder five times.

Denver	3	3	0	3	—	9
Los Angeles	0	0	14	0	—	14

Den — FG Treadwell 42
Den — FG Treadwell 44
L.A. — Robinson 5 interception return (Jaeger kick)
L.A. — McDaniel 42 fumble return (Jaeger kick)
Den — FG Treadwell 24
A: 54,206 T: 2:54

MONDAY, SEPTEMBER 10

SAN FRANCISCO 13, NEW ORLEANS 12—At the Superdome. Once again, 49er quarterback Joe Montana engineered a masterful game-winning drive in the final two minutes. With only 1:30 remaining and San Francisco out of timeouts, Montana marched the team 60 yards in six plays to set up placekicker Mike Cofer's winning 38-yard field goal. The Saints played a valiant game defensively, limiting the 49ers to 237 total yards, but the Saints offense couldn't muster a touchdown out of six trips inside the 49er 26. It was the 49ers' NFL-record-tying 11th consecutive road win.

San Francisco	3	0	7	3	—	13
New Orleans	3	6	0	3	—	12

S.F. — FG Cofer 52
N.O. — FG Andersen 41
N.O. — FG Andersen 39
N.O. — FG Andersen 28
S.F. — Jones 4 pass from Montana (Cofer kick)
N.O. — FG Andersen 32
S.F. — FG Cofer 38
A: 68,629 T: 3:06

WEEK 2 STANDINGS

AFC EAST	W	L	T	Pct.	PF	PA
Miami	2	0	0	1.000	57	31
Buffalo	1	1	0	.500	33	40
New England	1	1	0	.500	40	41
N.Y. Jets	1	1	0	.500	44	46
Indianapolis	0	2	0	.000	24	42

AFC CENTRAL	W	L	T	Pct.	PF	PA
Cincinnati	2	0	0	1.000	46	36
Cleveland	1	1	0	.500	34	27
Pittsburgh	1	1	0	.500	23	22
Houston	0	2	0	.000	36	67

AFC WEST	W	L	T	Pct.	PF	PA
L.A. Raiders	2	0	0	1.000	31	22
Denver	1	1	0	.500	33	37
Kansas City	1	1	0	.500	47	45
San Diego	0	2	0	.000	30	38
Seattle	0	2	0	.000	13	34

NFC EAST	W	L	T	Pct.	PF	PA
N.Y. Giants	2	0	0	1.000	55	27
Dallas	1	1	0	.500	24	42
Phoenix	1	1	0	.500	23	52
Washington	1	1	0	.500	44	26
Philadelphia	0	2	0	.000	41	50

NFC CENTRAL	W	L	T	Pct.	PF	PA
Chicago	2	0	0	1.000	48	13
Detroit	1	1	0	.500	42	52
Green Bay	1	1	0	.500	49	55
Minnesota	1	1	0	.500	53	27
Tampa Bay	1	1	0	.500	52	56

NFC WEST	W	L	T	Pct.	PF	PA
San Francisco	2	0	0	1.000	39	25
Atlanta	1	1	0	.500	61	48
L.A. Rams	1	1	0	.500	59	50
New Orleans	0	2	0	.000	15	45

RESULTS
N.Y. Giants 28, Dallas 7
Phoenix 23, Philadelphia 21
San Francisco 26, Washington 13
Chicago 31, Green Bay 13
Pittsburgh 20, Houston 9
Miami 30, Buffalo 7
N.Y. Jets 24, Cleveland 21
L.A. Raiders 17, Seattle 13
Detroit 21, Atlanta 14
New England 16, Indianapolis 14
Cincinnati 21, San Diego 16
L.A. Rams 35, Tampa Bay 14
Minnesota 32, New Orleans 3
Denver 24, Kansas City 23 (Monday night)

SUNDAY, SEPTEMBER 16

N.Y. GIANTS 28, DALLAS 7—At Texas Stadium. With the temperature reaching 122° on the field, the Giants controlled the ball for 41:40 to wear down the Cowboy defense. New York quarterback Phil Simms completed 16 of 21 passes for 208 yards, and running back Lewis Tillman rushed for 71 yards. Dallas could muster only 20 yards rushing and needed a 90-yard kickoff return for a TD by rookie speedster Alexander Wright to avoid a shutout.

New York	0	14	7	7	–	28
Dallas	0	7	0	0	–	7

N.Y. – Simms 4 run (Allegre kick)
N.Y. – Anderson 1 run (Allegre kick)
Dall – Wright 90 kickoff return (Willis kick)
N.Y. – Bavaro 4 pass from Simms (Allegre kick)
N.Y. – Taylor 11 interception return (Allegre kick)
A: 61,090 T: 2:47

PHOENIX 23, PHILADELPHIA 21—At Veterans Stadium. Cardinals kicker Al Del Greco booted three fourth-quarter field goals to help Phoenix to an upset victory over the Eagles and give rookie coach Joe Bugel his first NFL win. The turning point came in the second quarter when Philadelphia, leading 14–0, tried a pass on fourth-and-two from the Cardinals 37. Phoenix linebacker Ken Harvey sacked Eagle quarterback Randall Cunningham for a seven-yard loss, and the Cardinals scored seven plays later. Running back Johnny Johnson, a seventh-round draft choice, rushed for 88 yards, and Phoenix quarterback Timm Rosenbach ran for 50, including a 13-yard scramble to set up the winning kick with 25 seconds left.

Phoenix	0	7	7	9	–	23
Philadelphia	14	0	7	0	–	21

Phi – Hargrove 34 pass from Cunningham (Ruzek kick)
Phi – Cunningham 1 run (Ruzek kick)
Phoe – Johnson 22 run (Del Greco kick)
Phoe – Thompson 1 run (Del Greco kick)
Phi – Sherman 2 pass from Cunningham (Ruzek kick)
Phoe – FG Del Greco 25
Phoe – FG Del Greco 50
Phoe – FG Del Greco 42
A: 64,396 T: 2:53

SAN FRANCISCO 26, WASHINGTON 13—At Candlestick Park. Behind solid blocking by the offensive line, 49er QB Joe Montana passed for 390 yards and two touchdowns as San Francisco drubbed the Redskins. The 49ers built a 20–10 halftime lead, then blocked a field goal attempt and stopped the Redskins on three straight plays at the 49er one-yard line to throttle Washington in the second half. San Francisco wideout John Taylor caught eight passes for 160 yards, and Montana's day gave him 31,654 career passing yards to become the team's alltime leader.

Washington	0	10	3	0	–	13
San Francisco	3	17	3	3	–	26

S.F. – FG Cofer 31
S.F. – Rice 12 pass from Montana (Cofer kick)
Wash – FG Lohmiller 37
S.F. – Taylor 49 pass from Montana (Cofer kick)
Wash – Monk 35 pass from Rypien (Lohmiller kick)
Wash – FG Lohmiller 20
S.F. – FG Cofer 26
S.F. – FG Cofer 34
A: 64,287 T: 2:46

CHICAGO 31, GREEN BAY 13—At Lambeau Field. The Bears defense spent much of the day in the Packer backfield, sacking quarterback Anthony Dilweg six times, and Chicago quarterback Jim Harbaugh bounced back from an opening-play interception to complete 11 of 14 passes for 161 yards and two touchdowns. One of the scores was a perfectly lofted 40-yarder down the sideline to wideout Ron Morris. The Bears defense also forced three fumbles, two of which led to TDs. Don Majkowski relieved Dilweg at QB in the fourth quarter and was 8 for 12 for 84 yards with an interception.

Chicago	0	17	7	7	–	31
Green Bay	7	3	3	0	–	13

G.B. – Woodside 10 run (Jacke kick)
Chi – FG Butler 41
Chi – Anderson 1 run (Butler kick)
Chi – Harbaugh 2 run (Butler kick)
G.B. – FG Jacke 37
Chi – Morris 40 pass from Harbaugh (Butler kick)
G.B. – FG Jacke 37
Chi – Anderson 16 pass from Harbaugh (Butler kick)
A: 58,938 T: 2:56

PITTSBURGH 20, HOUSTON 9—At Three Rivers Stadium. The Steeler defense and kicking team provided all of Pittsburgh's points in a game marred by fights and penalties. Oiler QB Warren Moon suffered four interceptions, the first one on his first pass of the game, which Steeler cornerback David Johnson returned for a touchdown. With the Steelers holding a four-point lead in the fourth quarter, Pittsburgh cornerback Rod Woodson broke Houston's spirit with a 52-yard punt return for a TD. Steeler fans repeatedly booed QB Bubby Brister, who completed only nine of 23 passes for 81 yards.

Houston	0	7	2	0	–	9
Pittsburgh	7	3	0	10	–	20

Pitt – Johnson 26 interception return (Anderson kick)
Hou – White 1 run (Zendejas kick)
Pitt – FG Anderson 31
Hou – Safety, Brister tackled in end zone
Pitt – FG Anderson 27
Pitt – Woodson 52 punt return (Anderson kick)
A: 54,814 T: 3:08

MIAMI 30, BUFFALO 7—At Joe Robbie Stadium. No longer relying solely on the arm of Dan Marino, the Dolphins used a strong rushing game to end a six-game losing streak to the Bills and give Don Shula his 200th win as Miami coach. Three of the Dolphin scores came after turnovers by Buffalo. Late in the third quarter, Miami caught the Bills with six defensive backs on the field and went to a no-huddle offense for eight straight plays, giving the ball to running back Marc Logan five consecutive times for 31 yards. Running back Sammie Smith ended the drive with a one-yard TD plunge, his second score of the day. Buffalo was held to just 44 yards rushing.

Buffalo	0	0	0	7	–	7
Miami	0	16	7	7	–	30

Mia – Smith 2 run (Stoyanovich kick)
Mia – FG Stoyanovich 23
Mia – FG Stoyanovich 29
Mia – FG Stoyanovich 48
Mia – Smith 1 run (Stoyanovich kick)
Mia – Paige 17 pass from Marino (Stoyanovich kick)
Buff – Kinnebrew 1 run (Norwood kick)
A: 68,490 T: 2:46

N.Y. JETS 24, CLEVELAND 21—At Giants Stadium. Browns running back Eric Metcalf ran back the opening kickoff 98 yards for a touchdown, but the Jets answered with 24 straight points and then held on to give coach Bruce Coslet his first NFL win. New York's defense pounded Cleveland all day, sacking quarterback Bernie Kosar three times—causing two lost fumbles—and limiting the Browns to four of 13 third-down conversions. Jet QB Ken O'Brien turned in a solid performance, completing 13 of 21 passes for 218 yards.

Cleveland	7	0	7	7	–	21
New York	14	10	0	0	–	24

Cle – Metcalf 98 kickoff return (Kauric kick)
N.Y. – McNeil 2 run (Leahy kick)
N.Y. – Hector 6 run (Leahy kick)
N.Y. – FG Leahy 47
N.Y. – Baxter 1 run (Leahy kick)
Cle – Langhorne 4 pass from Kosar (Kauric kick)
Cle – Hoard 9 run (Kauric kick)
A: 67,354 T: 3:03

L.A. RAIDERS 17, SEATTLE 13—At the Kingdome. After three quarters of sluggish offensive play, the Raiders, keyed by quarterback Jay Schroeder, drove 80 and 65 yards in their final two possessions to come back against the Seahawks. Seattle quarterback Dave Krieg completed his first 14 passes for 171 yards, but the Seahawks stalled at the L.A. 18 and five in the first half. The key play in the fourth quarter was a controversial 45-yard completion to Raider wide receiver Mervyn Fernandez, who didn't appear to get both feet in bounds. The completion stood when play resumed, before the replay officials could contact the official on the field. Four plays later, Fernandez caught a pass to tie the game.

Los Angeles	3	0	0	14	–	17
Seattle	0	3	7	3	–	13

L.A. – FG Jaeger 47
Sea – FG Johnson 22
Sea – Williams 2 run (Johnson kick)
L.A. – Fernandez 12 pass from Schroeder (Jaeger kick)
Sea – FG Johnson 19
L.A. – Bell 1 run (Jaeger kick)
A: 61,889 T: 2:39

DETROIT 21, ATLANTA 14—At the Silverdome. Lion quarterback Rodney Peete led Detroit to a 21–7 lead, then watched backup QB Bob Gagliano preserve it. Peete passed for two touchdowns in the first half, but after he missed his first five attempts of the second half, Gagliano replaced him and locked up the win with a 22-yard scramble that allowed Detroit to run out the clock on the final possession. The Falcon defense keyed on the Lions' Barry Sanders, allowing him only 55 yards. Running back Steve Broussard had 88 yards on 19 carries for the Falcons.

Atlanta	7	0	7	0	–	14
Detroit	7	14	0	0	–	21

Det – Greer 12 pass from Peete (Murray kick)
Atl – Rison 10 pass from Miller (Davis kick)
Det – Johnson 5 pass from Peete (Murray kick)
Det – Sanders 17 run (Murray kick)
Atl – Broussard 3 run (Davis kick)
A: 48,961 T: 2:57

NEW ENGLAND 16, INDIANAPOLIS 14—At the Hoosier Dome. Colt quarterback Jeff George threw four interceptions, the last one late in the fourth quarter when the Patriots were clinging to a six-point lead. George's miscue allowed New England to drive for the winning field goal, a 25-yarder by Jason Staurovsky with 2:36 remaining. George's counterpart, Steve Grogan, methodically directed the Pats conservative offense, completing 16 of 24 passes for 187 yards. New England running back John Stephens helped the cause with 96 yards on 25 carries.

New England	0	7	3	6	–	16
Indianapolis	7	0	0	7	–	14

Ind – Bentley 1 run (Biasucci kick)
N.E. – Dykes 27 pass from Grogan (Staurovsky kick)
N.E. – FG Staurovsky 39
N.E. – FG Staurovsky 27
N.E. – FG Staurovsky 25
Ind – Brooks 68 pass from George (Biasucci kick)
A: 49,256 T: 2:49

CINCINNATI 21, SAN DIEGO 16—At Jack Murphy Stadium. Two key fourth-quarter turnovers by the Chargers allowed the Bengals to pull out a tough, come-from-behind victory. On third-and-five from the Bengal eight-yard line, San Diego quarterback Billy Joe Tolliver overthrew his receiver, and cornerback Lewis Billups intercepted the ball. Four minutes later, Cincinnati quarterback Boomer Esiason hit wide receiver Eddie Brown for the 23-yard touchdown that put the Bengals in front. With almost three minutes remaining, Charger wide receiver Anthony Miller fumbled after a 20-yard catch, and the Bengals were able to run out the clock. Brown had a big day, catching 10 passes for 178 yards and two TDs.

Cincinnati	0	14	0	7	–	21
San Diego	13	3	0	0	–	16

S.D. – Harmon 36 pass from Tolliver (Reveiz kick)
S.D. – Caravello 17 pass from Tolliver (kick failed)
Cin – Brooks 10 pass from Esiason (Breech kick)
S.D. – FG Reveiz 19
Cin – Brown 30 pass from Esiason (Breech kick)
Cin – Brown 23 pass from Esiason (Breech kick)
A: 48,098 T: 2:56

L.A. RAMS 35, TAMPA BAY 14—At Tampa Stadium. Ram quarterback Jim Everett threw four touchdown passes, three in the first half, in a Los Angeles rout. After watching the Rams jump out to a 21–0 lead, Buc quarterback Vinny Testaverde hit wide receiver Bruce Hill with a 48-yard scoring toss, but the comeback was short-lived as L.A. cornerback Bobby Humphery intercepted Testaverde on the last play of the first half and returned the ball 44 yards for a touchdown to restore the 21-point lead. Everett finished with 269 yards passing.

Los Angeles	14	14	7	0	–	35
Tampa Bay	0	7	0	7	–	14

L.A. – McGee 6 pass from Everett (Lansford kick)
L.A. – Ellard 14 pass from Everett (Lansford kick)
L.A. – Delpino 10 pass from Everett (Lansford kick)
T.B. – Hill 48 pass from Testaverde (Christie kick)
L.A. – Humphery 44 interception return (Lansford kick)
L.A. – Delpino 42 pass from Everett (Lansford kick)
T.B. – Anderson 1 run (Christie kick)
A: 59,705 T: 2:38

MINNESOTA 32, NEW ORLEANS 3—At the Metrodome. The Viking defense smothered the Saints, tackling New Orleans running back Dalton Hilliard in the end zone for a safety, sacking Saints QBs three times and forcing four interceptions, two by linebacker Mike Merriweather. The Minnesota offense didn't do so badly either, as quarterback Wade Wilson passed for three touchdowns, and wide receiver Hassan Jones caught four passes for 103 yards.

New Orleans	0	3	0	0	–	3
Minnesota	3	15	14	0	–	32

Minn – FG Igwebuike 30
Minn – Safety, Hilliard tackled in end zone
Minn – FG Igwebuike 48
N.O. – FG Andersen 37
Minn – Carter 15 pass from Wilson (Igwebuike kick)
Minn – FG Igwebuike 38
Minn – Walker 5 pass from Wilson (Igwebuike kick)
Minn – Jordan 15 pass from Wilson (Igwebuike kick)
A: 56,272 T: 3:04

MONDAY, SEPTEMBER 17

DENVER 24, KANSAS CITY 23—At Mile High Stadium. Trailing 23–21 late in the fourth quarter and facing a fourth-and-10, Bronco quarterback John Elway completed a pass across the middle to wide receiver Vance Johnson, who streaked to the Chiefs 34-yard line to set up David Treadwell's winning field goal with no time left on the clock. The Denver win overshadowed fine performances by Kansas City quarterback Steve DeBerg, who completed 26 of 45 passes for 395 yards, and wide receiver Stephone Paige, who caught 10 passes for 206 yards and two touchdowns. Denver running back Bobby Humphrey rushed for 132 yards on 19 carries.

Kansas City	3	6	0	14	–	23
Denver	7	7	7	3	–	24

K.C. – FG Lowery 39
Den – Humphrey 37 run (Treadwell kick)
K.C. – FG Lowery 29
Den – Humphrey 6 run (Treadwell kick)
K.C. – FG Lowery 31
Den – Elway 2 run (Treadwell kick)
K.C. – Paige 16 pass from DeBerg (Lowery kick)
K.C. – Paige 83 pass from DeBerg (Lowery kick)
Den – FG Treadwell 22
A: 75,277 T: 3:23

WEEK 3 STANDINGS

AFC EAST	W	L	T	Pct.	PF	PA
Buffalo	2	1	0	.667	63	47
Miami	2	1	0	.667	60	51
New England	1	2	0	.333	47	82
N.Y. Jets	1	2	0	.333	51	76
Indianapolis	0	3	0	.000	34	66

AFC CENTRAL	W	L	T	Pct.	PF	PA
Cincinnati	3	0	0	1.000	87	43
Cleveland	1	2	0	.333	48	51
Houston	1	2	0	.333	60	77
Pittsburgh	1	2	0	.333	26	42

AFC WEST	W	L	T	Pct.	PF	PA
L.A. Raiders	3	0	0	1.000	51	25
Denver	2	1	0	.667	67	68
Kansas City	2	1	0	.667	64	48
San Diego	1	2	0	.333	54	52
Seattle	0	3	0	.000	44	68

NFC EAST	W	L	T	Pct.	PF	PA
N.Y. Giants	3	0	0	1.000	75	30
Washington	2	1	0	.667	63	41
Dallas	1	2	0	.333	39	61
Philadelphia	1	2	0	.333	68	71
Phoenix	1	2	0	.333	30	80

NFC CENTRAL	W	L	T	Pct.	PF	PA
Chicago	3	0	0	1.000	67	29
Tampa Bay	2	1	0	.667	75	76
Detroit	1	2	0	.333	62	75
Green Bay	1	2	0	.333	52	72
Minnesota	1	2	0	.333	69	46

NFC WEST	W	L	T	Pct.	PF	PA
San Francisco	3	0	0	1.000	58	38
Atlanta	1	2	0	.333	74	67
L.A. Rams	1	2	0	.333	80	77
New Orleans	1	2	0	.333	43	52

RESULTS
Chicago 19, Minnesota 16
Philadelphia 27, L.A. Rams 21
L.A. Raiders 20, Pittsburgh 3
N.Y. Giants 20, Miami 3
San Diego 24, Cleveland 14
Kansas City 17, Green Bay 3
Denver 34, Seattle 31 (OT)
San Francisco 19, Atlanta 13
New Orleans 28, Phoenix 7
Washington 19, Dallas 15
Cincinnati 41, New England 7
Houston 24, Indianapolis 10
Tampa Bay 23, Detroit 20
Buffalo 30, N.Y. Jets 7 (Monday night)

SUNDAY, SEPTEMBER 23

CHICAGO 19, MINNESOTA 16—At Soldier Field. With 25 seconds remaining and the score tied, Viking punter Harry Newsome muffed a snap, allowing Bears kicker Kevin Butler to boot the winning 52-yard field goal with only four seconds left. Minnesota had tied the game at 16 when quarterback Wade Wilson hit wide receiver Hassan Jones with a 17-yard touchdown pass with 1:55 remaining. Under Chicago's conservative game plan, running backs Neal Anderson and Brad Muster combined for 181 yards on 37 carries, and quarterback Jim Harbaugh attempted just 16 passes, completing five for 40 yards.

Minnesota	0	6	3	7	–	16
Chicago	3	10	3	3	–	19

Chi – FG Butler 23
Chi – FG Butler 51
Minn – FG Igwebuike 26
Chi – Anderson 8 run (Butler kick)
Minn – FG Igwebuike 24
Minn – FG Igwebuike 22
Chi – FG Butler 32
Minn – Jones 17 pass from Wilson (Igwebuike kick)
Chi – FG Butler 52
A: 65,420 T: 2:56

PHILADELPHIA 27, L.A. RAMS 21—At Anaheim Stadium. The Eagles' Anthony Toney rushed for 103 yards on 24 carries, and Philadelphia controlled the ball for the final 8:04 of the game to seal the win. The Rams' running game produced only 35 yards, with nine yards being the longest gain of the day. Eagle quarterback Randall Cunningham confounded the Los Angeles defense with his scrambling and passing, running for 44 yards on seven tries and completing 18 of 29 passes for 248 yards and two touchdowns. Philadelphia tight end Keith Jackson ended his holdout this week and was the team's leading receiver, with four catches for 77 yards.

Philadelphia	3	14	3	7	–	27
Los Angeles	7	7	0	7	–	21

Phi – FG Ruzek 43
L.A. – Ellard 50 pass from Everett (Lansford kick)
Phi – Quick 15 pass from Cunningham (Ruzek kick)
L.A. – McGee 10 pass from Everett (Lansford kick)
Phi – Williams 11 pass from Cunningham (Ruzek kick)
Phi – FG Ruzek 18
Phi – Drummond 2 run (Ruzek kick)
L.A. – Gary 1 run (Lansford kick)
A: 63,644 T: 2:58

L.A. RAIDERS 20, PITTSBURGH 3—At Memorial Coliseum. The Raiders broke open a defensive battle with two fourth-quarter touchdowns—a one-yard plunge by Marcus Allen and a 66-yard pass from Jay Schroeder to wide receiver Mervyn Fernandez. Fernandez ended the day with five catches for 130 yards. The Los Angeles defense tormented Steeler quarterback Bubby Brister, who suffered six sacks, two lost fumbles and an interception. Raider rookie linebacker Aaron Wallace had two of the sacks. After three weeks, Pittsburgh has not scored an offensive touchdown.

Pittsburgh	3	0	0	0	–	3
Los Angeles	0	3	3	14	–	20

Pitt – FG Anderson 31
L.A. – FG Jaeger 40
L.A. – FG Jaeger 45
L.A. – Allen 1 run (Jaeger kick)
L.A. – Fernandez 66 pass from Schroeder (Jaeger kick)
A: 50,657 T: 2:48

N.Y. GIANTS 20, MIAMI 3—At Giants Stadium. The Giants defense harassed the Dolphins' young offensive line, shutting down Miami's newfound rushing game and limiting quarterback Dan Marino to 115 yards passing. On offense, New York's balanced attack ate up more than 40 minutes of the clock, with veteran running back Ottis Anderson leading the way with 72 yards and two touchdowns. With 9,433 career yards, Anderson moved into eighth place on the league's alltime rushing list, surpassing Earl Campbell.

Miami	0	0	3	0	–	3
New York	3	7	0	10	–	20

N.Y. – FG Allegre 22
N.Y. – Anderson 1 run (Allegre kick)
Mia – FG Stoyanovich 51
N.Y. – Anderson 2 run (Allegre kick)
N.Y. – FG Allegre 45
A: 76,483 T: 2:46

SAN DIEGO 24, CLEVELAND 14—At Cleveland Stadium. The Browns offensive line could not protect quarterback Bernie Kosar, who was sacked three times and threw three interceptions. The most costly one came early in the fourth quarter with the Chargers clinging to a three-point lead and Cleveland on the Charger 32-yard line. San Diego blitzed, and linebacker Henry Rolling picked off Kosar's pass, returning it to the Browns four-yard line to set up the final score. When Sam Seale picked off Kosar in the second quarter, he ended Kosar's string of pass attempts without an interception at 152. San Diego running back Marion Butts rushed for 90 yards on 24 carries, and running back Craig McEwen caught six passes for 60 yards .

San Diego	3	7	7	7	–	24
Cleveland	7	7	0	0	–	14

S.D. – FG Reveiz 42
Cle – Johnson 64 interception return (Kauric kick)
S.D. – Miller 19 pass from Tolliver (Reveiz kick)
Cle – Hoard 1 run (Kauric kick)
S.D. – Miller 23 pass from Tolliver (Reveiz kick)
S.D. – Bernstine 1 run (Reveiz kick)
A: 77,429 T: 3:07

KANSAS CITY 17, GREEN BAY 3—At Lambeau Field. The Chiefs defense gave former Packer holdout Don Majkowski a rude welcome in his first start at quarterback this season, sacking him six times and grabbing two interceptions, one of which cornerback Stan Petry returned for a touchdown. The crucial play of the game was a fumble by Green Bay running back Brent Fulwood at the Chiefs one-yard line in the third quarter. In the fourth quarter, with six minutes to play and Kansas City nursing a seven-point lead, Packer running back Michael Haddix fumbled at the Chiefs 44-yard line. Kansas City running back Christian Okoye rushed for 122 yards on 23 carries.

Kansas City	0	7	0	10	–	17
Green Bay	0	3	0	0	–	3

G.B. – FG Jacke 46
K.C. – Okoye 5 run (Lowery kick)
K.C. – FG Lowery 20
K.C. – Petry 33 interception return (Lowery kick)
A: 58,817 T: 2:52

DENVER 34, SEATTLE 31—At Mile High Stadium. Seahawk kicker Norm Johnson missed two field goals, a 39-yarder with seven seconds left in regulation and a 44-yarder 4:59 into overtime, allowing the Broncos' David Treadwell the chance to boot the winning field goal with 5:46 to go in overtime. Running backs for both teams had big games: Seattle's Derrick Fenner ran for 144 yards and three touchdowns, while Denver's Bobby Humphrey gained 129 yards. Denver quarterback John Elway completed 30 of 40 passes for 297 yards and three first-half touchdowns.

Seattle	7	7	10	7	0	–	31
Denver	14	14	0	3	3	–	34 (OT)

Sea – Fenner 4 run (Johnson kick)
Den – Jackson 6 pass from Elway (Treadwell kick)
Den – Mecklenberg 2 fumble return (Treadwell kick)
Sea – Fenner 2 run (Johnson kick)
Den – Jackson 29 pass from Elway (Treadwell kick)
Den – Bratton 1 pass from Elway (Treadwell kick)
Sea – FG Johnson 39
Sea – Heller 2 pass from Krieg (Johnson kick)
Den – FG Treadwell 27
Sea – Fenner 4 run (Johnson kick)
Den – FG Treadwell 25
A: 75,290 T: 3:22

SAN FRANCISCO 19, ATLANTA 13—At Candlestick Park. Trailing by six with just seven seconds remaining, Falcon quarterback Chris Miller fumbled a snap, and the 49ers recovered to end Atlanta's upset bid. Falcon coach Jerry Glanville argued that Miller was throwing the ball onto the turf to stop the clock, but the replay official disagreed. Atlanta's defense stopped the 49ers' running game cold, allowing only 66 rushing yards, and Falcon nosetackle Tory Epps blocked two field goal attempts. San Francisco quarterback Joe Montana led a second-half surge, completing 24 of 36 passes on the day for 398 yards and two touchdowns.

Atlanta	3	0	7	3	–	13
San Francisco	0	5	14	0	–	19

Atl – FG Davis 37
S.F. – Safety, Miller forced out of end zone
S.F. – FG Cofer 47
S.F. – Rice 35 pass from Montana (Cofer kick)
Atl – Collins 7 pass from Miller (Davis kick)
S.F. – Jones 67 pass from Montana (Cofer kick)
Atl – FG Davis 35
A: 62,858 T: 3:18

NEW ORLEANS 28, PHOENIX 7—At the Superdome. Saints backup running back Rueben Mayes entered the game halfway through the third quarter and carried the team rushing load as he ran for 99 yards and three TDs on 16 carries. With New Orleans leading by seven late in the third quarter, Cardinals quarterback Timm Rosenbach lost a fumble, and four plays later Mayes scored his second touchdown to give the Saints a comfortable lead. Two New Orleans TD drives were kept alive by 15-yard penalties after the Cardinals had stopped the Saints on third down.

Phoenix	0	0	7	0	–	7
New Orleans	0	7	7	14	–	28

N.O. – Martin 14 pass from Fourcade (Andersen kick)
Phoe – Proehl 37 pass from Rosenbach (Del Greco kick)
N.O. – Mayes 10 run (Andersen kick)
N.O. – Mayes 4 run (Andersen kick)
N.O. – Mayes 14 run (Andersen kick)
A: 61,110 T: 2:58

WASHINGTON 19, DALLAS 15—At RFK Stadium. Redskins cornerback Darrell Green scored the only Washington touchdown with an 18-yard interception return, and Washington's defense sacked Cowboy quarterback Troy Aikman eight times to avenge a loss that kept the Redskins from making the playoffs the season before. The Redskins offense could muster only 214 yards, but kicker Chip Lohmiller booted four field goals, including a 55-yarder. Washington quarterback Mark Rypien injured his knee in the second quarter and was replaced by Stan Humphries for the remainder of the game.

Dallas	0	3	3	9	–	15
Washington	3	3	6	7	–	19

Wash – FG Lohmiller 37
Dall – FG Willis 33
Wash – FG Lohmiller 23
Dall – FG Willis 41
Wash – FG Lohmiller 24
Wash – FG Lohmiller 55
Wash – Green 18 interception return (Lohmiller kick)
Dall – Smith 2 run (Willis kick)
Dall – Safety, Mojsiejenko ran out of end zone
A: 53,804 T: 3:14

CINCINNATI 41, NEW ENGLAND 7—At Riverfront Stadium. After two close come-from-behind games, the Bengals exploded for 31 points, burying the Patriots from the opening kickoff. With 2:09 gone in the game, Cincinnati kicker Jim Breech nailed a 46-yard field goal to score in his 152nd straight game, breaking the NFL record set by Fred Cox of the Vikings. On the next Bengal possession, quarterback Boomer Esiason rolled left after a fake handoff and found wideout Eddie Brown for a 42-yard touchdown. Wide receiver Tim McGee was Esiason's favorite target, catching six passes for 163 yards.

New England	0	7	0	0	–	7
Cincinnati	17	14	3	7	–	41

Cin – FG Breech 46
Cin – Brown 42 pass from Esiason (Breech kick)
Cin – Holman 4 pass from Johnson (Breech kick)
Cin – Green 3 run (Breech kick)
Cin – Brooks 6 run (Breech kick)
N.E. – Cook 7 pass from Wilson (Staurovsky kick)
Cin – FG Breech 23
Cin – Holman 3 pass from Esiason (Breech kick)
A: 56,470 T: 3:02

HOUSTON 24, INDIANAPOLIS 10—At the Astrodome. Oiler quarterback Warren Moon threw an interception on his first pass but thereafter executed the run-and-shoot to perfection to finish with 308 yards passing and three touchdowns. Moon's 19,289 career passing yards pushed him ahead of George Blanda to become the team's alltime leader. Houston scored twice in the second quarter after Colt fumbles, and the Oiler offense put together an 11-play, 87-yard drive to put the game away in the fourth quarter.

Indianapolis	0	0	10	0	–	10
Houston	0	14	3	7	–	24

Hou – White 13 pass from Moon (Zendejas kick)
Hou – White 7 pass from Moon (Zendejas kick)
Ind – FG Biasucci 33
Hou – FG Zendejas 30
Ind – Beach 16 pass from Trudeau (Biasucci kick)
Hou – Givins 6 pass from Moon (Zendejas kick)
A: 50,093 T: 3:08

TAMPA BAY 23, DETROIT 20—At Tampa Stadium. Buccaneer quarterback Vinny Testaverde threw a three-yard touchdown pass to running back John Harvey with 4:21 remaining to give Tampa Bay its second win over the Lions in three weeks. Testaverde's late-game heroics overshadowed a strong game by Lion quarterback Rodney Peete, who rushed eight times for 97 yards and completed 17 of 26 passes for 169 yards and one touchdown.

Detroit	3	3	7	7	–	20
Tampa Bay	0	6	3	14	–	23

Det – FG Murray 25
T.B. – FG Christie 55
T.B. – FG Christie 28
Det – FG Murray 33
Det – Peete 1 run (Murray kick)
T.B. – FG Christie 21
T.B. – Anderson 10 run (Christie kick)
Det – Clark 5 pass from Peete (Murray kick)
T.B. – Harvey 3 pass from Testaverde (Christie kick)
A: 55,075 T: 2:52

MONDAY, SEPTEMBER 24

BUFFALO 30, N.Y. JETS 7—At Giants Stadium. The Bills dominated the Jets on both offense and defense, running up 451 total yards and sacking New York quarterback Ken O'Brien three times. Buffalo running back Thurman Thomas shredded the Jet defense for a career-high 214 yards on 18 carries for an average of 11.89 yards per carry.

Buffalo	7	13	3	7	–	30
New York	7	0	0	0	–	7

N.Y. – Baxter 1 run (Leahy kick)
Buff – Davis 1 run (Norwood kick)
Buff – Rolle 2 pass from Kelly (Norwood kick)
Buff – FG Norwood 48
Buff – FG Norwood 42
Buff – FG Norwood 27
Buff – McKeller 6 pass from Kelly (Norwood kick)
A: 69,927 T: 3:00

WEEK 4 STANDINGS

AFC EAST	W	L	T	Pct.	PF	PA
Buffalo	3	1	0	.750	88	57
Miami	3	1	0	.750	92	75
N.Y. Jets	2	2	0	.500	88	89
New England	1	3	0	.250	60	119
Indianapolis	1	3	0	.250	58	89

AFC CENTRAL	W	L	T	Pct.	PF	PA
Cincinnati	3	1	0	.750	103	74
Houston	2	2	0	.500	77	84
Cleveland	1	3	0	.250	48	85
Pittsburgh	1	3	0	.250	32	70

AFC WEST	W	L	T	Pct.	PF	PA
L.A. Raiders	4	0	0	1.000	75	35
Kansas City	3	1	0	.750	98	48
Denver	2	2	0	.500	95	97
San Diego	1	3	0	.250	61	69
Seattle	1	3	0	.250	75	84

NFC EAST	W	L	T	Pct.	PF	PA
N.Y. Giants	4	0	0	1.000	106	47
Washington	3	1	0	.750	101	51
Phoenix	1	3	0	.250	40	118
Dallas	1	3	0	.250	56	92
Philadelphia	1	3	0	.250	91	95

NFC CENTRAL	W	L	T	Pct.	PF	PA
Chicago	3	1	0	.750	77	53
Tampa Bay	3	1	0	.750	98	96
Green Bay	2	2	0	.500	76	93
Detroit	1	3	0	.250	83	99
Minnesota	1	3	0	.250	89	69

NFC WEST	W	L	T	Pct.	PF	PA
San Francisco	3	0	0	1.000	58	38
Atlanta	1	2	0	.333	74	67
L.A. Rams	1	2	0	.333	80	77
New Orleans	1	2	0	.333	43	52

RESULTS
L.A. Raiders 24, Chicago 10
Buffalo 29, Denver 28
Indianapolis 24, Philadelphia 23
N.Y. Giants 31, Dallas 17
Houston 17, San Diego 7
Miami 28, Pittsburgh 6
N.Y. Jets 37, New England 13
Tampa Bay 23, Minnesota 20 (OT)
Green Bay 24, Detroit 21
Kansas City 34, Cleveland 0
Washington 38, Phoenix 10
Seattle 31, Cincinnati 16 (Monday night)
Open dates: San Francisco, Atlanta, New Orleans, L.A. Rams

SUNDAY, SEPTEMBER 30

L.A. RAIDERS 24, CHICAGO 10—At Memorial Coliseum. In a meeting of 3–0 teams, the Raider defense crushed the Bears and dominated the game. Los Angeles sacked Chicago quarterback Jim Harbaugh six times, forced a Harbaugh fumble that defensive end Greg Townsend turned into a touchdown and limited the Bears to only one of 11 third-down conversions. On offense, the Raiders were conservative, running the ball on 36 of 52 plays. Marcus Allen and Greg Bell combined for 22 carries and 103 yards. Los Angeles wide receiver Willie Gault, a former Bear, caught four passes for 103 yards.

Chicago	7	3	0	0	–	10
Los Angeles	10	7	0	7	–	24

L.A. – Allen 1 run (Jaeger kick)
Chi – Gentry 80 pass from Harbaugh (Butler kick)
L.A. – FG Jaeger 27
L.A. – Townsend 1 fumble return (Jaeger kick)
Chi – FG Butler 22
L.A. – Allen 3 run (Jaeger kick)
A: 80,156 T: 2:39

BUFFALO 29, DENVER 28—At Rich Stadium. Trailing 21–9 in the fourth quarter, the Bills scored three touchdowns in the space of 1:17 to pull out a win in a game otherwise dominated by the Broncos. The comeback began when Bills cornerback Nate Odomes blocked a David Treadwell field goal try and linebacker Cornelius Bennett scooped it up and dashed 80 yards for a touchdown. One minute later Buffalo safety Leonard Smith intercepted a pass from Denver quarterback John Elway and returned it 39 yards for a touchdown. Two plays from scrimmage later the Bills went up 29–21 when Bennett recovered an Elway fumble, setting up a two-yard touchdown run by Kenneth Davis. The Broncos outgained the Bills 410 yards to 197, and Denver running back Bobby Humphrey rushed 34 times for 177 yards, an average of 5.2 yards per carry.

Denver	7	7	7	7	–	28
Buffalo	0	3	6	20	–	29

Den – Humphrey 1 run (Treadwell kick)
Den – Sewell 3 run (Treadwell kick)
Buff – FG Norwood 37
Buff – Smith 12 run (kick failed)
Den – Winder 3 run (Treadwell kick)
Buff – Bennett 80 blocked field goal return (Norwood kick)
Buff – Smith 39 interception return (kick failed)
Buff – Davis 2 run (Norwood kick)
Den – Nattiel 7 pass from Elway (Treadwell kick)
A: 74,393 T: 3:08

INDIANAPOLIS 24, PHILADELPHIA 23—At Veterans Stadium. Colt backup quarterback Jack Trudeau, substituting for injured rookie Jeff George, threw a six-yard touchdown pass to wide receiver Bill Brooks with no time remaining to give Indianapolis its first win of the season. Brooks's catch was his sixth on the 14-play, 82-yard drive. For the Eagles, quarterback Randall Cunningham completed 22 of 34 passes for 274 yards and two touchdowns; he also rushed for 61 yards on 10 carries. Running back Keith Byars was his favorite target, catching 12 passes for 133 yards.

Indianapolis	7	3	7	7	–	24
Philadelphia	3	14	3	3	–	23

Phi – FG Ruzek 22
Ind – Hester 5 pass from Trudeau (Biasucci kick)
Phi – Jackson 35 pass from Cunningham (Ruzek kick)
Phi – Barnett 21 pass from Cunningham (Ruzek kick)
Ind – FG Biasucci 41
Phi – FG Ruzek 44
Ind – Bentley 26 run (Biasucci kick)
Phi – FG Ruzek 31
Ind – Brooks 6 pass from Trudeau (Biasucci kick)
A: 62,067 T: 3:10

N.Y. GIANTS 31, DALLAS 17—At Giants Stadium. The Giants continued to roll methodically over opponents, beating the Cowboys for the second time in three weeks to remain undefeated. New York veterans led the way, with running back Ottis Anderson rushing for 79 yards and quarterback Phil Simms completing 16 of 22 passes for 188 yards and three touchdowns in only three quarters of play. Simms upped his career completions to 2,040, moving him ahead of Terry Bradshaw for 20th place on the league's alltime completions list. Dallas quarterback Troy Aikman completed 21 of 26 passes for 233 yards and one touchdown. When Cowboy rookie running back Emmitt Smith scored from four yards out in the third quarter, it was the first time that the Giants defense had allowed a touchdown in 10 quarters.

Dallas	0	3	7	7	–	17
New York	7	10	0	14	–	31

N.Y. – Ingram 12 pass from Simms (Bahr kick)
Dall – FG Willis 22
N.Y. – FG Bahr 34
N.Y. – Mrosko 7 pass from Simms (Bahr kick)
Dall – Smith 4 run (Willis kick)
N.Y. – Hampton 27 pass from Simms (Bahr kick)
N.Y. – Hostetler 12 run (Bahr kick)
Dall – Novacek 7 pass from Aikman (Willis kick)
A: 75,923 T: 2:27

HOUSTON 17, SAN DIEGO 7—At Jack Murphy Stadium. Oiler quarterback Warren Moon threw to 11 different receivers, completing 27 of 46 passes for 355 yards and two touchdowns as Houston's run-and-shoot offense kept the Chargers off-balance. Ernest Givins led the receiving parade with six catches for 97 yards and a touchdown. In the fourth quarter, with the Oilers holding a seven-point lead, San Diego quarterback Billy Joe Tolliver threw an interception at the Houston 37, and Houston went on to kick a field goal for the final margin. Oiler linebacker Al Smith had nine tackles. Both kickers missed easy field goals: Houston's Tony Zendejas was wide with kicks from 36 and 27 yards, and the Chargers' Fuad Reveiz failed to convert from 45 and 27 yards.

Houston	7	7	0	3	–	17
San Diego	0	7	0	0	–	7

Hou – Hill 9 pass from Moon (Zendejas kick)
S.D. – Miller 27 pass from Tolliver (Reveiz kick)
Hou – Givins 22 pass from Moon (Zendejas kick)
Hou – FG Zendejas 34
A: 48,762 T: 2:59

MIAMI 28, PITTSBURGH 6—At Three Rivers Stadium. The Steeler offense remained punchless as it failed to score a touchdown for the fourth straight game. Seven of Pittsburgh's first 12 plays lost yardage, and the Steelers failed to pick up a first down until the Dolphins had jumped out to a 21–0 lead. Two fourth-down plays made that lead possible. On its first series Miami converted a fourth-and-one from the Steeler 10 and pushed in for the touchdown. Leading 7–0 and facing a fourth down from its own 48 on the first play of the second quarter, Miami faked a punt and upback Jim Jensen hit Ferrell Edmunds for a 31-yard gain, which set up the Dolphins' second touchdown. Miami nursed the lead with its running game and controlled the ball for almost two thirds of the game. Dolphin defensive end Jeff Cross had three sacks, and cornerback Tim McKyer had two interceptions.

Miami	7	14	0	7	–	28
Pittsburgh	0	3	3	0	–	6

Mia – Smith 1 run (Stoyanovich kick)
Mia – Smith 7 run (Stoyanovich kick)
Mia – Clayton 35 pass from Marino (Stoyanovich kick)
Pitt – FG Anderson 46
Pitt – FG Anderson 35
Mia – Paige 1 run (Stoyanovich kick)
A: 54,691 T: 2:41

N.Y. JETS 37, NEW ENGLAND 13—At Foxboro Stadium. Rocked by allegations that Patriots players sexually harassed a female newspaper reporter, New England folded under a stiff Jet defense and a balanced New York offense led by rookies Blair Thomas and Rob Moore. Running back Thomas gained 100 yards on 20 carries, and wide receiver Moore caught nine passes for 175 yards and one touchdown. The Jets outgained the Patriots 499 yards to 258. On defense, New York linebacker Kyle Clifton had two interceptions. New England owner Victor Kiam, who had been embroiled in the controversy, addressed the team before the game and appeared in the stands, greeting fans and trying to repair the franchise's image.

New York	7	17	10	3	–	37
New England	3	3	0	7	–	13

N.Y. – Baxter 1 run (Leahy kick)
N.E. – FG Staurovsky 46
N.Y. – Moore 69 pass from O'Brien (Leahy kick)
N.E. – FG Staurovsky 40
N.Y. – FG Leahy 24
N.Y. – McNeil 4 run (Leahy kick)
N.Y. – Baxter 28 run (Leahy kick)
N.Y. – FG Leahy 18
N.E. – Perryman 4 run (Staurovsky kick)
N.Y. – FG Leahy 46
A: 36,724 T: 2:55

TAMPA BAY 23, MINNESOTA 20—At the Metrodome. Viking kicker Donald Igwebuike, who had been released before the start of the season by the Bucaneers, missed a 48-yard field goal in overtime, then had to watch as Tampa Bay kicker Steve Christie, the man who took his job, booted the winner from 36 yards out. The field goal was set up when Buccaneer cornerback Wayne Haddix intercepted a pass that had deflected off the hands of wide receiver Anthony Carter and off the helmet of safety Mark Robinson. Haddix returned the ball to the Viking 26. With 1:19 left in regulation, Tampa Bay quarterback Vinny Testaverde marched the Buccaneers 74 yards in five plays, hitting Bruce Hill with an 11-yard touchdown pass to tie the score with only 24 seconds remaining. The victory by Tampa Bay ended Minnesota's 14-game home winning streak. The Bucaneers' Gary Anderson rushed for 108 yards on 22 carries. The 3–1 start for Tampa Bay is its best since 1979.

Tampa Bay	7	3	3	7	3	–	23
Minnesota	0	3	3	14	0	–	20

T.B. – Anderson 2 run (Christie kick)
Minn – FG Igwebuike 28
T.B. – FG Christie 39
T.B. – FG Christie 22
Minn – FG Igwebuike 32
Minn – Carter 7 pass from Gannon (Igwebuike kick)
Minn – Jones 41 pass from Gannon (Igwebuike kick)
T.B. – Hill 11 pass from Testaverde (Christie kick)
T.B. – FG Christie 36
A: 54,462 T: 3:10

GREEN BAY 24, DETROIT 21—At the Silverdome. Packer quarterback Don Majkowski fired a touchdown pass to leaping wide receiver Jeff Query with :55 to play to give Green Bay the victory. The Lions had jumped out to a 21–10 lead behind the running of Barry Sanders, who finished with 94 yards on 20 carries and one touchdown, and quarterback Rodney Peete, who rushed for 50 yards and one touchdown. But Majkowski brought back memories of his miraculous '89 season as he rallied his team, scrambling for 88 yards on eight carries and passing for 289 yards and three touchdowns. Detroit kicker Eddie Murray missed four field goals, including a 44-yarder with :08 remaining. Lion rookie linebacker Tracy Hayworth had two sacks.

Green Bay	0	10	0	14	–	24
Detroit	7	7	7	0	–	21

Det – Clark 4 pass from Peete (Murray kick)
G.B. – FG Jacke 34
G.B. – West 3 pass from Majkowski (Jacke kick)
Det – Sanders 3 run (Murray kick)
Det – Peete 7 run (Murray kick)
G.B. – Haddix 4 pass from Majkowski (Jacke kick)
G.B. – Query 26 pass from Majkowski (Jacke kick)
A: 64,509 T: 3:19

KANSAS CITY 34, CLEVELAND 0—At Arrowhead Stadium. The Chiefs' special teams ran back two blocked punts for touchdowns and set up another touchdown on Naz Worthen's 37-yard punt return in a rout of the Browns. Kansas City quarterback Steve DeBerg passed for two touchdowns, while Cleveland's Bernie Kosar was sacked for the 14th time in four games. Chiefs cornerback Albert Lewis had one of the punt blocks, his third in the last three games, and linebacker Derrick Thomas had two sacks. The loss was the worst regular-season shutout in Cleveland franchise history.

Cleveland	0	0	0	0	–	0
Kansas City	7	17	10	0	–	34

K.C. – Thomas 47 pass from DeBerg (Lowery kick)
K.C. – FG Lowery 39
K.C. – Martin 31 blocked punt return (Lowery kick)
K.C. – Harry 6 pass from DeBerg (Lowery kick)
K.C. – FG Lowery 34
K.C. – Ross 4 blocked punt return (Lowery kick)
A: 75,462 T: 2:59

WASHINGTON 38, PHOENIX 10—At Sun Devil Stadium. Stan Humphries, the Redskins' backup quarterback starting in place of injured Mark Rypien, connected on 20 of 25 passes for 257 yards and two touchdowns as coach Joe Gibbs beat former assistant Joe Bugel for the second time in four weeks. The Cardinals jumped out to a 10–7 halftime lead, but in the second half Humphries sneaked up the middle for a touchdown and completed 11 of 12 passes for 183 yards to lead Washington's comeback. The Redskins defense limited Phoenix to 192 total yards and allowed the Cardinals to convert only one of nine third-down plays. Phoenix rookie running back Johnny Johnson accounted for 93 yards on the ground and 15 yards on three receptions.

Washington	0	7	10	21	–	38
Phoenix	0	10	0	0	–	10

Phoe – FG Del Greco 32
Wash – Riggs 1 run (Lohmiller kick)
Phoe – Green 12 pass from Rosenbach (Del Greco kick)
Wash – FG Lohmiller 26
Wash – Clark 42 pass from Humphries (Lohmiller kick)
Wash – Humphries 1 run (Lohmiller kick)
Wash – Clark 42 pass from Humphries (Lohmiller kick)
Wash – Byner 1 run (Lohmiller kick)
A: 49,303 T: 2:39

MONDAY, OCTOBER 1

SEATTLE 31, CINCINNATI 16—At the Kingdome. The Seahawk defense harried the Bengal offense into two turnovers, and Seattle running back Derrick Fenner scored three touchdowns as the Seahawks pulled away from Cincinnati in the fourth quarter. Seattle's offensive line gave quarterback Dave Krieg time to throw, and Krieg responded by completing 17 of 24 passes for 217 yards and two touchdowns. Bengal quarterback Boomer Esiason fumbled three snaps from center, was sacked three times and completed only 10 of 23 passes for 128 yards. With the Seahawks leading 17–9 going into the fourth quarter, Cincinnati was still within striking distance, but on third-and-seven from his own 37, Krieg completed a 63-yard touchdown pass to wide receiver Tommy Kane, who had beaten safety Rickey Dixon in one-on-one coverage.

Cincinnati	0	6	3	7	–	16
Seattle	3	7	7	14	–	31

Sea – FG Johnson 51
Cin – FG Breech 34
Sea – Fenner 4 run (Johnson kick)
Cin – FG Breech 26
Sea – Fenner 3 run (Johnson kick)
Cin – FG Breech 43
Sea – Kane 63 pass from Krieg (Johnson kick)
Cin – Price 66 punt return (Breech kick)
Sea – Fenner 2 pass from Krieg (Johnson kick)
A: 60,135 T: 3:06

WEEK 5 STANDINGS

AFC EAST	W	L	T	Pct.	PF	PA
Buffalo	4	1	0	.800	130	99
Miami	4	1	0	.800	108	73
Indianapolis	2	3	0	.400	81	108
N.Y. Jets	2	3	0	.400	104	109
New England	1	4	0	.200	80	152

AFC CENTRAL	W	L	T	Pct.	PF	PA
Cincinnati	4	1	0	.800	137	105
Cleveland	2	3	0	.400	78	114
Houston	2	3	0	.400	98	108
Pittsburgh	2	3	0	.400	68	84

AFC WEST	W	L	T	Pct.	PF	PA
L.A. Raiders	4	1	0	.800	99	73
Kansas City	3	2	0	.600	117	71
Denver	2	3	0	.400	124	127
Seattle	2	3	0	.400	108	104
San Diego	1	4	0	.200	75	105

NFC EAST	W	L	T	Pct.	PF	PA
N.Y. Giants	4	0	0	1.000	106	47
Washington	3	1	0	.750	101	51
Dallas	2	3	0	.400	70	102
Philadelphia	1	3	0	.250	91	95
Phoenix	1	3	0	.250	40	118

NFC CENTRAL	W	L	T	Pct.	PF	PA
Chicago	4	1	0	.800	104	66
Tampa Bay	3	2	0	.600	108	110
Detroit	2	3	0	.400	117	126
Green Bay	2	3	0	.400	89	120
Minnesota	1	4	0	.200	116	103

NFC WEST	W	L	T	Pct.	PF	PA
San Francisco	4	0	0	1.000	82	59
Atlanta	2	2	0	.500	102	94
L.A. Rams	1	3	0	.250	111	111
New Orleans	1	3	0	.250	70	80

RESULTS
Chicago 27, Green Bay 13
Buffalo 38, L.A. Raiders 24
Miami 20, N.Y. Jets 16
Atlanta 28, New Orleans 27
Cincinnati 34, L.A. Rams 31 (OT)
Detroit 34, Minnesota 27
Pittsburgh 36, San Diego 14
San Francisco 24, Houston 21
Dallas 14, Tampa Bay 10
Seattle 33, New England 20
Indianapolis 23, Kansas City 19
Cleveland 30, Denver 29 (Monday night)
Open dates: N.Y. Giants, Philadelphia, Phoenix, Washington

SUNDAY, OCTOBER 7

CHICAGO 27, GREEN BAY 13—At Soldier Field. The Bears relied on a strong defense and conservative offense to beat the Packers. Neal Anderson was the offensive key, carrying the ball 21 times for 141 yards and one touchdown. Chicago's defense limited Green Bay quarterback Don Majkowski to 12 completions in 39 attempts and forced two interceptions. The defense was just as tough against the rush, allowing the Packers just 32 yards on the ground. Bears starting quarterback Jim Harbaugh left the game late in the second quarter with a rib injury and was replaced by Mike Tomczak. The game's crucial play came late in the third quarter with the Bears leading 10–6, when Chicago defensive end Richard Dent recovered a Majkowski fumble at the Green Bay 17-yard line; three plays later quarterback Mike Tomczak ran six yards for the score.

Green Bay	3	3	0	7	–	13
Chicago	7	3	7	10	–	27

G.B. – FG Jacke 38
Chi – Anderson 3 run (Butler kick)
G.B. – FG Jacke 27
Chi – FG Butler 50
Chi – Tomczak 6 run (Butler kick)
G.B. – Sharpe 76 pass from Majkowski (Jacke kick)
Chi – FG Butler 51
Chi – Boso 2 pass from Tomczak (Butler kick)
A: 59,929 T: 3:31

BUFFALO 38, L.A. RAIDERS 24—At Rich Stadium. The Bills exploded for 24 points in the fourth quarter to erase a 24–14 deficit and hand the Raiders their first defeat of the season. After pulling within three points to 24–21 on a 42-yard pass from Jim Kelly to wide receiver James Lofton, Buffalo blocked a Los Angeles punt on the next series, and J.D. Williams picked it up and ran 38 yards for a touchdown. Bills linebacker Cornelius Bennett caused a fumble on the next series to set up a field goal. The Bills' final touchdown came when cornerback Nate Odomes stole the ball from the grip of Raider wide receiver Willie Gault and ran 49 yards down the sideline for the score. Like Denver the week before, Los Angeles dominated Buffalo offensively, outgaining the Bills 347 yards to 280 and holding nearly a two-to-one edge in time of possession.

Los Angeles	7	3	7	7	–	24
Buffalo	0	7	7	24	–	38

L.A. – Gault 11 pass from Schroeder (Jaeger kick)
Buff – Reed 13 pass from Kelly (Norwood kick)
L.A. – FG Jaeger 19
L.A. – Allen 1 run (Jaeger kick)
Buff – McKeller 15 pass from Kelly (Norwood kick)
L.A. – Smith 4 pass from Schroeder (Jaeger kick)
Buff – Lofton 42 pass from Kelly (Norwood kick)
Buff – Williams 38 blocked punt return (Norwood kick)
Buff – FG Norwood 23
Buff – Odomes 49 fumble return (Norwood kick)
A: 80,076 T: 3:03

MIAMI 20, N.Y. JETS 16—At Joe Robbie Stadium. Trailing 16–13 midway through the fourth quarter, the Dolphins drove 80 yards in 14 plays to score the winning touchdown with 1:03 remaining. On the drive, Miami quarterback Dan Marino converted four third-down situations with completions before firing a 13-yard bullet to wide receiver Mark Duper on a crossing pattern for the game-winner. Duper, who had spent time on the bench for the past two seasons with injuries and a drug suspension, caught five passes for 125 yards and two touchdowns, as many touchdowns as he scored in the last two seasons. Jet quarterback Ken O'Brien completed 20 of 33 passes for 256 yards and a touchdown, but the Dolphin defense sacked him four times, with Jeff Cross getting two of those.

New York	3	10	0	3	–	16
Miami	0	0	13	7	–	20

N.Y. – FG Leahy 25
N.Y. – Moore 9 pass from O'Brien (Leahy kick)
N.Y. – FG Leahy 19
Mia – Logan 11 run (pass failed)
Mia – Duper 69 pass from Marino (Stoyanovich kick)
N.Y. – FG Leahy 30
Mia – Duper 13 pass from Marino (Stoyanovich kick)
A: 69,678 T: 2:49

ATLANTA 28, NEW ORLEANS 27—At Atlanta-Fulton County Stadium. With less than three minutes remaining, Falcon quarterback Chris Miller connected with wide receiver Andre Rison for a 45-yard completion on fourth-and-two and for a three-yard touchdown five plays later to give Atlanta the come-from-behind win. Rison, who was acquired from Indianapolis in the off-season, ended the day with 10 catches for 154 yards and two touchdowns, and Miller completed 23 of 44 passes for 366 yards and three touchdowns. Saints quarterback John Fourcade accounted for all three New Orleans touchdowns, passing for two and running for one.

New Orleans	7	10	7	3	–	27
Atlanta	7	7	7	7	–	28

Atl – Miller 1 run (Davis kick)
N.O. – Turner 68 pass from Fourcade (Andersen kick)
Atl – Collins 9 pass from Miller (Davis kick)
N.O. – Fourcade 5 run (Andersen kick)
N.O. – FG Andersen 46
Atl – Rison 20 pass from Miller (Davis kick)
N.O. – Brenner 3 pass from Fourcade (Andersen kick)
N.O. – FG Andersen 23
Atl – Rison 3 pass from Miller (Davis kick)
A: 57,401 T: 3:20

CINCINNATI 34, L.A. RAMS 31—At Anaheim Stadium. After a week of turmoil over coach Sam Wyche's decision to bar a female reporter from the locker room, the Bengals jumped out to a 21-0 lead, saw the Rams battle back to tie the game at 31 with 1:36 remaining, then won the pass-happy game with a 44-yard field goal by Jim Breech in overtime. Cincinnati quarterback Boomer Esiason threw for 471 yards—a club record—and three touchdowns. Bengal tight end Rodney Holman led all receivers, with 10 catches for 161 yards, including a crucial third-down catch on Cincinnati's winning drive. Bengal wide receiver Tim McGee caught eight passes for 142 yards, and Ram wideout Willie Anderson caught seven passes for 144 yards and a touchdown.

Cincinnati	14	7	7	3	3	–	34
Los Angeles	0	7	14	10	0	–	31

Cin – Brooks 27 pass from Esiason (Breech kick)
Cin – Brooks 9 pass from Esiason (Breech kick)
Cin – Ball 1 run (Breech kick)
L.A. – Gary 2 run (Lansford kick)
L.A. – Anderson 55 pass from Everett (Lansford kick)
Cin – Green 14 pass from Esiason (Breech kick)
L.A. – Johnson 9 pass from Everett (Lansford kick)
L.A. – Gary 1 run (Lansford kick)
Cin – FG Breech 40
L.A. – FG Lansford 40
Cin – FG Breech 44
A: 62,619 T: 3:39

DETROIT 34, MINNESOTA 27—At the Metrodome. Lion backup quarterback Bob Gagliano's two first-half interceptions led to 10 Viking points, but in the second half he passed for two touchdowns, sparking Detroit to score on four straight possessions in the Lions' comeback win. Detroit running back Barry Sanders rushed for 82 yards on 15 carries and caught three passes for 42 yards. In the fourth quarter with the score tied at 20, Minnesota, on the Lion 21-yard line, tried a pass on fourth-and-one that fell incomplete. The Lion defense sacked Minnesota quarterback Rich Gannon five times, but he completed 23 of 35 passes for 227 yards and two touchdowns.

Detroit	3	7	7	17	–	34
Minnesota	6	14	0	7	–	27

Minn – FG Igwebuike 36
Det – FG Murray 32
Minn – FG Igwebuike 48
Det – Sanders 22 pass from Gagliano (Murray kick)
Minn – Jones 11 pass from Gannon (Igwebuike kick)
Minn – Carter 8 pass from Gannon (Igwebuike kick)
Det – Johnson 5 pass from Gagliano (Murray kick)
Det – FG Murray 23
Det – Greer 16 pass from Gagliano (Murray kick)
Det – Sanders 1 run (Murray kick)
Minn – Walker 2 run (Igwebuike kick)
A: 57,586 T: 3:04

PITTSBURGH 36, SAN DIEGO 14—At Three Rivers Stadium. The Steeler offense scored its first touchdown of the season, on an eight-yard pass from quarterback Bubby Brister to rookie tight end Eric Green, and the defense held the Chargers to 188 total yards in a rout. Brister completed 11 of 14 passes for 132 yards and two touchdowns before leaving the game late in the first half with bruised ribs. Charger quarterback Billy Joe Tolliver threw three interceptions, two of which were hauled in by cornerback Dwayne Woodruff.

San Diego	7	0	7	0	–	14
Pittsburgh	3	14	7	12	–	36

Pitt – FG Anderson 45
S.D. – Plummer 2 pass from Tolliver (Carney kick)
Pitt – Green 8 pass from Brister (Anderson kick)
Pitt – Green 1 pass from Brister (Anderson kick)
Pitt – Williams 2 run (Anderson kick)
S.D. – Miller fumble recovery in end zone (Carney kick)
Pitt – Safety, Stowe blocked punt out of end zone
Pitt – FG Anderson 45
Pitt – Foster 2 run (Anderson kick)
A: 53,486 T: 2:51

SAN FRANCISCO 24, HOUSTON 21—At the Astrodome. The Oilers jumped out to a 14-0 first-quarter lead, but 49er quarterback Joe Montana led a San Francisco comeback that culminated in a 46-yard touchdown pass to wide receiver John Taylor with 6:31 left. The 49er defense stifled Houston's run-and-shoot offense in the fourth quarter, allowing the Oilers just six yards of total offense. San Francisco's Roger Craig caught two passes to set an NFL career receiving record for running backs, with 494 catches, surpassing the mark of the Bears' Walter Payton. Taylor finished the day with four catches for 132 yards and two touchdowns, including a 78-yarder in the third quarter.

San Francisco	0	7	7	10	–	24
Houston	14	0	7	0	–	21

Hou – Moon 1 run (Zendejas kick)
Hou – Hill 30 pass from Moon (Zendejas kick)
S.F. – Rice 6 pass from Montana (Cofer kick)
S.F. – Taylor 78 pass from Montana (Cofer kick)
Hou – Jeffires 18 pass from Moon (Zendejas kick)
S.F. – FG Cofer 23
S.F. – Taylor 46 pass from Montana (Cofer kick)
A: 59,931 T: 2:57

DALLAS 14, TAMPA BAY 10—At Texas Stadium. Cowboy rookie running back Emmitt Smith and a staunch defense combined to give Dallas its second win of the season. Smith ran for 121 yards on 23 carries, including a 14-yard touchdown run in the fourth quarter that put Dallas ahead for good. The Cowboys contained Buccaneer quarterback Vinny Testaverde, who passed for only 194 yards. Tampa Bay running back Gary Anderson rushed for 76 yards and caught passes for 88 yards to account for more than half of the Buccaneers' total offense, but he fumbled on first-and-goal at the Dallas seven-yard line midway through the third quarter. The star for the Cowboys on defense was tackle Jimmie Jones, who had 2.5 sacks.

Tampa Bay	0	3	7	0	–	10
Dallas	7	0	0	7	–	14

Dall – Novacek 12 pass from Aikman (Willis kick)
T.B. – FG Christie 33
T.B. – Anderson 58 pass from Testaverde (Christie kick)
Dall – Smith 14 run (Willis kick)
A: 60,076 T: 2:35

SEATTLE 33, NEW ENGLAND 20—At Foxboro Stadium. Trailing 20–19 with 2:37 remaining, the Seahawks scored two touchdowns in 24 seconds to pull out the win. The first score came on a 45-yard pass from quarterback Dave Krieg to wide receiver Jeff Chadwick. Seattle scored again two plays after Patriots running back Robert Perryman fumbled at the New England 21. Seahawk running back Derrick Fenner rushed 19 times for 77 yards and scored twice to give him a league-leading total of eight TDs.

Seattle	13	6	0	14	–	33
New England	3	7	7	3	–	20

Sea – Fenner 5 run (kick failed)
Sea – Kane 20 pass from Krieg (Johnson kick)
N.E. – FG Staurovsky 53
Sea – FG Johnson 31
Sea – FG Johnson 19
N.E. – Williams 45 fumble return (Staurovsky kick)
N.E. – Dykes 35 pass from Wilson (Staurovsky kick)
N.E. – FG Staurovsky 48
Sea – Chadwick 45 pass from Krieg (Johnson kick)
Sea – Fenner 5 run (Johnson kick)
A: 39,735 T: 2:53

INDIANAPOLIS 23, KANSAS CITY 19—At the Hoosier Dome. A fourth-quarter fumble by Chiefs running back Christian Okoye at the Kansas City 21 set up a 10-yard touchdown run by Colt running back Albert Bentley with 5:53 remaining as Indianapolis got its second straight win. Chiefs quarterback Steve DeBerg, who had not suffered an interception all season, threw three, and the Colts overcame seven sacks by the Kansas City defense, four by linebacker Derrick Thomas. The Chiefs moved the ball inside the Indianapolis 26 six times but could only come away with one touchdown. Bentley ended the day with 84 yards rushing on 20 carries and 30 yards receiving on four catches.

Kansas City	10	6	3	0	–	19
Indianapolis	0	10	0	13	–	23

K.C. – FG Lowery 37
K.C. – Thomas 21 pass from DeBerg (Lowery kick)
K.C. – FG Lowery 39
Ind – FG Biasucci 38
Ind – Bentley 9 pass from Trudeau (Biasucci kick)
K.C. – FG Lowery 44
K.C. – FG Lowery 35
Ind – FG Biasucci 21
Ind – Bentley 10 run (Biasucci kick)
Ind – FG Biasucci 18
A: 54,950 T: 3:16

MONDAY, OCTOBER 8

CLEVELAND 30, DENVER 29—At Mile High Stadium. Browns kicker Jerry Kauric booted a 30-yard field goal with no time remaining to give Cleveland a victory in Denver for the first time since 1972. The previously porous Browns offensive line allowed no sacks, and quarterback Bernie Kosar threw for 318 yards and three touchdowns. His favorite target was wide receiver Webster Slaughter, who caught seven passes for 123 yards. Denver running back Bobby Humphrey ran for 106 yards and one touchdown on 20 carries.

Cleveland	6	7	7	10	–	30
Denver	7	12	0	10	–	29

Den – Elway 13 run (Treadwell kick)
Cle – Metcalf 5 run (kick blocked)
Den – FG Treadwell 20
Cle – Slaughter 43 pass from Kosar (Kauric kick)
Den – Humphrey 19 run (Treadwell kick)
Den – Safety, Fletcher blocked punt out of end zone
Cle – Mack 11 pass from Kosar (Kauric kick)
Den – Jackson 16 run (Treadwell kick)
Den – FG Treadwell 25
Cle – Brennan 24 pass from Kosar (Kauric kick)
Cle – FG Kauric 30
A: 74,814 T: 3:06

WEEK 6 STANDINGS

AFC EAST	W	L	T	Pct.	PF	PA
Buffalo	4	1	0	.800	130	99
Miami	4	1	0	.800	108	73
Indianapolis	2	3	0	.400	81	108
N.Y. Jets	2	4	0	.333	107	148
New England	1	4	0	.200	80	152

AFC CENTRAL	W	L	T	Pct.	PF	PA
Cincinnati	4	2	0	.667	154	153
Houston	3	3	0	.500	146	125
Pittsburgh	3	3	0	.500	102	101
Cleveland	2	4	0	.333	98	139

AFC WEST	W	L	T	Pct.	PF	PA
L.A. Raiders	5	1	0	.833	123	90
Kansas City	4	2	0	.667	160	95
Denver	2	4	0	.333	141	161
San Diego	2	4	0	.333	114	108
Seattle	2	4	0	.333	125	128

NFC EAST	W	L	T	Pct.	PF	PA
N.Y. Giants	5	0	0	1.000	130	67
Washington	3	2	0	.600	121	75
Philadelphia	2	3	0	.400	123	119
Phoenix	2	3	0	.400	60	121
Dallas	2	4	0	.333	73	122

NFC CENTRAL	W	L	T	Pct.	PF	PA
Chicago	5	1	0	.833	142	75
Tampa Bay	4	2	0	.667	134	124
Detroit	2	4	0	.333	141	169
Green Bay	2	4	0	.333	103	146
Minnesota	1	5	0	.167	140	135

NFC WEST	W	L	T	Pct.	PF	PA
San Francisco	5	0	0	1.000	127	94
Atlanta	2	3	0	.400	137	139
New Orleans	2	3	0	.400	95	100
L.A. Rams	1	4	0	.250	120	149

RESULTS
N.Y. Giants 24, Washington 20
Chicago 38, L.A. Rams 9
New Orleans 25, Cleveland 20
L.A. Raiders 24, Seattle 17
Tampa Bay 26, Green Bay 14
Houston 48, Cincinnati 17
Kansas City 43, Detroit 24
Pittsburgh 34, Denver 17
San Francisco 45, Atlanta 35
San Diego 39, N.Y. Jets 3
Phoenix 20, Dallas 3
Philadelphia 32, Minnesota 24 (Monday night)
Open dates: Buffalo, Indianapolis, Miami, New England

SUNDAY, OCTOBER 14

N.Y. GIANTS 24, WASHINGTON 20—At RFK Stadium. The Giants used a big-play passing offense and took advantage of four Redskins turnovers to beat Washington for the fifth straight time. New York quarterback Phil Simms completed 13 of 22 passes, three of which went for more than 60 yards. The Redskins defense played tough, allowing only 57 yards on the ground and giving the offense a chance to pull within one point with 5:59 left. Washington stopped the Giants on their next possession, but the ensuing punt hit a Redskins blocker at the Washington five-yard line and allowed New York to kick a field goal for the final difference.

New York	0	7	14	3	–	24
Washington	3	0	10	7	–	20

Wash – FG Lohmiller 42
N.Y. – Baker 80 pass from Simms (Bahr kick)
Wash – FG Lohmiller 35
N.Y. – Anderson 5 run (Bahr kick)
Wash – Sanders 31 pass from Byner (Lohmiller kick)
N.Y. – Bavaro 2 pass from Simms (Bahr kick)
Wash – Riggs 1 run (Lohmiller kick)
N.Y. – FG Bahr 19
A: 54,737 T: 2:55

CHICAGO 38, L.A. RAMS 9—At Soldier Field. The Bears scored on their first four possessions as the Ram defense, ranked last in the league going into the game, looked helpless against the Chicago barrage. Bears quarterback Jim Harbaugh enjoyed his best passing day as a pro, completing 18 of 25 passes for 248 yards and two touchdowns. In the first half, Chicago converted seven out of seven third-down tries, including a 21-yard pass to running back Neal Anderson on a third-and-18 that set up the Bears' fourth touchdown.

Los Angeles	0	0	6	3	–	9
Chicago	14	14	3	7	–	38

Chi – Anderson 12 pass from Harbaugh (Butler kick)
Chi – Harbaugh 12 run (Butler kick)
Chi – Morris 18 pass from Harbaugh (Butler kick)
Chi – Muster 13 run (Butler kick)
Chi – FG Butler 27
L.A. – McGee 11 pass from Everett (kick failed)
L.A. – FG Lansford 35
Chi – Anderson 15 run (Butler kick)
A: 59,383 T: 2:51

NEW ORLEANS 25, CLEVELAND 20—At the Superdome. Quarterback Steve Walsh made his debut with the Saints a successful one as he relieved starter John Fourcade on New Orleans's third offensive series and led the Saints to a 25–6 lead that stood up in the face of a late Browns comeback. On Walsh's first series he directed a 14-play, 79-yard drive for a touchdown, hitting seven out of seven passes for 50 yards. He ended the day with 15 completions in 26 attempts for 243 yards and three touchdowns. Cleveland scored the second of two fourth-quarter touchdowns with 2:56 to play, but a 58-yard completion from Walsh to wide receiver Eric Martin on third-and-10 allowed the Saints to eat up the clock.

Cleveland	0	6	0	14	–	20
New Orleans	3	6	7	9	–	25

N.O. – FG Andersen 52
Cle – FG Kauric 37
N.O. – Hilliard 4 pass from Walsh (kick failed)
Cle – FG Kauric 39
N.O. – Turner 49 pass from Walsh (Andersen kick)
N.O. – Martin 13 pass from Walsh (Andersen kick)
N.O. – Safety, Massey blocked punt out of end zone
Cle – Slaughter 13 pass from Kosar (Kauric kick)
Cle – Mack 1 run (Kauric kick)
A: 68,608 T: 3:08

L.A. RAIDERS 24, SEATTLE 17—At Memorial Coliseum. Jay Schroeder's precision passing staked the Raiders to an early 21–0 lead, and Los Angeles held on to run coach Art Shell's home record to 10–0. The Raiders scored on their first three possessions with drives of 81, 80 and 48 yards, and at the half Schroeder was 14 of 17 for 167 yards and three touchdowns. Los Angeles defensive end Greg Townsend sacked Seahawk quarterback Dave Krieg twice and forced a Krieg fumble on the Raider six-yard line. Krieg ended the day with 22 completions in 36 attempts for 294 yards passing and two touchdowns.

Seattle	0	14	3	0	–	17
Los Angeles	7	14	0	3	–	24

L.A. – Smith 1 pass from Schroeder (Jaeger kick)
L.A. – Fernandez 3 pass from Schroeder (Jaeger kick)
L.A. – Horton 3 pass from Schroeder (Jaeger kick)
Sea – Skansi 5 pass from Krieg (Johnson kick)
Sea – Kane 31 pass from Krieg (Johnson kick)
Sea – FG Johnson 34
L.A. – FG Jaeger 22
A: 50,624 T: 2:52

TAMPA BAY 26, GREEN BAY 14—At Tampa Stadium. Packer quarterback Don Majkowski threw five interceptions, two of which were nabbed by cornerback Wayne Haddix, who returned one for a touchdown. Buccaneer quarterback Vinny Testaverde completed 17 of 29 passes for 292 yards, including a three-yarder to himself off a batted ball. Tampa Bay running back Gary Anderson was again the workhorse of the offense, accounting for 142 total yards on 11 rushes and four receptions. The Buccaneer defense held Green Bay to just 36 yards rushing. Packer wideout Sterling Sharpe caught seven passes for 139 yards.

Green Bay	0	0	14	0	–	14
Tampa Bay	3	13	10	0	–	26

T.B. – FG Christie 24
T.B. – FG Christie 32
T.B. – FG Christie 39
T.B. – Hall 14 pass from Testaverde (Christie kick)
T.B. – FG Christie 32
G.B. – Query recovered fumble in end zone (Jacke kick)
T.B. – Haddix 29 interception return (Christie kick)
G.B. – Fontenot 8 pass from Majkowski (Jacke kick)
A: 67,472 T: 3:05

HOUSTON 48, CINCINNATI 17—At the Astrodome. Oiler quarterback Warren Moon directed the run-and-shoot offense to perfection, throwing five touchdown passes to five different receivers as Houston avenged last season's 61–7 mauling by the Bengals. Moon connected on 21 of 33 attempts for 369 yards, 101 of which went to Ernest Givins. The Oiler defense also got into the scoring act as cornerback Richard Johnson intercepted a Boomer Esiason pass and returned it 30 yards for a touchdown. During the second and third quarters, Houston scored 31 unanswered points to break open a close game.

Cincinnati	7	3	7	0	–	17
Houston	7	24	7	10	–	48

Cin – Taylor 2 run (Breech kick)
Hou – Jones 33 pass from Moon (Zendejas kick)
Cin – FG Breech 29
Hou – Hill 33 pass from Moon (Zendejas kick)
Hou – Johnson 30 interception return (Zendejas kick)
Hou – Harris 42 pass from Moon (Zendejas kick)
Hou – FG Zendejas 22
Hou – Givins 11 pass from Moon (Zendejas kick)
Cin – Holman 5 pass from Esiason (Breech kick)
Hou – Jeffires 3 pass from Moon (Zendejas kick)
Hou – FG Zendejas 23
A: 53,501 T: 3:12

KANSAS CITY 43, DETROIT 24—At Arrowhead Stadium. Chiefs running back Barry Word set a club record for rushing as he ran for 200 yards and two touchdowns on 18 carries for an average of 11.1 yards per rush. Word broke away for runs of 45 and 53 yards, the latter going for a touchdown that made the score 36–17 and locked up the win for Kansas City. Christian Okoye also enjoyed a big day, rushing for 91 yards on 23 carries. Barry Sanders's rushing and receiving kept the Lions in the game; he ran for 90 yards and a touchdown and caught five passes for 135 yards and a touchdown. The Chiefs' 566 total yards on offense was the second best in team history.

Detroit	14	0	0	10	–	24
Kansas City	3	14	12	14	–	43

K.C. – FG Lowery 21
Det – Sanders 47 pass from Gagliano (Karlis kick)
Det – Sanders 13 run (Karlis kick)
K.C. – Hayes 1 pass from DeBerg (Lowery kick)
K.C. – Okoye 4 run (Lowery kick)
K.C. – FG Lowery 32
K.C. – Safety, Maas tackled Gagliano in end zone
K.C. – Okoye 1 run (Lowery kick)
Det – FG Karlis 21
K.C. – Word 53 run (Lowery kick)
Det – Wilder 8 pass from Ware (Karlis kick)
K.C. – Word 1 run (Lowery kick)
A: 74,312 T: 3:09

PITTSBURGH 34, DENVER 17—At Mile High Stadium. The combination of an injury-plagued Bronco defense and an emerging Steeler offense resulted in a Pittsburgh rout and Denver's third straight loss. Steeler quarterback Bubby Brister led the charge, completing 21 of 28 passes for 353 yards and four touchdowns. Rookie tight end Eric Green was on the receiving end of three of those touchdowns, and Louis Lipps caught nine of Brister's passes for 141 yards. The longest pass of Brister's career—a 90-yarder to running back Dwight Stone—didn't result in a touchdown or even a score, when Warren Williams fumbled at the goal line. The Broncos took an early 17–7 lead, but Pittsburgh touchdown drives of 55 and 65 yards erased the margin early in the third quarter as the crowd showered the home team with boos.

Pittsburgh	0	14	7	13	–	34
Denver	10	7	0	0	–	17

Den – Winder 1 run (Treadwell kick)
Den – FG Treadwell 24
Pitt – Lipps 6 pass from Brister (Anderson kick)
Den – Sewell 2 run (Treadwell kick)
Pitt – Green 3 pass from Brister (Anderson kick)
Pitt – Hoge 6 run (Anderson kick)
Pitt – Green 10 pass from Brister (kick failed)
Pitt – Green 3 pass from Brister (Anderson kick)
A: 74,285 T: 2:59

SAN FRANCISCO 45, ATLANTA 35—At Atlanta-Fulton County Stadium. The 49er battery of Joe Montana and Jerry Rice combined for five touchdowns as San Francisco built a big lead and held on to remain undefeated. Rice's touchdown receptions tied an NFL record, and Montana's 476 yards passing was the 10th-best total in NFL history. Rice ended the day with 13 catches for 225 yards, while Montana completed 32 of 49 with six touchdown tosses overall. The score was tied 14–14 midway through the second quarter when the Falcons failed to convert a fourth-down run at their own 42. San Francisco scored three plays later. As time expired in the first half, 49er kicker Mike Cofer hit a club-record 56-yard field goal. Two touchdown passes to Rice pushed the 49er advantage to 45–21 before Atlanta scored two fourth-quarter touchdowns for the final margin. Falcon wide receiver Andre Rison caught nine passes for 172 yards and two touchdowns.

San Francisco	14	17	7	7	–	45
Atlanta	7	14	0	14	–	35

S.F. – Rice 24 pass from Montana (Cofer kick)
Atl – Rison 75 pass from Miller (Davis kick)
S.F. – Rice 25 pass from Montana (Cofer kick)
Atl – Butler 62 blocked punt return (Davis kick)
S.F. – Sherrard 43 pass from Montana (Cofer kick)
S.F. – Rice 19 pass from Montana (Cofer kick)
Atl – Milling 5 pass from Miller (Davis kick)
S.F. – FG Cofer 56
S.F. – Rice 13 pass from Montana (Cofer kick)
S.F. – Rice 15 pass from Montana (Cofer kick)
Atl – Wilkins 3 pass from Miller (Davis kick)
Atl – Rison 13 pass from Campbell (Davis kick)
A: 57,921 T: 3:25

SAN DIEGO 39, N.Y. JETS 3—At Giants Stadium. The Charger defense stifled the Jets' offense, giving the San Diego offense a chance to show its steadiness as well as its explosiveness. New York gained just 148 total yards and converted only one of ten third-down plays. Charger running back Marion Butts rushed 26 times for 121 yards, 26 yards more than the entire Jet team. Backfield mate Rod Bernstine gained 80 yards on 11 carries. San Diego quarterback Billy Joe Tolliver completed 12 of 18 passes for 169 yards and one touchdown, with wide receiver Anthony Miller catching five passes for 100 yards. Jet punter Joe Prokop fumbled a snap in the first quarter that led to a safety and had to run on another punt attempt that set up a Charger touchdown.

San Diego	2	20	10	7	–	39
New York	3	0	0	0	–	3

S.D. – Safety, Grossman tackled O'Brien in end zone
N.Y. – FG Leahy 22
S.D. – Miller 29 pass from Tolliver (Carney kick)
S.D. – Butts 5 run (Carney kick)
S.D. – FG Carney 34
S.D. – FG Carney 42
S.D. – Butts 6 run (Carney kick)
S.D. – FG Carney 37
S.D. – Bernstine 40 run (Carney kick)
A: 63,311 T: 2:52

PHOENIX 20, DALLAS 3—At Sun Devil Stadium. Cardinals running back Johnny Johnson rushed for 120 yards, and the Cowboy offense gained only 85 total yards in a battle of NFC East also-rans. The margin would have been greater except for a fumble on the Dallas two-yard line by Johnson and a goal line stand when Dallas stopped running back Anthony Thompson three times from the one. The Phoenix defense chased quarterback Troy Aikman all over the field, sacking him four times and allowing him to complete only nine of 25 passes. Defensive end Freddie Joe Nunn had two sacks.

Dallas	0	0	3	0	–	3
Phoenix	7	3	0	10	–	20

Phoe – Thompson 1 run (Del Greco kick)
Phoe – FG Del Greco 28
Dall – FG Willis 37
Phoe – FG Del Greco 28
Phoe – Johnson 9 run (Del Greco kick)
A: 45,235 T: 2:59

MONDAY, OCTOBER 15

PHILADELPHIA 32, MINNESOTA 24—At Veterans Stadium. Trailing 24–15 with four minutes to play, the Eagles scored 17 points to beat the Vikings. The comeback started with a pass from Philadelphia quarterback Randall Cunningham that bounced off several players before Fred Barnett snagged it and ran it into the end zone for a 40-yard touchdown. A sack resulting in a lost fumble on the Vikings' next series led to a six-yard touchdown run by Eagle running back Anthony Toney. Philadelphia kicker Roger Ruzek completed the scoring outburst with a 19-yard field goal after an interception by Eagle cornerback William Frizzell. Cunningham scrambled 13 times for 90 yards.

Minnesota	7	14	0	3	–	24
Philadelphia	9	0	6	17	–	32

Phi – FG Ruzek 38
Phi – Williams 19 pass from Cunningham (kick blocked)
Minn – Carter 42 pass from Gannon (Igwebuike kick)
Minn – Fenney 1 run (Igwebuike kick)
Minn – Carter 78 pass from Gannon (Igwebuike kick)
Phi – FG Ruzek 30
Phi – FG Ruzek 29
Minn – FG Igwebuike 33
Phi – Barnett 40 pass from Cunningham (Ruzek kick)
Phi – Toney 6 run (Ruzek kick)
Phi – FG Ruzek 19
A: 66,296 T: 3:26

WEEK 7 STANDINGS

AFC EAST	W	L	T	Pct.	PF	PA
Buffalo	5	1	0	.833	160	126
Miami	5	1	0	.833	125	83
Indianapolis	2	4	0	.333	98	135
N.Y. Jets	2	5	0	.286	134	178
New England	1	5	0	.167	90	169

AFC CENTRAL	W	L	T	Pct.	PF	PA
Cincinnati	5	2	0	.714	188	166
Houston	4	3	0	.571	169	135
Pittsburgh	3	4	0	.429	109	128
Cleveland	2	5	0	.286	111	173

AFC WEST	W	L	T	Pct.	PF	PA
L.A. Raiders	6	1	0	.857	147	99
Kansas City	4	3	0	.571	167	114
Denver	3	4	0	.429	168	178
Seattle	3	4	0	.429	144	135
San Diego	2	5	0	.286	123	132

NFC EAST	W	L	T	Pct.	PF	PA
N.Y. Giants	6	0	0	1.000	150	86
Washington	4	2	0	.667	134	82
Dallas	3	4	0	.429	90	135
Philadelphia	2	4	0	.333	130	132
Phoenix	2	4	0	.333	79	141

NFC CENTRAL	W	L	T	Pct.	PF	PA
Chicago	5	1	0	.833	142	75
Tampa Bay	4	3	0	.571	147	141
Detroit	2	4	0	.333	141	169
Green Bay	2	4	0	.333	103	146
Minnesota	1	5	0	.167	140	135

NFC WEST	W	L	T	Pct.	PF	PA
San Francisco	6	0	0	1.000	154	101
Atlanta	2	4	0	.333	161	183
L.A. Rams	2	4	0	.333	164	173
New Orleans	2	4	0	.333	105	123

RESULTS
Miami 17, New England 10 (Thursday night)
Dallas 17, Tampa Bay 13
Washington 13, Philadelphia 7
Houston 23, New Orleans 10
San Francisco 27, Pittsburgh 7
Buffalo 30, N.Y. Jets 27
Denver 27, Indianapolis 17
N.Y. Giants 20, Phoenix 19
L.A. Raiders 24, San Diego 9
Seattle 19, Kansas City 7
L.A. Rams 44, Atlanta 24
Cincinnati 34, Cleveland 13 (Monday night)
Open dates: Chicago, Detroit, Green Bay, Minnesota

THURSDAY, OCTOBER 18

MIAMI 17, NEW ENGLAND 10—At Joe Robbie Stadium. Dolphin wide receiver Mark Clayton caught a 36-yard pass from Dan Marino in the third quarter to set up the two-yard touchdown run by Sammie Smith that provided Miami with the winning margin. The Patriots cut the lead to 17–10 on a Marc Wilson-to-George Adams touchdown pass in the fourth quarter but were held on their next possession when Miami linebacker David Griggs stopped Wilson on a quarterback sneak on fourth-and-one. In the second quarter the Dolphins' Mark Higgs blocked a punt and returned it for a touchdown to give Miami a 10–3 lead. The Dolphin defense held the Patriots to 49 yards rushing.

New England	0	3	0	7	—	10
Miami	0	10	7	0	—	17

N.E. — FG Staurovsky 41
Mia — FG Stoyanovich 47
Mia — Higgs 19 blocked punt return (Stoyanovich kick)
Mia — Smith 2 run (Stoyanovich kick)
N.E. — Adams 4 pass from Wilson (Staurovsky kick)
A: 62,630 T: 3:07

SUNDAY, OCTOBER 21

DALLAS 17, TAMPA BAY 13—At Tampa Stadium. Cowboy quarterback Troy Aikman hit wide receiver Michael Irvin deep in the left corner of the end zone for a 28-yard touchdown pass with 23 seconds remaining to give Dallas a two-game season sweep of the Buccaneers. The Cowboy offense was ineffectual until the final drive, which began after Tampa Bay went up 13–10 with 1:56 remaining. Dallas cornerback Issiac Holt had two interceptions, one of which he returned 64 yards for a touchdown in the fourth quarter to tie the game at 10. Cowboy linebacker Ken Norton Jr. was the defensive star, totaling 10 tackles, one sack and one fumble recovery. Overall, the Dallas defense sacked Buccaneer quarterback Vinny Testaverde six times, with defensive tackle Danny Noonan and defensive end Tony Tolbert getting two sacks apiece.

Dallas	0	0	3	14	—	17
Tampa Bay	3	7	0	3	—	13

T.B. — FG Christie 23
T.B. — Peebles 3 pass from Testaverde (Christie kick)
Dall — FG Willis 24
Dall — Holt 64 interception return (Willis kick)
T.B. — FG Christie 32
Dall — Irvin 28 pass from Aikman (Willis kick)
A: 68,315 T: 2:57

WASHINGTON 13, PHILADELPHIA 7—At RFK Stadium. The Redskins defense kept Eagle quarterback Randall Cunningham in check with five sacks—two by cornerback A.J. Johnson—and limited the other Philadelphia backs to 40 yards rushing in a frustrating day for the Eagle offense. In the second quarter Cunningham drove Philadelphia from its own one-yard line to the Washington 11, only to come up empty as Roger Ruzek missed a field goal attempt. On the Redskins' next possession, they drove 80 yards in six plays for a touchdown. The Eagles' only touchdown came with 43 seconds remaining, when Cunningham hit Fred Barnett with a nine-yard scoring pass. The Redskins offense was erratic as quarterback Stan Humphries hit only 14 of 31 passes and kicker Chip Lohmiller made only two of six field goal attempts. Defensive tackle Jerome Brown of the Eagles had 10 tackles.

Philadelphia	0	0	0	7	—	7
Washington	0	7	0	6	—	13

Wash — Riggs 1 run (Lohmiller kick)
Wash — FG Lohmiller 33
Wash — FG Lohmiller 39
Phil — Barnett 9 pass from Cunningham (Ruzek kick)
A: 53,567 T: 3:10

HOUSTON 23, NEW ORLEANS 10—At the Astrodome. The Oiler defense stifled the Saints, with linebacker Johnny Meads accounting for nine tackles, five assists, 1.5 sacks, three forced fumbles and a deflected pass. Defensive end Sean Jones was the other Houston star, blocking a field goal attempt, registering two sacks and forcing a fumble. The New Orleans defense took away the big play from the Oilers' run-and-shoot offense as quarterback Warren Moon threw for only 202 yards, more than 100 yards below his average. His counterpart for the Saints, Steve Walsh, completed 22 of 39 passes for 292 yards. Houston kicker Tony Zendejas suffered a broken fibula following a kickoff.

New Orleans	3	0	0	7	—	10
Houston	0	10	10	3	—	23

N.O. — FG Andersen 20
Hou — White 6 pass from Moon (Zendejas kick)
Hou — FG Zendejas 43
Hou — White 1 run (Zendejas kick)
Hou — FG Zendejas 45
N.O. — Brenner 31 pass from Walsh (Andersen kick)
Hou — FG Zendejas 33
A: 57,908 T: 3:08

SAN FRANCISCO 27, PITTSBURGH 7—At Candlestick Park. The 49ers, after taking a 13–7 lead on a Mike Cofer field goal in the third quarter, recovered the ensuing kickoff, which the Steelers left unfielded, and scored on a one-yard run by Tom Rathman three plays later to break open a close game. Pittsburgh's defense held Joe Montana in check with only 157 yards passing but allowed running back Dexter Carter to gain 90 yards rushing and 57 yards receiving. For the first time all season, the 49ers accumulated more than 100 yards on the ground. In the fourth quarter, San Francisco defensive end Charles Haley had sacks on back-to-back plays, the second one causing the fumble that led to the 49ers' final touchdown.

Pittsburgh	7	0	0	0	—	7
San Francisco	0	10	10	7	—	27

Pitt — Bell 2 pass from Brister (Anderson kick)
S.F. — FG Cofer 39
S.F. — Sherrard 5 pass from Montana (Cofer kick)
S.F. — FG Cofer 20
S.F. — Rathman 1 run (Cofer kick)
S.F. — Rathman 1 run (Cofer kick)
A: 64,301 T: 2:47

BUFFALO 30, N.Y. JETS 27—At Rich Stadium. Jim Kelly's fourth touchdown pass, a 14-yarder to fullback Jamie Mueller with 19 seconds left, gave the Bills their third consecutive fourth-quarter come-from-behind win. The winning score was set up by a 16-yard reception to the Jets' 13-yard line by Andre Reed on a third-and-10 play. New York held Buffalo to minus 10 yards in the first quarter and built a 21–7 second-quarter lead before allowing Buffalo to score twice in the final two minutes of the half to cut the margin to 21–17. Kelly finished the day with 19 completions in 32 attempts for 297 yards. The victory was the Bills' seventh straight over the Jets.

New York	7	14	3	3	—	27
Buffalo	0	17	7	6	—	30

N.Y. — McNeil 5 run (Leahy kick)
N.Y. — Boyer 1 pass from O'Brien (Leahy kick)
Buff — Reed 19 pass from Kelly (Norwood kick)
N.Y. — Toon 19 pass from O'Brien (Leahy kick)
Buff — Reed 14 pass from Kelly (Norwood kick)
Buff — FG Norwood 29
N.Y. — FG Leahy 28
Buff — Lofton 60 pass from Kelly (Norwood kick)
N.Y. — FG Leahy 25
Buff — Mueller 14 pass from Kelly (kick failed)
A: 79,002 T: 3:06

DENVER 27, INDIANAPOLIS 17—At the Hoosier Dome. Playing in his first game after a long holdout and suspension, Colts running back Eric Dickerson took the field to a chorus of boos that quickly changed to cheers after his first carry, an 11-yarder that moved him past O.J. Simpson to sixth on the alltime rushing list. Dickerson's presence was not enough to overcome the passing of Bronco quarterback John Elway, who threw for 317 yards and two touchdowns to help Denver pull away in the fourth quarter. Indianapolis quarterback Jack Trudeau also threw for more than 300 yards, finishing with 24 completions in 39 attempts for 312 yards and two touchdowns. Jessie Hester was his favorite target, catching eight passes for 152 yards.

Denver	7	10	0	10	—	27
Indianapolis	3	7	0	7	—	17

Den — Nattiel 52 pass from Elway (Treadwell kick)
Ind — FG Biasucci 32
Den — Jackson 5 pass from Elway (Treadwell kick)
Den — FG Treadwell 39
Ind — Johnson 1 pass from Trudeau (Biasucci kick)
Ind — Hester 5 pass from Trudeau (Biasucci kick)
Den — FG Treadwell 42
Den — Sewell 4 run (Treadwell kick)
A: 59,850 T: 3:06

N.Y. GIANTS 20, PHOENIX 19—At Giants Stadium. Trailing 19–10 with 5:38 remaining, the Giants mounted a comeback behind backup quarterback Jeff Hostetler to pull out the win. Hostetler, who took over for injured starter Phil Simms late in the first quarter, threw a 38-yard touchdown pass to a diving Stephen Baker to narrow the margin to two points with 3:21 left. After New York stopped the Cardinals on the next series, Hostetler completed passes of 26 yards to Mark Ingram and 18 yards to Lionel Manuel to set up the winning field goal by Matt Bahr as time expired. Cardinals running back Johnny Johnson gained 108 yards on 30 carries, the first time in 21 games the Giants defense had allowed an opposing player to go more than 100 yards. Defensive tackle Ken Harvey of the Cardinals had nine tackles, three sacks and one fumble recovery.

Phoenix	3	7	6	3	—	19
New York	7	3	0	10	—	20

N.Y. — Anderson 4 run (Bahr kick)
Phoe — FG Del Greco 39
N.Y. — FG Bahr 34
Phoe — Sharpe 1 pass from Rosenbach (Del Greco kick)
Phoe — FG Del Greco 18
Phoe — FG Del Greco 34
Phoe — FG Del Greco 45
N.Y. — Baker 38 pass from Hostetler (Bahr kick)
N.Y. — FG Bahr 40
A: 76,518 T: 2:56

L.A. RAIDERS 24, SAN DIEGO 9—At Jack Murphy Stadium. Bo Jackson, his baseball duties done, made his football debut an effective one by rushing for 53 yards on 12 carries and scoring two touchdowns on runs of five and seven yards. His first touchdown broke a 3–3 tie in the second quarter and came after an eight-yard punt by John Kidd gave the Raiders the ball at the San Diego 35. Jackson shared the rushing load with Marcus Allen, who ran for 45 yards and caught three passes for 50 yards. The Chargers penetrated the Los Angeles 20-yard line four times, but the Raider defense allowed them only three field goals. Raider quarterback Jay Schroeder completed 11 passes to five different receivers for 176 yards and one touchdown. San Diego running back Marion Butts gained 76 yards on 16 carries, but only 23 of those yards came in the second half.

Los Angeles	0	10	7	7	—	24
San Diego	3	3	3	0	—	9

S.D. — FG Carney 27
L.A. — FG Jaeger 24
L.A. — Jackson 5 run (Jaeger kick)
S.D. — FG Carney 37
L.A. — Jackson 7 run (Jaeger kick)
S.D. — FG Carney 37
L.A. — Gault 8 pass from Schroeder (Jaeger kick)
A: 60,569 T: 2:48

SEATTLE 19, KANSAS CITY 7—At the Kingdome. Seahawk kicker Norm Johnson, who had made only seven of his past 12 attempts, kicked four field goals, two in the final 10 minutes, to help Seattle to a win. Seahawks quarterback Dave Krieg threw four interceptions, but the Seattle defense held the Chiefs offense in check, allowing running backs Christian Okoye and Barry Word to gain only 66 yards. Seahawk running backs Derrick Fenner and John L. Williams combined for 128 yards on the ground. On defense, safety Nesby Glasgow was everywhere, making six tackles, one sack and one fumble recovery.

Kansas City	0	7	0	0	—	7
Seattle	0	3	3	13	—	19

K.C. — Birden 33 pass from DeBerg (Lowery kick)
Sea — FG Johnson 39
Sea — FG Johnson 27
Sea — FG Johnson 39
Sea — FG Johnson 43
Sea — Williams 4 run (Johnson kick)
A: 60,358 T: 3:06

L.A. RAMS 44, ATLANTA 24—At Anaheim Stadium. The Rams came back from a 10–0 first quarter deficit and scored 20 straight points in the second quarter on the way to a rout of the Falcons. At one point the Rams scored on eight consecutive possessions, led by the running of Cleveland Gary, who finished with 102 yards rushing, and the passing of Jim Everett, who completed 24 of 38 passes for 302 yards and three touchdowns. Los Angeles receiver Henry Ellard caught six passes for 109 yards and a touchdown, but Atlanta's Andre Rison bested him with five catches for 161 yards and two touchdowns. The Ram defense broke through for four sacks.

Atlanta	10	0	7	7	—	24
Los Angeles	0	20	14	10	—	44

Atl — FG Davis 41
Atl — Dixon 5 pass from Miller (Davis kick)
L.A. — Gary 23 run (Lansford kick)
L.A. — FG Lansford 46
L.A. — Johnson 1 pass from Everett (Lansford kick)
L.A. — FG Lansford 24
Atl — Rison 71 pass from Miller (Davis kick)
L.A. — Ellard 35 pass from Everett (Lansford kick)
L.A. — Anderson 37 pass from Everett (Lansford kick)
L.A. — Gary 1 run (Lansford kick)
L.A. — FG Lansford 32
Atl — Rison 14 pass from Campbell (Davis kick)
A: 54,761 T: 3:07

MONDAY, OCTOBER 22

CINCINNATI 34, CLEVELAND 13—At Cleveland Stadium. The Bengals relied on a strong running game and two touchdown passes from quarterback Boomer Esiason to bury the Browns. Esiason completed only seven of 17 passes for 85 yards, but Cincinnati ran for 233 total yards as the rushing load was shared evenly between running backs Harold Green with 75 yards, Craig Taylor with 73 and James Brooks with 63. Ickey Woods made an appearance in the Bengals' backfield for the first time since major knee surgery last season, scoring a short touchdown to cap the scoring in the fourth quarter. A one-yard touchdown run by Cleveland running back Leroy Hoard as the second quarter ended pulled the Browns within four points, but Cincinnati controlled the ball with its ground game in the second half and never let Cleveland back in the game. Browns QB Bernie Kosar continued to have his troubles, suffering four sacks and two interceptions.

Cincinnati	7	10	3	14	—	34
Cleveland	3	10	0	0	—	13

Cin — Holman 19 pass from Esiason (Breech kick)
Cle — FG Kauric 21
Cin — Brooks 28 run (Breech kick)
Cin — FG Breech 20
Cle — FG Kauric 30
Cle — Hoard 1 run (Kauric kick)
Cin — FG Breech 21
Cin — Barber 2 pass from Esiason (Breech kick)
Cin — Woods 1 run (Breech kick)
A: 78,567 T: 3:05

WEEK 8 STANDINGS

FC EAST	W	L	T	Pct.	PF	PA
uffalo	6	1	0	.857	187	136
iami	6	1	0	.857	152	90
.Y. Jets	3	5	0	.375	151	190
idianapolis	2	5	0	.286	105	162
ew England	1	6	0	.143	100	196

FC CENTRAL	W	L	T	Pct.	PF	PA
incinnati	5	3	0	.625	205	204
ouston	4	4	0	.500	181	152
ittsburgh	4	4	0	.500	150	138
leveland	2	6	0	.250	128	193

FC WEST	W	L	T	Pct.	PF	PA
.A. Raiders	6	1	0	.857	147	99
ansas City	4	3	0	.571	167	114
enver	3	4	0	.429	168	178
eattle	3	4	0	.429	144	135
an Diego	3	5	0	.375	164	142

FC EAST	W	L	T	Pct.	PF	PA
.Y. Giants	7	0	0	1.000	171	96
ashington	4	3	0	.571	144	103
hiladelphia	3	4	0	.429	151	152
allas	3	5	0	.375	110	156
hoenix	2	5	0	.286	100	172

FC CENTRAL	W	L	T	Pct.	PF	PA
hicago	6	1	0	.857	173	96
ampa Bay	4	4	0	.500	157	182
etroit	3	4	0	.429	168	179
reen Bay	3	4	0	.429	127	156
innesota	1	6	0	.143	150	159

FC WEST	W	L	T	Pct.	PF	PA
an Francisco	7	0	0	1.000	174	118
tlanta	3	4	0	.429	199	200
.A. Rams	2	5	0	.286	174	214
ew Orleans	2	5	0	.286	115	150

ESULTS
hiladelphia 21, Dallas 20
an Francisco 20, Cleveland 17
hicago 31, Phoenix 21
tlanta 38, Cincinnati 17
an Diego 41, Tampa Bay 10
etroit 27, New Orleans 10
.Y. Jets 17, Houston 12
uffalo 27, New England 10
iami 27, Indianapolis 7
.Y. Giants 21, Washington 10
reen Bay 24, Minnesota 10
ittsburgh 41, L.A. Rams 10 (Monday night)
pen dates: Denver, L.A. Raiders, Kansas City, Seattle

SUNDAY, OCTOBER 28

HILADELPHIA 21, DALLAS 20—At Texas Stadium. After wo fourth-quarter touchdowns put the Cowboys up 20–14, Eagle uarterback Randall Cunningham directed a 13-play, 85-yard drive hat ended with a 10-yard touchdown pass to leaping wide receiver alvin Williams with 44 seconds left to give Philadelphia the win. he second of Dallas's two touchdowns came with 4:02 remaining n a three-yard run by Emmitt Smith after Issiac Holt blocked an agle punt, the first punt blocked by Dallas since 1987. Cowboy ght end Jay Novacek caught seven passes for 105 yards and a ouchdown.

Philadelphia	7	0	0	14	–	21
Dallas	0	3	3	14	–	20

hi – Toney 10 pass from Cunningham (Ruzek kick)
)all – FG Willis 43
)all – FG Willis 43
hi – Sherman 19 run (Ruzek kick)
)all – Novacek 29 pass from Aikman (Willis kick)
)all – Smith 3 run (Willis kick)
hi – Williams 10 pass from Cunningham (Ruzek kick)
: 62,605 T: 3:10

SAN FRANCISCO 20, CLEVELAND 17—At Candlestick Park. The Browns scored two fourth-quarter touchdowns to overcome a 7–3 lead but saw their comeback bid end when San Francisco icker Mike Cofer booted a 45-yard field goal with five seconds emaining to give the 49ers the win. Joe Montana had a rare subpar day, completing 17 of 37 passes for 185 yards with two nterceptions, but he still set up the game-winning kick by hitting vide receiver Mike Sherrard with a 35-yard completion on third-and-14. Sherrard broke his right ankle on the catch, the the third ime he had broken a bone in that leg. Browns backup quarterback Mike Pagel replaced an ineffective Bernie Kosar in the fourth quarter and passed for Cleveland's two touchdowns. Safety Ronnie ott led the 49er defense with four tackles, one interception and a umble recovery.

Cleveland	0	0	3	14	–	17
San Francisco	0	14	3	3	–	20

S.F. – Rice 14 pass from Montana (Cofer kick)
S.F. – Rathman 1 run (Cofer kick)
Cle – FG Kauric 45
S.F. – FG Cofer 40
Cle – Slaughter 11 pass from Pagel (Kauric kick)
Cle – Newsome 4 pass from Pagel (Kauric kick)
S.F. – FG Cofer 45
A: 63,672 T: 3:07

CHICAGO 31, PHOENIX 21—At Sun Devil Stadium. The Bears umped out to a 28–0 lead, then held off a Cardinals comeback to secure the win on a scorching 93° day. The crucial play was a disputed in-the-grasp sack midway through the fourth quarter, which prevented Phoenix from getting a first down at the Chicago 20-yard line. The Bears defense allowed 331 total yards but stopped the Cardinals when it counted, limiting them to only one of seven third-down conversions. The Bears running backs carried the offensive load: Neal Anderson ran 20 times for 74 yards and two touchdowns and caught three passes for 55 yards, while Brad Muster rushed 12 times for 99 yards. Chicago quarterback Jim Harbaugh completed all six of his passes in the first half, including a short pass that wide receiver Ron Morris took for a 67-yard touchdown.

Chicago	7	21	0	3	–	31
Phoenix	0	7	7	7	–	21

Chi – Anderson 2 run (Butler kick)
Chi – Harbaugh 1 run (Butler kick)
Chi – Morris 67 pass from Harbaugh (Butler kick)
Chi – Anderson 2 run (Butler kick)
Phoe – Smith 3 pass from Rosenbach (Del Greco kick)
Phoe – Johnson 21 run (Del Greco kick)
Chi – FG Butler 33
Phoe – Green 40 pass from Rosenbach (Del Greco kick)
A: 71,233 T: 3:04

ATLANTA 38, CINCINNATI 17—At Atlanta-Fulton County Stadium. Falcon linebacker Scott Case intercepted a pass and recovered a fumble to set up two first-half touchdowns and give Atlanta an early lead, then Deion Sanders returned a punt 79 yards for a touchdown early in the third quarter to break open the game. Atlanta quarterback Chris Miller completed 13 of 18 passes for 124 yards and two touchdowns. Linebacker Jessie Tuggle of the Falcons was in on 13 tackles. The Bengals, playing their fifth straight road game, gained only 84 yards rushing and committed five turnovers.

Cincinnati	0	7	3	7	–	17
Atlanta	10	7	14	7	–	38

Atl – FG Davis 27
Atl – Rozier 1 run (Davis kick)
Cin – Brooks 6 run (Breech kick)
Atl – Dixon 3 pass from Miller (Davis kick)
Atl – Sanders 79 punt return (Davis kick)
Cin – FG Breech 35
Atl – Dixon 11 pass from Miller (Davis kick)
Cin – Brown 4 pass from Esiason (Breech kick)
Atl – Broussard 50 run (Davis kick)
A: 53,214 T: 2:52

SAN DIEGO 41, TAMPA BAY 10—At Jack Murphy Stadium. The Chargers defense caused seven turnovers and running back Marion Butts rushed for 73 yards and three touchdowns in a San Diego rout. Backfield mate Rod Bernstine added 75 yards and one touchdown on 15 carries. The Buccaneers were able to gain only 38 yards rushing and 157 total yards behind backup quarterback Chris Chandler, who started in place of the injured Vinny Testaverde. The Charger offense scored on its first four possessions in running up its highest point total since 1987. On defense, cornerback Gill Byrd had two interceptions, and defensive end Burt Grossman had two sacks.

Tampa Bay	0	7	3	0	–	10
San Diego	7	17	0	17	–	41

S.D. – Butts 1 run (Carney kick)
S.D. – Miller 31 pass from Tolliver (Carney kick)
T.B. – Carrier 68 pass from Chandler (Christie kick)
S.D. – FG Carney 28
S.D. – Butts 2 run (Carney kick)
T.B. – FG Christie 48
S.D. – Bernstine 20 run (Carney kick)
S.D. – FG Carney 27
S.D. – Butts 5 run (Carney kick)
A: 40,653 T: 2:53

DETROIT 27, NEW ORLEANS 10—At the Superdome. By committing eight turnovers—seven in the second half—the Saints turned a close game into a walkover for the Lions, who scored twenty unanswered points after New Orleans took a 10–7 halftime lead. Detroit made plenty of its own mistakes in the first half, including a fumbled kickoff, a dropped interception, a holding penalty on a kickoff return that nullified a touchdown and a muffed punt that led to the Saints' only TD. The Lions scored all of their points following turnovers, but their offense was far from sharp. Running back Barry Sanders carried the ball 12 times for only 10 yards, and quarterback Rodney Peete, starting his first game since he suffered a leg injury on Sept. 30, was sacked five times. The Saints also held the Lions to one of 10 third-down conversions. The most effective Detroit player on offense was wide receiver Robert Clark, who caught six passes for 127 yards.

Detroit	0	7	10	10	–	27
New Orleans	7	3	0	0	–	10

N.O. – Martin 6 pass from Walsh (Andersen kick)
Det – Clark 5 pass from Peete (Karlis kick)
N.O. – FG Andersen 47
Det – FG Karlis 25
Det – Williams 53 fumble return (Karlis kick)
Det – FG Karlis 39
Det – Sanders 2 run (Karlis kick)
A: 64,368 T: 2:53

N.Y. JETS 17, HOUSTON 12—At the Astrodome. Early in the fourth quarter, Jet defensive end Darrell Davis sacked Oiler quarterback Warren Moon in the end zone, forcing a fumble that Davis recovered for the touchdown that put the Jets up for good. Houston outgained New York 425 to 229, but the Jets held the ball when they had to, driving 50 yards in 6:01 to set up a Pat Leahy field goal with only 44 seconds remaining. Leahy's counterpart for the Oilers, Teddy Garcia, who was substituting for injured regular Tony Zendejas, missed two field goals and an extra point. Wide receiver Al Toon of the Jets caught seven passes for 119 yards, including a 42-yard touchdown. Toon also made a crucial 28-yard reception on a third-and-14 play during the Jets' final scoring drive. The New York defense, which had only 12 sacks going into the game, dumped Moon five times.

New York	0	7	0	10	–	17
Houston	3	3	6	0	–	12

Hou – FG Garcia 42
N.Y. – Toon 42 pass from O'Brien (Leahy kick)
Hou – FG Garcia 49
Hou – Jeffires 9 pass from Moon (kick failed)
N.Y. – Davis recovered fumble in the end zone (Leahy kick)
N.Y. – FG Leahy 32
A: 56,337 T: 2:53

BUFFALO 27, NEW ENGLAND 10—At Foxboro Stadium. Bills running back Thurman Thomas rushed for 136 yards and one touchdown as Buffalo powered past the Patriots. On the Bills' first possession, quarterback Jim Kelly completed five passes for 60 yards before handing the ball to running back Don Smith for a one-yard touchdown run. New England answered with a 66-yard drive to the Buffalo five-yard line, but Bills cornerback Nate Odomes ended the Patriots' scoring threat with a diving interception in the end zone. New England running back John Stephens rushed for 93 yards on 19 carries. Buffalo's defense sacked veteran quarterback Steve Grogan three times and pressured him into two interceptions and a sub-50-% passing day.

Buffalo	7	7	13	0	–	27
New England	0	3	0	7	–	10

Buff – Smith 1 run (Norwood kick)
Buff – Thomas 3 run (Norwood kick)
N.E. – FG Staurovsky 32
Buff – FG Norwood 35
Buff – FG Norwood 35
Buff – McKeller 20 pass from Kelly (Norwood kick)
N.E. – Martin 19 pass from Grogan (Staurovsky kick)
A: 51,959 T: 2:43

MIAMI 27, INDIANAPOLIS 7—At the Hoosier Dome. The Dolphins defense scored the opening touchdown—a fumble recovery in the end zone by linebacker Cliff Odom—and knocked Colt quarterbacks Jack Trudeau and Jeff George out of the game in crushing Indianapolis. Taking over at quarterback for the Colts was 40-year-old Joe Ferguson, who finished with two completions in eight attempts and had two passes intercepted. The Miami offense kept the ball for all but 18:55 in racking up 206 yards rushing and 23 first downs, while the Miami defense allowed the Colts only 31 yards rushing and seven first downs, just one of which came on a third-down play. Dolphin quarterback Dan Marino completed 15 of his first 17 passes and finished at 21 of 29 for 161 yards. Miami's defense held Eric Dickerson to 27 yards on 10 carries.

Miami	10	7	3	7	–	27
Indianapolis	0	7	0	0	–	7

Mia – Odom recovered fumble in end zone (Stoyanovich kick)
Mia – FG Stoyanovich 34
Ind – Goode 54 fumble return (Biasucci kick)
Mia – Jensen 5 pass from Marino (Stoyanovich kick)
Mia – FG Stoyanovich 53
Mia – Paige 2 run (Stoyanovich kick)
A: 59,213 T: 2:41

N.Y. GIANTS 21, WASHINGTON 10—At Giants Stadium. Two fourth-quarter interceptions by the Giants ended the Redskins' hopes of victory as New York swept its season series with Washington. The Redskins had closed an early lead by the Giants to 14–10 and had driven to the New York three-yard line with 6:31 left when safety Greg Jackson intercepted a pass that deflected off the hands of running back Earnest Byner. Less than two minutes later, cornerback Everson Walls picked off a pass—his second of the day—and returned it for a touchdown to seal the victory. Giants running back Ottis Anderson rushed for 92 yards on 24 carries, and quarterback Phil Simms directed the steady offense, completing 15 of 24 passes for 145 yards and two touchdowns.

Washington	0	3	7	0	–	10
New York	0	14	0	7	–	21

N.Y. – Baker 4 pass from Simms (Bahr kick)
N.Y. – Bavaro 13 pass from Simms (Bahr kick)
Wash – FG Lohmiller 45
Wash – Humphries 5 run (Lohmiller kick)
N.Y. – Walls 28 interception return (Bahr kick)
A: 75,321 T: 2:44

GREEN BAY 24, MINNESOTA 10—At Milwaukee County Stadium. Viking quarterback Rich Gannon threw five interceptions, two of which led to touchdowns, as the Packers defeated the troubled Vikings. Herschel Walker, who has been the focus of much of the criticism of Minnesota, gained six yards on three carries and fumbled the first time he touched the ball, a miscue that led to another Green Bay touchdown. Wide receiver Anthony Carter shone in defeat for the Vikings, catching nine passes for 141 yards, including a touchdown late in the game that deflected off defensive back Mark Lee. The Packers were leading only 10–3 late in the third quarter when Green Bay defensive lineman Shawn Patterson deflected a Gannon pass and returned it nine yards for a touchdown. Quarterback Don Majkowski was efficient, totaling 11 completions in 22 attempts for 203 yards and scoring one touchdown on a six-yard run in the fourth quarter that put the game out of reach.

Minnesota	0	3	0	7	–	10
Green Bay	3	7	7	7	–	24

G.B. – FG Jacke 35
Minn – FG Igwebuike 20
G.B. – Thompson 12 run (Jacke kick)
G.B. – Patterson 9 interception return (Jacke kick)
G.B. – Majkowski 6 run (Jacke kick)
Minn – Carter 49 pass from Gannon (Igwebuike kick)
A: 55,125 T: 2:59

MONDAY, OCTOBER 29

PITTSBURGH 41, L.A. RAMS 10—At Three Rivers Stadium. The Rams' Gaston Green returned the opening kickoff 100 yards for a touchdown, but it was L.A.'s only one of the night as the Steelers answered with a 75-yard touchdown drive and then pulled away for the easy victory. After Los Angeles closed to 14–10 early in the second quarter, Pittsburgh scored the last 27 points of the game. Steeler quarterback Bubby Brister threw four touchdown passes, and running backs Warren Williams, Barry Foster and Merril Hoge rushed for better than 50 yards each. Pittsburgh's defense intercepted Ram quarterback Jim Everett twice and held him to 15-of-34 passing for 176 yards. Steeler return man Rod Woodson set up two field goals with kickoff returns of 49 and 45 yards.

Los Angeles	7	3	0	0	–	10
Pittsburgh	14	3	10	14	–	41

L.A. – Green 100 kickoff return (Lansford kick)
Pitt – Hoge 6 pass from Brister (Anderson kick)
Pitt – Green 17 pass from Brister (Anderson kick)
L.A. – FG Lansford 32
Pitt – FG Anderson 42
Pitt – FG Anderson 30
Pitt – Hoge 1 run (Anderson kick)
Pitt – Stone 8 pass from Brister (Anderson kick)
Pitt – Hoge 2 pass from Brister (Anderson kick)
A: 56,466 T: 3:00

WEEK 9 STANDINGS

AFC EAST	W	L	T	Pct.	PF	PA
Buffalo	7	1	0	.875	229	136
Miami	7	1	0	.875	175	93
N.Y. Jets	4	5	0	.444	175	199
Indianapolis	2	6	0	.250	112	186
New England	1	7	0	.125	120	244

AFC CENTRAL	W	L	T	Pct.	PF	PA
Cincinnati	5	4	0	.556	212	225
Pittsburgh	5	4	0	.556	171	147
Houston	4	5	0	.444	194	169
Cleveland	2	7	0	.222	128	235

AFC WEST	W	L	T	Pct.	PF	PA
L.A. Raiders	6	2	0	.750	154	108
Kansas City	5	3	0	.625	176	121
San Diego	4	5	0	.444	195	156
Denver	3	5	0	.375	190	205
Seattle	3	5	0	.375	158	166

NFC EAST	W	L	T	Pct.	PF	PA
N.Y. Giants	8	0	0	1.000	195	103
Washington	5	3	0	.625	185	141
Philadelphia	4	4	0	.500	199	172
Dallas	3	6	0	.333	119	180
Phoenix	2	6	0	.250	103	195

NFC CENTRAL	W	L	T	Pct.	PF	PA
Chicago	7	1	0	.875	199	102
Tampa Bay	4	5	0	.444	163	208
Detroit	3	5	0	.375	206	220
Green Bay	3	5	0	.375	147	180
Minnesota	2	6	0	.250	177	181

NFC WEST	W	L	T	Pct.	PF	PA
San Francisco	8	0	0	1.000	198	138
Atlanta	3	5	0	.375	208	221
L.A. Rams	3	5	0	.375	191	227
New Orleans	3	5	0	.375	136	157

RESULTS
Kansas City 9, L.A. Raiders 7
N.Y. Jets 24, Dallas 9
New Orleans 21, Cincinnati 7
Buffalo 42, Cleveland 0
San Francisco 24, Green Bay 20
Chicago 26, Tampa Bay 6
Washington 41, Detroit 38 (OT)
L.A. Rams 17, Houston 13
Miami 23, Phoenix 3
Philadelphia 48, New England 20
Pittsburgh 21, Atlanta 9
San Diego 31, Seattle 14
Minnesota 27, Denver 22
N.Y. Giants 24, Indianapolis 7 (Monday night)

SUNDAY, NOVEMBER 4

KANSAS CITY 9, L.A. RAIDERS 7—At Arrowhead Stadium. In bitterly cold weather with freezing rain, the Chiefs and the Raiders relied on their defenses in an AFC West slugfest. Kansas City totaled negative yardage in the first quarter yet held a 6–0 lead as Nick Lowery kicked two field goals after Los Angeles turnovers, one a blocked punt and the other a Bo Jackson fumble. Neither offense had success until the fourth quarter, when the Raiders scored their only touchdown and the Chiefs kicked the winning field goal. Kansas City running back Christian Okoye converted two critical third-down plays in the fourth quarter to help the Chiefs run time off the clock.

Los Angeles	0	0	0	7	—	7
Kansas City	6	0	0	3	—	9

K.C. — FG Lowery 36
K.C. — FG Lowery 48
L.A. — Smith 2 run (Jaeger kick)
K.C. — FG Lowery 41
A: 70,951 T: 3:05

N.Y. JETS 24, DALLAS 9—At Giants Stadium. Jet rookie Terance Mathis tied a league record with a 98-yard punt return for a TD to give New York a second-quarter boost on the way to a win over the Cowboys. The play seemed to spark the Jets, who came alive in the second half, scoring their first two fourth-quarter TDs of the season. Dallas dominated the first half, holding New York to two first downs and 46 total yards. After the Cowboys pulled within one point in the fourth quarter, Dallas safety James Washington roughed Ken O'Brien on a third-down play, giving the Jets a first down. New York went on to score a touchdown on the drive and put the game out of reach.

Dallas	3	3	0	3	—	9
New York	0	7	3	14	—	24

Dall — FG Willis 37
N.Y. — Mathis 98 punt return (Leahy kick)
Dall — FG Willis 35
N.Y. — FG Leahy 24
Dall — FG Willis 32
N.Y. — Baxter 2 run (Leahy kick)
N.Y. — McNeil 1 run (Leahy kick)
A: 68,086 T: 2:50

NEW ORLEANS 21, CINCINNATI 7—At Riverfront Stadium. Playing their first home game in six weeks, the Bengals listened to a chorus of boos as the Saints used a devastating running attack to rout Cincinnati. Craig (Ironhead) Heyward and Rueben Mayes both had 100-yard games, with Heyward rushing for 122 on 19 carries and Mayes gaining 115 on 30 carries. On the first play of the game, Heyward broke loose for a 39-yard gain. Six plays later, the Saints completed a 60-yard drive for their first TD. Overall, New Orleans ran 52 rushing plays to only 17 passing.

New Orleans	7	7	0	7	—	21
Cincinnati	0	7	0	0	—	7

N.O. — Fenerty 5 pass from Walsh (Andersen kick)
N.O. — Mayes 6 run (Andersen kick)
Cin — Brown 9 pass from Esiason (Breech kick)
N.O. — Heyward 1 run (Andersen kick)
A: 60,067 T: 2:50

BUFFALO 42, CLEVELAND 0—At Cleveland Stadium. The Browns' woes continued in the face of a dominant Bills defense and the versatility of Buffalo running back Thurman Thomas, who rushed for two touchdowns and caught a Jim Kelly pass for a third. Mike Pagel started at QB for Cleveland in place of Bernie Kosar, but Pagel was no more successful in getting the offense moving. He threw two interceptions and had six passes batted down.

Buffalo	7	7	7	21	—	42
Cleveland	0	0	0	0	—	0

Buff — Thomas 3 run (Norwood kick)
Buff — Thomas 11 run (Norwood kick)
Buff — Mueller 1 run (Norwood kick)
Buff — Thomas 11 pass from Kelly (Norwood kick)
Buff — Davis 3 run (Norwood kick)
Buff — Talley 60 interception return (Norwood kick)
A: 78,331 T: 3:00

SAN FRANCISCO 24, GREEN BAY 20—At Lambeau Field. The 49ers spotted the Packers a 10-point lead then surged back behind Joe Montana to avenge their last loss, a 21–17 defeat to Green Bay in Week 11 of the 1989 season. With 38 seconds left in the first half, Green Bay quarterback Don Majkowski fired a 20-yard TD pass to Sterling Sharpe to give the Packers a 10–0 lead. Three plays from scrimmage later, with only 11 seconds remaining before halftime, Montana hit John Taylor on a 23-yard slant pattern for a TD. In the second half, Montana threw two more touchdowns, including a 64-yarder to Jerry Rice. Green Bay's final chance for a win ended when Perry Kemp fumbled deep in 49er territory with 1:38 left. Montana ended the day with 411 yards passing, and Rice caught six passes for 187 yards.

San Francisco	0	7	3	14	—	24
Green Bay	3	7	0	10	—	20

G.B. — FG Jacke 30
G.B. — Sharpe 20 pass from Majkowski (Jacke kick)
S.F. — Taylor 23 pass from Montana (Cofer kick)
S.F. — FG Cofer 22
S.F. — Jones 6 pass from Montana (Cofer kick)
G.B. — FG Jacke 37
S.F. — Rice 64 pass from Montana (Cofer kick)
G.B. — Sharpe 17 pass from Majkowski (Jacke kick)
A: 58,835 T: 3:11

CHICAGO 26, TAMPA BAY 6—At Tampa Stadium. Bears safety Mark Carrier intercepted Buccaneer QB Vinny Testaverde twice and forced a fumble as Chicago thoroughly controlled the game. Bears quarterback Jim Harbaugh completed 14 of 23 passes for 213 yards and a TD. Running back Brad Muster rushed for 78 yards on only nine carries.

Chicago	0	17	9	0	—	26
Tampa Bay	0	0	0	6	—	6

Chi — Muster 12 run (Butler kick)
Chi — Anderson 1 run (Butler kick)
Chi — FG Butler 30
Chi — Gentry 19 pass from Harbaugh (kick failed)
Chi — FG Butler 22
T.B. — Perkins 5 pass from Testaverde (run failed)
A: 68,575 T: 3:38

WASHINGTON 41, DETROIT 38—At the Silverdome. Twelve-year veteran backup QB Jeff Rutledge entered the game in the third quarter and led the Redskins from a 35–14 deficit to a 41–38 overtime victory. He was in control of the offense for eight possessions and directed Washington to three touchdowns and two field goals, including the game-winner with 5:50 remaining in overtime. He finished the day with 30 completions in 42 attempts for 363 yards passing, and his 12-yard QB-draw for a touchdown with eight seconds left in regulation sent the game into overtime.

Washington	7	7	7	17	3	—	41
Detroit	7	21	10	0	0	—	38

Det — Clark 33 pass from Peete (Karlis kick)
Wash — Riggs 8 run (Lohmiller kick)
Det — Peete 10 run (Karlis kick)
Det — White interception return (Karlis kick)
Wash — Johnson 3 pass from Humphries (Lohmiller kick)
Det — Matthews 24 pass from Peete (Karlis kick)
Det — Sanders 45 run (Karlis kick)
Wash — Riggs 3 run (Lohmiller kick)
Det — FG Karlis 26
Wash — FG Lohmiller 38
Wash — Clark 34 pass from Rutledge (Lohmiller kick)
Wash — Rutledge 12 run (Lohmiller kick)
Wash — FG Lohmiller 34
A: 69,326 T: 3:38

L.A. RAMS 17, HOUSTON 13—At Anaheim Stadium. Ram cornerback Bobby Humphery stepped in front of Allen Pinkett at the goal line and knocked down a Warren Moon pass on fourth down to preserve a Ram victory with 40 seconds left. The Oilers had trouble getting into the end zone all day; they were inside the Los Angeles 20-yard line five times but came away with only two field goals. The Rams came back from a 10–3 deficit with two second-quarter touchdowns to take the lead, and their defense held Houston to one field goal in the second half. Moon finished with 343 yards passing.

Houston	10	0	0	3	—	13
Los Angeles	3	14	0	0	—	17

Hou — Hill 40 pass from Moon (Garcia kick)
L.A. — FG Lansford 19
Hou — FG Garcia 27
L.A. — Gary 1 run (Lansford kick)
L.A. — Johnson 2 pass from Everett (Lansford kick)
Hou — FG Garcia 31
A: 52,628 T: 2:56

MIAMI 23, PHOENIX 3—At Joe Robbie Stadium. Dan Marino directed a controlled offensive attack as Miami crushed the Cardinals. The Dolphin defense held NFC rushing leader Johnny Johnson to 27 yards and sacked Phoenix QB Timm Rosenbach five times, with former Cardinals linebacker E.J. Junior getting two. Marino completed 18 of 25 passes for 205 yards and two TDs.

Phoenix	0	3	0	0	—	3
Miami	3	10	10	0	—	23

Mia — FG Stoyanovich 19
Mia — Paige 17 pass from Marino (Stoyanovich kick)
Mia — FG Stoyanovich 21
Phoe — FG Del Greco 44
Mia — Clayton 7 pass from Marino (Stoyanovich kick)
Mia — FG Stoyanovich 19
A: 54,924 T: 2:41

PHILADELPHIA 48, NEW ENGLAND 20—At Veterans Stadium. Eagle QB Randall Cunningham riddled the Patriots defense with his running and passing as Philadelphia won in a rout. He rushed for 124 yards on eight carries—including a 52-yard run for a TD—and passed for 240 yards and four touchdowns. Eagle running back Heath Sherman also bettered the 100-yard mark, gaining 113 yards on 24 carries. New England was still in the game at halftime, trailing by only 10 points, but Philadelphia took the second-half kickoff and drove 80 yards in eight plays for the TD. Patriots wideout Irving Fryar caught four passes for 115 yards and one touchdown.

New England	3	7	3	7	—	20
Philadelphia	10	10	7	21	—	48

Phi — FG Ruzek 27
N.E. — FG Staurovsky 39
Phi — Barnett 37 pass from Cunningham (Ruzek kick)
Phi — FG Ruzek 34
N.E. — Fryar 36 pass from Wilson (Staurovsky kick)
Phi — Jackson 37 pass from Cunningham (Ruzek kick)
Phi — Williams 23 pass from Cunningham (Ruzek kick)
N.E. — FG Staurovsky 44
Phi — Jackson 3 pass from Cunningham (Ruzek kick)
N.E. — Cook 14 pass from Wilson (Staurovsky kick)
Phi — Cunningham 52 run (Ruzek kick)
Phi — Vick 1 run (Ruzek kick)
A: 65,514 T: 3:07

PITTSBURGH 21, ATLANTA 9—At Three Rivers Stadium. The Falcons jumped out to a 9–0 first-half lead, then watched as the Steeler offense revived and scored three second-half TDs (two on Atlanta turnovers) to pull out the win, Pittsburgh's fourth in five games. Falcon QB Chris Miller, who had not thrown an interception in his last 115 attempts, threw three. The Steeler defense was led by linebacker Bryan Hinkle, who made 11 tackles, forced one fumble and recovered another.

Atlanta	6	3	0	0	—	9
Pittsburgh	0	0	7	14	—	21

Atl — FG Davis 41
Atl — FG Davis 43
Atl — FG Davis 38
Pitt — Lipps 11 pass from Brister (Anderson kick)
Pitt — Mularkey 19 pass from Brister (Anderson kick)
Pitt — Williams 70 run (Anderson kick)
A: 57,093 T: 2:53

SAN DIEGO 31, SEATTLE 14—At the Kingdome. After the two teams traded touchdowns, San Diego scored 24 unanswered points to win the game and stay out of the cellar in the AFC West. Two of the Charger touchdowns came within 32 seconds of one another at the end of the third quarter without San Diego's offense taking the field. Nate Lewis returned a Seahawk punt 63 yards up the middle of the field for a touchdown, and on the next series of downs, defensive end Leslie O'Neal sacked Seattle QB Dave Krieg who fumbled into the end zone, where the ball was recovered by defensive tackle Les Miller. The Chargers held the Seahawk offense to 98 total yards through the first three quarters.

San Diego	7	7	17	0	—	31
Seattle	0	7	0	7	—	14

S.D. — Harmon 11 pass from Tolliver (Carney kick)
Sea — Williams 21 run (Johnson kick)
S.D. — Early 45 pass from Tolliver (Carney kick)
S.D. — FG Carney 20
S.D. — Lewis 63 punt return (Carney kick)
S.D. — Miller fumble recovery in end zone (Carney kick)
Sea — Blades 18 pass from Krieg (Johnson kick)
A: 59,646 T: 2:53

MINNESOTA 27, DENVER 22—At the Metrodome. The Broncos built a 16–0 lead under the direction of QB John Elway, but when he left with a foot injury late in the second quarter, backup Gary Kubiak allowed the Vikings to come back, throwing three interceptions, one of which was returned for a touchdown. The score that put Minnesota up for good was a flea-flicker from QB Rich Gannon to wideout Anthony Carter that resulted in a 56-yard touchdown. The star for the Vikings on the other side of the ball was defensive end Chris Doleman, who had two sacks. When Elway left the game, he had completed eight of 10 passes for 88 yards and one touchdown. Denver running back Bobby Humphrey rushed for 92 yards on 21 carries. The victory ended the Vikings' losing streak at five.

Denver	6	10	6	0	—	22
Minnesota	0	7	10	10	—	27

Den — Johnson 3 pass from Elway (kick blocked)
Den — Bratton 1 run (Treadwell kick)
Den — FG Treadwell 31
Minn — Fenney 4 run (Igwebuike kick)
Minn — FG Igwebuike 38
Minn — Browner 26 interception return (Igwebuike kick)
Den — FG Treadwell 46
Minn — Carter 56 pass from Gannon (Igwebuike kick)
Minn — FG Igwebuike 41
A: 57,331 T: 2:51

MONDAY, NOVEMBER 5

N.Y. GIANTS 24, INDIANAPOLIS 7—At the Hoosier Dome. The Giants dominated the Colts from start to finish in another display of methodical efficiency. For its three first-half scores, New York's offense drove 74 yards in 13 plays, 58 yards in eight plays and 74 yards in nine plays. Ottis Anderson finished off two of the drives with short TD runs. In the second half, safety Dave Duerson picked up a fumble after a Pepper Johnson sack of Indianapolis QB Jeff George and ran 31 yards for the TD that capped the scoring. Giants QB Phil Simms completed 17 of 21 passes for 172 yards.

New York	3	14	0	7	—	24
Indianapolis	0	0	7	0	—	7

N.Y. — FG Bahr 23
N.Y. — Anderson 2 run (Bahr kick)
N.Y. — Anderson 3 run (Bahr kick)
Ind — Bentley 1 run (Biasucci kick)
N.Y. — Duerson 31 fumble return (Bahr kick)
A: 58,688 T: 2:42

WEEK 10 STANDINGS

FC EAST	W	L	T	Pct	PF	PA
uffalo	8	1	0	.889	274	150
iami	8	1	0	.889	192	96
.Y. Jets	4	6	0	.400	178	216
ndianapolis	3	6	0	.333	125	196
ew England	1	8	0	.111	130	257

FC CENTRAL	W	L	T	Pct	PF	PA
incinnati	5	4	0	.556	212	225
ittsburgh	5	4	0	.556	171	147
ouston	4	5	0	.444	194	169
leveland	2	7	0	.222	128	235

FC WEST	W	L	T	Pct	PF	PA
.A. Raiders	6	3	0	.667	170	137
ansas City	5	4	0	.556	192	138
an Diego	5	5	0	.500	214	163
eattle	4	5	0	.444	175	182
enver	3	6	0	.333	197	224

FC EAST	W	L	T	Pct	PF	PA
.Y. Giants	9	0	0	1.000	226	110
hiladelphia	5	4	0	.556	227	186
ashington	5	4	0	.556	199	169
allas	3	7	0	.300	125	204
hoenix	2	7	0	.222	117	240

FC CENTRAL	W	L	T	Pct	PF	PA
hicago	8	1	0	.889	229	126
reen Bay	4	5	0	.444	176	196
ampa Bay	4	6	0	.400	170	243
etroit	3	6	0	.333	213	237
innesota	3	6	0	.333	194	188

FC WEST	W	L	T	Pct	PF	PA
an Francisco	9	0	0	1.000	222	144
ew Orleans	4	5	0	.444	171	164
tlanta	3	6	0	.333	232	251
.A. Rams	3	6	0	.333	198	258

ESULTS

hicago 30, Atlanta 24
ndianapolis 13, New England 10
iami 17, N.Y. Jets 3
innesota 17, Detroit 7
uffalo 45, Phoenix 14
eattle 17, Kansas City 16
ew Orleans 35, Tampa Bay 7
an Diego 19, Denver 7
reen Bay 29, L.A. Raiders 16
.Y. Giants 31, L.A. Rams 7
an Francisco 24, Dallas 6
hiladelphia 28, Washington 14 (Monday night)
pen dates: Cincinnati, Cleveland, Houston, Pittsburgh

SUNDAY, NOVEMBER 11

CHICAGO 30, ATLANTA 24—At Soldier Field. The Falcons shut down the Bears' NFL-leading rushing game but could not overcome their own blunders or take advantage of Chicago's. Leading 24–3 early in the third quarter, Bears punter Maury Buford fumbled after trying to run, but an interception by Lemuel Stinson, his second of the day, stopped Atlanta's drive. Buford had his next punt blocked, which allowed the Falcons to pull within a touchdown with 4:17 remaining. With 1:28 left, Chicago's Vestee Jackson picked off a Chris Miller pass, the Bears' fifth takeaway of the day, and returned it 45 yards for a touchdown to put the game away. Emotions ran high, fueled by game-week feuding between Stinson and Atlanta players Deion Sanders and Andre Rison. Chicago quarterback Jim Harbaugh left the game in the fourth quarter with a bruised chest, and his replacement Mike Tomczak, failed to complete any of his five passes.

Atlanta	3	0	7	14	–	24
Chicago	0	17	7	6	–	30

Atl – FG Davis 36
Chi – FG Butler 21
Chi – Anderson 8 run (Butler kick)
Chi – Davis 8 pass from Harbaugh (Butler kick)
Chi – Muster 1 run (Butler kick)
Atl – Johnson 5 pass from Miller (Davis kick)
Atl – Broussard 1 run (Davis kick)
Chi – Jackson 45 interception return (kick failed)
Atl – Rison 11 pass from Miller (Davis kick)
A: 62,855 T: 3:31

INDIANAPOLIS 13, NEW ENGLAND 10—At Foxboro Stadium. Lack of interest was the only thing in abundance during a meeting between two of the league's worst teams. Before only 28,924 fans, the smallest crowd in the NFL so far this year, Jeff George hit Bill Brooks with a 26-yard touchdown pass with 2:05 remaining to give the Colts the win. The completion was one of only six by George in 24 attempts on the day. His counterpart for the Pats, Marc Wilson, did little better, completing eight of 23 passes for 87 yards. Midway through the fourth quarter, the Colts had a first-and-goal from the six but couldn't score. In the one bright spot for New England, running backs John Stephens and Marvin Allen combined for 135 yards rushing. Eric Dickerson, in his third start since his season-opening suspension, was held to 25 yards on 14 carries.

Indianapolis	0	3	3	7	–	13
New England	7	3	0	0	–	10

N.E. – Allen 1 run (Staurovsky kick)
Ind – FG Biasucci 54
N.E. – FG Staurovsky 29
Ind – FG Biasucci 38
Ind – Brooks 26 pass from George (Biasucci kick)
A: 28,924 T: 2:56

MIAMI 17, N.Y. JETS 3—At Giants Stadium. The Dolphins got a couple of lucky bounces and an outstanding performance from their defense. With Miami leading 10–3 in the third quarter, Dolphin cornerback Tim McKyer intercepted a pass and returned it to the Jet 34, where he fumbled. It appeared that Jet running back Johnny Hector recovered the ball, but the official on the field ruled that McKyer was out of bounds when he fumbled. The play was not subject to replay review because the official had blown his whistle when he judged McKyer to be out of bounds. The Dolphins subsequently scored to go up 17–3. Miami's other TD came after a punt by Miami kicker Reggie Roby hit a Jet blocker on the leg and was recovered by the Dolphins on the New York six-yard line. Miami linebacker David Griggs had 2.5 sacks.

Miami	3	0	7	7	–	17
New York	0	3	0	0	–	3

Mia – FG Stoyanovich 23
N.Y. – FG Leahy 24
Mia – Paige 4 pass from Marino (Stoyanovich kick)
Mia – Logan 1 run (Stoyanovich kick)
A: 68,362 T: 2:59

MINNESOTA 17, DETROIT 7—At the Silverdome. Lion rookie Andre Ware, last year's Heisman Trophy winner, started his first pro game and threw two interceptions on his first two possessions. Bob Gagliano, who had rallied Detroit to a win over Minnesota earlier in the season, relieved Ware after halftime and also had two passes intercepted, one of which defensive end Al Noga returned for a touchdown with 1:49 remaining and the Vikings leading by three. Minnesota quarterback Rich Gannon performed efficiently, running for a touchdown on fourth-and-goal from the one and hitting 12 of 17 passes for 146 yards. Viking safety Joey Browner had an excellent game, accounting for two interceptions, two deflections and three solo tackles.

Minnesota	0	7	3	7	–	17
Detroit	0	0	7	0	–	7

Minn – Gannon 1 run (Reveiz kick)
Minn – FG Reveiz 27
Det – Campbell 18 pass from Gagliano (Karlis kick)
Minn – Noga 26 interception return (Reveiz kick)
A: 68,264 T: 2:40

BUFFALO 45, PHOENIX 14—At Rich Stadium. Even with his favorite target, Andre Reed, out with an ankle injury, Bills quarterback Jim Kelly threw four touchdown passes as Buffalo scored more than 40 points for the second straight game. Bills tight end Butch Rolle broke a 7–7 tie in the second quarter with a one-yard touchdown reception; his last eight catches have been for TDs. The Cardinals stayed close until the fourth quarter, when, with Buffalo leading 21–14, Kelly engineered a 13-play, 64-yard drive for a field goal. With a 30-mph wind blowing for the entire game, the Bills made liberal use of Thurman Thomas, who rushed for 112 yards on 26 carries. The success of the rushing game helped Buffalo control the clock for 38 minutes. Bruce Smith had two sacks for the Bills to bring his season total to 10.

Phoenix	7	0	7	0	–	14
Buffalo	0	21	0	24	–	45

Phoe – Johnson 1 run (Del Greco kick)
Buff – McKeller 18 pass from Kelly (Norwood kick)
Buff – Rolle 1 pass from Kelly (Norwood kick)
Buff – Tasker 24 pass from Kelly (Norwood kick)
Phoe – Jones 29 pass from Rosenbach (Del Greco kick)
Buff – FG Norwood 25
Buff – Beebe 11 pass from Kelly (Norwood kick)
Buff – Mueller 1 run (Norwood kick)
Buff – Davis 13 run (Norwood kick)
A: 74,904 T: 2:57

SEATTLE 17, KANSAS CITY 16—At Arrowhead Stadium. Chiefs linebacker Derrick Thomas set an NFL record by sacking Seahawk quarterback Dave Krieg seven times, but on the final play of the game, Krieg escaped Thomas's rush and threw a 25-yard strike to Paul Skansi for the winning touchdown. Krieg put Seattle in position for the winning play by moving the Seahawks from their own 34 to the Chiefs 25 in 44 seconds. The previous record for sacks was held by San Francisco's Fred Dean, who had six against New Orleans in 1983. When he escaped from Kansas City's defense, Krieg played well, completing 16 of 23 passes for 306 yards and two touchdowns.

Seattle	0	3	7	7	–	17
Kansas City	0	6	10	0	–	16

K.C. – FG Lowery 25
Sea – FG Johnson 43
K.C. – FG Lowery 30
Sea – Chadwick 54 pass from Krieg (Johnson kick)
K.C. – FG Lowery 24
K.C. – Saleaumua recovered fumble in end zone (Lowery kick)
Sea – Skansi 25 pass from Krieg (Johnson kick)
A: 71,285 T: 3:04

NEW ORLEANS 35, TAMPA BAY 7—At the Superdome. Saints running back Craig Heyward rushed for 155 yards and two touchdowns on 20 carries as New Orleans broke open a close game in the third quarter to hand the Buccaneers their fourth straight loss. Heyward's longest run was a 47-yard TD jaunt just before halftime that put the Saints up 14–7. Chris Chandler started at quarterback for Tampa Bay, but when he suffered a concussion in the third quarter, Vinny Testaverde replaced him and lost a fumble on the first snap he took, giving New Orleans the ball on the Buccaneer five-yard line. The Saints defense was all over the Tampa Bay quarterbacks, sacking them six times, with linebacker Pat Swilling getting four and nosetackle Jim Wilks getting the other two. The Buccaneers have scored only one offensive touchdown in each of the last six games.

Tampa Bay	7	0	0	0	–	7
New Orleans	0	14	14	7	–	35

T.B. – Chandler 12 run (Christie kick)
N.O. – Perriman 26 pass from Walsh (Andersen kick)
N.O. – Heyward 47 run (Andersen kick)
N.O. – Mayes 4 run (Andersen kick)
N.O. – Heyward 2 run (Andersen kick)
N.O. – Mayes 1 run (Andersen kick)
A: 67,865 T: 2:45

SAN DIEGO 19, DENVER 7—At Jack Murphy Stadium. With their third straight win in a workmanlike performance over the Broncos, the Chargers pulled to 5–5. Kicker John Carney led the way with four field goals, and linebacker Gary Plummer, inserted into San Diego's offense, scored a touchdown on a one-yard run. The game featured the NFL's two leading runners, the Chargers' Marion Butts and Denver's Bobby Humphrey. Butts rushed for 114 yards on 16 carries, and the San Diego defense held Humphrey to 62 yards on 22 carries. Charger cornerback Gill Byrd had two interceptions, the second coming with the Broncos behind 12–7 and threatening at the Charger10-yard line. Byrd leads the NFL with seven pickoffs.

Denver	7	0	0	0	–	7
San Diego	0	9	3	7	–	19

Den – Johnson 22 pass from Elway (Treadwell kick)
S.D. – FG Carney 19
S.D. – FG Carney 23
S.D. – FG Carney 43
S.D. – FG Carney 32
S.D. – Plummer 1 run (Carney kick)
A: 59,557 T: 2:51

GREEN BAY 29, L.A. RAIDERS 16—At Memorial Coliseum. Packer quarterback Don Majkowski overcame eight sacks to throw two touchdown passes and set up a club-record five field goals by Chris Jacke as Green Bay handed the Raiders their second straight defeat and ended their 10-game home winning streak. Green Bay's defense allowed Los Angeles only 165 total yards and forced four turnovers, the most crucial being a Johnny Holland interception on the first snap of the second half to set up a 23-yard field goal that broke a 16–16 tie. In the fourth quarter, a 28-yard punt by the Raiders' Jeff Gossett gave the Packers good field position to start a drive, which ended in a 28-yard touchdown pass from Majkowski to wide receiver Perry Kemp. Green Bay's offense dominated time of possession, holding the ball slightly more than 39 minutes. On defense, Shawn Patterson and Tim Harris each had two sacks.

Green Bay	3	13	3	10	–	29
Los Angeles	13	3	0	0	–	16

L.A. – Allen 5 run (Jaeger kick)
G.B. – FG Jacke 39
L.A. – Allen 2 run (kick failed)
G.B. – FG Jacke 51
G.B. – FG Jacke 32
G.B. – Workman 5 pass from Majkowski (Jacke kick)
L.A. – FG Jaeger 24
G.B. – FG Jacke 23
G.B. – Kemp 28 pass from Majkowski (Jacke kick)
G.B. – FG Jacke 20
A: 50,855 T: 2:59

N.Y. GIANTS 31, L.A. RAMS 7—At Anaheim Stadium. The Giants used a second-half surge to break away from the Rams and win their club-record 12th straight regular-season game. The Rams let the game slip from their grasp when they failed to move the ball after a Sean Landeta punt pinned them on their own three. Dave Meggett returned the subsequent L.A. punt 22 yards to the Ram 30. Six plays later, Ottis Anderson scored on a three-yard run to give the Giants a 24–7 lead early in the fourth quarter. In the second half, Landeta nailed three straight punts at the L.A. three-yard line and averaged 46.8 yards on five punts. New York's defense hounded Jim Everett into three interceptions, two of them by linebacker Gary Reasons. Phil Simms turned in another steady performance for the Giants, hitting 19 of 26 passes for 213 yards and a touchdown. Marcus Dupree, the former Oklahoma and USFL running back who had not played professionally since 1985, made his NFL debut for the Rams, gaining 22 yards on four carries.

New York	3	7	7	14	–	31
Los Angeles	0	0	7	0	–	7

N.Y. – FG Bahr 44
N.Y. – Bavaro 9 pass from Simms (Bahr kick)
L.A. – Gary 3 run (Lansford kick)
N.Y. – Hampton 19 run (Bahr kick)
N.Y. – Anderson 3 run (Bahr kick)
N.Y. – Tillman 1 run (Bahr kick)
A: 64,632 T: 2:51

SAN FRANCISCO 24, DALLAS 6—At Texas Stadium. The 49ers continued to roll, extending their undefeated streak to 17 games. San Francisco turned to the rushing game more than usual, running the ball 35 times for 107 yards and retaining possession for more than 40 minutes. Joe Montana and Jerry Rice connected on 12 passes for 147 yards and a touchdown. The 49ers took control of the game midway into the second quarter when fullback Tom Rathman scored on a fourth-and-goal from the one to give San Francisco a 7–3 lead. Linebacker Matt Millen intercepted a Troy Aikman pass on the next series, and six plays later, Rice caught a seven-yard TD pass from Montana. The 49er defense limited the Cowboys to 158 total yards and only one of 10 third-down conversions.

San Francisco	0	17	0	7	–	24
Dallas	3	3	0	0	–	6

Dall – FG Willis 23
S.F. – Rathman 1 run (Cofer kick)
S.F. – Rice 7 pass from Montana (Cofer kick)
Dall – FG Willis 37
S.F. – FG Cofer 42
S.F. – Montana 4 run (Cofer kick)
A: 62,966 T: 2:58

MONDAY, NOVEMBER 12

PHILADELPHIA 28, WASHINGTON 14—At Veterans Stadium. Second-year running back Heath Sherman rushed for 124 yards—his second straight 100-yard game—and caught two touchdown passes to lead the Eagles to a win over the Redskins. Philadelphia broke open a tied game in the third quarter after QB Randall Cunningham hit Sherman with a six-yard pass to convert a fourth-and-four from the Washington 27 and a nine-yard TD pass three plays later. The Eagle defense held Washington in check, allowing only 200 total yards and one of 13 third-down conversions. Jeff Rutledge, the Redskins' hero the week before, completed just six of 19 passes for 62 yards before leaving in the third quarter with a sprained thumb. Stan Humphries was little more effective when he took over, throwing an interception and completing six of 11 passes before he also became injured. Washington finished with running back Brian Mitchell at QB.

Washington	0	7	0	7	–	14
Philadelphia	7	0	21	0	–	28

Phi – Frizzell 30 interception return (Ruzek kick)
Wash – Warren 8 pass from Rutledge (Lohmiller kick)
Phi – Sherman 9 pass from Byars (Ruzek kick)
Phi – Simmons 18 fumble return (Ruzek kick)
Phi – Sherman 2 pass from Cunningham (Ruzek kick)
Wash – Mitchell 1 run (Lohmiller kick)
A: 65,857 T: 3:09

WEEK 11 STANDINGS

AFC EAST	W	L	T	Pct.	PF	PA
Buffalo	9	1	0	.900	288	150
Miami	8	2	0	.800	202	109
Indianapolis	4	6	0	.400	142	210
N.Y. Jets	4	7	0	.364	192	233
New England	1	9	0	.100	130	271

AFC CENTRAL	W	L	T	Pct.	PF	PA
Cincinnati	6	4	0	.600	239	228
Houston	5	5	0	.500	229	192
Pittsburgh	5	5	0	.500	174	174
Cleveland	2	8	0	.200	151	270

AFC WEST	W	L	T	Pct.	PF	PA
L.A. Raiders	7	3	0	.700	183	147
Kansas City	6	4	0	.600	219	148
San Diego	5	6	0	.455	224	190
Seattle	4	6	0	.400	196	206
Denver	3	7	0	.300	210	240

NFC EAST	W	L	T	Pct.	PF	PA
N.Y. Giants	10	0	0	1.000	246	110
Philadelphia	6	4	0	.600	251	209
Washington	6	4	0	.600	230	186
Dallas	4	7	0	.364	149	225
Phoenix	2	8	0	.200	138	264

NFC CENTRAL	W	L	T	Pct.	PF	PA
Chicago	9	1	0	.900	245	139
Green Bay	5	5	0	.500	200	217
Minnesota	4	6	0	.400	218	209
Tampa Bay	4	7	0	.364	177	274
Detroit	3	7	0	.300	213	257

NFC WEST	W	L	T	Pct.	PF	PA
San Francisco	10	0	0	1.000	253	151
New Orleans	4	6	0	.400	188	195
Atlanta	3	7	0	.300	255	275
L.A. Rams	3	7	0	.300	219	282

RESULTS
N.Y. Giants 20, Detroit 0
Houston 35, Cleveland 23
Buffalo 14, New England 0
Washington 31, New Orleans 17
Philadelphia 24, Atlanta 23
Kansas City 27, San Diego 10
Chicago 16, Denver 13 (OT)
Dallas 24, L.A. Rams 21
Green Bay 24, Phoenix 21
Minnesota 24, Seattle 21
Indianapolis 17, N.Y. Jets 14
San Francisco 31, Tampa Bay 7
Cincinnati 27, Pittsburgh 3
L.A. Raiders 13, Miami 10 (Monday night)

SUNDAY, NOVEMBER 18

N.Y. GIANTS 20, DETROIT 0—At Giants Stadium. The Giants racked up their 10th win of the season by scoring all their points in the first half and allowing the Lions no closer than the 29-yard line. Ottis Anderson carried the rushing load, totaling 91 yards on 23 carries. Phil Simms completed 13 of 18 passes for 170 yards and two touchdowns. Through 10 games, the Giants have outscored opponents 125–36 in the first half.

Detroit	0	0	0	0	–	0
New York	7	13	0	0	–	20

N.Y. — Baker 33 pass from Simms (Bahr kick)
N.Y. — FG Bahr 24
N.Y. — Ingram 57 pass from Simms (Bahr kick)
N.Y. — FG Bahr 49
A: 76,109 T: 2:32

HOUSTON 35, CLEVELAND 23—At Cleveland Stadium. Oiler quarterback Warren Moon celebrated his 34th birthday by throwing for five touchdowns as Houston handed new Cleveland coach Jim Shofner a loss in his first game since replacing the fired Bud Carson. Curtis Duncan was the leading receiver for the Oilers, catching seven passes for 130 yards and one TD. Moon completed 24 of 32 passes for 322 yards on the day. The loss was Cleveland's fifth straight.

Houston	7	7	0	21	–	35
Cleveland	6	7	3	7	–	23

Cle — Newsome 13 pass from Kosar (kick failed)
Hou — White 3 pass from Moon (Garcia kick)
Cle — Gainer 1 run (Kauric kick)
Hou — Jeffires 46 pass from Moon (Garcia kick)
Cle — FG Kauric 22
Hou — Duncan 37 pass from Moon (Garcia kick)
Hou — Jones 23 pass from Moon (Garcia kick)
Hou — Givins 7 pass from Moon (Garcia kick)
Cle — Langhorne 4 pass from Kosar (Kauric kick)
A: 76,726 T: 3:00

BUFFALO 14, NEW ENGLAND 0—At Rich Stadium. The woeful Patriots hung close to the powerful Bills for 58 minutes, but Buffalo got the big play when rookie cornerback James Williams intercepted a pass as New England was marching for a possible tying score. On the next play, Bills running back Thurman Thomas broke loose on an 80-yard run for a touchdown to ice the game. Thomas rushed for 165 yards on 22 carries, an average of 7.5 per carry. In the second quarter, the Bills kept the Patriots from scoring after New England had a first-and-goal from the one. Buffalo quarterback Jim Kelly's 79 yards and five completions were both career lows. Irving Fryar had a good day in defeat, catching seven passes for 85 yards for the losers.

New England	0	0	0	0	–	0
Buffalo	7	0	0	7	–	14

Buff — Thomas 5 run (Norwood kick)
Buff — Thomas 80 run (Norwood kick)
A: 74,720 T: 2:47

WASHINGTON 31, NEW ORLEANS 17—At RFK Stadium. After missing six weeks because of surgery on a sprained knee, Mark Rypien returned as the Redskins' starting quarterback and threw four touchdown passes as Washington turned the game into a romp with a pair of touchdown drives in the third quarter. Running back Earnest Byner contributed 116 yards to the Redskins' offensive show, and Gary Clark totaled 131 yards on eight catches, two of them for touchdowns. After gaining 277 yards in his previous two games, Saints running back Craig (Ironhead) Heyward was held to 57 yards on 13 carries.

New Orleans	7	3	0	7	–	17
Washington	3	14	14	0	–	31

N.O. — Perriman 16 pass from Walsh (Andersen kick)
Wash — FG Lohmiller 39
Wash — Clark 8 pass from Rypien (Lohmiller kick)
N.O. — FG Andersen 38
Wash — Monk 7 pass from Rypien (Lohmiller kick)
Wash — Clark 19 pass from Rypien (Lohmiller kick)
Wash — Bryant 3 pass from Rypien (Lohmiller kick)
N.O. — Turner 8 pass from Walsh (Andersen kick)
A: 52,573 T: 2:45

PHILADELPHIA 24, ATLANTA 23—At Atlanta-Fulton County Stadium. Down 16–7 with 13:29 remaining, the Eagles scored 17 fourth-quarter points to pull out a 24–23 victory. Roger Ruzek's game-winning 46-yard field goal with 1:45 remaining was set up by a weak 29-yard punt by Atlanta's Scott Fulhage. Randall Cunningham connected with wide receiver Calvin Williams on a 30-yard scoring pass one play after the Falcons fumbled to give the Eagles a brief lead and keep them in the game. Cunningham threw three touchdown passes in all.

Philadelphia	0	7	0	17	–	24
Atlanta	0	10	3	10	–	23

Atl — Johnson 1 run (Davis kick)
Phi — Jackson 1 pass from Cunningham (Ruzek kick)
Atl — FG Davis 53
Atl — FG Davis 46
Atl — FG Davis 28
Phi — Jackson 17 pass from Cunningham (Ruzek kick)
Phi — Williams 30 pass from Cunningham (Ruzek kick)
Atl — Rison 23 pass from Miller (Davis kick)
Phi — FG Ruzek 46
A: 53,755 T: 3:16

KANSAS CITY 27, SAN DIEGO 10—At Arrowhead Stadium. Chiefs quarterback Steve DeBerg threw three touchdown passes, including a 90-yarder to J.J. Birden on the third play of the game, as Kansas City ended a streak of five straight losses to the Chargers. After the Chiefs' first TD, San Diego QB Billy Joe Tolliver fumbled on its own 14, setting up a Nick Lowery field goal, which gave Kansas City a 10–0 lead with 4:07 gone. Tolliver accounted for all five of the Chargers' turnovers, throwing three interceptions and fumbling twice. Barry Word of the Chiefs led all rushers with 90 yards on 17 carries.

San Diego	3	0	7	0	–	10
Kansas City	10	7	3	7	–	27

K.C. — Birden 90 pass from DeBerg (Lowery kick)
K.C. — FG Lowery 36
S.D. — FG Carney 42
K.C. — Jones 2 pass from DeBerg (Lowery kick)
S.D. — Walker 2 pass from Tolliver (Carney kick)
K.C. — FG Lowery 37
K.C. — Jones 6 pass from DeBerg (Lowery kick)
A: 63,717 T: 3:09

CHICAGO 16, DENVER 13—At Mile High Stadium. Kevin Butler missed a game-winning 41-yard field goal on the final play of regulation but redeemed himself with a 44-yarder in overtime as the Bears won their sixth consecutive game. Denver quarterback John Elway tied the game by scoring on a nine-yard bootleg with 1:14 left, capping a 70-yard drive. The contest was a defensive struggle, with the Bears sacking Elway six times and linebacker Mike Singletary racking up 11 solo tackles and three assists. Neal Anderson rushed 28 times for 111 yards

Chicago	0	3	10	0	3	–	16
Denver	3	3	0	7	0	–	13

Den — FG Treadwell 27
Chi — FG Butler 37
Den — FG Treadwell 24
Chi — FG Butler 32
Chi — Muster 10 run (Butler kick)
Den — Elway 9 run (Treadwell kick)
Chi — FG Butler 44
A: 75,013 T: 3:30

DALLAS 24, L.A. RAMS 21—At Anaheim Stadium. The Cowboys, who hadn't scored a touchdown in the last two games, got two TD catches from Michael Irvin and a 23-yard field goal from Ken Willis with 4:24 left to drop the Rams to 3–7 for the year. Running backs led the way for both teams as L.A.'s Cleveland Gary rushed for 103 yards and three touchdowns and Emmitt Smith of the Cowboys had 54 yards rushing and 117 yards receiving. Gary, however, committed a crucial error when he fumbled at the Cowboy five-yard line with the score tied 21–21 in the third quarter. Dallas linebacker Ken Norton Jr. recovered, and the Cowboys drove 89 yards for the winning field goal.

Dallas	7	14	0	3	–	24
Los Angeles	7	7	7	0	–	21

L.A. — Gary 16 run (Lansford kick)
Dall — Irvin 10 pass from Aikman (Willis kick)
L.A. — Gary 4 run (Lansford kick)
Dall — Agee 6 pass from Aikman (Willis kick)
Dall — Irvin 61 pass from Aikman (Willis kick)
L.A. — Gary 1 run (Lansford kick)
Dall — FG Willis 23
A: 58,589 T: 3:06

GREEN BAY 24, PHOENIX 21—At Sun Devil Stadium. Backup quarterback Anthony Dilweg replaced injured Don Majkowski with 8:58 left in the first half and threw two touchdowns in the final 6:30 to give Green Bay the come-from-behind win. The winning drive was set up when Phoenix failed to convert a fourth-down play from the Packer 43 with 2:10 remaining. Johnny Johnson, the Cardinals' rookie running back, had 103 yards on 15 carries, and Sterling Sharpe of the Packers caught 10 passes for 157 yards.

Green Bay	7	3	0	14	–	24
Phoenix	0	7	7	7	–	21

G.B. — Sharpe 54 pass from Majkowski (Jacke kick)
G.B. — FG Jacke 54
Phoe — Jones 22 pass from Rosenbach (Del Greco kick)
Phoe — Green 27 pass from Rosenbach (Del Greco kick)
Phoe — Jones 25 pass from Rosenbach (Del Greco kick)
G.B. — Weathers 15 pass from Dilweg (Jacke kick)
G.B. — West 1 pass from Dilweg (Jacke kick)
A: 46,878 T: 3:02

MINNESOTA 24, SEATTLE 21—At the Kingdome. Herschel Walker finally broke out of his slump and rushed for 99 yards on 16 carries, including a 58-yard TD run to tie the game late in the fourth quarter. The Vikings got the win, their third in a row, when Fuad Reveiz booted a 24-yard field goal with no time left on the clock. Minnesota safety Joey Browner set up the winning kick with an interception of a Dave Krieg pass, which deflected off the hands of receiver Paul Skansi. The Viking defense held Seattle to four of 13 third-down conversions.

Minnesota	7	7	0	10	–	24
Seattle	7	7	0	7	–	21

Sea — Blades 9 pass from Krieg (Johnson kick)
Minn — Jones 8 pass from Gannon (Reveiz kick)
Minn — Carter 11 pass from Gannon (Reveiz kick)
Sea — Blades 5 pass from Krieg (Johnson kick)
Sea — Fenner 1 run (Johnson kick)
Minn — Walker 58 run (Reveiz kick)
Minn — FG Reveiz 24
A: 59,735 T: 3:04

INDIANAPOLIS 17, N.Y. JETS 14—At the Hoosier Dome. The Colts bounced back from a 14–0 deficit with 17 unanswered points for the victory as the Jet offense stalled again in the fourth quarter. Kicker Dean Biasucci booted the winning 38-yard field goal with 1:46 remaining. Two unusual plays keyed the win for Indianapolis. Midway through the third quarter, Jet safety Erik McMillian intercepted a Jeff George pass, but in attempting to lateral to a teammate on the return, McMillian instead tossed the ball back to George, who was preparing to make the tackle. On the next play, George threw deep to Jessie Hester, the ball was tipped by Hester and Jet DB James Hasty, and Hester came down with the ball in the end zone for the TD.

New York	3	5	6	0	–	14
Indianapolis	0	0	7	10	–	17

N.Y. — FG Leahy 32
N.Y. — Safety, George tackled in end zone
N.Y. — FG Leahy 21
N.Y. — FG Leahy 29
N.Y. — FG Leahy 39
Ind — Hester 43 pass from George (Biasucci kick)
Ind — Morgan 3 pass from George (Biasucci kick)
Ind — FG Biasucci 38
A: 47,283 T: 3:05

SAN FRANCISCO 31, TAMPA BAY 7—At Candlestick Park. The 49ers tied the NFL record for the longest winning streak at 18 games with a systematic dismantling of the Buccaneers, whose losing streak reached five games. San Francisco's defense allowed the Tampa Bay offense only 180 total yards, while the 49er offense amassed 393 yards. San Francisco rushed the ball effectively, with running backs Dexter Carter, Harry Sydney and Roger Craig gaining more than 40 yards each. Joe Montana also had a good day, completing 23 of 35 for 230 yards and two TDs, both to tight end Brent Jones.

Tampa Bay	0	0	7	0	–	7
San Francisco	7	10	7	7	–	31

S.F. — Jones 11 pass from Montana (Cofer kick)
S.F. — FG Cofer 24
S.F. — Jones 4 pass from Montana (Cofer kick)
T.B. — Haddix 65 interception return (Christie kick)
S.F. — Craig 10 run (Cofer kick)
S.F. — Sydney 1 run (Cofer kick)
A: 62,221 T: 2:57

CINCINNATI 27, PITTSBURGH 3—At Riverfront Stadium. The Bengals took over first place in the AFC Central with their fifth straight win over the Steelers. Cincinnati opened the scoring with a 13-play, 63-yard drive that ended in a five-yard TD run by Ickey Woods. James Brooks of the Bengals led all rushers with 105 yards on 20 carries as the Bengals totaled 178 yards on the ground. Entering the game, the Steeler defense had allowed just 91.4 rushing yards per game. On offense, Pittsburgh had only one turnover, but it was a costly one as the Bengals' Barney Bussey picked up a fumble late in the third quarter and returned it 70 yards for a touchdown.

Pittsburgh	0	0	0	3	–	3
Cincinnati	7	3	14	3	–	27

Cin — Woods 5 run (Breech kick)
Cin — FG Breech 21
Cin — Taylor 1 run (Breech kick)
Cin — Bussey 70 fumble return (Breech kick)
Pitt — FG Anderson 31
Cin — FG Breech 33
A: 60,064 T: 2:40

MONDAY, NOVEMBER 19

L.A. RAIDERS 13, MIAMI 10—At Joe Robbie Stadium. The Dolphin defense, ranked No. 1 in the league, was shredded by the Raiders' rushing tandem of Marcus Allen (79 yards) and Bo Jackson (99 yards) as L.A. built an early lead and held on for the win. The Raiders challenged Miami's defense from the opening kick as Allen carried the ball on the Raiders' first nine plays from scrimmage. On defense L.A. held the Dolphins to 14 yards on the ground, with Miami's leading rusher, Sammie Smith, gaining -3 yards on six carries. Smith was just as unsuccessful on the receiving end, catching one pass for -1 yard. Quarterback Dan Marino kept the Dolphins in the game, completing 20 of 36 passes for 214 yards and one TD. Another Marino TD pass, a three-yarder to Mark Duper, was nullified when the referee ruled that Miami had not gotten the snap off before the 45-second clock expired. Jim Jensen was the leading receiver for the Dolphins, catching seven passes for 79 yards.

Los Angeles	0	10	3	0	–	13
Miami	0	7	0	3	–	10

L.A. — FG Jaeger 23
L.A. — Allen 2 run (Jaeger kick)
Mia — Schwedes 14 pass from Marino (Stoyanovich kick)
L.A. — FG Jaeger 43
Mia — FG Stoyanovich 26
A: 70,553 T: 2:47

WEEK 12 STANDINGS

AFC EAST	W	L	T	Pct.	PF	PA
Buffalo	9	2	0	.818	312	177
Miami	9	2	0	.818	232	122
Indianapolis	5	6	0	.455	176	230
N.Y. Jets	4	8	0	.333	199	257
New England	1	10	0	.091	144	305

AFC CENTRAL	W	L	T	Pct.	PF	PA
Cincinnati	6	5	0	.545	259	262
Houston	6	5	0	.545	256	216
Pittsburgh	6	5	0	.545	198	181
Cleveland	2	9	0	.182	164	300

AFC WEST	W	L	T	Pct.	PF	PA
Kansas City	7	4	0	.636	246	172
L.A. Raiders	7	4	0	.636	207	174
Seattle	5	6	0	.455	209	216
San Diego	5	7	0	.417	234	203
Denver	3	8	0	.273	237	280

NFC EAST	W	L	T	Pct.	PF	PA
N.Y. Giants	10	1	0	.909	259	141
Philadelphia	7	4	0	.636	282	222
Washington	6	5	0	.545	247	213
Dallas	5	7	0	.417	176	242
Phoenix	3	8	0	.273	172	278

NFC CENTRAL	W	L	T	Pct.	PF	PA
Chicago	9	2	0	.818	258	180
Green Bay	6	5	0	.545	220	227
Minnesota	5	6	0	.455	259	222
Detroit	4	7	0	.364	253	284
Tampa Bay	4	8	0	.333	187	294

NFC WEST	W	L	T	Pct.	PF	PA
San Francisco	10	1	0	.909	270	179
New Orleans	5	6	0	.455	198	202
L.A. Rams	4	7	0	.364	247	299
Atlanta	3	8	0	.273	262	285

RESULTS
Dallas 27, Washington 17 (Thursday)
Detroit 40, Denver 27 (Thursday)
New Orleans 10, Atlanta 7
Minnesota 41, Chicago 13
Indianapolis 34, Cincinnati 20
Miami 30, Cleveland 13
Philadelphia 31, N.Y. Giants 13
Green Bay 20, Tampa Bay 10
Kansas City 27, L.A. Raiders 24
L.A. Rams 28, San Francisco 17
Phoenix 34, New England 14
Pittsburgh 24, N.Y. Jets 7
Seattle 13, San Diego 10 (OT)
Houston 27, Buffalo 24 (Monday night)

THURSDAY, NOVEMBER 22

DALLAS 27, WASHINGTON 17—At Texas Stadium. Trailing Washington 17–10 late in the third quarter, the Cowboys erupted for 17 unanswered points to upset the Redskins. Rookie running back Emmitt Smith rushed for 132 yards on 23 carries and two touchdowns, including a 48-yard scamper to put the game away in the fourth quarter. Troy Aikman completed 20 of 31 passes for 222 yards.

Washington	0	7	10	0	–	17
Dallas	10	0	7	10	–	27

Dall – FG Willis 49
Dall – Irvin 12 pass from Aikman (Willis kick)
Wash – Byner 5 run (Lohmiller kick)
Wash – FG Lohmiller 25
Wash – Sanders 6 pass from Rypien (Lohmiller kick)
Dall – Smith 1 run (Willis kick)
Dall – FG Willis 41
Dall – Smith 48 run (Willis kick)
A: 60,355 T: 3:16

DETROIT 40, DENVER 27—At the Silverdome. Barry Sanders rushed for 147 yards on 23 carries and scored two TDs as the Lions crushed the Broncos. Denver pulled within a TD early in the fourth quarter, but two Eddie Murray field goals ended hopes of a Bronco comeback. Detroit QB Bob Gagliano completed 18 of 30 passes for 248 yards and two touchdowns.

Denver	7	10	3	7	–	27
Detroit	21	6	7	6	–	40

Det – Johnson 11 pass from Gagliano (Murray kick)
Den – Bratton 1 run (Treadwell kick)
Det – Sanders 7 run (Murray kick)
Det – Johnson 43 pass from Gagliano (Murray kick)
Det – FG Murray 24
Den – FG Treadwell 24
Den – Henderson 49 interception return (Treadwell kick)
Det – FG Murray 32
Den – FG Treadwell 32
Det – Sanders 35 pass from Gagliano (Murray kick)
Den – Bratton 1 run (Treadwell kick)
Det – FG Murray 43
Det – FG Murray 45
A: 73,896 T: 3:02

SUNDAY, NOVEMBER 25

NEW ORLEANS 10, ATLANTA 7—At the Superdome. The Falcons suffered the sixth loss in their last seven games as Saints QB Steve Walsh directed an 86-yard drive that ended with a blitz-beating six-yard pass to Eric Martin for the winning TD with 2:10 left. On that drive, Walsh completed seven of nine passes for 67 yards. The Falcons had taken the lead in the defensive game with a 51-yard throw to wide receiver George Thomas midway through the fourth quarter before New Orleans answered with its long drive. Atlanta had a chance to tie the score, but Greg Davis's 51-yard field goal with 1:08 remaining was wide left. Saints running back Craig Heyward carried most of the offensive load with 24 rushes for 88 yards and five receptions for 35 yards.

Atlanta	0	0	0	7	–	7
New Orleans	0	3	0	7	–	10

N.O. – FG Andersen 20
Atl – Thomas 51 pass from Miller (Davis kick)
N.O. – Martin 6 pass from Walsh (Andersen kick)
A: 68,229 T: 3:07

MINNESOTA 41, CHICAGO 13—At the Metrodome. The Vikings scored on all six of their first-half possessions to hand the Bears their second loss of the season. The rout began when Herschel Walker returned the opening kickoff 64 yards to the Chicago 31 to set up a Fuad Reveiz 41-yard field goal. On their next series, Bears QB Jim Harbaugh fumbled—one of three overall—to set up another Reveiz field goal. After forcing the Bears to punt, Minnesota got a 30-yard punt return from Leo Lewis, which led to the Vikings' first TD on a two-yard run by Walker. The Minnesota defense sacked Harbaugh seven times.

Chicago	0	3	7	3	–	13
Minnesota	13	21	7	0	–	41

Minn – FG Reveiz 41
Minn – FG Reveiz 45
Minn – Walker 2 run (Reveiz kick)
Minn – Walker 17 pass from Gannon (Reveiz kick)
Minn – Jones 5 pass from Gannon (Reveiz kick)
Chi – FG Butler 41
Minn – Carter 22 pass from Gannon (Reveiz kick)
Minn – Merriweather 33 fumble return (Reveiz kick)
Chi – Green 10 pass from Harbaugh (Butler kick)
Chi – FG Butler 43
A: 58,866 T: 3:00

INDIANAPOLIS 34, CINCINNATI 20—At Riverfront Stadium. The Colts won their third game in a row as rookie QB Jeff George had his best game of the season and Eric Dickerson rushed for 143 yards. Dickerson's 100-yard game was the 59th of his career, putting him in second place behind Walter Payton (77) and breaking a tie with Jim Brown. After the Bengals scored first on a one-yard run by Ickey Woods, the Colts countered with 31 unanswered points.

Indianapolis	7	10	14	3	–	34
Cincinnati	6	0	14	0	–	20

Cin – Woods 1 run (kick failed)
Ind – Hester 19 pass from George (Biasucci kick)
Ind – Dickerson 1 run (Biasucci kick)
Ind – FG Biasucci 22
Ind – Brooks 5 pass from George (Biasucci kick)
Ind – Morgan 6 pass from George (Biasucci kick)
Cin – Brown 21 pass from Esiason (Breech kick)
Cin – Brown 20 pass from Esiason (Breech kick)
Ind – FG Breech 26
A: 60,051 T: 3:00

MIAMI 30, CLEVELAND 13—At Cleveland Stadium. The Dolphins jumped out to a 27–3 first-half lead, then used a ball-control offense to salt the game away. The loss was the sixth in a row for the Browns. Cleveland's defense looked hapless, allowing Miami to convert 11 of 16 third-down plays. Dolphin QB Dan Marino completed 16 of 29 passes to eight different receivers for 245 yards and two TDs. His yardage put him over 30,000 yards passing, a mark he has reached faster than any QB in NFL history.

Miami	14	13	3	0	–	30
Cleveland	0	3	3	7	–	13

Mia – Duper 5 pass from Marino (Stoyanovich kick)
Mia – Pruitt 35 pass from Marino (Stoyanovich kick)
Mia – Smith 4 run (kick failed)
Mia – Glenn 31 interception return (Stoyanovich kick)
Cle – FG Kauric 36
Cle – FG Kauric 42
Mia – FG Stoyanovich 40
Cle – Mack 2 run (Kauric kick)
A: 70,225 T: 2:45

PHILADELPHIA 31, N.Y. GIANTS 13—At Veterans Stadium. Two deflected passes in the fourth quarter resulted in touchowns for the Eagles, breaking open a close game and ending the Giants' hopes of a perfect season. It was the fifth straight win for Philadelphia. Two minutes into the fourth quarter, with the Eagles leading 17–13, Philadelphia QB Randall Cunningham threw a pass intended for wide receiver Fred Barnett. The ball deflected off Barnett into the hands of Eagle receiver Calvin Williams for a six-yard TD. Two plays after the Eagles kicked off, Giants QB Phil Simms, who had thrown only two interceptions all year, also had a pass deflected—this one by onrushing lineman Clyde Simmons—and Philadelphia linebacker Byron Evans caught the ball and returned it 23 yards for a TD.

N.Y. Giants	7	6	0	0	–	13
Philadelphia	7	7	3	14	–	31

N.Y. – Ingram 15 pass from Simms (Bahr kick)
Phi – Barnett 49 pass from Cunningham (Ruzek kick)
Phi – Cunningham 1 run (Ruzek kick)
N.Y. – Bavaro 4 pass from Simms (Bahr kick)
Phi – FG Ruzek 39
Phi – Williams 6 pass from Cunningham (Ruzek kick)
Phi – Evans 23 interception return (Ruzek kick)
A: 66,706 T: 3:01

GREEN BAY 20, TAMPA BAY 10—At Milwaukee County Stadium. Packer backup Anthony Dilweg, subbing for injured starter Don Majkowski, threw two touchdown passes in a Green Bay win. For the Bucs, QB Vinny Testaverde, benched for two games, started and threw for 281 yards and a TD, but Tampa Bay's offense has not scored more than one TD in a game in six weeks.

Tampa Bay	0	3	7	0	–	10
Green Bay	0	7	10	3	–	20

G.B. – Sharpe 4 pass from Dilweg (Jacke kick)
T.B. – FG Christie 33
G.B. – Haddix 2 pass from Dilweg (Jacke kick)
G.B. – FG Jacke 25
T.B. – Hill 11 pass from Testaverde (Christie kick)
G.B. – FG Jacke 25
A: 53,677 T: 2:53

KANSAS CITY 27, L.A. RAIDERS 24—At Memorial Coliseum. The Chiefs, behind three TD passes by Steve DeBerg, swept their season series with the Raiders and moved into a tie for first place in the AFC West. The game went back and forth, with L.A. answering every Kansas City score, until DeBerg found running back Bill Jones open in the end zone for an 11-yard TD with 6:32 remaining that gave the Chiefs a 27–17 lead. Marcus Allen scored three TDs for the Raiders, and L.A.'s defense held Kansas City backs Christian Okoye and Barry Word to a combined 82 yards rushing, but L.A. QB Jay Schroeder lost two fumbles, which led to Kansas City TDs. The Chiefs defense sacked Schroeder five times and held Bo Jackson to 25 yards rushing.

Kansas City	0	10	10	7	–	27
Los Angeles	0	10	7	7	–	24

K.C. – FG Lowery 35
L.A. – Allen 3 run (Jaeger kick)
K.C. – Harry 19 pass from DeBerg (Lowery kick)
L.A. – FG Jaeger 50
K.C. – Jones 11 pass from DeBerg (Lowery kick)
L.A. – Allen 10 run (Jaeger kick)
K.C. – FG Lowery 36
K.C. – Jones 11 pass from DeBerg (Lowery kick)
L.A. – Allen 5 run (Jaeger kick)
A: 69,326 T: 3:38

L.A. RAMS 28, SAN FRANCISCO 17—At Candlestick Park. The Rams ended the 49ers' 18-game winning streak and handed San Francisco its first loss of the season. In the second half, the 49ers rallied from a 14-point halftime deficit to pull to 21–17, but L.A. responded with a 17-play, 90-yard drive for a TD that consumed 10:37 of the fourth quarter. Cleveland Gary ended the drive with a one-yard plunge for his third TD of the game. Ram cornerback Bobby Humphery clinched the victory with an interception of a Joe Montana pass with 2:09 remaining. The 49ers suffered six turnovers: three interceptions and three fumbles.

Los Angeles	7	14	0	7	–	28
San Francisco	0	7	10	0	–	17

L.A. – Gary 22 pass from McGee (Lansford kick)
L.A. – Gary 10 run (Lansford kick)
S.F. – Taylor 5 pass from Montana (Cofer kick)
L.A. – McGee 6 run (Lansford kick)
S.F. – Sydney 23 pass from Montana (Cofer kick)
S.F. – FG Cofer 42
L.A. – Gary 1 run (Lansford kick)
A: 62,633 T: 3:05

PHOENIX 34, NEW ENGLAND 14—At Sun Devil Stadium. Rookie running back Anthony Thompson of the Cardinals, who was filling in for injured fellow rookie Johnny Johnson, rushed for 136 yards and a TD in leading Phoenix to a win over the hapless Patriots. The victory ended a five-game Cardinals' losing streak.

New England	7	7	0	0	–	14
Phoenix	7	7	10	10	–	34

Phoe – Thompson 5 run (Del Greco kick)
N.E. – Stephens 18 pass from Hodson (Staurovsky kick)
Phoe – Rosenbach 2 run (Del Greco kick)
N.E. – Cook 22 pass from Hodson (Staurovsky kick)
Phoe – FG Del Greco 29
Phoe – Rosenbach 6 run (Del Greco kick)
Phoe – Flagler 29 run (Del Greco kick)
Phoe – FG Del Greco 50
A: 30,110 T: 2:52

PITTSBURGH 24, N.Y. JETS 7—At Giants Stadium. In a sloppy game, the Steelers spotted the Jets a touchdown before scoring 24 straight points and blanking New York. Pittsburgh fumbled eight times (losing one), had two passes intercepted and was penalized eight times for 62 yards. The Jets' offensive woes continued as they totaled only 173 net yards.

Pittsburgh	0	7	3	14	–	24
New York	0	7	0	0	–	7

N.Y. – Moore 53 pass from O'Brien (Leahy kick)
Pitt – Williams 5 pass from Brister (Anderson kick)
Pitt – FG Anderson 33
Pitt – Hoge 1 run (Anderson kick)
Pitt – Lipps 3 pass from Brister (Anderson kick)
A: 57,806 T: 2:38

SEATTLE 13, SAN DIEGO 10—At Jack Murphy Stadium. The Seahawks overcame a 128-yard rushing performance by Charger running back Marion Butts and five fumbles (one lost) by QB Dave Krieg to beat San Diego in overtime. The big play in the extra period came when Charger tight end Arthur Cox fumbled at his own 23-yard line. Seattle linebacker Rufus Porter recovered, and two plays later, kicker Norm Johnson booted a 40-yard field goal to end the game. With less than a minute to go in regulation and the score tied, Cox lost a fumble after catching a pass, allowing Seattle to run out the clock and send the game into OT.

Seattle	0	3	0	7	3	–	13
San Diego	0	3	7	0	0	–	10

S.D. – FG Carney 20
Sea – FG Johnson 26
S.D. – Cox 8 pass from Tolliver (Carney kick)
Sea – Fenner 1 run (Johnson kick)
Sea – FG Johnson 40
A: 50,096 T: 2:57

MONDAY, NOVEMBER 26

HOUSTON 27, BUFFALO 24—At the Astrodome. The Oilers upset the Bills to keep pace with Pittsburgh and Cincinnati for the lead in the AFC Central. Houston running back Lorenzo White had the team's first 100-yard rushing day of the year as he churned out 125 yards on 18 carries. White also caught five passes for 89 yards. Oiler QB Warren Moon threw for 300 yards, his fourth straight game of 300 yards or better passing. Buffalo stayed right with the Oilers until the fourth quarter when Moon led an 88-yard drive, flipping three yards to Leonard Harris for a TD. The Bills answered with a Thurman Thomas TD with 3:29 remaining, but the Oilers were able to run out the clock.

Buffalo	7	7	3	7	–	24
Houston	7	6	7	7	–	27

Hou – Jeffires 37 pass from Moon (Garcia kick)
Buff – Metzelaars 1 pass from Kelly (Norwood kick)
Hou – FG Garcia 25
Hou – FG Garcia 36
Buff – McKeller 12 pass from Kelly (Norwood kick)
Buff – FG Norwood 43
Hou – White 1 run (Garcia kick)
Hou – Harris 3 pass from Moon (Garcia kick)
Buff – Thomas 2 run (Norwood kick)
A: 60,130 T: 2:47

WEEK 13 STANDINGS

AFC EAST	W	L	T	Pct.	PF	PA
Buffalo	10	2	0	.833	342	200
Miami	9	3	0	.750	252	164
Indianapolis	5	7	0	.417	193	250
N.Y. Jets	4	9	0	.308	216	295
New England	1	11	0	.083	151	342

AFC CENTRAL	W	L	T	Pct.	PF	PA
Cincinnati	7	5	0	.583	275	274
Houston	6	6	0	.500	266	229
Pittsburgh	6	6	0	.500	210	197
Cleveland	2	10	0	.167	187	338

AFC WEST	W	L	T	Pct.	PF	PA
Kansas City	8	4	0	.667	283	179
L.A. Raiders	8	4	0	.667	230	194
Seattle	6	6	0	.500	222	226
San Diego	6	7	0	.462	272	220
Denver	3	9	0	.250	257	303

NFC EAST	W	L	T	Pct.	PF	PA
N.Y. Giants	10	2	0	.833	262	148
Philadelphia	7	5	0	.583	305	252
Washington	7	5	0	.583	289	233
Dallas	6	7	0	.462	193	255
Phoenix	4	8	0	.333	192	295

NFC CENTRAL	W	L	T	Pct.	PF	PA
Chicago	10	2	0	.833	281	197
Green Bay	6	6	0	.500	227	250
Minnesota	6	6	0	.500	282	229
Tampa Bay	5	8	0	.364	210	311
Detroit	4	8	0	.333	270	307

NFC WEST	W	L	T	Pct.	PF	PA
San Francisco	11	1	0	.909	277	182
L.A. Rams	5	7	0	.417	285	322
New Orleans	5	7	0	.417	211	219
Atlanta	3	9	0	.250	279	308

RESULTS

Chicago 23, Detroit 17 (OT)
Tampa Bay 23, Atlanta 17
Cincinnati 16, Pittsburgh 12
Kansas City 37, New England 7
L.A. Rams 38, Cleveland 23
Buffalo 30, Philadelphia 23
Washington 42, Miami 20
Seattle 13, Houston 10 (OT)
San Deigo 38, N.Y. Jets 17
Phoenix 20, Indianapolis 17
L.A. Raiders 23, Denver 20
Dallas 17, New Orleans 13
Minnesota 23, Green Bay 7
San Francisco 7, N.Y. Giants 3 (Monday night)

SUNDAY, DECEMBER 2

CHICAGO 23, DETROIT 17—At Soldier Field. Neal Anderson of the Bears caught a 50-yard touchdown pass in overtime to give Chicago the win. The Bears elected to take the wind in the overtime period and give the ball to Detroit first, a strategy that nearly backfired when the Lions moved into position for a 35-yard field goal. But Eddie Murray missed on the attempt, and the Bears scored on their next possession. A Detroit miscue helped send the game into overtime. The Lions had the ball at the Chicago 22 and were leading 17–14 with less than three minutes remaining when Bears linebacker Ron Rivera intercepted a Bob Gagliano pass. Chicago drove to the Detroit one-yard line, tying the game with a 19-yard field goal by Kevin Butler. Bears QB Jim Harbaugh passed more than usual, completing 23 of 39 passes for 208 yards without an interception.

Detroit	7	3	0	7	0	—	17
Chicago	0	14	0	3	6	—	23

Det — Peete 1 run (Murray kick)
Chi — Muster 6 run (Butler kick)
Det — FG Murray 34
Chi — Harbaugh 2 run (Butler kick)
Det — Johnson 22 pass from Gagliano (Murray kick)
Chi — FG Butler 19
Chi — Anderson 50 pass from Harbaugh
A: 66,946 T: 3:25

TAMPA BAY 23, ATLANTA 17—At Tampa Stadium. Vinny Testaverde hit Mark Carrier with a 35-yard pass with 39 seconds remaining to give the Buccaneers a win and end their six-game losing streak. The Falcons suffered their 17th straight road loss. Testaverde finished the game 17 of 33 for 351 yards, including an 89-yard touchdown pass to Willie Drewrey, the longest TD pass in Tampa Bay history. Atlanta was up 14–13 in the fourth quarter when a Buccaneer punt hit a Falcon player in the back, allowing Tampa Bay to recover and take the lead on a 21-yard field goal by Steve Christie. Atlanta took the lead again on a 46-yard field goal by Greg Davis before Carrier caught the winning TD pass. Falcon quarterback Chris Miller left the game with a broken collarbone and will miss the rest of the season.

Atlanta	7	0	0	10	—	17
Tampa Bay	0	13	0	10	—	23

Atl — Johnson 3 run (Davis kick)
T.B. — Drewrey 89 pass from Testaverde (Christie kick)
T.B. — FG Christie 39
T.B. — FG Christie 44
Atl — Rozier 9 run (Davis kick)
T.B. — FG Christie 21
Atl — FG Davis 46
T.B. — Carrier 35 pass from Testaverde (Christie kick)
A: 42,839 T: 2:49

CINCINNATI 16, PITTSBURGH 12—At Three Rivers Stadium. The Bengals jumped out to a 10-point halftime lead, then came up with a crucial goal-line stand to preserve the win late in the fourth quarter, holding the Steelers scoreless after they had a first down on the seven. Cincinnati's defense allowed Pittsburgh 305 total yards, but the Steelers could get only four field goals out of eight trips across the 50. The Bengals moved the ball well on the ground, rushing for 165 yards—James Brooks had 81 of them—but two missed field goals in the second half by Jim Breech allowed Pittsburgh to stay in the game. On one drive in the second quarter, the Bengals covered 63 yards in 12 plays and ran 7:01 off the clock.

Cincinnati	7	9	0	0	—	16
Pittsburgh	6	0	3	3	—	12

Pitt — FG Anderson 32
Cin — Brown 50 pass from Esiason (Breech kick)
Pitt — FG Anderson 36
Cin — Safety, Francis tackled Brister in end zone
Cin — Brooks 7 run (Breech kick)
Pitt — FG Anderson 29
Pitt — FG Anderson 48
A: 58,200 T: 2:52

KANSAS CITY 37, NEW ENGLAND 7—At Foxboro Stadium. The Chiefs had little trouble with the Patriots, handing New England its club-record 10th straight loss. Kansas City started off hot, with Stephone Paige burning Ronnie Lippett for an 86-yard touchdown reception on the first play from scrimmage. Chiefs QB Steve DeBerg, who finished at 15 of 21 for 331 yards, also hit J.J. Birden with a 61-yard pass in the first quarter to set up a 19-yard Nick Lowery field goal. After bolting ahead for a 23–0 halftime lead, the Chiefs were content to give the ball to Barry Word, who rushed 19 times for 112 yards. Christian Okoye had only five yards on 11 carries, but two of his carries went for touchdowns.

Kansas City	13	10	7	7	—	37
New England	0	0	7	0	—	7

K.C. — Paige 86 pass from DeBerg (Lowery kick)
K.C. — FG Lowery 19
K.C. — FG Lowery 32
K.C. — FG Lowery 45
K.C. — Thomas 11 pass from DeBerg (Lowery kick)
K.C. — Okoye 1 run (Lowery kick)
N.E. — Cook 2 pass from Hodson (Staurovsky kick)
K.C. — Okoye 1 run (Lowery kick)
A: 26,280 T: 2:56

L.A. RAMS 38, CLEVELAND 23—At Cleveland Stadium. The Rams moved the ball consistently on offense as Cleveland proved to be an easy opponent. After the Browns tied the score 3–3 on a Jerry Kauric field goal near the end of the first quarter, L.A. scored 21 unanswered points. Jim Everett was the catalyst for the Ram offense, throwing four touchdown passes to four different receivers and completing 22 of 29 passes for 261 yards. Henry Ellard caught six passes for 90 yards and passed Tom Fears as the Rams' alltime leading receiver, with 402 receptions. On defense for L.A., Kevin Greene sacked Bernie Kosar three times.

Los Angeles	3	14	14	7	—	38
Cleveland	3	0	14	6	—	23

L.A. — FG Lansford 30
Cle — FG Kauric 27
L.A. — Holohan 1 pass from Everett (Lansford kick)
L.A. — Green 16 pass from Everett (Lansford kick)
L.A. — Gary 1 run (Lansford kick)
Cle — Slaughter 17 pass from Kosar (Kauric kick)
L.A. — Delpino 21 pass from Everett (Lansford kick)
Cle — Mack 3 pass from Kosar (Kauric kick)
L.A. — McGee 9 pass from Everett (Lansford kick)
Cle — Mack 1 run (kick failed)
A: 61,981 T: 2:47

BUFFALO 30, PHILADELPHIA 23—At Rich Stadium. The Bills jumped out to a 24–0 first-quarter lead and seemed set to run away with the game, but the Eagles closed to 24–23 midway through the third quarter. After a Scott Norwood field goal gave the Bills a four-point cushion, Eagle linebacker Seth Joyner intercepted a Jim Kelly pass, but when Joyner attempted a lateral, the ball didn't reach his intended target and Buffalo receiver James Lofton came away with the ball to preserve the win. Lofton was the big star on offense, catching five passes for 174 yards and a TD. The Bills defense sacked Randall Cunningham six times.

Philadelphia	0	16	7	0	—	23
Buffalo	24	0	3	3	—	30

Buff — Lofton 63 pass from Kelly (Norwood kick)
Buff — FG Norwood 43
Buff — Reed 56 pass from Kelly (Norwood kick)
Buff — Thomas 4 pass from Kelly (Norwood kick)
Phi — Jackson 18 pass from Cunningham (Ruzek kick)
Phi — FG Ruzek 32
Phi — Barnett 95 pass from Cunningham (Ruzek kick)
Phi — Byars 1 pass from Cunningham (Ruzek kick)
Buff — FG Norwood 21
Buff — FG Norwood 45
A: 79,320 T: 3:08

WASHINGTON 42, MIAMI 20—At RFK Stadium. The Redskins offense dominated Miami's league-leading defense, with most of the damage done by running back Earnest Byner, who rushed for 157 yards and scored three touchdowns on 32 carries. Wide receiver Art Monk and quarterback Mark Rypien teamed up for 10 completions totaling 92 yards and two touchdowns. Washington's defense held the Dolphins to 34 yards on the ground.

Miami	0	3	3	14	—	20
Washington	7	14	14	7	—	42

Wash — Byner 2 run (Lohmiller kick)
Wash — Monk 6 pass from Rypien (Lohmiller kick)
Wash — Byner 7 run (Lohmiller kick)
Mia — FG Stoyanovich 21
Mia — FG Stoyanovich 44
Wash — Johnson 3 pass from Rypien (Lohmiller kick)
Wash — Byner 13 run (Lohmiller kick)
Mia — Pruitt 24 pass from Marino (Stoyanovich kick)
Mia — Williams 42 interception return (Stoyanovich kick)
Wash — Monk 7 pass from Rypien (Lohmiller kick)
A: 53,599 T: 2:48

SEATTLE 13, HOUSTON 10—At the Kingdome. For the fourth week in a row, the Seahawks' game came down to the final play, and for the third time, Seattle won, this time beating the Oilers on a 42-yard field goal by Norm Johnson in overtime. Seattle got the chance to kick the field goal when linebacker Tony Woods forced a fumble by wide receiver Bernard Ford at the Houston 25 and linebacker David Wyman recovered. Ball control helped the Seahawks keep the Oilers' high-powered offense in check, with Seattle dominating time of possession 36:50 to 27:35. Houston quarterback Warren Moon's streak of games with 300-plus passing yards was stopped at four.

Houston	0	3	0	7	0	—	10
Seattle	0	7	3	0	3	—	13

Hou — FG Garcia 29
Sea — Warren 1 run (Johnson kick)
Sea — FG Johnson 39
Hou — Givins 2 pass from Moon (Garcia kick)
Sea — FG Johnson 42
A: 57,592 T: 3:09

SAN DIEGO 38, N.Y. JETS 17—At Jack Murphy Stadium. The Jets performed yet another second-half swandive, allowing the Chargers to pull away for the win. New York had pulled to within 24–17 early in the fourth quarter, but San Diego embarked on a six-play, 84-yard drive to extend its lead to 14 points. Marion Butts scored two touchdowns and rushed 26 times for 159 yards.

New York	3	7	0	7	—	17
San Diego	7	10	7	14	—	38

N.Y. — FG Leahy 38
S.D. — Butts 1 run (Carney kick)
S.D. — Butts 4 run (Carney kick)
N.Y. — Toon 21 pass from O'Brien (Leahy kick)
S.D. — FG Carney 22
S.D. — Miller 24 pass from Tolliver (Carney kick)
N.Y. — Toon 8 pass from O'Brien (Leahy kick)
S.D. — Lewis 19 pass from Tolliver (Carney kick)
S.D. — Lewis 10 run (Carney kick)
A: 40,877 T: 2:59

PHOENIX 20, INDIANAPOLIS 17—At Sun Devil Stadium. Taking a lateral from Cedric Mack after Mack's interception of Colt QB Jeff George, Marcus Turner scampered 21 yards for the winning touchdown with 10:19 left, to give the Cards their second straight win and end Indianapolis's three-game winning streak. George had thrown 147 straight passes without an interception.

Indianapolis	10	0	7	0	—	17
Phoenix	0	6	0	14	—	20

Ind — FG Biasucci 49
Ind — Johnson 15 pass from George (Biasucci kick)
Phoe — FG Del Greco 32
Phoe — FG Del Greco 39
Ind — Hester 6 pass from George (Biasucci kick)
Phoe — Rosenbach 1 run (Del Greco kick)
Phoe — Turner 21 return of Mack interception (Del Greco kick)
A: 31,885 T: 2:57

L.A. RAIDERS 23, DENVER 20—At Mile High Stadium. With seven seconds remaining, Scott Davis of the Raiders blocked a 41-yard field goal try by David Treadwell to preserve a Los Angeles win. The Raiders took the lead in the third quarter when Bo Jackson, who gained 117 yard on 13 carries, scored on an 11-yard run two plays after Terry McDaniel's interception. Jackson also had a 62-yard run for a TD in the fourth quarter.

Los Angeles	7	0	7	9	—	23
Denver	3	7	0	10	—	20

Den — FG Treadwell 45
L.A. — Smith 4 run (Jaeger kick)
Den — Johnson 21 pass from Elway (Treadwell kick)
L.A. — Jackson 11 run (Jaeger kick)
Den — FG Treadwell 21
L.A. — Jackson 62 run (Jaeger kick)
L.A. — FG Jaeger 46
Den — Young 8 pass from Elway (Treadwell kick)
A: 74,162 T: 3:04

DALLAS 17, NEW ORLEANS 13—At Texas Stadium. The Cowboys surged back from a 10-point halftime deficit to beat the Saints. On the first play of the second half, Dallas QB Troy Aikman hit Kelvin Martin with a 45-yard pass, which began an eight-play, 80-yard drive for the TD that got the Cowboys back in the game. Late in the fourth quarter with the score tied, New Orleans punter Tommy Barnhardt's boot traveled only 17 yards, setting up Ken Willis's winning 47-yard field goal with 53 seconds remaining.

New Orleans	3	7	3	0	—	13
Dallas	0	0	7	10	—	17

N.O. — FG Andersen 43
N.O. — Mayes 15 run (Andersen kick)
Dall — Smith 1 run (Willis kick)
N.O. — FG Andersen 50
Dall — Johnston 5 pass from Aikman (Willis kick)
Dall — FG Willis 47
A: 60,087 T: 2:45

MINNESOTA 23, GREEN BAY 7—At the Metrodome. The Vikings extended their winning streak to five games with a victory over the Packers. Minnesota fell behind 7–6 in the third quarter when Green Bay's Tiger Greene blocked a punt and returned the ball for a TD, but the Vikings rallied for 17 points in the final three minutes. Packer QB Anthony Dilweg fumbled twice and threw an interception, miscues that produced 13 of Minnesota's points.

Green Bay	0	0	7	0	—	7
Minnesota	3	3	17	0	—	23

Minn — FG Reveiz 29
Minn — FG Reveiz 32
G.B. — Greene 36 blocked punt return (Jacke kick)
Minn — FG Reveiz 41
Minn — Carter 56 pass from Gannon (Reveiz kick)
Minn — Noga fumble recovery in end zone (Reveiz kick)
A: 62,058 T: 3:00

MONDAY, DECEMBER 3

SAN FRANCISCO 7, N.Y. GIANTS 3—At Candlestick Park. In a fierce defensive struggle, the 49ers won the battle of the two teams with the best records in the league after stopping the Giants twice on first-and-goal opportunities. After New York failed on a fourth-and-nine play with 3:59 left, the 49ers were able to eat some of the clock before the Giants got the ball back for one last shot, which failed when Phil Simms was sacked on the last play of the game. John Taylor scored the day's only TD when Joe Montana found him on a 23-yard post pattern in the first half.

New York	0	3	0	0	—	3
San Francisco	0	7	0	0	—	7

N.Y. — FG Bahr 20
S.F. — Taylor 23 pass from Montana (Cofer kick)
A: 66,413 T: 2:50

WEEK 14 STANDINGS

AFC EAST	W	L	T	Pct.	PF	PA
Buffalo	11	2	0	.846	373	207
Miami	10	3	0	.769	275	184
Indianapolis	5	8	0	.385	200	281
N.Y. Jets	4	9	0	.308	216	295
New England	1	12	0	.077	154	366

AFC CENTRAL	W	L	T	Pct.	PF	PA
Cincinnati	7	6	0	.538	292	294
Houston	7	6	0	.538	324	243
Pittsburgh	7	6	0	.538	234	200
Cleveland	2	11	0	.154	201	396

AFC WEST	W	L	T	Pct.	PF	PA
Kansas City	9	4	0	.692	314	199
L.A. Raiders	9	4	0	.692	268	225
Seattle	7	6	0	.538	242	240
San Diego	6	7	0	.462	272	220
Denver	3	10	0	.231	277	334

NFC EAST	W	L	T	Pct.	PF	PA
N.Y. Giants	11	2	0	.846	285	163
Washington	8	5	0	.615	299	242
Philadelphia	7	6	0	.538	325	275
Dallas	6	7	0	.462	193	255
Phoenix	5	8	0	.385	206	308

NFC CENTRAL	W	L	T	Pct.	PF	PA
Chicago	10	3	0	.769	290	207
Green Bay	6	7	0	.462	241	270
Minnesota	6	7	0	.462	297	252
Tampa Bay	5	8	0	.385	210	311
Detroit	4	9	0	.308	301	345

NFC WEST	W	L	T	Pct.	PF	PA
San Francisco	12	1	0	.923	297	199
New Orleans	6	7	0	.462	235	239
L.A. Rams	5	8	0	.385	305	346
Atlanta	3	10	0	.231	292	332

RESULTS
Buffalo 31, Indianapolis 7
Houston 58, Cleveland 14
N.Y. Giants 23, Minnesota 15
Pittsburgh 24, New England 3
Phoenix 24, Atlanta 13
San Francisco 20, Cincinnati 17 (OT)
Seattle 20, Green Bay 14
Washington 10, Chicago 9
Kansas City 31, Denver 20
New Orleans 24, L.A. Rams 20
Miami 23, Philadelphia 20 (OT)
L.A. Raiders 38, Detroit 31 (Monday night)
Open dates: Dallas, N.Y. Jets, San Diego, Tampa Bay

SUNDAY, DECEMBER 9

BUFFALO 31, INDIANAPOLIS 7—At the Hoosier Dome. Bills defensive end Bruce Smith sacked Colt quarterback Jeff George four times as Buffalo enjoyed a rout. The Bills defense held George to 13 of 25 passing for 93 yards as Indianapolis totaled only 127 offensive yards. The Bills offense got two touchdowns each from wide receiver Andre Reed and running back Thurman Thomas, who rushed for 76 yards and caught four passes for 91 yards. With 37 career touchdown catches, Reed now holds the club record.

Buffalo	14	7	3	7	–	31
Indianapolis	0	0	7	0	–	7

Buff – Reed 34 pass from Kelly (Norwood kick)
Buff – Reed 7 pass from Kelly (Norwood kick)
Buff – Thomas 5 run (Norwood kick)
Ind – George 1 run (Biasucci kick)
Buff – FG Norwood 25
Buff – Thomas 23 run (Norwood kick)
A: 53,268 T: 2:39

HOUSTON 58, CLEVELAND 14—At the Astrodome. The Browns hit rock bottom in a disappointing season as the Oilers set a team record for number of points scored in a game. Houston began the point parade by scoring six touchdowns and a field goal on its first seven possessions, totaling 31 points in the second quarter alone. Warren Moon, the Oiler quarterback, had only an average game, completing 17 of 25 passes for 190 yards and two touchdowns, but running back Lorenzo White put the run in the run-and-shoot by rushing for 116 yards and four touchdowns, tying a team record set by Earl Campbell in 1978. The Oiler defense intercepted Browns quarterback Bernie Kosar twice and sacked him four times. With a 101-yard return in the second quarter, Cleveland's Eric Metcalf became the first Brown to score two touchdowns on kickoff returns in one season.

Cleveland	0	7	7	0	–	14
Houston	14	31	7	6	–	58

Hou – White 10 run (Garcia kick)
Hou – White 1 run (Garcia kick)
Hou – Kinard 72 fumble return (Garcia kick)
Hou – Givins 6 pass from Moon (Garcia kick)
Cle – Metcalf 101 kickoff return (Kauric kick)
Hou – FG Garcia 45
Hou – White 7 run (Garcia kick)
Hou – Harris 17 pass from Moon (Garcia kick)
Hou – White 5 run (Garcia kick)
Cle – Metcalf 31 pass from Kosar (Kauric kick)
Hou – Jones 9 pass from Carlson (kick failed)
A: 54,469 T: 3:11

N.Y. GIANTS 23, MINNESOTA 15—At Giants Stadium. Linebacker Lawrence Taylor, who had only 1.5 sacks in the Giants' previous nine games, got 2.5 against the Vikings as New York came back from a halftime deficit to clinch the NFC East title. Taylor also had nine tackles, three assists and a forced fumble. Trailing by two midway through the fourth quarter, New York forced the Vikings to punt from their own 10, then embarked on a 42-yard drive that culminated in the go-ahead TD on a two-yard plunge by Ottis Anderson. Anderson ran for 26 yards on the day to extend his career total to 10,012 and become the eighth runner in NFL history to gain more than 10,000 yards. Rookie running back Rodney Hampton rushed for 78 yards on 19 carries. Coach Bill Parcells was on the sidelines despite a painful kidney stone, which later required hospitalization.

Minnesota	5	7	3	0	–	15
New York	3	7	0	13	–	23

Minn – Safety, Simms sacked in the end zone by Doleman
Minn – FG Reveiz 22
N.Y. – FG Bahr 36
Minn – Anderson 1 run (Reveiz kick)
N.Y. – Anderson 1 run (Bahr kick)
Minn – FG Reveiz 37
N.Y. – FG Bahr 48
N.Y. – Anderson 2 run (Bahr kick)
N.Y. – FG Bahr 18
A: 76,121 T: 3:03

PITTSBURGH 24, NEW ENGLAND 3—At Three Rivers Stadium. Steeler coach Chuck Noll got his 200th career victory as Pittsburgh remained in a three-way tie for the AFC Central lead. The Steeler defense set up the first score of the game, a Gary Anderson field goal, with a recovery of a fumble by John Stephens in the first quarter. Midway through the second quarter, Pittsburgh added to its lead with a seven-play, 80-yard drive that ended with an eight-yard run by Merril Hoge, who rushed for 117 yards and two touchdowns. The Steeler defense allowed New England only 182 total yards and just 56 yards on the ground. Pittsburgh nosetackle Gerald Williams had two sacks. The loss was the 11th in a row for the Patriots.

New England	0	3	0	0	–	3
Pittsburgh	3	7	7	7	–	24

Pitt – FG Anderson 42
Pitt – Hoge 8 run (Anderson kick)
N.E. – FG Staurovsky 49
Pitt – Green 14 pass from Brister (Anderson kick)
Pitt – Hoge 41 run (Anderson kick)
A: 48,354 T: 2:40

PHOENIX 24, ATLANTA 13—At Atlanta–Fulton County Stadium. With less than five minutes to go and the Cardinals leading by four, Phoenix cornerback Marcus Turner intercepted a pass by Falcon quarterback Scott Campbell and returned it 47 yards to put the game away. Atlanta had four turnovers for the day as well as 104 yards in penalties, the most crucial one an offside call with only one second left in the half, which allowed Phoenix to kick a field goal. The Cardinals converted 10 of 17 third-down plays, amassed 20 first downs (three by penalty), gained 361 net yards and were led on offense by rookie wide receiver Ricky Proehl, who caught six passes for 102 yards.

Phoenix	0	10	7	7	–	24
Atlanta	3	7	0	3	–	13

Atl – FG Davis 41
Phoe – Proehl 45 pass from Rosenbach (Del Greco kick)
Atl – Wilkins 20 pass from Campbell (Davis kick)
Phoe – FG Del Greco 37
Phoe – Thompson 1 run (Del Greco kick)
Atl – FG Davis 24
Phoe – Turner 47 interception return (Del Greco kick)
A: 36,222 T: 3:10

SAN FRANCISCO 20, CINCINNATI 17—At Riverfront Stadium. The 49ers unveiled a surprisingly effective running game with an unsurprising result as they beat the Bengals in overtime. Mike Cofer's 23-yard field goal with 6:12 gone in the extra period capped a 75-yard drive to give San Francisco its 17th consecutive road victory. Another 23-yard Cofer field goal had tied the game with 57 seconds left in regulation. The 49ers gained 202 rushing yards for the day, with Roger Craig totaling 97 yards on 21 carries and Tom Rathman and Harry Sydney contributing 53 and 36 yards, respectively. The win was San Francisco's seventh in a row over the Bengals.

San Francisco	7	0	7	3	3	–	20
Cincinnati	7	0	10	0	0	–	17

Cin – Taylor 2 pass from Esiason (Breech kick)
S.F. – Rathman 1 run (Cofer kick)
Cin – FG Breech 38
S.F. – Sydney 3 run (Cofer kick)
Cin – Woods 1 run (Breech kick)
S.F. – FG Cofer 23
S.F. – FG Coer 23
A: 60,084 T: 3:00

SEATTLE 20, GREEN BAY 14—At Milwaukee County Stadium. Blair Kiel, the third-string quarterback for the Packers, threw two fourth-quarter touchdown passes, but Green Bay could not come back from a 20–0 deficit. The Packers got the ball in scoring position one last time with 3:36 remaining when the Seahawks' Nesby Glasgow fumbled on a kickoff return, but on a fourth-and-six from the Seattle eight-yard line, Kiel missed receiver Jeff Query with a pass. The Seahawks dominated the first half in building a 17–0 lead, gaining 198 yards to the Packers' 65. Seattle's defense held Green Bay to 13 yards on the ground, a team-record low for the Packers. Running back Derrick Fenner rushed for 112 yards on 20 carries, and linebacker David Wyman had 10 tackles for Seattle.

Seattle	7	10	3	0	–	20
Green Bay	0	0	0	14	–	14

Sea – Chadwick 8 pass from Krieg (Johnson kick)
Sea – FG Johnson 37
Sea – Fenner 14 run (Johnson kick)
Sea – FG Johnson 22
G.B. – Kemp 13 pass from Kiel (Jacke kick)
G.B. – West 1 pass from Kiel (Jacke kick)
A: 52,015 T: 3:07

WASHINGTON 10, CHICAGO 9—At RFK Stadium. Chip Lohmiller kicked a 35-yard field goal with 2:14 remaining to give the Redskins the win. The Bears defense stifled Washington in the first half, picking off three Mark Rypien passes, but the Redskins bounced back with a 12-play, 72-yard drive in the third quarter for a touchdown and also with a fumble recovery in the fourth quarter that set up the winning field goal. Rypien threw five interceptions overall, with Chicago rookie Mark Carrier picking off three to tie a club record. Earnest Byner led the Washington offense with 121 yards on 28 carries. The Redskins defense shut out the Bears in the second half, intercepting Chicago QB Jim Harbaugh twice in the final two minutes to secure the victory.

Chicago	3	6	0	0	–	9
Washington	0	0	7	3	–	10

Chi – FG Butler 29
Chi – FG Butler 23
Chi – FG Butler 46
Wash – Clark 8 pass from Rypien (Lohmiller kick)
Wash – FG Lohmiller 35
A: 53,920 T: 3:05

KANSAS CITY 31, DENVER 20—At Arrowhead Stadium. Chiefs quarterback Steve DeBerg, facing a fourth-and-three from the Bronco 27 with his team ahead by four points, hit Robb Thomas with a touchdown pass to seal the victory over Denver. In the third quarter, Kansas City's Barry Word had scored the go-ahead touchdown on a fourth-down play from the one. Two John Elway touchdown passes gave the Broncos a 13–10 lead at halftime, but the Chiefs stormed back in the second half, with the defense forcing Denver turnovers on the Broncos' first three possessions. DeBerg completed 18 of 27 passes for 254 yards and three touchdowns, including a 49-yarder to Stephone Paige off a flea-flicker. Kansas City linebacker Derrick Thomas had two sacks.

Denver	0	13	0	7	–	20
Kansas City	7	3	7	14	–	31

K.C. – Paige 49 pass from DeBerg (Lowery kick)
Den – Sharpe 5 pass from Elway (kick failed)
Den – Young 16 pass from Elway (Treadwell kick)
K.C. – FG Lowery 33
K.C. – Word 1 run (Lowery kick)
K.C. – Whitaker 1 pass from DeBerg (Lowery kick)
Den – Humphrey 2 run (Treadwell kick)
K.C. – Thomas 27 pass from DeBerg (Lowery kick)
A: 74,347 T: 3:14

NEW ORLEANS 24, L.A. RAMS 20—At Anaheim Stadium. The Saints came back from a 10-point deficit and got a big defensive play to keep the Rams from scoring after they had reached the New Orleans six-yard line on their final possession. Linebacker Pat Swilling forced L.A. quarterback Jim Everett to fumble on what would have been the final play of the game had an offside penalty not given the Rams another chance. But Swilling came up big yet again, forcing Everett to throw incomplete. Steve Walsh had put the Saints ahead in the fourth quarter with a four-yard TD pass to wide receiver Eric Martin. Reserve running back Gill Fenerty carried the ball 10 times for 104 yards, breaking loose for a 60-yard touchdown run in the fourth quarter. For the Rams, running back Cleveland Gary had four receptions for 118 yards but fumbled twice, once at the New Orleans goal line.

New Orleans	0	3	7	14	–	24
Los Angeles	0	10	7	3	–	20

L.A. – FG Lansford 38
N.O. – FG Andersen 48
L.A. – Everett 2 run (Lansford kick)
N.O. – Maxie 50 interception return (Andersen kick)
L.A. – Ellard 42 pass from Everett (Lansford kick)
L.A. – FG Lansford 18
N.O. – Fenerty 60 run (Andersen kick)
N.O. – Martin 4 pass from Walsh (Andersen kick)
A: 56,864 T: 3:01

MIAMI 23, PHILADELPHIA 20—At Joe Robbie Stadium. Dan Marino led the Dolphins back from a 20–10 fourth-quarter deficit, and Pete Stoyanovich kicked the winning field goal with 2:28 left in overtime to clinch a playoff spot. Marino completed 27 of 54 passes for 365 yards and two touchdowns, but no completion was bigger than a 12-yard pass to Mark Duper on a fourth-and-10 to set up Stoyanovich's game-tying 34-yard field goal with three seconds to go in regulation. In the overtime period, Miami got a break when Eagle punter Jeff Feagles bobbled a low snap and illegally kicked the ball 23 yards. The Dolphins refused the illegal kick penalty and began a six-play, 35-yard drive to set up the winning field goal. Philadelphia was able to run the ball well against the Miami defense, totaling 257 yards, 94 by QB Randall Cunningham.

Philadelphia	0	10	3	7	0	–	20
Miami	10	0	0	10	3	–	23

Mia – Martin 28 pass from Marino (Stoyanovich kick)
Mia – FG Stoyanovich 24
Phi – Byars 3 pass from Cunningham (Ruzek kick)
Phi – FG Ruzek 53
Phi – FG Ruzek 33
Phi – Williams 45 pass from Cunningham (Ruzek kick)
Mia – Duper 6 pass from Marino (Stoyanovich kick)
Mia – FG Stoyanovich 34
Mia – FG Stoyanovich 39
A: 67,034 T: 3:22

MONDAY, DECEMBER 10

L.A. RAIDERS 38, DETROIT 31—At the Silverdome. Four Heisman Trophy winners—Barry Sanders, Marcus Allen, Bo Jackson and Tim Brown—scored TDs as the teams combined for 35 points in the first quarter. Sanders began the scoring with a 35-yard touchdown dash with only 2:09 gone. One play from scrimmage later, L.A. quarterback Jay Schroeder hit Willie Gault with a 68-yard TD pass. Sanders scored again on a five-yard run set up by a 56-yard pass from Rodney Peete to wide receiver Jeff Campbell. The Raiders answered with a two-yard TD run by Allen, and Campbell closed out the first quarter barrage with an 11-yard TD reception. Jackson scored on a 55-yard run midway through the second quarter to bring L.A. within three points of Detroit, and the Raiders pulled away in the second half on two TD passes from Schroeder, one of which went to Brown. Sanders finished the game with 176 yards rushing, while Jackson led L.A. with 129.

Los Angeles	14	7	14	3	–	38
Detroit	21	3	0	7	–	31

Det – Sanders 35 run (Murray kick)
L.A. – Gault 68 pass from Schroeder (Jaeger kick)
Det – Sanders 5 run (Murray kick)
L.A. – Allen 2 run (Jaeger kick)
Det – Campbell 11 pass from Peete (Murray kick)
Det – FG Murray 47
L.A. – Jackson 55 run (Jaeger kick)
L.A. – Fernandez 10 pass from Schroeder (Jaeger kick)
L.A. – Brown 3 pass from Schroeder (Jaeger kick)
Det – Peete 6 run (Murray kick)
L.A. – FG Jaeger 37
A: 72,190 T: 3:19

WEEK 15 STANDINGS

AFC EAST	W	L	T	Pct.	PF	PA
Buffalo	12	2	0	.857	390	220
Miami	11	3	0	.786	299	201
Indianapolis	6	8	0	.429	229	302
N.Y. Jets	4	10	0	.286	237	324
New England	1	13	0	.071	164	391

AFC CENTRAL	W	L	T	Pct.	PF	PA
Pittsburgh	8	6	0	.571	243	206
Houston	8	6	0	.571	351	253
Cincinnati	7	7	0	.500	299	318
Cleveland	3	11	0	.214	214	406

AFC WEST	W	L	T	Pct.	PF	PA
L.A. Raiders	10	4	0	.714	292	232
Kansas City	9	5	0	.643	324	226
Seattle	7	7	0	.500	259	264
San Diego	6	8	0	.429	282	240
Denver	4	10	0	.286	297	344

NFC EAST	W	L	T	Pct.	PF	PA
N.Y. Giants	11	3	0	.786	298	180
Washington	9	5	0	.643	324	252
Philadelphia	8	6	0	.571	356	275
Dallas	7	7	0	.500	234	265
Phoenix	5	9	0	.357	216	349

NFC CENTRAL	W	L	T	Pct.	PF	PA
Chicago	10	4	0	.714	311	245
Tampa Bay	6	8	0	.429	236	324
Green Bay	6	8	0	.429	241	301
Minnesota	6	8	0	.429	310	278
Detroit	5	9	0	.357	339	366

NFC WEST	W	L	T	Pct.	PF	PA
San Francisco	13	1	0	.929	323	209
New Orleans	6	8	0	.429	241	248
L.A. Rams	5	9	0	.357	315	372
Atlanta	3	11	0	.214	302	345

RESULTS
Buffalo 17, N.Y. Giants 13 (Saturday)
Washington 25, New England 10 (Saturday)
Cleveland 13, Atlanta 10
Philadelphia 31, Green Bay 0
Indianapolis 29, N.Y. Jets 21
Tampa Bay 26, Minnesota 13
Dallas 41, Phoenix 10
Miami 24, Seattle 17
Pittsburgh 9, New Orleans 6
L.A. Raiders 24, Cincinnati 7
Denver 20, San Diego 10
Detroit 38, Chicago 21
Houston 27, Kansas City 10
San Francisco 26, L.A. Rams 10 (Monday night)

SATURDAY, DECEMBER 15

BUFFALO 17, N.Y. GIANTS 13—At Giants Stadium. Both the Bills and the Giants lost their starting quarterbacks to injuries—Jim Kelly for four weeks and Phil Simms for the season—but Frank Reich stepped in for Buffalo and led the Bills to a victory. Reich was 8 of 15 for 97 yards, including a 43-yard completion to Don Beebe that set up the winning field goal. New York rookie running back Rodney Hampton rushed for 105 yards on 21 carries.

Buffalo	7	7	0	3	–	17
New York	7	3	3	0	–	13

N.Y. – Anderson 1 run (Bahr kick)
Buff – Reed 6 pass from Kelly (Norwood kick)
Buff – Thomas 2 run (Norwood kick)
N.Y. – FG Bahr 23
N.Y. – FG Bahr 22
Buff – FG Norwood 29
A: 66,893 T: 2:57

WASHINGTON 25, NEW ENGLAND 10—At Foxboro Stadium. In a driving rain before the NFL's smallest crowd of the season, Earnest Byner of the Redskins rushed for 149 yards on 39 carries to go over 1,000 yards for the second time in his career. Washington's two first-quarter scores came on Patriots miscues, one a New England fumble that linebacker Kurt Gouveia picked up and ran back 39 yards for a TD, and the other a botched snap on a punt attempt that sailed through the end zone for a safety.

Washington	9	10	0	6	–	25
New England	0	0	7	3	–	10

Wash – Gouveia 39 fumble return (Lohmiller kick)
Wash – Safety, ball snapped out of end zone
Wash – Byner 5 run (Lohmiller kick)
Wash – FG Lohmiller 19
N.E. – Stephens 4 run (Staurovsky kick)
N.E. – FG Staurovsky 42
Wash – FG Lohmiller 38
Wash – FG Lohmiller 26
A: 22,286 T: 2:49

SUNDAY, DECEMBER 16

CLEVELAND 13, ATLANTA 10—At Cleveland Stadium. The Browns victimized Atlanta quarterbacks with eight sacks—2.5 by nosetackle Michael Dean Perry—as Cleveland broke an eight-game losing streak in a meeting between two teams going nowhere. Atlanta wide receiver Andre Rison caught six passes for 100 yards, while the Browns, the worst rushing team in the league, gained 142 yards on the ground. Cleveland's Kevin Mack had 80 yards on 16 carries.

Atlanta	0	3	0	7	–	10
Cleveland	0	10	3	0	–	13

Atl – FG Davis 30
Cle – Mack 5 run (Kauric kick)
Cle – FG Kauric 23
Cle – FG Kauric 41
Atl – Dixon 11 pass from Millen (Davis kick)
A: 46,536 T: 3:17

PHILADELPHIA 31, GREEN BAY 0—At Veterans Stadium. The Eagle defense dominated the game, holding the Packers to 158 total yards and sacking Green Bay quarterbacks five times. Randall Cunningham, the Philadelphia quarterback, completed 13 of 27 passes for 241 yards and a touchdown, but his most spectacular play came in the fourth quarter on a 17-yard TD run that ended with a diving leap into the end zone.

Green Bay	0	0	0	0	–	0
Philadelphia	7	10	0	14	–	31

Phi – Toney 8 pass from Byars (Ruzek kick)
Phi – FG Ruzek 34
Phi – Byars 12 pass from Cunningham (Ruzek kick)
Phi – Cunningham 17 run (Ruzek kick)
Phi – Sanders 2 run (Ruzek kick)
A: 65,627 T: 3:00

INDIANAPOLIS 29, N.Y. JETS 21—At Giants Stadium. After taking a 14–3 lead in the second quarter, the Jets allowed the Colts to score 26 unanswered points and claim the win. Indianapolis's defense gave up 300 total yards but did not surrender a third-down conversion. Colt running back Eric Dickerson rushed 26 times for 117 yards and scored on two one-yard runs, one after a fake punt gained 40 yards to the New York six.

Indianapolis	3	7	13	6	–	29
New York	7	7	0	7	–	21

Ind – FG Biasucci 35
N.Y. – Moore 6 pass from O'Brien (Leahy kick)
N.Y. – Baxter 1 run (Leahy kick)
Ind – Verdin 23 pass from George (Biasucci kick)
Ind – Dickerson 1 run (Biasucci kick)
Ind – Dickerson 1 run (kick failed)
Ind – FG Biasucci 20
Ind – FG Biasucci 37
N.Y. – Moore 10 pass from Taylor (Leahy kick)
A: 41,423 T: 2:57

TAMPA BAY 26, MINNESOTA 13—At Tampa Stadium. The Buccaneers, playing their first game under interim coach Richard Williamson, relied on the legs and the arm of Vinny Testaverde to secure a win over the Vikings, quashing Minnesota's playoff hopes. Testaverde ran for a career-high 105 yards and a TD and passed for 148 yards and another TD. Tampa Bay's defense forced eight turnovers, including two interceptions by safety Mark Robinson, and held the Vikings to 56 yards rushing.

Minnesota	0	0	13	0	–	13
Tampa Bay	7	16	3	0	–	26

T.B. – Testaverde 48 run (Christie kick)
T.B. – FG Christie 50
T.B. – FG Christie 43
T.B. – FG Christie 42
T.B. – Carrier 25 pass from Testaverde (Christie kick)
Minn – Jones 75 pass from Wilson (Reveiz kick)
T.B. – FG Christie 30
Minn – Walker 1 run (pass failed)
A: 47,272 T: 3:16

DALLAS 41, PHOENIX 10—At Texas Stadium. Rookie running back Emmitt Smith scored four touchowns and safety James Washington intercepted two passes and recovered a fumble as the Cowboys trounced Phoenix for their fourth straight win to remain in the playoff picture. The Dallas defense held the Cardinals to 49 yards on the ground and 200 yards overall. After allowing a first-quarter field goal, the Cowboys scored 34 straight points. Smith rushed for 103 yards on 24 carries, including an 11-yard TD run in the first quarter during which he eluded six tacklers. Dallas wide receiver Michael Irvin caught four passes for 91 yards and a TD.

Phoenix	3	0	0	7	–	10
Dallas	13	7	7	14	–	41

Phoe – FG Del Greco 38
Dall – Smith 1 run (Willis kick)
Dall – Smith 11 run (kick failed)
Dall – Irvin 8 pass from Aikman (Willis kick)
Dall – Smith 1 run (Willis kick)
Dall – Smith 6 run (Willis kick)
Phoe – Johnson 1 run (Del Greco kick)
Dall – Johnston 6 run (Willis kick)
A: 60,190 T: 3:07

MIAMI 24, SEATTLE 17—At Joe Robbie Stadium. The Dolphin defense shut down the Seahawk running game, allowing only 83 yards, and intercepted quarterback Dave Krieg three times as Miami ran its record to 11–3. After Seattle took a 10–3 lead, a fumbled punt by the Seahawks' Chris Warren set up a four-yard pass from Dan Marino to James Pruitt to tie the score. With only a seven-point lead in the third quarter, Marino faked into the line on a fourth-and-one and hit tight end Ferrell Edmunds with an 11-yard touchdown pass that proved to be the difference in the game. Seattle wide receiver Tommy Kane caught 10 passes for 162 yards.

Seattle	3	7	0	7	–	17
Miami	3	14	7	0	–	24

Sea – FG Johnson 24
Mia – FG Stoyanovich 32
Sea – Fenner 2 run (Johnson kick)
Mia – Pruitt 4 pass from Marino (Stoyanovich kick)
Mia – Stradford 6 run (Stoyanovich kick)
Mia – Edmunds 11 pass from Marino (Stoyanovich kick)
Sea – Chadwick 12 pass from Krieg
A: 57,851 T: 2:51

PITTSBURGH 9, NEW ORLEANS 6—At the Superdome. The two kickers—Gary Anderson of the Steelers and Morton Andersen of the Saints—did all the scoring, with a 43-yard Anderson field goal with 1:44 remaining providing the final margin of victory. One play before the winning field goal, Saints defensive back Toi Cook dropped a sure interception of a Bubby Brister pass. New Orleans quarterback Steve Walsh, amid the boos of the fans, completed only eight of 26 passes for 95 yards. Though he was the game's leading rusher with 49 yards, the Saints' Gil Fenerty fumbled at the Pittsburgh one-yard line with 41 seconds left in the half after New Orleans had driven 77 yards. Despite their loss, the Saints remain in contention for a playoff spot.

Pittsburgh	0	3	0	6	–	9
New Orleans	0	0	3	3	–	6

Pitt – FG Anderson 29
N.O. – FG Andersen 50
N.O. – FG Andersen 43
Pitt – FG Anderson 42
Pitt – FG Anderson 43
A: 68,582 T: 2:49

L.A. RAIDERS 24, CINCINNATI 7—At Memorial Coliseum. The Raiders clinched their first playoff spot in five years with a victory over the Bengals. L.A.'s part-time running back Bo Jackson provided most of the excitement with 117 yards on eight carries. He broke loose on an 88-yard run in the third quarter but was caught from behind at the one-yard line by Cincinnati defensive back Rod Jones. Bengal quarterback Boomer Esiason threw two interceptions, both of which led to Los Angeles scores. Raider quarterback Jay Schroeder provided steady, if unspectacular passing, completing 10 of 20 passes for 163 yards and three touchdowns, two to wideout Tim Brown.

Cincinnati	7	0	0	0	–	7
Los Angeles	7	10	7	0	–	24

Cin – McGee 41 pass from Esiason (Breech kick)
L.A. – Brown 5 pass from Schroeder (Jaeger kick)
L.A. – Brown 44 pass from Schroeder (Jaeger kick)
L.A. – FG Jaeger 39
L.A. – Horton 1 pass from Schroeder (Jaeger kick)
A: 54,132 T: 2:50

DENVER 20, SAN DIEGO 10—At Mile High Stadium. John Elway, looking like his old self in the midst of a disappointing season, extinguished the Chargers' playoff hopes by throwing two touchdown passes, both to Michael Young, and scrambling for 34 yards on seven carries. The win ended a four-game losing streak at home for the Broncos. Elway finished with 18 completions in 29 attempts for 248 yards. San Diego missed a scoring opportunity in the first quarter when tight end Derrick Walker fumbled at the Denver goal line and safety Randy Robbins picked it up and ran it out to the 26. The Broncos later pulled away to a 14-point lead, then held on for the win.

San Diego	0	3	0	7	–	10
Denver	0	7	7	6	–	20

S.D. – FG Carney 30
Den – Young 25 pass from Elway (Treadwell kick)
Den – Young 3 pass from Elway (Treadwell kick)
Den – FG Treadwell 49
S.D. – McEwen 22 pass from Tolliver (Carney kick)
Den – FG Treadwell 26
A: 64,919 T: 3:09

DETROIT 38, CHICAGO 21—At the Silverdome. The Bears were dominated by the Lions on both offense and defense as Detroit quarterback Rodney Peete threw for 316 yards and four touchdowns. After taking a 7–0 lead in the first quarter, the Bears gave up three second-quarter touchdown passes to fall into a deep hole. Chicago lost quarterback Jim Harbaugh for the season to a dislocated shoulder after a sack, one of six the Lions inflicted on the Bears' quarterbacks. Neal Anderson was the only bright spot for Chicago, rushing for 100 yards on 22 carries.

Chicago	7	0	7	7	–	21
Detroit	0	21	7	10	–	38

Chi – Muster 1 run (Butler kick)
Det – Clark 20 pass from Peete (Murray kick)
Det – Johnson 44 pass from Peete (Murray kick)
Det – Clark 1 pass from Peete (Murray kick)
Chi – Dent 45 fumble return (Butler kick)
Det – Greer 68 pass from Peete (Murray kick)
Det – Sanders 1 run (Murray kick)
Det – FG Murray 26
Chi – Davis 8 pass from Willis (Butler kick)
A: 67,759 T: 3:06

HOUSTON 27, KANSAS CITY 10—At Arrowhead Stadium. Warren Moon had the second-best passing day in NFL history as he shredded the Chiefs defense for 527 yards, just 27 yards short of Norm Van Brocklin's total of 554 in 1951. The game was tight until midway through the third quarter when Moon hit wideout Haywood Jeffires with an 87-yard touchown pass to give Houston a 17–7 lead. Kansas City quarterback Steve DeBerg saw *his* chase for a record end when cornerback Richard Johnson picked off a pass, stopping his streak of passes without an interception at 234, 60 short of Bart Starr's mark. DeBerg later suffered a broken bone in his pinkie finger and had to leave the game. Jeffires was the recipient of nine Moon passes for a total of 245 yards, a whopping average of 27.2 per catch.

Houston	7	3	7	10	–	27
Kansas City	7	3	0	0	–	10

Hou – Jones 24 pass from Moon (Garcia kick)
Hou – FG Garcia 32
K.C. – Birden 62 pass from DeBerg (Lowery kick)
Hou – Jeffires 87 pass from Moon (Garcia kick)
K.C. – FG Lowery 35
Hou – FG Garcia 26
Hou – Jones 2 pass from Moon (Garcia kick)
A: 61,756 T: 3:21

MONDAY, DECEMBER 17

SAN FRANCISCO 26, L.A. RAMS 10—At Anaheim Stadium. The 49ers avenged their only loss of the season and clinched the home-field advantage throughout the playoffs with a victory over the Rams. San Francisco jumped out to an early lead but didn't put Los Angeles away until the fourth quarter when backup running back Dexter Carter sprung loose for a 74-yard touchdown run off left tackle. The score gave the 49ers a comfortable 16-point lead. Carter finished the game with 124 yards on 13 carries as San Francisco gained 173 yards on the ground overall while holding the Rams to 53 yards rushing. Los Angeles had closed to 16–7 in the third quarter when 49er linebacker Matt Millen came up with a big defensive play, recovering a fumble at the Ram 42 to stop a Los Angeles drive. Jerry Rice had five catches for 104 yards.

San Francisco	3	13	3	7	–	26
Los Angeles	0	7	3	0	–	10

S.F. – FG Cofer 23
S.F. – Rathman 1 run (pass failed)
S.F. – Rice 60 pass from Montana (Cofer kick)
L.A. – Faison 8 pass from Everett (Lansford kick)
S.F. – FG Cofer 31
L.A. – FG Lansford 21
S.F. – Carter 74 run (Cofer kick)
A: 65,619 T: 3:08

WEEK 16 STANDINGS

AFC EAST	W	L	T	Pct.	PF	PA
Buffalo	13	2	0	.867	414	234
Miami	11	4	0	.733	313	225
Indianapolis	7	8	0	.467	264	330
N.Y. Jets	5	10	0	.333	279	331
New England	1	14	0	.067	171	433

AFC CENTRAL	W	L	T	Pct.	PF	PA
Pittsburgh	9	6	0	.600	278	206
Cincinnati	8	7	0	.533	339	338
Houston	8	7	0	.533	371	293
Cleveland	3	12	0	.200	214	441

AFC WEST	W	L	T	Pct.	PF	PA
L.A. Raiders	11	4	0	.733	320	256
Kansas City	10	5	0	.667	348	247
Seattle	8	7	0	.533	276	276
San Diego	6	9	0	.400	303	264
Denver	4	11	0	.267	309	361

NFC EAST	W	L	T	Pct.	PF	PA
N.Y. Giants	12	3	0	.800	322	201
Philadelphia	9	6	0	.600	373	278
Washington	9	6	0	.600	352	287
Dallas	7	8	0	.467	237	282
Phoenix	5	10	0	.333	237	373

NFC CENTRAL	W	L	T	Pct.	PF	PA
Chicago	11	4	0	.733	338	259
Tampa Bay	6	9	0	.400	250	351
Green Bay	6	9	0	.400	258	325
Detroit	6	9	0	.400	363	383
Minnesota	6	9	0	.400	334	306

NFC WEST	W	L	T	Pct.	PF	PA
San Francisco	13	2	0	.867	333	222
New Orleans	7	8	0	.467	254	258
L.A. Rams	5	10	0	.333	328	393
Atlanta	4	11	0	.267	322	358

RESULTS
Detroit 24, Green Bay 17 (Saturday)
Indianapolis 35, Washington 28 (Saturday)
L.A. Raiders 28, Minnesota 24 (Saturday)
Kansas City 24, San Diego 21
Atlanta 20, L.A. Rams 13
Buffalo 24, Miami 14
Chicago 27, Tampa Bay 14
Cincinnati 40, Houston 20
New Orleans 13, San Francisco 10
N.Y. Giants 24, Phoenix 21
N.Y. Jets 42, New England 7
Philadelphia 17, Dallas 3
Pittsburgh 35, Cleveland 0
Seattle 17, Denver 12

SATURDAY, DECEMBER 22

DETROIT 24, GREEN BAY 17—At Lambeau Field. In frigid weather of 2°, Lion defensive back Ray Crockett returned a fumble 22 yards for a touchdown to tie the game in the fourth quarter, and Barry Sanders scored the winning touchdown on a six-yard run with 3:37 remaining to end the Packers' playoff hopes. Crockett had another big play when he intercepted third-string quarterback Blair Kiel, who had moved Green Bay to the Detroit 14-yard line with 1:51 left. Sanders rushed for 133 yards on 19 carries.

Detroit	7	0	3	14	—	24
Green Bay	7	0	10	0	—	17

G.B. — Kiel 3 run (Jacke kick)
Det — Peete 26 run (Murray kick)
G.B. — Thompson 76 kickoff return (Jacke kick)
Det — FG Murray 22
G.B. — FG Jacke 25
Det — Crockett 22 fumble return (Murray kick)
Det — Sanders 6 run (Murray kick)
A: 46,700 T: 2:59

INDIANAPOLIS 35, WASHINGTON 28—At the Hoosier Dome. The Colts exploded for 21 points in the fourth quarter, including a 25-yard interception return by Alan Grant for the winning touchdown with 50 seconds remaining, to upset the Redskins. Just 31 seconds earlier, Indianapolis had tied the game with an 12-yard touchdown pass to Billy Brooks from Jeff George, who kept the Colts in the game with 18 of 33 passing for 252 yards and three touchdowns. Washington completely shut down Indianapolis's running game, limiting Eric Dickerson to 31 yards on 10 carries, and led by as many as 11 points in the fourth quarter before the Colts made their comeback.

Washington	7	6	5	10	—	28
Indianapolis	0	14	0	21	—	35

Wash — Monk 12 pass from Rypien (Lohmiller kick)
Ind — Dickerson 4 run (Biasucci kick)
Ind — Morgan 42 pass from George (Biasucci kick)
Wash — FG Lohmiller 53
Wash — FG Lohmiller 56
Wash — Safety, George intentionally grounded ball in end zone
Wash — FG Lohmiller 29
Wash — Clark 53 pass from Rypien (Lohmiller kick)
Ind — Morgan 8 pass from George (Biasucci kick)
Wash — FG Lohmiller 27
Ind — Brooks 12 pass from George (Biasucci kick)
Ind — Grant 25 interception return (Biasucci kick)
A: 58,173 T: 3:23

L.A. RAIDERS 28, MINNESOTA 24—At the Metrodome. Jay Schroeder threw four touchdown passes on only 10 completions as the Raiders bounced the Vikings from the playoff race. Los Angeles led the entire game, completing a 56-yard pass to Willie Gault on the first play from scrimmage to set up a 17-yard pass to Mervyn Fernandez for the touchdown. Trailing 28–10 in the fourth quarter, Minnesota charged back with two touchdowns, the last a three-yard pass from Rich Gannon to tight end Steve Jordan to pull the Vikings within four points with 15 seconds left. Gault had two catches for 117 yards. Linebacker Aaron Wallace had two sacks for the Raiders.

Los Angeles	14	0	7	7	—	28
Minnesota	0	10	0	14	—	24

L.A. — Fernandez 17 pass from Schroeder (Jaeger kick)
L.A. — Graddy 47 pass from Schroeder (Jaeger kick)
Minn — FG Reveiz 28
Minn — Carter 27 pass from Wilson (Reveiz kick)
L.A. — Allen 19 pass from Schroeder (Jaeger kick)
L.A. — Horton 3 pass from Schroeder (Jaeger kick)
Minn — Jones 4 pass from Gannon (Reveiz kick)
Minn — Jordan 3 pass from Gannon (Reveiz kick)
A: 53,899 T: 2:57

SUNDAY, DECEMBER 23

KANSAS CITY 24, SAN DIEGO 21—At Jack Murphy Stadium. After building a 21–7 halftime lead, the Chiefs needed a Nick Lowery field goal with 2:46 remaining and an interception by Deron Cherry with less than two minutes left to seal a win over the Chargers. In the first half, Kansas City quarterback Steve DeBerg, playing with a splint on his left pinkie, threw two touchdown passes to give the Chiefs a comfortable lead. San Diego surged back in the second half behind a short TD run by Rod Bernstine and a 55-yard punt return by Kitrick Taylor early in the fourth quarter. With 3:22 left in the game and the Chiefs at their own one-yard line, DeBerg found running back Todd McNair at the 10-yard line, and he broke loose to the Charger 30 to help set up Lowery's winning field goal.

Kansas City	7	14	0	3	—	24
San Diego	7	0	7	7	—	21

K.C. — Paige 8 pass from DeBerg (Lowery kick)
S.D. — Miller 5 pass from Tolliver (Carney kick)
K.C. — Word 11 run (Lowery kick)
K.C. — McNair 40 pass from DeBerg (Lowery kick)
S.D. — Bernstine 3 run (Carney kick)
S.D. — Taylor 55 punt return (Carney kick)
K.C. — FG Lowery 32
A: 45,135 T: 2:46

ATLANTA 20, L.A. RAMS 13—At Atlanta–Fulton County Stadium. Falcon safety Scott Case returned an interception for a touchdown less than two minutes into the game, and the Rams played catch-up the rest of the way as Atlanta ended a four-game losing streak. Both defenses were stingy around the goal line: The Rams twice held the Falcons to field goals after Atlanta had been inside the 10, and the Falcons blocked a 24-yard field goal and held the Rams to a three-pointer after L.A. had a first down at the two. QB Hugh Millen started for Atlanta and was 13 of 21 for 178 yards.

Los Angeles	7	3	3	0	—	13
Atlanta	10	10	0	0	—	20

Atl — Case 36 interception return (Davis kick)
Atl — FG Davis 21
L.A. — Gary 7 run (Lansford kick)
Atl — Rozier 11 run (Davis kick)
L.A. — FG Lansford 19
Atl — FG Davis 23
L.A. — FG Lansford 25
A: 30,021 T: 3:08

BUFFALO 24, MIAMI 14—At Rich Stadium. Backup QB Frank Reich threw two touchdown passes, and Buffalo's defense sacked Dolphin quarterback Dan Marino three times as the Bills took their third consecutive AFC East title and won the home field advantage throughout the playoffs. The Buffalo rushing game dominated the Dolphins, producing 206 yards, 154 from Thurman Thomas. The Bills were already leading 7–0 when they recovered Marc Logan's fumble of the second-half kickoff, which set up an 11-yard TD pass from Reich to Andre Reed. The Dolphins never got back in the game after that.

Miami	0	0	7	7	—	14
Buffalo	0	7	10	7	—	24

Buff — Lofton 7 pass from Reich (Norwood kick)
Buff — Reed 11 pass from Reich (Norwood kick)
Mia — Duper 30 pass from Marino (Stoyanovich kick)
Buff — FG Norwood 21
Buff — Thomas 13 run (Norwood kick)
Mia — Clayton 11 pass from Marino (Stoyanovich kick)
A: 80,235 T: 2:59

CHICAGO 27, TAMPA BAY 14—At Soldier Field. The Bears, playing under a pall cast by the death of rookie defensive tackle Fred Washington in an auto accident, went about their methodical business and beat the Buccaneers. Mike Tomczak started at quarterback in place of the injured Jim Harbaugh and threw for 239 yards and two TDs, as well as running for another touchdown. Tampa Bay jumped on top with a five-yard pass from Vinny Testaverde to wide receiver Mark Carrier, but Chicago came back with 27 unanswered points, scoring the go-ahead touchdown after the defense stopped the Buccaneers on fourth-and-one from the Bears 11. Testaverde threw three interceptions, one to Chicago's Mark Carrier, who set a club record with 10 pickoffs.

Tampa Bay	7	0	0	7	—	14
Chicago	0	14	10	3	—	27

T.B. — Carrier 5 pass from Testaverde (Christie kick)
Chi — Tomczak 1 run (Butler kick)
Chi — Davis 18 pass from Tomczak (Butler kick)
Chi — Thornton 12 pass from Tomczak (Butler kick)
Chi — FG Butler 46
Chi — FG Butler 43
T.B. — Hill 4 pass from Testaverde (Christie kick)
A: 46,456 T: 3:07

CINCINNATI 40, HOUSTON 20—At Riverfront Stadium. Bengal running back James Brooks rushed for a team-record 201 yards as Cincinnati kept up with Pittsburgh in the chase for the AFC Central title. The Oilers took a 10–0 lead, but Cincinnati stormed back to tie the game at 13 by halftime and dominate the second half with 27 unanswered points. Bengal quarterback Boomer Esiason threw two fourth-quarter touchdown passes to tight end Eric Kattus to clinch the win. Oiler QB Warren Moon suffered a dislocated thumb that put him out for the season.

Houston	0	13	7	0	—	20
Cincinnati	0	13	14	13	—	40

Hou — FG Garcia 29
Hou — Jeffires 21 pass from Moon (Garcia kick)
Cin — Woods 1 run (Breech kick)
Hou — FG Garcia 36
Cin — Brooks 56 run (Breech kick)
Hou — Moon 1 run (Garcia kick)
Cin — Jennings 1 run (Breech kick)
Cin — Woods 1 run (Breech kick)
Cin — Kattus 16 pass from Esiason (Breech kick)
Cin — Kattus 22 pass from Esiason (kick blocked)
A: 60,044 T: 3:17

NEW ORLEANS 13, SAN FRANCISCO 10—At Candlestick Park. In a must-win game for the Saints, New Orleans played tough defense, forcing four fumbles to beat the 49ers, who chose to rest many of their starters with the homefield advantage guaranteed throughout the playoffs. With 4:43 left, Morton Andersen booted the winning field goal, a 40-yarder set up by a Vaughan Johnson fumble recovery. The Saints' Renaldo Turnbull had two sacks.

New Orleans	7	3	0	3	—	13
San Francisco	7	0	0	3	—	10

S.F. — Rathman 1 run (Cofer kick)
N.O. — Scales 5 pass from Walsh (Andersen kick)
N.O. — FG Andersen 30
S.F. — FG Cofer 30
N.O. — FG Andersen 40
A: 60,012 T: 3:05

N.Y. GIANTS 24, PHOENIX 21—At Sun Devil Stadium. Backup quarterback Jeff Hostetler, in his first start of the season, threw for 190 yards and a TD and ran for another touchdown as the Giants held off the stubborn Cardinals. Phoenix had a chance to win the game when Ricky Proehl reduced the lead to seven with a three-yard TD catch with 2:09 left and then recovered the following onside kick. But the Giants defense, led by a Lawrence Taylor sack, held the Cardinals and took over on downs with 52 seconds remaining. Phoenix quarterback Timm Rosenbach completed 23 of 41 passes for 381 yards and three TDs.

New York	3	7	7	7	—	24
Phoenix	0	7	7	7	—	21

N.Y. — FG Bahr 27
N.Y. — Hampton 2 run (Bahr kick)
Phoe — Flagler 11 pass from Rosenbach (Del Greco kick)
N.Y. — Ingram 44 pass from Hostetler (Bahr kick)
Phoe — Jones 68 pass from Rosenbach (Del Greco kick)
N.Y. — Hostetler 4 run (Bahr kick)
Phoe — Proehl 3 pass from Rosenbach (Del Greco kick)
A: 41,212 T: 3:02

N.Y. JETS 42, NEW ENGLAND 7—At Giants Stadium. The Jets had lost five in a row entering the game, but they thrashed the lowly Patriots, gaining 465 total yards. Ken O'Brien completed 11 of 12 passes for 210 yards and two TDs. New York's running game accumulated 239 yards, with Blair Thomas gaining a game-high 88 on 12 carries.

New England	0	7	0	0	—	7
New York	7	14	14	7	—	42

N.Y. — Hector 7 run (Leahy kick)
N.E. — Fryar 24 pass from Wilson (Staurovsky kick)
N.Y. — Moore 2 pass from O'Brien (Leahy kick)
N.Y. — McNeil 9 run (Leahy kick)
N.Y. — McNeil 1 run (Leahy kick)
N.Y. — Thomas 6 pass from O'Brien (Leahy kick)
N.Y. — Taylor 5 run (Leahy kick)
A: 30,250 T: 2:48

PHILADELPHIA 17, DALLAS 3—At Veterans Stadium. The Cowboys' four-game winning streak came to an abrupt end as did the season of quarterback Troy Aikman, who went down with a separated shoulder after a first-quarter sack by Clyde Simmons. The Eagles held only a 10–3 lead until midway through the fourth quarter when cornerback Eric Allen intercepted a Babe Laufenberg pass, one of four he surrendered on the day, and dashed 35 yards for a touchdown. Despite the loss, the Cowboys remained in contention for a wildcard spot.

Dallas	0	3	0	0	—	3
Philadelphia	7	3	0	7	—	17

Phi — Williams 18 pass from Byars (Ruzek kick)
Dall — FG Willis 46
Phi — FG Ruzek 29
Phi — Allen 35 interception return (Ruzek kick)
A: 63,895 T: 3:00

PITTSBURGH 35, CLEVELAND 0—At Three Rivers Stadium. The Browns tied an NFL record by losing eight fumbles, and Steeler quarterback Bubby Brister threw four touchdown passes on only 10 completions as Pittsburgh took over the lead in the AFC Central with the easy win. The Browns gave up an interception as well; the nine takeaways tie the Pittsburgh team record. The Steelers also enjoyed success on the ground with rookie running back Barry Foster rushing for 100 yards on 16 carries.

Cleveland	0	0	0	0	—	0
Pittsburgh	21	14	0	0	—	35

Pitt — Mularkey 20 pass from Brister (Anderson kick)
Pitt — Calloway 20 pass from Brister (Anderson kick)
Pitt — Mularkey 2 pass from Brister (Anderson kick)
Pitt — Hoge 12 pass from Brister (Anderson kick)
Pitt — Williams 1 run (Anderson kick)
A: 51,665 T: 2:45

SEATTLE 17, DENVER 12—At the Kingdome. Once again, the Seahawks' game came down to the final play, their fifth nail-biter this season. In this one, with the Broncos trailing by five, John Elway threw a 49-yard Hail Mary that was batted around before finally landing in the hands of Michael Young for an apparent Denver touchdown. The Broncos, however, incurred a motion penalty on the play, and the TD was nullified. The Seahawk defense sacked Elway three times and intercepted him in the end zone with 1:36 left after the Broncos had advanced to the Seattle 36. Safety Eugene Robinson set up the winning TD for the Seahawks with a 39-yard interception return in the third quarter. The win left Seattle in playoff contention entering the final week.

Denver	3	7	2	0	—	12
Seattle	3	7	7	0	—	17

Den — FG Treadwell 49
Sea — FG Johnson 21
Den — Humphrey 1 run (Treadwell kick)
Sea — Kane 5 pass from Krieg (Johnson kick)
Den — Safety, Krieg intentional grounding in end zone
Sea — Fenner 1 run (Johnson kick)
A: 55,845 T: 3:08

WEEK 17 STANDINGS

AFC EAST	W	L	T	Pct.	PF	PA
Buffalo	13	3	0	.813	428	263
Miami	12	4	0	.750	336	242
Indianapolis	7	9	0	.438	281	353
N.Y. Jets	6	10	0	.375	295	345
New England	1	15	0	.063	181	446

AFC CENTRAL	W	L	T	Pct.	PF	PA
Cincinnati	9	7	0	.563	360	352
Houston	9	7	0	.563	405	307
Pittsburgh	9	7	0	.563	292	240
Cleveland	3	13	0	.188	228	462

AFC WEST	W	L	T	Pct.	PF	PA
L.A. Raiders	12	4	0	.750	337	268
Kansas City	11	5	0	.688	369	257
Seattle	9	7	0	.563	306	286
San Diego	6	10	0	.375	315	281
Denver	5	11	0	.313	331	374

NFC EAST	W	L	T	Pct.	PF	PA
N.Y. Giants	13	3	0	.813	335	211
Philadelphia	10	6	0	.625	396	299
Washington	10	6	0	.625	381	301
Dallas	7	9	0	.438	244	308
Phoenix	5	11	0	.313	268	396

NFC CENTRAL	W	L	T	Pct.	PF	PA
Chicago	11	5	0	.688	348	280
Tampa Bay	6	10	0	.375	264	367
Detroit	6	10	0	.375	373	413
Green Bay	6	10	0	.375	271	347
Minnesota	6	10	0	.375	351	326

NFC WEST	W	L	T	Pct.	PF	PA
San Francisco	14	2	0	.875	353	239
New Orleans	8	8	0	.500	274	275
L.A. Rams	5	11	0	.313	345	412
Atlanta	5	11	0	.313	348	365

RESULTS
Kansas City 21, Chicago 10 (Saturday)
Philadelphia 23, Phoenix 21 (Saturday)
Washington 29, Buffalo 14
Cincinnati 21, Cleveland 14
Atlanta 26, Dallas 7
Miami 23, Indianapolis 17
N.Y. Giants 13, New England 10
San Francisco 20, Minnesota 17
Seattle 30, Detroit 10
Denver 22, Green Bay 13
N.Y. Jets 16, Tampa Bay 14
L.A. Raiders 17, San Diego 12
Houston 34, Pittsburgh 14
New Orleans 20, L.A. Rams 17 (Monday night)

SATURDAY, DECEMBER 29

KANSAS CITY 21, CHICAGO 10—At Soldier Field. The Chiefs finished the season with a surprisingly easy win over the Bears, who limp into the playoffs beset by injuries. Kansas City's defense limited Chicago to six first downs, recovered three fumbles and harried quarterback Mike Tomczak into a five for 23 passing performance. On offense, Chiefs running back Barry Word gained 73 yards to give him 1,015 for the season. Despite playing with a broken pinkie for the second straight week, Steve DeBerg completed 25 of 32 passes for 276 yards. Nick Lowery kicked five field goals to run his streak of successful three-pointers to 21.

Kansas City	6	6	6	3	–	21
Chicago	3	7	0	0	–	10

K.C. – FG Lowery 19
Chi – FG Butler 24
K.C. – FG Lowery 30
K.C. – FG Lowery 43
Chi – Bailey 95 punt return (Butler kick)
K.C. – FG Lowery 32
K.C. – Okoye 3 run (kick failed)
K.C. – FG Lowery 38
A: 60,262 T: 2:54

PHILADELPHIA 23, PHOENIX 21—At Sun Devil Stadium. Leading 23–7 in the fourth quarter, the Eagles withstood a late two-touchdown rally by the Cardinals to hold on to a victory and win the home field advantage for their wild-card playoff game. Phoenix QB Timm Rosenbach hit Ricky Proehl with a 38-yard TD with 5:56 left and J.T. Smith with a 45-yarder with 1:51 remaining, but the Eagles were able to run out the clock on their final possession. Philadelphia QB Randall Cunningham threw three TDs and ran for 60 yards, giving him 942 for the season, just 26 shy of the NFL rushing record for quarterbacks, set by Bobby Douglass in 1972.

Philadelphia	7	6	7	3	–	23
Phoenix	0	7	0	14	–	21

Phi – Barnett 16 pass from Cunningham (Ruzek kick)
Phi – Williams 27 pass from Cunningham (kick failed)
Phoe – Green 12 pass from Rosenbach (Del Greco kick)
Phi – Barnett 3 pass from Cunningham (Ruzek kick)
Phi – FG Ruzek 44
Phoe – Proehl 38 pass from Rosenbach (Del Greco kick)
Phoe – Smith 45 pass from Rosenbach (Del Greco kick)
A: 31,796 T: 2:57

SUNDAY, DECEMBER 30

WASHINGTON 29, BUFFALO 14—At RFK Stadium. With the home field advantage through the playoffs wrapped up and little to play for, the Bills proved to be an easy opponent for the Redskins. Chip Lohmiller tied a Washington record with five field goals, but there were few other highlights. Buffalo coach Marv Levy emptied his bench after halftime, but even so, the Redskins couldn't get into the end zone until midway through the fourth quarter. Thurman Thomas had five carries for zero yards in one half of work, a lost day that allowed Detroit's Barry Sanders to win the league rushing title by seven yards.

Buffalo	0	0	7	7	–	14
Washington	3	6	3	17	–	29

Wash – FG Lohmiller 37
Wash – FG Lohmiller 24
Wash – FG Lohmiller 19
Buff – Davis 13 pass from Gilbert (Norwood kick)
Wash – FG Lohmiller 43
Wash – FG Lohmiller 32
Wash – Riggs 3 run (Lohmiller kick)
Wash – Hobbs 18 pass from Rypien (Lohmiller kick)
Buff – Tasker 20 pass from Gilbert (Norwood kick)
A: 52,397 T: 2:53

CINCINNATI 21, CLEVELAND 14—At Riverfront Stadium. The Bengals squeaked by the Browns, then had to wait to see if Houston would beat Pittsburgh to give Cincinnati the AFC Central championship and a playoff spot. Cleveland gave the Bengals a tough fight, pulling to a 14–14 tie late in the third quarter, but fell behind by seven when Cincinnati scored on a 48-yard swing pass to running back Eric Ball. The Browns moved to the Cincinnati seven-yard line with 55 seconds remaining, but Bengals safety David Fulcher stepped in front of a Mike Pagel pass for the interception that clinched the win.

Cleveland	0	0	14	0	–	14
Cincinnati	0	14	0	7	–	21

Cin – Francis 17 interception return (Breech kick)
Cin – Holman 22 pass from Esiason (Breech kick)
Cle – Mack 2 run (Kauric kick)
Cle – Brennan 16 pass from Pagel (Kauric kick)
Cin – Ball 48 pass from Esiason (Breech kick)
A: 60,041 T: 2:55

ATLANTA 26, DALLAS 7—At Atlanta–Fulton County Stadium. The Falcons harried backup quarterback Babe Laufenberg with a non-stop assault of linebacker blitzes as Atlanta trounced the Cowboys 26–7. The loss, coupled with the Saints victory over the Rams on Monday night, ended Dallas's hopes of making the playoffs just one season after going 1–15. Laufenberg completed only 10 of 24 passes for 129 yards with two interceptions. The Atlanta defense held the Cowboys to 47 yards rushing, and on offense, Falcons running back Mike Rozier rushed for 155 yards on 21 carries. Atlanta's Deion Sanders had an electrifying 61-yard interception return for a touchdown in the fourth quarter.

Dallas	0	0	0	7	–	7
Atlanta	0	7	9	10	–	26

Atl – Johnson 1 run (Davis kick)
Atl – Jones 76 kickoff return (Davis kick)
Atl – Safety, Green tackled Smith in end zone
Atl – FG Davis 23
Atl – Sanders 61 interception return (Davis kick)
Dall – Novacek 27 pass from Laufenberg (Willis kick)
A: 50,097 T: 2:55

MIAMI 23, INDIANAPOLIS 17—At Joe Robbie Stadium. The Dolphins held off the Colts behind a big-play defense to secure the home field for their first-round playoff game. In the fourth quarter, safety Jarvis Williams intercepted Colts quarterback Jeff George at the goal line, and Brian Sochia picked up a George fumble and ran 13 yards for the game-clinching TD. Otherwise, the Miami defense had a hard time stopping either George (18 completions in 30 attempts for 222 yards and two TDs) or running back Eric Dickerson (110 yards on 20 carries). Dolphins quarterback Dan Marino, finished with 14 completions in 26 attempts for 192 yards and one TD.

Indianapolis	7	7	0	3	–	17
Miami	7	9	0	7	–	23

Ind – Bentley 15 pass from George (Biasucci kick)
Mia – Smith 53 pass from Marino (Stoyanovich kick)
Mia – Smith 1 run (Stoyanovich kick)
Ind – Hester 64 pass from George (Biasucci kick)
Mia – Safety, George intentionally grounding in end zone
Mia – Sochia 13 fumble return (Stoyanovich kick)
Ind – FG Biasucci 55
A: 59,547 T: 2:50

N.Y. GIANTS 13, NEW ENGLAND 10—At Foxboro Stadium. Giants cornerback Mark Collins intercepted a pass from Patriots quarterback Tommy Hodson with 40 seconds left to preserve a 13–10 win. Matt Bahr put the winning points on the board just before the half after linebacker Gary Reasons recovered a Hodson fumble on the New England 24. Backup quarterback Jeff Hostetler improved his career record to 4–0 as a starter.

New York	10	3	0	0	–	13
New England	0	10	0	0	–	10

N.Y. – Meggett 17 pass from Hostetler (Bahr kick)
N.Y. – FG Bahr 44
N.E. – Fryar 40 pass from Hodson (Staurovsky kick)
N.E. – FG Staurovsky 19
N.Y. – FG Bahr 27
A: 60,410 T: 2:39

SAN FRANCISCO 20, MINNESOTA 17—At the Metrodome. Backup quarterback Steve Young rallied the 49ers from a 10-point deficit at halftime to a victory over the Vikings, who went from first to last in the NFC Central in just one year. Young, replacing Joe Montana at halftime as coach George Seifert had planned, completed 15 of 24 passes for 205 yards and two TDs, as well as gaining 59 yards on the ground. The winning play was a 34-yard touchdown pass to John Taylor with only 29 seconds left.

San Francisco	0	0	3	17	–	20
Minnesota	3	7	0	7	–	17

Minn – FG Reveiz 34
Minn – Walker 9 run (Reveiz kick)
S.F. – FG Cofer 29
S.F. – FG Cofer 35
S.F. – Rice 14 pass from Young (Cofer kick)
Minn – Anderson 1 run (Reveiz kick)
S.F. – Taylor 34 pass from Young (Cofer kick)
A: 51,590 T: 3:14

SEATTLE 30, DETROIT 10—At the Kingdome. A battered Seahawk defense, led by Jacob Green with three sacks, stifled the Lions' run-and-shoot offense as Seattle broke away from Detroit in the second half for the victory. The win left the Seahawks at 9–7, but they were eliminated from a playoff spot when Houston beat Pittsburgh. After kicking a field goal to tie the game 10–10 at halftime, Seattle got two big defensive plays in the third quarter to go up by 10 points: Safety Eugene Robinson picked up a fumble and ran it in from 16 yards out for a TD, and linebacker David Wyman intercepted a tipped pass to set up a field goal. The Seahawks defense held Barry Sanders to 23 yards on the ground, but he still won the league rushing title with 1,304 yards, seven more than Buffalo's Thurman Thomas.

Detroit	0	10	0	0	–	10
Seattle	7	3	10	10	–	30

Sea – Fenner 1 run (Johnson kick)
Det – FG Murray 24
Det – Sanders 16 run (Murray kick)
Sea – FG Johnson 43
Sea – Robinson 16 fumble return (Johnson kick)
Sea – FG Johnson 25
Sea – FG Johnson 37
Sea – Fenner 9 run (Johnson kick)
A: 50,681 T: 2:53

DENVER 22, GREEN BAY 13—At Mile High Stadium. The Broncos (5–11) and the Packers (6–10) ended miserable seasons, with Denver's Sammy Winder, the nine-year veteran playing in his last game before retirement, getting 80 yards on 15 carries.

Green Bay	3	3	0	7	–	13
Denver	3	3	14	2	–	22

Den – FG Treadwell 22
G.B. – FG Jacke 37
Den – FG Treadwell 31
G.B. – FG Jacke 24
Den – Humphrey 5 run (Treadwell kick)
Den – Jackson 15 pass from Elway (Treadwell kick)
G.B. – Sharpe 9 pass from Dilweg (Jacke kick)
Den – Safety, Dilweg tackled in end zone
A: 46,943 T: 2:56

N.Y. JETS 16, TAMPA BAY 14—At Tampa Stadium. The Jets handed the Buccaneers their eighth loss in their last ten games as both teams finished 6–10. Tampa Bay pulled to within two points with 3:32 remaining when Vinny Testaverde directed a seven-play, 62-yard drive that ended with a seven-yard TD pass to wideout Bruce Hill. But New York held on to win after Tony Eason found wide receiver Dale Dawkins for a leaping 31-yard reception that allowed the Jets to run out the clock.

New York	0	13	3	0	–	16
Tampa Bay	0	7	0	7	–	14

N.Y. – FG Leahy 21
T.B. – Cobb 1 run (Christie kick)
N.Y. – FG Leahy 32
N.Y. – Thomas 5 run (Leahy kick)
N.Y. – FG Leahy 25
T.B. – Hill 7 pass from Testaverde (Christie kick)
A: 46,543 T: 2:41

L.A. RAIDERS 17, SAN DIEGO 12—At Memorial Coliseum. The Raiders won the AFC West title for the first time since 1985, but to do it they had to mount a rally against the stubborn Chargers. After a field goal put the Raiders up by one in the fourth quarter, Donnie Elder raced 90 yards to the L.A. seven with the ensuing kickoff. But San Diego was forced to settle for a field goal and the Raiders promptly drove 80 yards in 11 plays for the winning score, a 17-yard pass from Jay Schroeder to running back Steve Smith. Running back Rod Bernstine tore apart the L.A. defense for 114 yards on 27 carries.

San Diego	3	6	0	3	–	12
Los Angeles	0	7	0	10	–	17

S.D. – FG Carney 19
L.A. – Allen 1 run (Jaeger kick)
S.D. – McEwen 7 pass from Friesz (kick blocked)
L.A. – FG Jaeger 45
S.D. – FG Carney 21
L.A. – Smith 17 pass from Schroeder (Jaeger kick)
A: 59,547 T: 2:50

HOUSTON 34, PITTSBURGH 14—At the Astrodome. Cody Carlson, subbing for the injured Warren Moon, completed 22 of 29 passes for 247 yards and three touchdowns to knock Pittsburgh out of first place in the AFC Central and earn a wild-card spot for the Oilers. Houston and Carlson started off hot, scoring on four of the team's first five first-half possessions and building a 24–0 lead. After the Steelers got on the board in the third quarter with a four-yard TD run by Merril Hoge, Carlson led the Oilers on an 80-yard drive that ended with a 53-yard touchdown pass to Haywood Jeffires that put the game out of reach. Houston's Lorenzo White helped to consume the clock by rushing for 90 yards on 18 carries.

Pittsburgh	0	0	7	7	–	14
Houston	7	17	7	3	–	34

Hou – White 1 run (Garcia kick)
Hou – Givins 14 pass from Carlson (Garcia kick)
Hou – Hill 3 pass from Carlson (Garcia kick)
Hou – FG Garcia 47
Pitt – Hoge 4 run (Anderson kick)
Hou – Jeffires 53 pass from Carlson (Garcia kick)
Pitt – Hoge 3 run (Anderson kick)
Hou – FG Garcia 45
A: 56,906 T: 2:52

MONDAY, DECEMBER 31

NEW ORLEANS 20, L.A. RAMS 17—At the Superdome. The Saints' Morton Andersen got a second chance at a field goal and his team got a second chance to make the playoffs when Rams nosetackle Alvin Wright blocked a potential winning field goal but was called offside on the play. Anderson kicked from five yards closer and made the 24-yarder with two seconds remaining to defeat L.A. The Rams had fought back from a 14–3 deficit, tying the game on an 81-yard fourth-quarter drive. But the Saints responded with their own six-play, 44-yard drive to get into field goal range, the key being a 34-yard pass from Steve Walsh to Eric Martin.

Los Angeles	0	3	0	14	–	17
New Orleans	7	7	0	6	–	20

N.O. – Turner 26 pass from Walsh (Andersen kick)
L.A. – FG Lansford 24
N.O. – Heyward 1 run (Andersen kick)
L.A. – Anderson 47 pass from Everett (Lansford kick)
N.O. – FG Andersen 41
L.A. – Delpino 1 pass from Everett (Lansford kick)
N.O. – FG Andersen 24
A: 68,647 T: 3:02

PLAYOFFS

AFC FIRST ROUND

Miami 17, Kansas City 16
Cincinnati 41, Houston 14

NFC FIRST ROUND

Chicago 16, New Orleans 6
Washington 20, Philadelphia 6

AFC SECOND ROUND

L.A. Raiders 20, Cincinnati 10
Buffalo 44, Miami 34

NFC SECOND ROUND

N.Y. Giants 31, Chicago 3
San Francisco 28, Washington 10

AFC CHAMPIONSHIP

Buffalo 51, L.A. Raiders 3

NFC CHAMPIONSHIP

N.Y. Giants 15, San Francisco 13

SUPER BOWL XXV

N.Y. Giants 20, Buffalo 19

SATURDAY, JANUARY 5

MIAMI 17, KANSAS CITY 16—At Joe Robbie Stadium. With the Dolphins trailing 16–3 entering the fourth quarter, Miami quarterback Dan Marino completed nine of nine passes for 101 yards and two touchdowns to eliminate the Chiefs from the playoffs. The first touchdown, a one-yard pass to Tony Paige, capped a 10-play, 66-yard drive, during which the crucial gain was a run by Sammie Smith on fourth-and-two that kept the drive alive. The second touchdown was a 12-yard pass to Mark Clayton that cornerback Albert Lewis just missed intercepting. That play, with 3:28 remaining, concluded an 11-play, 85-yard drive. Kansas City had one more chance to win the game, but with 56 seconds left Nick Lowery's 52-yard field goal, which would have been his 25th straight without a miss, fell short. Earlier in that drive, the Chiefs had advanced to the Dolphin 26, but guard David Szott was flagged for a holding call that moved the ball to the 36, which proved to be just out of Lowery's range. Marino finished the game with 19 completions in 30 attempts for 221 yards, while Smith gained 82 yards on 20 carries. For the Chiefs, Steve DeBerg completed 17 of 30 passes for 269 yards and a touchdown, and Christian Okoye gained 83 yards on 13 carries. The Dolphins held the Chiefs to one of 11 third-down conversions, the biggest stop coming in the third quarter after Kansas City had recovered a Mark Duper fumble at the Miami 29 and had to settle for a field goal that kept the Dolphins within two touchdowns of the lead.

Kansas City	3	7	6	0	–	16
Miami	0	3	0	14	–	17

K.C. – FG Lowery 27
Mia – FG Stoyanovich 58
K.C. – Paige 26 pass from DeBerg (Lowery kick)
K.C. – FG Lowery 25
K.C. – FG Lowery 38
Mia – Paige 1 pass from Marino (Stoyanovich kick)
Mia – Clayton 12 pass from Marino (Stoyanovich kick)
A: 67,276 T: 2:59

WASHINGTON 20, PHILADELPHIA 6—At Veterans Stadium. After falling behind 6–0 , the Redskins knuckled down on defense and produced enough offense to dump the Eagles. The biggest play of the game came with less than a minute left in the first half, when the replay official nullified a touchdown that would have given Philadelphia the lead. Washington running back Earnest Byner caught a swing pass and was tackled at the Eagle 11 when the ball came loose and was scooped up by Ben Smith, who dashed 89 yards for an apparent Philadelphia TD. The replay official, however, ruled that the ball was jarred loose by the ground, not by the tackle, and so was not a fumble. The Redskins went on to kick a field goal before the half, which gave Washington a four-point lead. The Redskins' crucial defensive series came in the third quarter, when, with Philadelphia trailing by only seven points, Eagle coach Buddy Ryan replaced Randall Cunningham with Jim McMahon for one series. Washington blitzed on three straight pass plays, and McMahon threw three incompletions. On the next series, the Redskins drove 55 yards for the touchdown that put the game out of reach. The defensive stars for Washington were Tim Johnson, with two sacks and a forced fumble, and linebacker Andre Collins, who had nine tackles, a fumble recovery and a shared sack. In his first playoff start, Mark Rypien was 15 of 31 for 206 yards and two touchdowns.

Washington	0	10	10	0	–	20
Philadelphia	3	3	0	0	–	6

Phi – FG Ruzek 37
Phi – FG Ruzek 28
Wash – Monk 16 pass from Rypien (Lohmiller kick)
Wash – FG Lohmiller 20
Wash – FG Lohmiller 19
Wash – Clark 3 pass from Rypien (Lohmiller kick)
A: 65,287 T: 2:55

SUNDAY, JANUARY 6

CHICAGO 16, NEW ORLEANS 6—At Soldier Field. Holding a 10–3 lead early in the third quarter, the Bears attempted a 45-yard field goal that was blocked by the Saints' Renaldo Turnbull and returned by Vince Buck for an apparent New Orleans TD. The play came back, however, when the linesman ruled that one of the Saints had been offside. The Bears got a first down from the penalty and went on to kick a field goal for a 10-point lead. The other crucial play was an over-the-shoulder catch by Dennis Gentry of a 38-yard Mike Tomczak pass that set up Kevin Butler's third field goal of the game to stretch Chicago's lead to 10 points again. The Bears defense shut down the Saints' big back attack, holding Craig (Ironhead) Heyward to 10 yards on four carries. Chicago's backs ran at will against the New Orleans defense, with Neal Anderson gaining 102 yards on 27 carries and Brad Muster rushing for 71 yards on 12 carries.

New Orleans	0	3	0	3	–	6
Chicago	3	7	3	3	–	16

Chi – FG Butler 19
Chi – Thornton 18 pass from Tomczak (Butler kick)
N.O. – FG Andersen 47
Chi – FG Butler 22
N.O. – FG Andersen 38
Chi – FG Butler 21
A: 60,767 T: 3:14

CINCINNATI 41, HOUSTON 14—At Riverfront Stadium. The Bengals dominated the Oilers from the outset, scoring on eight of their first nine possessions, outgaining Houston 222 yards to 36 in the first half and throwing confusing defenses at backup QB Cody Carlson. He completed only four of his first 13 passes as the Oilers fell behind 20–0 before getting a first down. Esiason, on the other hand, was enjoying success at just about everything he tried. He finished with 14 completions in 20 attempts for 150 yards and two TDs, and he ran for a touchdown as well. The only bad news for the Bengals was that James Brooks, their leading rusher, dislocated his thumb and probably would have to sit out the next playoff game.

Houston	0	0	7	7	–	14
Cincinnati	10	10	14	7	–	41

Cin – Woods 1 run (Breech kick)
Cin – FG Breech 27
Cin – Green 2 pass from Esiason (Breech kick)
Cin – FG Breech 30
Cin – Ball 3 run (Breech kick)
Cin – Esiason 10 run (Breech kick)
Hou – Givins 16 pass from Carlson (Garcia kick)
Cin – Kattus 9 pass from Esiason (Breech kick)
Hou – Givins 5 pass from Carlson (Garcia kick)
A: 60,012 T: 3:05

SATURDAY, JANUARY 12

BUFFALO 44, MIAMI 34—At Rich Stadium. Jim Kelly, who had not played since Week 15 when he sprained his knee, passed for 339 yards and three touchdowns in leading the Bills to a win over Miami. In spite of snowy conditions, the game was a passing shootout between Kelly and Dan Marino, who finished at 23 of 49 for 323 yards and three touchdowns. Buffalo used its no-huddle offense nearly the whole game as the Bills scored less than two minutes into the game and never trailed, at one point building a 17-point lead in the second quarter. Miami closed to 30–27 with less than a minute gone in the fourth quarter, but Buffalo answered with a 10-play, 63-yard drive, capped by a five-yard touchdown run by Thurman Thomas. The Bills scored again 36 seconds later, on a 26-yard pass to Andre Reed, after Marc Logan had fumbled the kickoff, and Scott Norwood had recovered for Buffalo. In addition to his passing heroics, Kelly also ran the ball five times for 37 yards, and when he wasn't running or passing himself, he handed off to Thomas, who rushed 32 times for 117 yards. For the Bills, James Lofton caught seven passes for 149 yards, and Andre Reed caught four balls for 122.

Miami	3	14	3	14	–	34
Buffalo	13	14	3	14	–	44

Buff – Reed 40 pass from Kelly (Norwood kick)
Mia – FG Stoyanovich 49
Buff – FG Norwood 24
Buff – FG Norwood 22
Buff – Thomas 5 run (Norwood kick)
Mia – Duper 64 pass from Marino (Stoyanovich kick)
Buff – Lofton 13 pass from Kelly (Norwood kick)
Mia – Marino 2 run (Stoyanovich kick)
Mia – FG Stoyanovich 22
Buff – FG Norwood 28
Mia – Foster 2 pass from Marino (Stoyanovich kick)
Buff – Thomas 5 run (Norwood kick)
Buff – Reed 26 pass from Kelly (Norwood kick)
Mia – Martin 8 pass from Marino (Stoyanovich kick)
A: 77,087 T: 3:23

SAN FRANCISCO 28, WASHINGTON 10—At Candlestick Park. Joe Montana and the 49ers looked in top form in easily dispatching the Redskins. Montana completed 22 of 31 passes for 274 yards and two touchdowns as he picked apart the Washington defense, building a 21–10 halftime lead. In the second half, the San Francisco defense came up with two critical interceptions of Redskins quarterback Mark Rypien. Both pickoffs came in the 49er end zone as Washington was driving for a score. San Francisco iced the game when nosetackle Michael Carter intercepted a tipped pass in the fourth quarter and rumbled 61 yards for the only points of the second half. Tight end Brent Jones was Montana's most effective target, with four catches for 103 yards. Earnest Byner, the Redskins' leading rusher, suffered a bruised shoulder in the second quarter and didn't return until late in the game.

Washington	10	0	0	0	–	10
San Francisco	7	14	0	7	–	28

Wash – Monk 31 pass from Rypien (Lohmiller kick)
S.F. – Rathman 1 run (Cofer kick)
Wash – FG Lohmiller 44
S.F. – Rice 10 pass from Montana (Cofer kick)
S.F. – Sherrard 8 pass from Montana (Cofer kick)
S.F. – Carter 61 interception return (Cofer kick)
A: 65,292 T: 2:57

SUNDAY, JANUARY 13

L.A. RAIDERS 20, CINCINNATI 10—At Memorial Coliseum. With the score tied at 10 midway through the fourth quarter, Jay Schroeder hit tight end Ethan Horton with a 41-yard touchdown pass to lift the Raiders to a win over the Bengals. From that point on, the L.A. defense shut down Cincinnati's offense, and the Raider offense was able to eat the clock by giving the ball to Marcus Allen. He ended up gaining 140 yards on 21 carries, including runs of 20 and 18 yards on L.A.'s final possession to help set up the field goal with 19 seconds remaining that sealed the game. Raider defensive end Greg Townsend kept the pressure on Bengal quarterback Boomer Esiason, sacking him three times. Howie Long got the other Raider sack. Esiason completed only eight of 15 passes for 104 yards and one touchdown, while his counterpart Schroeder had another efficient passing game, completing 11 out of 21 passes for 172 yards. Bo Jackson gained 77 yards on six carries before leaving with an injury.

Cincinnati	0	3	0	7	–	10
Los Angeles	0	7	3	10	–	20

Cin – FG Breech 27
L.A. – Fernandez 13 pass from Schroeder (Jaeger kick)
L.A. – FG Jaeger 49
Cin – Jennings 8 pass from Esiason (Breech kick)
L.A. – Horton 41 pass from Schroeder (Jaeger kick)
L.A. – FG Jaeger 25
A: 92,045 T: 2:35

N.Y. GIANTS 31, CHICAGO 3—At Giants Stadium. Jeff Hostetler converted four fourth-down plays, and the Giants defense stopped the Bears at the goal line on a fourth-and-goal to key the New York win. Hostetler led the Giants with both his arm and his legs, passing for two TDs and running for another. With the Giants in Bears territory and up by a field goal in the first quarter, Hostetler faked into the line on a fourth-and-one and lofted a pass to tight end Bob Mrosko for six yards and a first down that kept New York's first touchdown drive alive. Hostetler's 10-yard bootleg on fourth-and-one in the second quarter set up the Giants second TD. On a fourth-and-six in the third quarter, Hostetler ran for nine yards to set up New York's third TD for a 24–3 lead. The Giants defense held the Bears running game to 27 yards rushing.

Chicago	0	3	0	0	–	3
New York	10	7	7	7	–	31

N.Y. – FG Bahr 46
N.Y. – Baker 21 pass from Hostetler (Bahr kick)
Chi – FG Butler 33
N.Y. – Cross 5 pass from Hostetler (Bahr kick)
N.Y. – Hostetler 3 run (Bahr kick)
N.Y. – Carthon 1 run (Bahr kick)
A: 77,025 T: 2:52

SUNDAY, JANUARY 20

BUFFALO 51, L.A. RAIDERS 3—At Rich Stadium. The Bills exploded for the biggest scoring half in NFL playoff history as they dismantled the Raiders in the AFC championship. In the first half, employing a no-huddle offense, Jim Kelly threw for 247 yards and two touchdowns, and Thurman Thomas rushed for 109 yards as Buffalo bolted out to a 41–3 lead. On one play, Kelly dropped the snap from center, picked up the ball and fired a 13-yard TD pass to James Lofton. The Bills defense also contributed points, on a TD by Darryl Talley after an interception of L.A. quarterback Jay Schroeder, one of five pickoffs of Schroeder and six overall for Buffalo. The 48-point margin was the second largest in playoff history, second only to the Bears' 73–0 victory over the Redskins in 1940. Kelly ended the game 17 of 23 for 300 yards and two TDs, Thurman Thomas gained 138 yards on 25 carries, and backup running back Kenneth Davis scored three TDs on short runs.

Los Angeles	3	0	0	0	–	3
Buffalo	21	20	0	10	–	51

Buff – Lofton 13 pass from Kelly (Norwood kick)
L.A. – FG Jaeger 41
Buff – Thomas 12 run (Norwood kick)
Buff – Talley 27 interception return (Norwood kick)
Buff – Davis 1 run (Norwood kick)
Buff – Davis 3 run (Norwood kick)
Buff – Lofton 8 pass from Kelly (Norwood kick)
Buff – Davis 1 run (Norwood kick)
Buff – FG Norwood 39
A: 80,324 T: 3:17

N.Y. GIANTS 15, SAN FRANCISCO 13—At Candlestick Park. The Giants' Matt Bahr kicked a 42-yard field goal on the last play of the game to end the 49ers' hopes of winning a third straight Super Bowl. With 2:36 remaining, the 49ers were driving in Giants territory when Erik Howard's tackle caused Roger Craig to fumble. Lawrence Taylor recovered the ball, and quarterback Jeff Hostetler got New York into field goal position with passes of 19 yards to Mark Bavaro and 13 yards to Stephen Baker. The Giants had pulled within one point of the 49ers with 5:47 to go on a Bahr field goal, set up by a 30-yard run off a fake punt by linebacker Gary Reasons. Joe Montana left the game with nearly 10 minutes remaining after a bruising, blindside hit from Leonard Marshall.

New York	3	3	3	6	–	15
San Francisco	3	3	7	0	–	13

S.F. – FG Cofer 47
N.Y. – FG Bahr 28
N.Y. – FG Bahr 42
S.F. – FG Cofer 35
S.F. – Taylor 61 pass from Montana (Cofer kick)
N.Y. – FG Bahr 46
N.Y. – FG Bahr 38
N.Y. – FG Bahr 42
A: 65,750 T: 3:07

SUNDAY, JANUARY 27

N.Y. GIANTS 20, BUFFALO 19—At Tampa Stadium. In the closest Super Bowl ever, the Giants defeated the Bills when Scott Norwood's 47-yard field goal with four seconds remaining stayed wide right. The Bills' no-huddle offense kept the Giants off-balance in building a 12–3 second-quarter lead, but New York came back behind Jeff Hostetler, who threw a 14-yard TD pass to Stephen Baker to make the score 12–10 at halftime. The Giants carried their momentum into the third quarter, taking the second-half kickoff and embarking on a nine-minute, 75-yard touchdown drive to take the lead. Key on the drive was a catch on third-and-13 by Mark Ingram, who squirmed 14 yards for a first down. MVP Ottis Anderson of the Giants gained 102 yards on 21 carries, while Thurman Thomas of the Bills gained 135 yards on 15 carries, including the 31-yard TD run in the fourth quarter that gave the Bills a two-point lead. After Thomas's TD, New York drove 74 yards in 14 plays to set up the winning 21-yard field goal by Matt Bahr with 7:20 left.

Buffalo	3	9	0	7	–	19
New York	3	7	7	3	–	20

N.Y. – FG Bahr 28
Buff – FG Norwood 23
Buff – Smith 1 run (Norwood kick)
Buff – Safety, Hostetler tackled in end zone
N.Y. – Baker 14 pass from Hostetler (Bahr kick)
N.Y. – Anderson 1 run (Bahr kick)
Buff – Thomas 31 run (Norwood kick)
N.Y. – FG Bahr 21
A: 73,813 T: 3:19

ATLANTA

1990 TEAM RECORD

REGULAR SEASON (5-11)

Date	Result	Opponent	Att.
9/9	W 47-27	Houston	56,222
9/16	L 14-21	at Detroit	48,961
9/23	L 13-19	at San Francisco	62,858
10/7	W 28-27	New Orleans	57,401
10/14	L 35-45	San Francisco	57,921
10/21	L 24-44	at L.A. Rams	54,761
10/28	W 38-17	Cincinnati	53,214
11/4	L 9-21	at Pittsburgh	57,093
11/11	L 24-30	at Chicago	62,855
11/18	L 23-24	Philadelphia	53,755
11/25	L 7-10	at New Orleans	68,629
12/2	L 17-23	at Tampa Bay	42,839
12/9	L 13-24	Phoenix	36,222
12/16	L 10-13	at Cleveland	46,536
12/23	W 20-13	L.A. Rams	30,021
12/30	W 26-7	Dallas	50,097

1990 TEAM STATISTICS

	FALCONS	Opp.
Total First Downs	274	300
Rushing	85	79
Passing	168	179
Penalty	21	42
Third Down: Made/Att.	78/209	68/197
Fourth Down: Made/Att.	9/21	5/14
Total Net Yards	5055	5270
Avg. Per Game	315.9	329.4
Total Plays	994	983
Avg. Per Play	5.1	5.4
Net Yards Rushing	1594	1357
Avg. Per Game	99.6	84.8
Total Rushes	420	413
Net Yards Passing	3461	3913
Avg. Per Game	216.3	244.6
Sacked/Yards Lost	46/265	33/214
Gross Yards	3726	4127
Att./Completions	528/293	537/297
Completion Pct.	55.5	55.3
Had Intercepted	18	17
Punts/Avg.	70/41.6	74/40.2
Net Punting Avg.	36.0	34.5
Penalties/Yards Lost	125/1004	95/811
Fumbles/Ball Lost	40/21	26/18
Touchdowns	40	44
Rushing	11	11
Passing	21	31
Returns	8	2
Avg. Time of Possession	31:05	28:55

1990 INDIVIDUAL STATISTICS

Scoring	TD Run	TD Pass	TD Ret.	PAT	FG	Saf.	Tot.
Davis	0	0	0	40/40	22/33	0	106
Rison	0	10	0	0/0	0/0	0	60
Broussard	4	0	0	0/0	0/0	0	24
Dixon	0	4	0	0/0	0/0	0	24
Johnson	3	1	0	0/0	0/0	0	24
Rozier	3	0	0	0/0	0/0	0	18
Sanders	0	0	3	0/0	0/0	0	18
Butler	0	0	2	0/0	0/0	0	12
Collins	0	2	0	0/0	0/0	0	12
Wilkins	0	2	0	0/0	0/0	0	12
Case	0	0	1	0/0	0/0	0	6
Jones	0	0	1	0/0	0/0	0	6
Miller	1	0	0	0/0	0/0	0	6
Milling	0	1	0	0/0	0/0	0	6
Thomas	0	1	0	0/0	0/0	0	6
Tuggle	0	0	1	0/0	0/0	0	6
Green	0	0	0	0/0	0/0	1	2
FALCONS	11	21	8	40/40	22/33	1	348
OPP.	11	31	2	42/44	18/28	1	365

Passing	Att.	Comp.	Yds.	Pct.	TD	Int.	Tkld.	Rate
Miller	388	222	2735	57.2	17	14	26/167	78.7
Campbell	76	36	527	47.4	3	4	9/55	61.7
Millen	63	34	427	54.0	1	0	11/43	80.6
Jones	1	1	37	100.0	0	0	0/0	118.8
FALCONS	528	293	3726	55.5	21	18	46/265	76.8
OPP.	534	297	4127	55.3	31	17	33/214	86.2

Rushing	Att.	Yds.	Avg.	LG	TD
Rozier, H-A	163	717	4.4	67	3
Rozier, Atl.	153	675	4.4	67	3
Broussard	126	454	3.6	t50	4
Jones	49	185	3.8	22	0
Johnson	30	106	3.5	12	3
Miller	26	99	3.8	18	1
Campbell	9	38	4.2	20	0
Lang	9	24	2.7	9	0
Settle	9	16	1.8	4	0
Pringle	2	9	4.5	9	0
Millen	7	-12	-1.7	2	0
FALCONS	420	1594	3.8	67	11
OPP.	413	1357	3.3	t70	11

Receiving	No.	Yds.	Avg.	LG	TD
Rison	82	1208	14.7	t75	10
Dixon	38	399	10.5	34	4
Collins	34	503	14.8	61	2
Haynes	31	445	14.4	60	0
Broussard	24	160	6.7	18	0
Thomas	18	383	21.3	72	1
Milling	18	161	8.9	24	1
Rozier	8	59	7.4	20	0
Jones	13	103	7.9	16	1
Wilkins	12	175	14.6	37	2
Johnson	10	79	7.9	16	1
Bailey	4	44	11.0	13	0
Lang	1	7	7.0	7	0
FALCONS	293	3726	12.7	t75	21
OPP.	297	4127	13.9	t89	31

Intercepts.	No.	Yds.	Avg.	LG	TD
Sanders	3	153	51.0	t82	2
Case	3	38	12.7	t36	1
Dimry	3	16	5.3	13	0
Jordan	3	14	4.7	14	0
Butler	3	0	0.0	0	0
Mitchell	2	16	8.0	16	0
FALCONS	17	237	13.9	t82	3
OPP.	18	368	20.4	59	2

Punting	No.	Yds.	Avg.	In 20	LG
Fulhage	70	2913	41.6	15	59
FALCONS	70	2913	41.6	15	59
OPP.	74	2974	40.2	18	62

Punt Returns	No.	FC	Yds.	Avg.	LG	TD
Sanders	29	13	250	8.6	t79	1
Jordan	2	4	19	9.5	10	0
Rison	2	0	10	5.0	8	0
Mitchell	1	0	0	0.0	0	0
Reid	1	0	0	0.0	0	0
FALCONS	35	17	279	8.0	t79	1
OPP.	39	12	314	8.1	39	0

Kickoff Returns	No.	Yds.	Avg.	LG	TD
Sanders	39	851	21.8	50	0
Jones	8	236	29.5	t76	1
Broussard	3	45	15.0	23	0
Johnson	2	2	1.0	6	0
Case	1	13	13.0	13	0
Dixon	1	0	0.0	0	0
Gordon	1	43	43.0	43	0
Haynes	1	0	0.0	0	0
Lang	1	18	18.0	18	0
Pringle	1	14	14.0	14	0
Wilkins	1	7	7.0	7	0
FALCONS	59	1229	20.8	t76	1
OPP.	49	814	16.6	37	0

Sacks	No.
Green	6.0
Tuggle	5.0
Bruce	4.0
Gann	3.5
Case	3.0
Epps	3.0
Reid	3.0
Conner	2.0
Lyles	1.5
Bryan	1.0
Casillas	1.0
FALCONS	33.0
OPP.	46.0

BUFFALO

1990 TEAM RECORD

REGULAR SEASON (13-3)

Date	Result	Opponent	Att.
9/9	W 26-10	Indianapolis	78,899
9/16	L 7-30	at Miami	68,142
9/23	W 30-7	at N.Y. Jets	69,927
9/30	W 29-28	Denver	74,393
10/7	W 38-24	L.A. Raiders	80,076
10/21	W 30-27	N.Y. Jets	79,002
10/28	W 27-10	at New England	51,959
11/4	W 42-0	at Cleveland	78,331
11/11	W 45-14	Phoenix	74,904
11/18	W 14-0	New England	74,720
11/26	L 24-27	at Houston	60,130
12/2	W 30-23	Philadelphia	79,320
12/9	W 31-7	at Indianapolis	53,268
12/15	W 17-13	at N.Y. Giants	66,893
12/23	W 24-14	Miami	80,235
12/30	L 14-29	at Washington	52,397
	PLAYOFFS (2-1)		
1/12	W 44-34	Miami	77,087
1/20	W 51-3	L.A. Raiders	80,324
1/27	L 19-20	N.Y. Giants, at Tampa	73,813

1990 TEAM STATISTICS

	BILLS	Opp.
Total First Downs	302	288
Rushing	123	105
Passing	161	159
Penalty	18	24
Third Down: Made/Att.	81/184	89/208
Fourth Down: Made/Att.	5/11	10/19
Total Net Yards	5276	4607
Avg. Per Game	329.8	287.9
Total Plays	931	981
Avg. Per Play	5.7	4.7
Net Yards Rushing	2080	1808
Avg. Per Game	130.0	113.0
Total Rushes	479	483
Net Yards Passing	3196	2799
Avg. Per Game	199.8	174.9
Sacked/Yards Lost	27/208	43/326
Gross Yards	3404	3125
Att./Completions	425/263	455/254
Completion Pct.	61.9	55.8
Had Intercepted	11	18
Punts/Avg.	58/39.3	66/38.2
Net Punting Avg.	33.6	34.0
Penalties/Yards Lost	92/683	107/839
Fumbles/Ball Lost	17/10	33/17
Touchdowns	53	30
Rushing	20	13
Passing	28	17
Returns	5	0
Avg. Time of Possession	28:39	31:21

1990 INDIVIDUAL STATISTICS

Scoring	TD Run	TD Pass	TD Ret.	PAT	FG	Saf.	Tot.
Norwood	0	0	0	50/52	20/29	0	110
Thomas	11	2	0	0/0	0/0	0	78
Reed	0	8	0	0/0	0/0	0	48
Davis	4	1	0	0/0	0/0	0	30
McKeller	0	5	0	0/0	0/0	0	30
Lofton	0	4	0	0/0	0/0	0	24
Mueller	2	1	0	0/0	0/0	0	18
Rolle	0	3	0	0/0	0/0	0	18
Smith	2	0	0	0/0	0/0	0	12
Tasker	0	2	0	0/0	0/0	0	12
Beebe	0	1	0	0/0	0/0	0	6
Bennett	0	0	1	0/0	0/0	0	6
Kinnebrew	1	0	0	0/0	0/0	0	6
Metzelaars	0	1	0	0/0	0/0	0	6
Odomes	0	0	1	0/0	0/0	0	6
Smith	0	0	1	0/0	0/0	0	6
Talley	0	0	1	0/0	0/0	0	6
Williams	0	0	1	0/0	0/0	0	6
BILLS	20	28	5	50/53	20/29	0	428
OPP.	13	17	0	29/30	18/24	0	263

Passing	Att.	Comp.	Yds.	Pct.	TD	Int.	Tkld.	Rate
Kelly	346	219	2829	63.3	24	9	20/158	101.2
Reich	63	36	469	57.1	2	0	6/41	91.3
Gilbert	15	8	106	53.3	2	2	1/9	76.0
Smith	1	0	0	0.0	0	0	0/0	39.6
BILLS	425	263	3404	61.9	28	11	27/208	98.2
OPP.	455	254	3125	55.8	17	18	43/326	82.7

Rushing	Att.	Yds.	Avg.	LG	TD
Thomas	271	1297	4.8	t80	11
Davis	64	302	4.7	47	4
Mueller	59	207	3.5	20	2
Smith	20	82	4.1	13	2
Kelly	22	63	2.9	15	0
Gardner	15	41	2.7	14	0
Reich	15	24	1.6	9	0
Beebe	1	23	23.0	23	0
Reed	3	23	7.7	26	0
Kinnebrew	9	18	2.0	4	1
BILLS	479	2080	4.3	t80	20
OPP.	483	1808	3.7	51	13

Receiving	No.	Yds.	Avg.	LG	TD
Reed	71	945	13.3	t56	8
Thomas	49	532	10.9	63	2
Lofton	35	712	20.3	71	4
McKeller	34	464	13.6	43	5
Smith	21	225	10.7	39	0
Mueller	16	106	6.6	30	1
Beebe	11	221	20.1	49	1
Metzelaars	10	60	6.0	12	1
Davis	9	78	8.7	16	1
Rolle	3	6	2.0	t3	3
Tasker	2	44	22.0	t24	2
Edwards	2	11	5.5	6	0
BILLS	263	3404	12.9	71	28
OPP.	254	3125	12.3	t95	17

Intercepts.	No.	Yds.	Avg.	LG	TD
Jackson	3	16	5.3	14	0
Talley	2	60	30.0	t60	1
Smith	2	39	19.5	t39	1
Hagy	2	23	11.5	23	0
Kelso	2	0	0.0	0	0
Williams	2	0	0.0	0	0
Bentley	1	13	13.0	13	0
Hicks	1	0	0.0	0	0
Odomes	1	0	0.0	0	0
Pool	1	0	0.0	0	0
Seals	1	0	0.0	0	0
BILLS	18	151	8.4	t60	2
OPP.	11	156	14.2	61	0

Punting	No.	Yds.	Avg.	In 20	LG
Tuten	53	2107	39.8	12	55
Nies	5	174	34.8	0	39
BILLS	58	2281	39.3	12	55
OPP.	66	2523	38.2	18	61

Punt Returns	No.	FC	Yds.	Avg.	LG	TD
Edwards	14	5	92	6.6	16	0
Hale	10	4	76	7.6	25	0
Odomes	1	0	9	9.0	9	0
BILLS	25	9	177	7.1	25	0
OPP.	31	12	251	8.1	21	0

Kickoff Returns	No.	Yds.	Avg.	LG	TD
Smith	32	643	20.1	38	0
Edwards	11	256	23.3	54	0
Beebe	6	119	19.8	27	0
Rolle	2	22	11.0	11	0
BILLS	51	1040	20.4	54	0
OPP.	73	1129	15.5	35	0

Sacks	No.
Smith	19.0
Wright	5.0
Bennett	4.0
Seals	4.0
Talley	4.0
Bailey	2.0
Lodish	2.0
Conlan	1.0
Hicks	1.0
Garner	0.5
Patton	0.5
BILLS	43.0
OPP.	27.0

CHICAGO

1990 TEAM RECORD

REGULAR SEASON (11-5)

Date	Result	Opponent	Att.
9/9	W 17-0	Seattle	64,400
9/16	W 31-13	at Green Bay	58,938
9/23	W 19-16	Minnesota	65,420
9/30	L 10-24	at L.A. Raiders	80,156
10/7	W 27-13	Green Bay	59,929
10/14	W 38-9	L.A. Rams	59,383
10/28	W 31-21	at Phoenix	71,233
11/4	W 26-6	at Tampa Bay	68,555
11/11	L 30-24	Atlanta	62,855
11/18	W 16-13	at Denver	75,013
11/25	L 13-41	at Minnesota	58,866
12/2	W 23-17	Detroit	62,313
12/9	L 9-10	at Washington	53,920
12/16	L 21-38	at Detroit	67,759
12/23	W 27-14	Tampa Bay	46,456
12/29	L 10-21	Kansas City	60,262
PLAYOFFS (1-1)			
1/6	W 16-6	New Orleans	60,767
1/13	L 3-31	at N.Y. Giants	77,025

1990 TEAM STATISTICS

	BEARS	Opp.
Total First Downs	295	256
Rushing	142	102
Passing	134	136
Penalty	19	18
Third Down: Made/Att.	81/221	65/188
Fourth Down: Made/Att.	5/13	6/11
Total Net Yards	4980	4492
Avg. Per Game	311.3	280.8
Total Plays	1024	927
Avg. Per Play	4.9	4.8
Net Yards Rushing	2436	1572
Avg. Per Game	152.3	98.3
Total Rushes	551	391
Net Yards Passing	2544	2920
Avg. Per Game	159.0	182.5
Sacked/Yards Lost	43/283	41/300
Gross Yards	2827	3220
Att./Completions	430/229	495/258
Completion Pct.	53.3	52.1
Had Intercepted	12	31
Punts/Avg.	78/39.4	74/37.9
Net Punting Avg.	33.5	31.7
Penalties/Yards Lost	75/615	84/676
Fumbles/Ball Lost	29/14	38/14
Touchdowns	39	31
Rushing	22	10
Passing	14	19
Returns	3	2
Avg. Time of Possession	33:06	26:54

1990 INDIVIDUAL STATISTICS

Scoring	TD Run	TD Pass	TD Ret.	PAT	FG	Saf.	Tot.
Butler	0	0	0	36/37	26/37	0	114
Anderson	10	3	0	0/0	0/0	0	78
Muster	6	0	0	0/0	0/0	0	36
Harbaugh	4	0	0	0/0	0/0	0	24
Davis	0	3	0	0/0	0/0	0	18
Morris	0	3	0	0/0	0/0	0	18
Gentry	0	2	0	0/0	0/0	0	121
Tomczak	2	0	0	0/0	0/0	0	12
Bailey	0	0	1	0/0	0/0	0	6
Boso	0	1	0	0/0	0/0	0	6
Dent	0	0	1	0/0	0/0	0	6
Green	0	1	0	0/0	0/0	0	6
Jackson	0	0	1	0/0	0/0	0	6
Thornton	0	1	0	0/0	0/0	0	6
BEARS	22	14	3	36/38	26/37	0	348
OPP.	10	19	2	28/31	22/28	0	280

Passing	Att.	Comp.	Yds.	Pct.	TD	Int.	Tkld.	Rate
Harbaugh	312	180	2178	57.7	10	6	31/206	81.9
Tomczak	104	39	521	37.5	3	5	11/70	43.8
Willis	13	9	106	69.2	1	1	1/7	87.3
Bailey	1	1	22	100.0	0	0	0/0	118.8
BEARS	430	229	2827	53.3	14	12	43/283	73.1
OPP.	495	258	3220	52.1	19	31	41/300	59.3

Rushing	Att.	Yds.	Avg.	LG	TD
Anderson	260	1078	4.1	52	10
Muster	141	664	4.7	28	6
Harbaugh	51	321	6.3	17	4
Green	27	126	4.7	14	0
Bailey	26	86	3.3	9	0
Rouse	16	56	3.5	10	0
Gentry	11	43	3.9	11	0
Tomczak	12	41	3.4	14	2
Morris	2	26	13.0	16	0
Tate	3	5	1.7	4	0
Perry	1	-1	-1.0	-1	0
Buford	1	-9	-9.0	-9	0
BEARS	551	2436	4.4	52	22
OPP.	391	1572	4.0	25	10

Receiving	No.	Yds.	Avg.	LG	TD
Muster	47	452	9.6	48	0
Anderson	42	484	11.5	t50	3
Davis	39	572	14.7	51	3
Morris	31	437	14.1	t67	3
Gentry	23	320	13.9	t80	2
Thornton	19	254	13.4	32	1
Boso	11	135	12.3	25	1
Kozlowski	7	83	11.9	32	0
Green	4	26	6.5	t10	1
Waddle	2	32	16.0	23	0
Smith	2	20	10.0	12	0
Coley	1	7	7.0	7	0
Tomczak	1	5	5.0	5	0
BEARS	229	2827	12.3	t80	14
OPP.	258	3220	12.5	t76	19

Intercepts	No.	Yds.	Avg.	LG	TD
Carrier	10	39	3.9	14	0
Stinson	6	66	11.0	30	0
Dent	3	21	7.0	15	0
Woolford	3	18	6.0	9	0
Paul	2	49	24.5	26	0
Rivera	2	13	6.5	13	0
Morrissey	2	12	6.0	12	0
Gayle	2	5	2.5	5	0
Jackson	1	45	45.0	t45	1
BEARS	31	268	8.6	t45	1
OPP.	12	164	13.7	46	0

Punting	No.	Yds.	Avg.	In 20	LG
Buford	76	3073	40.4	22	59
BEARS	78	3073	39.4	22	59
OPP.	74	2804	37.9	13	56

Punt Returns	No.	FC	Yds.	Avg.	LG	TD
Bailey	36	13	399	11.1	t95	1
BEARS	36	13	399	11.1	t95	1
OPP.	39	6	322	8.3	30	0

Kickoff Returns	No.	Yds.	Avg.	LG	TD
Bailey	23	363	15.8	30	0
Gentry	18	388	21.6	59	0
Green	7	112	16.0	20	0
Rouse	3	17	5.7	10	0
Roper	1	0	0.0	0	0
Ryan	1	-1	-1.0	-1	0
Tate	1	0	0.0	0	0
BEARS	54	879	16.3	59	0
OPP.	73	1494	20.5	64	0

Sacks	No.
Dent	12.0
Armstrong	10.0
McMichael	4.0
Perry	4.0
Cox	3.0
Jones	2.0
Woolford	2.0
Gayle	1.0
Pruitt	1.0
Roper	1.0
Singletary	1.0
BEARS	41.0
OPP.	43.0

CINCINNATI

1990 TEAM RECORD

REGULAR SEASON (9-7)

Date	Result	Opponent	Att.
9/9	W 25-20	N.Y. Jets	56,467
9/16	W 21-16	at San Diego	48,098
9/23	W 41-7	New England	56,470
10/1	L 16-31	at Seattle	60,135
10/7	W 34-31	at L.A. Rams	62,619
10/14	L 17-48	at Houston	53,501
10/22	W 34-13	at Cleveland	78,567
10/28	L 17-38	at Atlanta	53,214
11/4	L 7-21	New Orleans	60,067
11/18	W 27-3	Pittsburgh	60,064
11/25	L 20-34	Indianapolis	60,051
12/2	W 16-12	at Pittsburgh	58,200
12/9	L 17-20	San Francisco	60,084
12/16	L 7-24	at L.A. Raiders	54,132
12/23	W 40-20	Houston	60,044
12/30	W 21-14	Cleveland	60,041
PLAYOFFS (1-1)			
1/6	W 41-14	Houston	60,012
1/13	L 10-20	at L.A. Raiders	77,087

1990 TEAM STATISTICS

	BENGALS	Opp.
Total First Downs	277	308
Rushing	107	116
Passing	151	180
Penalty	19	12
Third Down: Made/Att.	79/196	93/213
Fourth Down: Made/Att.	12/19	2/12
Total Net Yards	5063	5605
Avg. Per Game	316.4	350.3
Total Plays	943	1010
Avg. Per Play	5.4	5.5
Net Yards Rushing	2120	2085
Avg. Per Game	132.5	130.3
Total Rushes	485	442
Net Yards Passing	2943	3520
Avg. Per Game	183.9	220.0
Sacked/Yards Lost	33/209	25/205
Gross Yards	3152	3725
Att./Completions	425/237	543/300
Completion Pct.	55.8	55.2
Had Intercepted	23	15
Punts/Avg.	65/42.1	63/41.8
Net Punting Avg.	34.0	36.5
Penalties/Yards Lost	83/627	101/824
Fumbles/Ball Lost	25/12	32/16
Touchdowns	44	41
Rushing	16	15
Passing	25	24
Returns	3	2
Avg. Time of Possession	29:21	30:39

1990 INDIVIDUAL STATISTICS

Scoring	TD Run	TD Pass	TD Ret.	PAT	FG	Saf.	Tot.
Breech	0	0	0	41/44	17/21	0	92
Brooks	5	4	0	0/0	0/0	0	54
Brown	0	9	0	0/0	0/0	0	54
Woods	6	0	0	0/0	0/0	0	36
Holman	0	5	0	0/0	0/0	0	30
Taylor	2	1	0	0/0	0/0	0	18
Ball	1	1	0	0/0	0/0	0	12
Green	1	1	0	0/0	0/0	0	12
Kattus	0	2	0	0/0	0/0	0	12
Francis	0	0	1	0/0	0/0	1	8
Barber	0	1	0	0/0	0/0	0	6
Bussey	0	0	1	0/0	0/0	0	6
Jennings	1	0	0	0/0	0/0	0	6
McGee	0	1	0	0/0	0/0	0	6
Price	0	0	1	0/0	0/0	0	6
Fulcher	0	0	0	0/0	0/0	1	2
BENGALS	16	25	3	41/44	17/22	2	360
OPP.	15	24	2	40/41	22/29	0	352

Passing	Att.	Comp.	Yds.	Pct.	TD	Int.	Tkld.	Rate
Esiason	402	224	3031	55.7	24	22	30/198	77.0
Wilhelm	19	12	117	63.2	0	0	1/2	80.4
Philcox	2	0	0	0.0	0	1	2/9	0.0
James	1	0	0	0.0	0	0	0/0	39.6
Johnson	1	1	4	100.0	1	0	0/0	122.9
BENGALS	425	237	3152	55.8	25	23	33/209	76.5
OPP.	543	300	3725	55.2	24	15	25/205	79.9

Rushing	Att.	Yds.	Avg.	LG	TD
Brooks	195	1004	5.1	t56	5
Green	83	353	4.3	39	1
Woods	64	268	4.2	32	6
Taylor	51	216	4.2	24	2
Esiason	50	157	3.1	21	0
Ball	22	72	3.3	15	1
Jennings	12	46	3.8	13	1
James	1	11	11.0	11	0
Wilhelm	6	6	1.0	4	0
Barber	1	-13	-13.0	-13	0
BENGALS	485	2120	4.4	t56	16
OPP.	442	2085	4.7	88	15

Receiving	No.	Yds.	Avg.	LG	TD
Brown	44	706	16.0	t50	9
McGee	43	737	17.1	52	1
Holman	40	596	14.9	53	5
Brooks	26	269	10.3	35	4
Woods	20	162	8.1	22	0
Barber	14	196	14.0	28	1
Green	12	90	7.5	22	1
Kattus	11	145	13.2	31	2
Riggs	8	79	9.9	21	0
Smith	7	45	6.4	11	0
Jennings	4	23	5.8	13	0
James	3	36	12.0	16	0
Taylor	3	22	7.3	20	1
Ball	2	46	23.0	t48	1
BENGALS	237	3152	13.3	53	25
OPP.	300	3725	12.4	75	24

Intercepts.	No.	Yds.	Avg.	LG	TD
Bussey	4	37	9.3	18	0
Fulcher	4	20	5.0	18	0
Billups	3	39	13.0	29	0
White	1	21	21.0	21	0
Francis	1	17	17.0	t17	1
Zander	1	12	12.0	12	0
Price	1	0	0.0	0	0
BENGALS	15	146	9.7	29	1
OPP.	23	233	10.1	t30	1

Punting	No.	Yds.	Avg.	In 20	LG
Johnson	64	2705	42.3	12	70
Breech	1	34	34.0	0	34
BENGALS	65	2739	42.1	12	70
OPP.	63	2634	41.8	19	65

Punt Returns	No.	FC	Yds.	Avg.	LG	TD
Price	29	14	251	8.7	t66	1
Smith	1	0	4	4.0	4	0
BENGALS	30	14	255	8.5	t66	1
OPP.	36	11	352	9.8	t79	1

Kickoff Returns	No.	Yds.	Avg.	LG	TD
Jennings	29	584	20.1	33	0
Ball	16	366	22.9	38	0
Price	10	191	19.1	33	0
Smith	2	35	17.5	20	0
Barber	1	14	14.0	14	0
James	1	43	43.0	43	0
Kattus	1	10	10.0	10	0
Riggs	1	7	7.0	7	0
Taylor	1	16	16.0	16	0
BENGALS	62	1266	20.4	43	0
OPP.	43	945	22.0	64	0

Sacks	No.
Francis	8.0
Tuatagaloa	4.5
Bussey	2.0
Hammerstein	2.0
Krumrie	2.0
McClendon	2.0
Fulcher	1.0
Grant	1.0
Walker	1.0
White	1.0
Buck	0.5
BENGALS	25.0
OPP.	33.0

CLEVELAND

1990 TEAM RECORD

REGULAR SEASON (3-13)

Date	Result	Opponent	Att.
9/9	W 13-3	Pittsburgh	78,298
9/16	L 21-24	at New York Jets	67,354
9/23	L 14-24	San Diego	77,429
9/30	L 0-34	at Kansas City	75,462
10/8	W 30-29	at Denver	74,814
10/14	L 20-25	at New Orleans	68,608
10/22	L 13-34	Cincinnati	78,567
10/28	L 17-20	at San Francisco	63,672
11/4	L 0-42	Buffalo	78,331
11/18	L 23-35	Houston	76,726
11/25	L 13-30	Miami	70,225
12/2	L 23-38	L.A. Rams	61,981
12/9	L 14-58	at Houston	54,469
12/16	W 13-10	Atlanta	46,536
12/23	L 0-35	at Pittsburgh	51,665
12/30	L 14-21	at Cincinnati	60,041

1990 TEAM STATISTICS

	BROWNS	Opp.
Total First Downs	259	314
Rushing	74	117
Passing	167	169
Penalty	18	28
Third Down: Made/Att.	81/207	104/211
Fourth Down: Made/Att.	7/19	2/3
Total Net Yards	4367	5190
Avg. Per Game	272.9	324.4
Total Plays	980	987
Avg. Per Play	4.5	5.3
Net Yards Rushing	1220	2105
Avg. Per Game	76.3	131.6
Total Rushes	345	511
Net Yards Passing	3147	3085
Avg. Per Game	196.7	192.8
Sacked/Yards Lost	42/260	32/211
Gross Yards	3407	3296
Att./Completions	573/301	444/253
Completion Pct.	52.5	57.0
Had Intercepted	23	13
Punts/Avg.	78/36.9	68/38.1
Net Punting Avg.	30.9	33.8
Penalties/Yards Lost	122/922	95/684
Fumbles/Ball Lost	37/23	24/9
Touchdowns	27	59
Rushing	10	21
Passing	13	32
Returns	4	6
Avg. Time of Possession	27:12	32:49

1990 INDIVIDUAL STATISTICS

Scoring	TD Run	TD Pass	TD Ret.	PAT	FG	Saf.	Tot.
Karuic	0	0	0	24/27	14/20	0	66
Mack	5	2	0	0/0	0/0	0	42
Metcalf	1	1	2	0/0	0/0	0	24
Slaughter	0	4	0	0/0	0/0	0	24
Hoard	3	0	0	0/0	0/0	0	18
Brennan	0	2	0	0/0	0/0	0	12
Langhorne	0	2	0	0/0	0/0	0	12
Newsome	0	2	0	0/0	0/0	0	12
Blaylock	0	0	1	0/0	0/0	0	6
Gainer	1	0	0	0/0	0/0	0	6
Johnson	0	0	1	0/0	0/0	0	6
BROWNS	10	13	4	24/27	14/20	0	228
OPP.	21	32	6	56/59	16/27	2	462

Passing	Att.	Comp.	Yds.	Pct.	TD	Int.	Tkld.	Rate
Kosar	423	230	2562	54.4	10	15	37/220	65.7
Pagel	148	69	819	46.6	3	8	5/40	48.2
Francis	2	2	26	100.0	0	0	0/0	118.8
BROWNS	573	301	3407	52.5	13	23	42/260	61.5
OPP.	444	253	3296	57.0	32	13	32/211	92.3

Rushing	Att.	Yds.	Avg.	LG	TD
Mack	158	702	4.4	26	5
Metcalf	80	248	3.1	17	1
Hoard	58	149	2.6	42	3
Gainer	30	81	2.7	9	1
Slaughter	5	29	5.8	17	0
Kosar	10	13	1.3	5	0
Redden	1	-1	-1.0	-1	0
Pagel	3	-1	-0.3	0	0
BROWNS	345	1220	3.5	42	10
OPP.	511	2105	4.1	39	21

Receiving	No.	Yds.	Avg.	LG	TD
Slaughter	59	847	14.4	50	4
Metcalf	57	452	7.9	35	1
Langhorne	45	585	13.0	39	2
Brennan	45	568	12.6	28	2
Mack	42	360	8.6	30	2
Newsome	23	240	10.4	38	2
Hoard	10	73	7.3	17	0
Gainer	7	85	12.1	20	0
Joines	6	86	14.3	24	0
Galbraith	4	62	15.5	28	0
Talley	2	28	14.0	19	0
Kauric	1	21	21.0	21	0
BROWNS	301	3407	11.3	50	13
OPP.	253	3296	13.0	59	32

Intercepts.	No.	Yds.	Avg.	LG	TD
Wright	3	56	18.7	36	0
Blaylock	2	45	22.5	45	0
Braggs	2	13	6.5	11	0
Minnifield	2	0	0.0	0	0
Johnson	1	64	64.0	t64	1
Gash	1	16	16.0	16	0
Waiters	1	15	15.0	15	0
Grayson	1	3	3.0	3	0
BROWNS	13	212	16.3	t64	1
OPP.	23	422	18.3	67	3

Punting	No.	Yds.	Avg.	In 20	LG
Wagner	74	2879	38.9	13	65
Team Stat	4	0	0.0	0	0
BROWNS	78	2879	36.9	13	65
OPP.	68	2589	38.1	15	70

Punt Returns	No.	FC	Yds.	Avg.	LG	TD
Adams	13	4	81	6.2	15	0
Brennan	9	4	72	8.0	15	0
Lewis	8	7	56	7.0	18	0
Waiters	1	0	0	0.0	0	0
BROWNS	31	15	209	6.7	25	0
OPP.	41	13	425	10.4	37	0

Kickoff Returns	No.	Yds.	Avg.	LG	TD
Metcalf	52	1052	20.2	t101	2
Fullwood	6	119	19.8	27	0
Adams	3	33	11.0	15	0
Galbraith	3	16	5.3	10	0
Hoard	2	18	9.0	10	0
Johnson	2	17	8.5	11	0
Barnett	1	15	15.0	15	0
Talley	1	6	6.0	6	0
Gainer	1	0	0.0	0	0
BROWNS	71	1276	18.0	t101	2
OPP.	45	805	17.9	39	0

Sacks	No.
Perry	11.5
Matthews	3.5
Pleasant	3.5
Baker	3.0
Braggs	2.5
Johnson	2.0
Burnett	2.0
Grayson	1.0
Gibson	1.0
Blaylock	1.0
Buckowski	0.5
Waiters	0.5
BROWNS	32.0
OPP.	42.0

DALLAS

1990 TEAM RECORD

REGULAR SEASON (7-9)

Date	Result	Opponent	Att.
9/9	W 17-14	San Diego	48,063
9/16	L 7-28	N.Y. Giants	61,090
9/23	L 15-19	at Washington	53,804
9/30	L 17-31	at N.Y. Giants	75,923
10/7	W 14-10	Tampa Bay	60,076
10/14	L 3-20	at Phoenix	45,235
10/21	W 17-13	at Tampa Bay	68,315
10/28	L 20-21	Philadelphia	62,605
11/4	L 9-24	at N.Y. Jets	68,086
11/11	L 6-24	San Francisco	62,966
11/18	W 24-21	at L.A. Rams	58,589
11/22	W 27-17	Washington	60,355
12/2	W 17-13	New Orleans	60,087
12/16	W 41-10	Phoenix	60,190
12/23	L 3-17	at Philadelphia	63,895
12/30	L 7-26	at Atlanta	50,097

1990 TEAM STATISTICS

	COWBOYS	Opp.
Total First Downs	250	280
Rushing	88	109
Passing	135	153
Penalty	27	18
Third Down: Made/Att.	67/198	85/208
Fourth Down: Made/Att.	5/10	8/16
Total Net Yards	4081	4615
Avg. Per Game	255.1	288.4
Total Plays	911	988
Avg. Per Play	4.5	4.7
Net Yards Rushing	1500	1976
Avg. Per Game	93.8	123.5
Total Rushes	393	482
Net Yards Passing	2581	2639
Avg. Per Game	161.3	164.9
Sacked/Yards Lost	43/317	36/292
Gross Yards	2898	2931
Att./Completions	475/254	470/271
Completion Pct.	53.5	57.7
Had Intercepted	18	11
Punts/Avg.	79/43.2	70/40.9
Net Punting Avg.	35.6	36.2
Penalties/Yards Lost	98/729	104/911
Fumbles/Ball Lost	27/9	32/19
Touchdowns	27	36
Rushing	13	18
Passing	12	12
Returns	2	6
Avg. Time of Possession	28:44	31:16

1990 INDIVIDUAL STATISTICS

Scoring	TD Run	TD Pass	TD Ret.	PAT	FG	Saf.	Tot.
Willis	0	0	0	18/25	26/26	0	80
Smith	11	0	0	0/0	0/0	0	66
Irvin	0	5	0	0/0	0/0	0	30
Novacek	0	4	0	0/0	0/0	0	24
Johnston	1	1	0	0/0	0/0	0	12
Agee	0	1	0	0/0	0/0	0	6
Aikman	1	0	0	0/0	0/0	0	6
Holt	0	0	1	0/0	0/0	0	6
McKinnon	0	1	0	0/0	0/0	0	6
Wright	0	0	1	0/0	0/0	0	6
COWBOYS	13	12	2	18/25	26/27	0	244
OPP.	18	12	6	18/26	36/36	1	308

Passing	Att.	Comp.	Yds.	Pct.	TD	Int.	Tkld.	Rate
Aikman	399	226	2579	56.6	11	18	39/288	66.6
Laufenberg	67	24	279	35.8	1	6	4/29	16.9
Walsh	9	4	40	44.4	0	0	0/0	57.6
COWBOYS	475	254	2898	53.5	12	24	43/317	59.4
OPP.	470	271	2931	57.7	12	11	36/292	74.9

Rushing	Att.	Yds.	Avg.	LG	TD
Smith	241	937	3.9	t48	11
Agee	53	213	4.0	28	0
Aikman	40	172	4.3	20	1
Highsmith	19	48	2.5	7	0
Dixon	11	43	3.9	18	0
Johnston	10	35	3.5	8	1
Wright	3	26	8.7	14	0
Saxon	1	20	20.0	20	0
Laufenberg	2	6	3.0	5	0
Smith	6	6	1.0	6	0
Bates	1	4	4.0	4	0
Walsh	1	0	0.-	0	0
Martin	4	-2	-0.5	3	0
McKinnon	1	-8	-8.0	-8	0
COWBOYS	393	1500	3.8	t48	13
OPP.	482	1976	4.1	67	18

Receiving	No.	Yds.	Avg.	LG	TD
Martin	64	732	11.4	45	0
Novacek	59	657	11.1	41	4
Agee	30	272	9.1	30	1
Smith	24	228	9.5	57	0
Irvin	20	413	20.7	t61	5
McKinnon	14	172	12.3	t28	1
Johnston	14	148	10.6	26	1
Awalt	13	133	10.2	25	0
Wright	11	104	9.5	20	0
Highsmith	3	13	4.3	7	0
Dixon	2	26	13.0	21	0
COWBOYS	254	2898	11.4	t61	12
OPP.	271	2931	10.8	t58	12

Intercepts.	No.	Yds.	Avg.	LG	TD
Holt	3	72	24.0	t64	1
Washington	3	24	8.0	13	0
Bates	1	4	4.0	4	0
Gant	1	26	26.0	26	0
Hendrix	1	0	0.0	0	0
Horton	1	0	0.0	0	0
Williams	1	0	0.0	0	0
COWBOYS	11	126	11.5	t64	1
OPP.	24	353	14.7	t61	4

Punting	No.	Yds.	Avg.	In 20	LG
Saxon	79	3413	43.2	20	62
COWBOYS	79	3413	43.2	20	62
OPP.	70	2866	40.9	15	62

Punt Returns	No.	FC	Yds.	Avg.	LG	TD
Shepard	20	1	121	6.1	13	0
Harris	12	6	63	5.3	12	0
Martin	5	3	46	9.2	17	0
McKinnon	2	1	20	10.0	20	0
COWBOYS	39	11	250	6.4	20	0
OPP.	43	8	438	10.2	t98	1

Kickoff Returns	No.	Yds.	Avg.	LG	TD
Dixon	36	736	20.4	47	0
Wright	12	276	23.0	t90	1
Shepard	4	75	18.8	22	0
Stepnoski	1	15	15.0	15	0
Harris	1	0	0.0	0	0
COWBOYS	54	1102	20.4	t90	1
OPP.	55	1136	20.7	t76	1

Sacks	No.
Jones	7.5
Stubbs	7.5
Tolbert	6.0
Noonan	4.5
Jeffcoat	3.5
Norton	2.5
Del Rio	1.5
Hamel	1.0
Lockhart	1.0
Solomon	1.0
COWBOYS	36.0
OPP.	43.0

D E N V E R

1990 TEAM RECORD

REGULAR SEASON (5–11)

Date	Result	Opponent	Att.
9/9	L 9–14	at L.A. Raiders	54,206
9/17	W 24–23	Kansas City	75,277
9/23	W 34–31	Seattle	75,290
9/30	L 28–29	at Buffalo	74,393
10/8	L 29–30	Cleveland	74,814
10/14	L 17–34	Pittsburgh	74,285
10/21	W 27–17	at Indianapolis	59,850
11/4	L 22–27	at Minnesota	57,331
11/11	L 7–19	at San Diego	59,557
11/18	L 13–16	Chicago	75,013
11/22	L 27–40	at Detroit	73,896
12/2	L 20–23	L.A. Raiders	74,162
12/9	L 20–31	at Kansas City	74,347
12/16	W 20–10	San Diego	64,919
12/23	L 12–17	at Seattle	55,845
12/30	W 22–13	Green Bay	46,943

1990 TEAM STATISTICS

	BRONCOS	Opp.
Total First Downs	323	306
Rushing	126	110
Passing	170	181
Penalty	27	15
Third Down: Made/Att.	86/207	84/195
Fourth Down: Made/Att.	7/14	7/12
Total Net Yards	5213	5345
Avg. Per Game	325.8	334.1
Total Plays	1035	969
Avg. Per Play	5.0	5.5
Net Yards Rushing	1872	1963
Avg. Per Game	117.0	122.7
Total Rushes	462	456
Net Yards Passing	3341	3382
Avg. Per Game	208.8	211.4
Sacked/Yards Lost	46/330	34/289
Gross Yards	3671	3671
Att./Completions	527/305	479/284
Completion Pct.	57.9	59.3
Had Intercepted	18	10
Punts/Avg.	60/43.5	61/41.4
Net Punting Avg.	38.5	35.6
Penalties/Yards Lost	108/775	105/824
Fumbles/Ball Lost	30/14	36/15
Touchdowns	36	43
Rushing	19	16
Passing	15	22
Returns	2	5
Avg. Time of Possession	30:50	29:10

1990 INDIVIDUAL STATISTICS

Scoring	TD Run	TD Pass	TD Ret.	PAT	FG	Saf.	Tot.
Treadwell	0	0	0	34/36	25/34	0	109
Humphrey	7	0	0	0/0	0/0	0	42
Jackson	1	4	0	0/0	0/0	0	30
Bratton	3	1	0	0/0	0/0	0	24
Young	0	4	0	0/0	0/0	0	24
Elway	3	0	0	0/0	0/0	0	18
Johnson	0	3	0	0/0	0/0	0	18
Sewell	3	0	0	0/0	0/0	0	18
Nattiel	0	2	0	0/0	0/0	0	12
Winder	2	0	0	0/0	0/0	0	12
Mecklenburg	0	0	1	0/0	0/0	1	8
Henderson	0	0	1	0/0	0/0	0	6
Sharpe	0	1	0	0/0	0/0	0	6
Fletcher	0	0	0	0/0	0/0	1	2
BRONCOS	19	15	2	34/36	25/34	3	331
OPP.	16	22	5	38/43	26/33	3	374

Passing	Att.	Comp.	Yds.	Pct.	TD	Int.	Tkld.	Rate
Elway	502	294	3526	58.6	15	14	43/311	78.5
Kubiak	22	11	145	50.0	0	4	3/19	31.6
Humphrey	2	0	0	0.0	0	0	0/0	39.6
Sewell	1	0	0	0.0	0	0	0/0	39.6
BRONCOS	527	305	3671	57.9	15	18	46/330	74.6
OPP.	479	284	3671	59.3	22	10	34/289	90.0

Rushing	Att.	Yds.	Avg.	LG	TD
Humphrey	288	1202	4.2	t37	7
Elway	50	258	5.2	21	3
Winder	42	120	2.9	19	2
Bratton	27	82	3.0	10	3
Ezor	23	81	3.5	15	0
Kubiak	9	52	5.8	18	0
Sewell	17	46	2.7	8	3
Jackson	5	28	5.6	t16	1
Porter	1	3	3.0	3	0
BRONCOS	462	1872	4.1	t37	19
OPP.	456	1963	4.3	t62	16

Receiving	No.	Yds.	Avg.	LG	TD
Jackson	57	926	16.2	66	4
Johnson	54	747	13.8	49	3
Kay	29	282	9.7	22	0
Bratton	29	276	9.5	63	1
Young	28	385	13.8	42	4
Sewell	26	268	10.3	36	0
Humphrey	24	152	6.3	26	0
Nattiel	18	297	16.5	t52	2
Winder	17	145	8.5	17	0
Mobley	8	41	5.1	9	0
Sharpe	7	99	14.1	33	1
Porter	4	44	11.0	16	0
Verhulst	3	13	4.3	6	0
Lanier	1	−4	−4.0	−4	0
BRONCOS	305	3671	12.0	66	15
OPP.	284	3671	12.9	90	22

Intercepts.	No.	Yds.	Avg.	LG	TD
Henderson	2	71	35.5	t49	1
Montgomery	2	43	21.5	24	0
Atwater	2	32	16.0	27	0
Plummer	1	16	16.0	16	0
Smith	1	13	13.0	13	0
Braxton	1	10	10.0	10	0
Lang	1	5	5.0	5	0
BRONCOS	10	190	19.0	t49	1
OPP.	18	169	9.4	t39	3

Punting	No.	Yds.	Avg.	In 20	LG
Horan	58	2575	44.4	14	67
Elway	1	37	37.0	0	37
BRONCOS	60	2612	43.5	14	67
OPP.	62	2565	41.4	15	59

Punt Returns	No.	FC	Yds.	Avg.	LG	TD
Clark	21	1	159	7.6	32	0
Johnson	11	11	92	8.4	29	0
Nattiel	1	0	5	5.0	5	0
BRONCOS	33	12	256	7.8	32	0
OPP.	22	9	159	7.2	22	0

Kickoff Returns	No.	Yds.	Avg.	LG	TD
Clark	20	505	25.3	75	0
Montgomery	14	286	20.4	59	0
Ezor	13	214	16.5	50	0
Johnson	6	126	21.0	39	0
Winder	4	55	13.8	24	0
Bratton	3	37	12.3	18	0
Kay	2	10	5.0	7	0
Atwater	1	0	0.0	0	0
Jackson	1	18	18.0	18	0
Mobley	1	9	9.0	9	0
Nattiel	1	0	0.0	0	0
BRONCOS	66	1260	19.1	75	0
OPP.	69	1319	19.1	71	0

Sacks	No.
Fletcher	11.0
Mecklenburg	5.0
Powers	4.0
Holmes	3.0
Brooks	2.0
Galloway	2.0
Kragen	2.0
Atwater	1.0
Dennison	1.0
Lucas	1.0
Townsend	1.0
BRONCOS	34.0
OPP.	46.0

D E T R O I T

1990 TEAM RECORD

REGULAR SEASON (6–10)

Date	Result	Opponent	Att.
9/9	L 21–38	Tampa Bay	54,728
9/16	W 21–14	Atlanta	48,961
9/23	L 20–23	at Tampa Bay	55,075
9/30	L 21–24	Green Bay	64,509
10/7	W 34–27	at Minnesota	57,586
10/14	L 24–43	at Kansas City	74,312
10/28	W 27–10	at New Orleans	64,368
11/4	L 38–41	Washington	69,326
11/11	L 7–17	Minnesota	68,264
11/18	L 0–20	at N.Y. Giants	76,109
11/22	W 40–27	Denver	73,896
12/2	L 17–23	at Chicago	62,313
12/10	L 31–38	L.A. Raiders	72,190
12/16	W 38–21	Chicago	67,759
12/23	W 24–17	at Green Bay	46,700
12/30	L 10–30	at Seattle	50,681

1990 TEAM STATISTICS

	LIONS	Opp.
Total First Downs	281	335
Rushing	112	141
Passing	152	175
Penalty	17	19
Third Down: Made/Att.	53/164	106/222
Fourth Down: Made/Att.	7/14	12/16
Total Net Yards	4984	5734
Avg. Per Game	311.5	358.4
Total Plays	871	1080
Avg. Per Play	5.7	5.3
Net Yards Rushing	1929	2388
Avg. Per Game	120.6	149.3
Total Rushes	367	532
Net Yards Passing	3055	3346
Avg. Per Game	190.9	209.1
Sacked/Yards Lost	44/273	41/279
Gross Yards	3328	3625
Att./Completions	460/242	507/319
Completion Pct.	52.6	62.9
Had Intercepted	20	17
Punts/Avg.	63/40.6	62/40.8
Net Punting Avg.	35.3	33.0
Penalties/Yards Lost	88/731	97/798
Fumbles/Ball Lost	29/16	30/18
Touchdowns	46	49
Rushing	19	22
Passing	24	21
Returns	3	6
Avg. Time of Possession	26:04	35:10

1990 INDIVIDUAL STATISTICS

Scoring	TD Run	TD Pass	TD Ret.	PAT	FG	Saf.	Tot.
Sanders	13	3	0			0	96
Murray	0	0	0	34/34	13/19	0	73
Clark	0	8	0	0/0	0/0	0	48
Johnson	0	6	0	0/0	0/0	0	36
Peete	6	0	0	0/0	0/0	0	36
Karlis	0	0	0	12/12	4/7	0	24
Greer	0	3	0	0/0	0/0	0	18
Campbell	0	2	0	0/0	0/0	0	12
Wilder	0	1	0	0/0	0/0	0	6
Williams	0	0	1	0/0	0/0	0	6
Matthews	0	1	0	0/0	0/0	0	6
White	0	0	1	0/0	0/0	0	6
Crockett	0	0	1	0/0	0/0	0	6
LIONS	19	24	3	48/48	17/26	0	373
OPP.	22	21	6	48/48	23/30	1	413

Passing	Att.	Comp.	Yds.	Pct.	TD	Int.	Tkld.	Rate
Peete	271	142	1974	52.4	13	8	27/168	79.6
Gagliano	159	87	1190	54.7	10	10	13/83	73.6
Ware	30	13	164	43.3	1	2	4/22	44.1
LIONS	460	242	3328	52.6	24	20	44/273	75.5
OPP.	507	319	3625	62.9	21	17	41/279	83.8

Rushing	Att.	Yds.	Avg.	LG	TD
Sanders	255	1304	5.1	t45	13
Peete	48	365	7.6	37	6
Gagliano	46	145	3.2	22	0
Ware	7	64	9.1	30	0
Wilder	11	51	4.6	13	0
LIONS	367	1929	5.3	t45	19
OPP.	532	2388	4.5	t55	22

Receiving	No.	Yds.	Avg.	LG	TD
Johnson	64	727	11.4	t44	6
Clark	53	932	17.6	57	8
Sanders	35	462	13.2	t47	3
Matthews	30	349	11.6	52	1
Greer	20	332	16.6	t68	3
Campbell	19	236	12.4	51	2
Farr	12	170	14.2	29	0
Phillips	8	112	14.0	29	1
Wilder	1	8	8.0	t8	1
LIONS	242	3328	13.8	t68	24
OPP.	319	3625	11.4	t68	21

Intercepts.	No.	Yds.	Avg.	LG	TD
White	5	120	24.0	48	1
Crockett	3	17	5.7	9	0
Blades	2	25	12.5	21	0
McNorton	1	33	33.0	33	0
Oldham	1	28	28.0	28	0
Irvin	1	22	22.0	22	0
Welch	1	16	16.0	16	0
Spielman	1	12	12.0	12	0
Cofer	1	0	0.0	0	0
Jones	1	0	0.0	0	0
LIONS	17	273	16.1	48	1
OPP.	20	346	17.3	t62	3

Punting	No.	Yds.	Avg.	In 20	LG
Arnold	63	2560	40.6	10	59
LIONS	63	2560	40.6	10	59
OPP.	62	2530	40.8	8	57

Punt Returns	No.	FC	Yds.	Avg.	LG	TD
Gray	34	7	362	10.6	39	0
Campbell	1	0	0	0.0	0	0
LIONS	35	7	362	10.3	39	0
OPP.	29	10	234	8.1	24	0

Kickoff Returns	No.	Yds.	Avg.	LG	TD
Gray	41	939	22.9	65	0
Oldham	13	234	18.0	42	0
Campbell	12	238	19.8	38	0
Phillips	2	43	21.5	23	0
Andolsek	1	12	12.0	12	0
McKnight	1	0	0.0	0	0
LIONS	70	1466	20.9	65	0
OPP.	70	1229	17.6	t76	1

Sacks	No.
Cofer	10.0
Hayworth	4.0
Duckens	3.0
Ferguson	3.0
Hunter	3.0
Owens	3.0
Williams	3.0
Ball	2.0
Jamison	2.0
Spielman	2.0
Blades	1.0
Brooks	1.0
Cline	1.0
Crockett	1.0
Jones	1.0
Spindler	1.0
LIONS	41.0
OPP.	44.0

G R E E N   B A Y

1 9 9 0   T E A M   R E C O R D

REGULAR SEASON (6-10)

Date	Result	Opponent	Att.
9/9	W 36-24	L.A. Rams	57,685
9/16	L 13-31	Chicago	58,938
9/23	L 3-17	Kansas City	58,817
9/30	W 24-21	at Detroit	64,509
10/7	L 13-27	at Chicago	59,929
10/14	L 14-26	at Tampa Bay	67,472
10/28	W 24-10	Minnesota	55,125
11/4	L 20-24	San Francisco	58,835
11/11	W 29-16	at L.A. Raiders	50,855
11/18	W 24-21	at Phoenix	46,878
11/25	W 20-10	Tampa Bay	53,677
12/2	L 7-23	at Minnesota	62,058
12/9	L 14-20	Seattle	52,015
12/16	L 0-31	at Philadelphia	65,627
12/22	L 17-24	Detroit	46,700
12/30	L 13-22	at Denver	46,943

1 9 9 0   T E A M   S T A T I S T I C S

	PACKERS	Opp.
Total First Downs	276	286
Rushing	72	113
Passing	183	160
Penalty	21	13
Third Down: Made/Att.	76/196	85/210
Fourth Down: Made/Att.	5/14	3/9
Total Net Yards	4675	5442
Avg. Per Game	292.2	340.1
Total Plays	953	981
Avg. Per Play	4.9	5.5
Net Yards Rushing	1369	2059
Avg. Per Game	85.6	128.7
Total Rushes	350	475
Net Yards Passing	3306	3383
Avg. Per Game	206.6	211.4
Sacked/Yards Lost	62/390	27/172
Gross Yards	3696	3555
Att./Completions	541/302	479/256
Completion Pct.	55.8	53.4
Had Intercepted	21	16
Punts/Avg.	65/37.4	69/39.1
Net Punting Avg.	32.7	31.7
Penalties/Yards Lost	84/674	109/854
Fumbles/Ball Lost	37/22	26/14
Touchdowns	29	40
Rushing	5	16
Passing	20	20
Returns	4	4
Avg. Time of Possession	29:34	30:26

1 9 9 0   I N D I V I D U A L   S T A T I S T I C S

Scoring	TD Run	TD Pass	TD Ret.	PAT	FG	Saf.	Tot.
Jacke	0	0	0	28/29	23/30	0	97
Sharpe	0	6	0	0/0	0/0	0	36
West	0	5	0	0/0	0/0	0	30
Query	0	2	1	0/0	0/0	0	18
Haddix	0	2	0	0/0	0/0	0	12
Kemp	0	2	0	0/0	0/0	0	12
Thompson	1	0	1	0/0	0/0	0	12
Fontenot	0	1	0	0/0	0/0	0	6
Fullwood	1	0	0	0/0	0/0	0	6
Greene	0	0	1	0/0	0/0	0	6
Kiel	1	0	0	0/0	0/0	0	6
Majkowski	1	0	0	0/0	0/0	0	6
Patterson	0	0	1	0/0	0/0	0	6
Weathers	0	1	0	0/0	0/0	0	6
Woodside	1	0	0	0/0	0/0	0	6
Workman	0	1	0	0/0	0/0	0	6
PACKERS	5	20	4	28/29	23/30	0	271
OPP.	16	20	4	39/40	22/34	1	347

Passing	Att.	Comp.	Yds.	Pct.	TD	Int.	Tkld.	Rate
Majkowski	264	150	1925	56.8	10	12	32/178	73.5
Dilweg	192	101	1267	52.6	8	7	22/150	72.1
Kiel	85	51	504	60.0	2	2	8/62	74.8
PACKERS	541	302	3696	55.8	20	21	62/390	73.2
OPP.	479	256	3555	53.4	20	16	27/172	77.5

Rushing	Att.	Yds.	Avg.	LG	TD
Haddix	98	311	3.2	13	0
Thompson	76	264	3.5	37	1
Majkowski	29	186	6.4	24	1
Woodside	46	182	4.0	21	1
Fullwood	44	124	2.8	16	1
Dilweg	21	114	5.4	22	0
Fontenot	17	76	4.5	18	0
Workman	8	51	6.4	31	0
Query	3	39	13.0	18	0
Sharpe	2	14	7.0	10	0
Kiel	5	9	1.8	4	1
Kemp	1	-1	-1.0	-1	0
PACKERS	350	1369	3.9	37	5
OPP.	475	2059	4.3	52	16

Receiving	No.	Yds.	Avg.	LG	TD
Sharpe	67	1105	16.5	t76	6
Kemp	44	527	12.0	29	2
Query	34	458	13.5	t47	2
Weathers	33	390	11.8	29	1
Fontenot	31	293	9.5	59	1
West	27	356	13.2	50	5
Woodside	24	184	7.7	25	0
Haddix	13	94	7.2	28	2
Harris	12	157	13.1	26	0

Wilson	7	84	12.0	18	0
Workman	4	30	7.5	9	1
Fullwood	3	17	5.7	10	0
Thompson	3	1	0.3	1	0
PACKERS	302	3696	12.2	t76	20
OPP.	256	3555	13.9	74	20

Interceps.	No.	Yds.	Avg.	LG	TD
Butler	3	42	14.0	28	0
Holmes	3	39	13.0	24	0
Murphy	3	6	2.0	4	0
Stephen	2	26	13.0	26	0
Holland	1	32	32.0	32	0
Patterson	1	9	9.0	t9	1
Cecil	1	0	0.0	0	0
Lee	1	0	0.0	0	0
Pitts	1	0	0.0	0	0
PACKERS	16	154	9.6	32	1
OPP.	21	293	14.0	47	2

Punting	No.	Yds.	Avg.	In 20	LG
Bracken	64	2431	38.0	17	59
PACKERS	65	2431	37.4	17	59
OPP.	69	2698	39.1	16	61

Punt Returns	No.	FC	Yds.	Avg.	LG	TD
Query	32	7	308	9.6	25	0
Pitts	0	2	0	0.0	0	0
PACKERS	32	9	308	9.6	25	0
OPP.	34	13	266	7.8	30	0

Kickoff Returns	No.	Yds.	Avg.	LG	TD
Wilson	35	798	22.8	36	0
Workman	14	210	15.0	26	0
Bland	7	104	14.9	24	0
Fontenot	3	88	29.3	50	0
Thompson	3	103	34.3	t76	1
West	1	0	0.0	0	0
PACKERS	63	1303	20.7	t76	1
OPP.	56	1125	20.1	87	0

Sacks	No.
Harris	7.0
Brock	4.0
Patterson	4.0
Bennett	3.0
Brown	3.0
Dent	1.0
Holmes	1.0
Murphy	1.0
Nelson	1.0
Noble	1.0
Stephen	1.0
PACKERS	27.0
OPP.	62.0

H O U S T O N

1 9 9 0   T E A M   R E C O R D

REGULAR SEASON (13-3)

Date	Result	Opponent	Att.
9/9	L 27-47	at Atlanta	56,222
9/16	L 9-20	at Pittsburgh	54,814
9/23	W 24-10	Indianapolis	50,093
9/30	W 17-7	at San Diego	48,762
10/7	L 21-24	San Francisco	59,931
10/14	W 48-17	Cincinnati	53,501
10/21	W 23-10	New Orleans	57,908
10/28	L 12-17	N.Y. Jets	56,337
11/4	L 13-17	at L.A. Rams	52,628
11/18	W 35-23	at Cleveland	76,726
11/26	W 27-24	Buffalo	60,130
12/2	L 10-13	at Seattle	57,592
12/9	W 58-14	Cleveland	54,469
12/16	W 27-10	at Kansas City	61,756
12/23	L 20-40	at Cincinnati	60,044
12/30	W 34-14	Pittsburgh	56,906

PLAYOFFS (0-1)

1/6	L 14-41	at Cincinnati	60,012

1 9 9 0   T E A M   S T A T I S T I C S

	OILERS	Opp.
Total First Downs	376	279
Rushing	97	88
Passing	251	160
Penalty	28	31
Third Down: Made/Att.	94/181	67/175
Fourth Down: Made/Att.	3/12	6/13
Total Net Yards	6222	4635
Avg. Per Game	388.9	289.7
Total Plays	1006	890
Avg. Per Play	6.2	5.2
Net Yards Rushing	1417	1575
Avg. Per Game	88.6	98.4
Total Rushes	328	392
Net Yards Passing	4805	3060
Avg. Per Game	300.3	191.3
Sacked/Yards Lost	39/267	38/272
Gross Yards	5072	3332
Att./Completions	639/399	460/267
Completion Pct.	62.4	58.0
Had Intercepted	15	21
Punts/Avg.	34/45.0	62/38.7
Net Punting Avg.	36.6	35.0
Penalties/Yards Lost	135/1009	134/1015
Fumbles/Ball Lost	34/21	22/12
Touchdowns	49	37
Rushing	10	12
Passing	37	18
Returns	2	7
Avg. Time of Possession	31:35	28:25

1 9 9 0   I N D I V I D U A L   S T A T I S T I C S

Scoring	TD Run	TD Pass	TD Ret.	PAT	FG	Saf.	Tot.
White	8	4	0	0/0	0/0	0	72
Garcia	0	0	0	26/28	14/20	0	68
Givins	0	9	0	0/0	0/0	0	54
Jeffires	0	8	0	0/0	0/0	0	48
Zendejas	0	0	0	20/21	7/12	0	41
Jones	0	6	0	0/0	0/0	0	36
Hill	0	5	0	0/0	0/0	0	30
Harris	0	3	0	0/0	0/0	0	18
Moon	2	0	0	0/0	0/0	0	12
Duncan	0	1	0	0/0	0/0	0	6
Ford	0	1	0	0/0	0/0	0	6
Johnson	0	0	1	0/0	0/0	0	6
Kinard	0	0	1	0/0	0/0	0	6
Childress	0	0	0	0/0	0/0	1	2
OILERS	10	37	2	46/49	21/32	1	405
OPP.	12	18	7	34/37	17/21	0	307

Passing	Att.	Comp.	Yds.	Pct.	TD	Int.	Tkld.	Rate
Moon	584	362	4689	62.0	33	13	36/252	96.8
Carlson	55	37	383	67.3	4	2	3/15	96.3
OILERS	639	399	5072	62.4	37	15	39/267	96.7
OPP.	460	267	3332	58.0	18	21	38/272	74.7

Rushing	Att.	Yds.	Avg.	LG	TD
White	168	702	4.2	22	8
Pinkett	66	268	4.1	19	0
Moon	55	215	3.9	17	2
Jones	14	75	5.4	14	0
Givins	3	65	21.7	31	0
Carlson	11	52	4.7	16	0
Rozier	10	42	4.2	11	0
Jones	1	-2	-2.0	-2	0
OILERS	328	1417	4.3	31	10
OPP.	392	1575	4.0	t56	12

Receiving	No.	Yds.	Avg.	LG	TD
Jeffires	74	1048	14.2	t87	8
Hill	74	1019	13.8	57	5
Givins	72	979	13.6	t80	9
Duncan	66	785	11.9	t37	1
White	39	368	9.4	29	4
Jones	30	409	13.6	47	6
Harris	13	172	13.2	t42	3
Pinkett	11	85	7.7	38	0
Ford	10	98	9.8	24	1
NcNeil	5	63	12.6	16	0
Rozier	5	46	9.2	24	0
OILERS	399	5072	12.7	t87	37
OPP.	267	3332	12.5	t78	18

Intercepts.	No.	Yds.	Avg.	LG	TD
Johnson	8	100	12.5	35	1
Kinard	4	75	18.8	47	0
Dishman	4	50	12.5	42	0
McDowell	2	11	5.5	11	0
Meads	1	32	32.0	32	0
Allen	1	27	27.0	27	0
Knight	1	0	0.0	0	0
OILERS	21	295	14.0	47	1
OPP.	15	237	15.8	t82	2

Punting	No.	Yds.	Avg.	In 20	LG
Montgomery	34	1530	45.0	7	60
OILERS	34	1530	45.0	7	60
OPP.	62	2402	38.7	20	55

Punt Returns	No.	FC	Yds.	Avg.	LG	TD
McNeil	30	20	172	5.7	26	0
Duncan	0	1	0	0.0	0	0
OILERS	30	21	172	5.7	26	0
OPP.	23	0	186	8.1	t52	1

Kickoff Returns	No.	Yds.	Avg.	LG	TD
McNeil	27	551	20.4	64	0
Ford	14	219	15.6	23	0
Pinkett	4	91	15.6	23	0
Norgard	2	0	0.0	0	0
OILERS	47	861	18.3	64	0
OPP.	71	1329	18.7	t101	1

Sacks	No.
S. Jones	12.5
Childress	8.0
Fuller	8.0
E. Johnson	2.5
Meads	2.5
Smith	2.0
Smith	1.0
Alm	0.5
Montgomery	0.5
McDowell	0.5
OILERS	38.0
OPP.	39.0

INDIANAPOLIS

1990 TEAM RECORD

REGULAR SEASON (7–9)

Date	Result	Opponent	Att.
9/9	L 10–26	at Buffalo	78,899
9/16	L 14–16	New England	49,256
9/23	L 10–24	at Houston	50,093
9/30	W 24–23	at Philadelphia	62,067
10/7	W 23–19	Kansas City	54,950
10/21	L 17–27	Denver	59,850
10/28	L 7–27	Miami	59,213
11/5	L 7–24	N.Y. Giants	58,688
11/11	W 13–10	at New England	28,924
11/18	W 17–14	N.Y. Jets	47,283
11/25	W 34–20	at Cincinnati	60,051
12/2	L 17–20	at Phoenix	31,885
12/9	L 7–31	Buffalo	53,268
12/16	W 29–21	at N.Y. Jets	41,423
12/22	W 35–28	Washington	58,173
12/30	L 17–23	at Miami	59,547

1990 TEAM STATISTICS

	COLTS	Opp.
Total First Downs	245	320
Rushing	81	130
Passing	142	176
Penalty	22	14
Third Down: Made/Att.	56/185	87/204
Fourth Down: Made/Att.	11/18	7/14
Total Net Yards	4155	5614
Avg. Per Game	259.7	350.9
Total Plays	874	1034
Avg. Per Play	4.8	5.4
Net Yards Rushing	1282	2212
Avg. Per Game	80.1	138.3
Total Rushes	335	513
Net Yards Passing	2873	3402
Avg. Per Game	179.6	212.6
Sacked/Yards Lost	51/424	29/203
Gross Yards	3297	3605
Att./Completions	488/269	492/301
Completion Pct.	55.1	61.2
Had Intercepted	21	9
Punts/Avg.	72/42.8	58/42.0
Net Punting Avg.	37.4	34.4
Penalties/Yards Lost	78/590	104/781
Fumbles/Ball Lost	23/10	25/15
Touchdowns	33	36
Rushing	9	12
Passing	22	20
Returns	2	4
Avg. Time of Possession	27:27	33:33

1990 INDIVIDUAL STATISTICS

Scoring	TD Run	TD Pass	TD Ret.	PAT	FG	Saf.	Tot.
Biasucci	0	0	0	32/33	17/24	0	83
Bentley	4	2	0	0/0	0/0	0	36
Hester	0	6	0	0/0	0/0	0	36
Brooks	0	5	0	0/0	0/0	0	30
Morgan	0	5	0	0/0	0/0	0	30
Dickerson	4	0	0	0/0	0/0	0	24
Johnson	0	2	0	0/0	0/0	0	12
Beach	0	1	0	0/0	0/0	0	6
George	1	0	0	0/0	0/0	0	6
Goode	0	0	1	0/0	0/0	0	6
Grant	0	0	1	0/0	0/0	0	6
Verdin	0	1	0	0/0	0/0	0	6
COLTS	9	22	2	32/33	17/24	0	281
OPP.	12	20	4	35/36	32/43	3	353

Passing	Att.	Comp.	Yds.	Pct.	TD	Int.	Tkld.	Rate
George	334	181	2152	54.2	16	13	37/320	73.8
Trudeau	144	84	1078	58.3	6	6	14/104	78.4
Ferguson	8	2	21	25.0	0	2	0/0	0.0
Herrmann	1	1	6	100.0	0	0	0/0	91.7
Stark	1	1	40	100.0	0	0	0/0	118.8
COLTS	488	269	3297	55.1	22	21	51/424	73.3
OPP.	492	301	3605	61.2	20	9	29/203	89.5

Rushing	Att.	Yds.	Avg.	LG	TD
Dickerson	166	677	4.1	43	4
Bentley	137	556	4.1	t26	4
Trudeau	10	28	2.8	9	0
Clark	7	10	1.4	11	0
Hester	4	9	2.3	10	0
George	11	2	0.2	6	1
COLTS	335	1282	3.8	43	9
OPP.	513	2212	4.3	32	12

Receiving	No.	Yds.	Avg.	LG	TD
Bentley	71	664	9.4	73	2
Brooks	62	823	13.3	75	5
Hester	54	924	17.1	t64	6
Morgan	23	364	15.8	t42	5
Dickerson	18	92	5.1	17	0
Verdin	14	178	12.7	45	1
Beach	12	124	10.3	21	1
Mobley, Den.–Ind	8	41	4.1	9	0
Johnson	5	32	6.4	t15	2
Clark	5	23	4.6	11	0
Simmons	4	33	8.3	12	0
Prior	1	40	40.0	40	0
COLTS	269	3297	12.3	75	22
OPP.	301	3605	12.0	66	20

Intercepts	No.	Yds.	Avg.	LG	TD
Prior	3	66	22.0	36	0
Taylor	2	51	25.5	40	0
Grant	1	25	25.0	t25	1
Herrod	1	12	12.0	12	0
Goode	1	10	10.0	10	0
Bickett	1	9	9.0	9	0
COLTS	9	173	19.2	40	1
OPP.	21	221	10.5	t35	1

Punting	No.	Yds.	Avg.	In 20	LG
Stark	71	3084	43.4	24	61
COLTS	72	3084	42.8	24	61
OPP.	58	2435	42.0	13	68

Punt Returns	No.	FC	Yds.	Avg.	LG	TD
Verdin	31	3	396	12.8	36	0
Grant	2	0	6	3.0	6	0
Prior	2	6	0	0.0	0	0
Daniel	1	0	0	0.0	0	0
COLTS	36	9	402	11.2	36	0
OPP.	42	15	334	8.0	32	0

Kickoff Returns	No.	Yds.	Avg.	LG	TD
Simmons	19	348	18.3	34	0
Verdin	18	350	19.4	44	0
Grant	15	280	18.7	29	0
Bentley	11	211	19.2	36	0
Ball	1	0	0.0	0	0
Jarvis	1	0	0.0	0	0
Mobley, Den.–Ind.	1	9	9.0	9	0
COLTS	65	1189	18.3	44	0
OPP.	49	961	19.6	38	0

Sacks	No.
Clancy	7.5
Banks	4.5
Bickett	4.5
Herrod	4.0
Hand	3.0
Faulkner	2.0
Thompson	1.5
Siragusa	1.0
COLTS	29.0
OPP.	51.0

KANSAS CITY

1990 TEAM RECORD

REGULAR SEASON (11–5)

Date	Result	Opponent	Att.
9/9	W 24–21	Minnesota	68,363
9/17	L 23–24	at Denver	75,277
9/23	W 17–3	at Green Bay	58,817
9/30	W 34–0	Cleveland	75,462
10/7	L 19–23	at Indianapolis	54,950
10/14	W 43–24	Detroit	74,312
10/21	L 7–19	at Seattle	60,358
11/4	W 9–7	L.A. Raiders	70,951
11/11	L 16–17	Seattle	71,285
11/18	W 27–10	San Diego	63,717
11/25	W 27–24	at L.A. Raiders	65,710
12/2	W 37–7	at New England	26,280
12/9	W 31–20	Denver	74,347
12/16	L 10–27	Houston	61,756
12/24	W 24–21	at San Diego	45,135
12/29	W 21–10	at Chicago	60,262

PLAYOFFS (0–1)

Date	Result	Opponent	Att.
1/5	L...16–17	at Miami	67,276

1990 TEAM STATISTICS

	CHIEFS	Opp.
Total First Downs	280	268
Rushing	115	85
Passing	142	164
Penalty	23	19
Third Down: Made/Att.	91/222	81/204
Fourth Down: Made/Att.	7/10	3/15
Total Net Yards	5215	4881
Avg. Per Game	325.9	305.1
Total Plays	975	945
Avg. Per Play	5.3	5.2
Net Yards Rushing	1948	1640
Avg. Per Game	121.8	102.5
Total Rushes	504	373
Net Yards Passing	3267	3241
Avg. Per Game	204.2	202.6
Sacked/Yards Lost	22/191	60/421
Gross Yards	3458	3662
Att./Completions	449/260	512/267
Completion Pct.	57.9	52.1
Had Intercepted	5	20
Punts/Avg.	81/38.7	72/37.0
Net Punting Avg.	32.9	32.3
Penalties/Yards Lost	111/886	122/859
Fumbles/Ball Lost	30/14	38/25
Touchdowns	38	30
Rushing	11	12
Passing	23	16
Returns	4	2
Avg. Time of Possession	31:30	28:30

1990 INDIVIDUAL STATISTICS

Scoring	TD Run	TD Pass	TD Ret.	PAT	FG	Saf.	Tot.
Lowery	0	0	0	37/38	34/37	0	139
Okoye	7	0	0	0/0	0/0	0	42
Jones	0	5	0	0/0	0/0	0	30
Paige	0	5	0	0/0	0/0	0	30
Thomas	0	4	0	0/0	0/0	0	24
Word	4	0	0	0/0	0/0	0	24
Birden	0	3	0	0/0	0/0	0	18
Harry	0	2	0	0/0	0/0	0	12
McNair	0	2	0	0/0	0/0	0	12
Hayes	0	1	0	0/0	0/0	0	6
Martin	0	0	1	0/0	0/0	0	6
Petry	0	0	1	0/0	0/0	0	6
Ross	0	0	1	0/0	0/0	0	6
Saleaumua	0	1	0	0/0	0/0	0	6
Whitaker	0	0	1	0/0	0/0	0	6
Maas	0	0	0	0/0	0/0	1	2
CHIEFS	11	23	4	37/38	34/37	1	369
OPP.	12	16	2	29/30	16/20	2	257

Passing	Att.	Comp.	Yds.	Pct.	TD	Int.	Tkld.	Rate
DeBerg	444	258	3444	58.1	23	4	22/191	96.3
Pelluer	5	2	14	40.0	0	1	0/0	8.3
CHIEFS	449	260	3458	57.9	23	5	22/191	94.9
OPP.	512	267	3662	52.1	16	20	60/421	69.5

Rushing	Att.	Yds.	Avg.	LG	TD
Word	204	1015	5.0	t53	4
Okoye	245	805	3.3	32	7
McNair	14	61	4.4	13	0
Jones	10	47	4.7	14	0
Saxon	3	15	5.0	8	0
Pelluer	5	6	1.2	5	0
Goodburn	1	5	5.0	5	0
Jones	1	-1	-1.0	-1	0
DeBerg	21	-5	-0.2	6	0
CHIEFS	504	1948	3.9	t53	11
OPP.	373	1640	4.4	42	12

Receiving	No.	Yds.	Avg.	LG	TD
Paige	65	1021	15.7	t86	5
Thomas	41	545	13.3	t47	4
Harry	41	519	12.7	60	2
McNair	40	507	12.7	65	2
B. Jones	19	137	7.2	19	5
Birden	15	352	23.5	t90	3
Roberts	11	119	10.8	27	0
Hayes	9	83	9.2	21	1
Mandley	7	97	13.9	24	0
Word	4	28	7.0	10	0
Okoye	4	23	5.8	8	0
Whitaker	2	17	8.5	16	1
Jones	1	5	5.0	5	0
Saxon	1	5	5.0	5	0
CHIEFS	260	3458	13.3	t90	23
OPP.	267	3662	13.7	t87	16

Intercepts	No.	Yds.	Avg.	LG	TD
Ross	5	97	19.4	40	0
Cherry	3	40	13.3	21	0
Petry	3	33	11.0	t33	1
Donaldson	3	28	9.3	14	0
Lewis	2	15	7.5	15	0
Burruss	1	14	14.0	14	0
Porter	1	13	13.0	13	0
Pearson	1	10	10.0	10	0
Snow	1	0	0.0	0	0
CHIEFS	20	250	12.5	40	1
OPP.	5	86	17.2	40	0

Punting	No.	Yds.	Avg.	In 20	LG
Barker	64	2479	38.7	16	56
Goodburn	17	653	38.4	6	58
CHIEFS	81	3132	38.7	22	58
OPP.	72	2662	37.0	19	58

Punt Returns	No.	FC	Yds.	Avg.	LG	TD
Worthen	25	3	180	7.2	37	0
Birden	10	3	72	7.2	22	0
Harry	1	0	2	2.0	2	0
Whitaker	1	0	0	0.0	0	0
CHIEFS	37	6	254	6.9	37	0
OPP.	44	19	411	9.3	t95	2

Kickoff Returns	No.	Yds.	Avg.	LG	TD
McNair	14	227	16.2	23	0
Worthen	11	226	20.5	32	0
Jones	9	175	19.4	46	0
Saxon	5	81	16.2	23	0
Mandley	4	51	12.8	23	0
Birden	1	41	14.0	14	0
Roberts	1	0	0.0	0	0
Word	1	10	10.0	10	0
CHIEFS	46	784	17.0	46	0
OPP.	81	1391	17.2	50	0

Sacks	No.
Thomas	20.0
Smith	9.5
Saleaumua	7.0
Maas	5.5
Martin	5.5
Griffin	3.5
Hackett	3.0
Cooper	2.0
Snow	2.0
Bell	1.0
Meisner	1.0
CHIEFS	60.0
OPP.	22.0

L. A. RAIDERS

1990 TEAM RECORD

REGULAR SEASON (12–4)

Date	Result	Opponent	Att.
9/9	W 14–9	Denver	55,684
9/16	W 17–13	at Seattle	64,531
9/23	W 20–3	Pittsburgh	51,063
9/30	W 24–10	Chicago	81,237
10/7	L 24–38	at Buffalo	80,332
10/14	W 24–17	Seattle	51,101
10/21	W 24–9	at San Diego	62,505
11/4	L 7–9	at Kansas City	77,937
11/11	L 16–29	Green Bay	52,638
11/19	W 13–10	at Miami	72,393
11/25	L 24–27	Kansas City	65,303
12/2	W 23–20	at Denver	76,109
12/10	W 38–31	at Detroit	80,066
12/16	W 24–7	Cincinnati	55,110
12/22	W 28–24	at Minnesota	63,314
12/30	W 17–13	San Diego	64,445

PLAYOFFS (1–1)

1/13	W 20–10	Cincinnati	92,045
1/20	L 3–51	at Buffalo	80,324

1990 TEAM STATISTICS

	RAIDERS	Opp.
Total First Downs	258	266
Rushing	110	95
Passing	133	152
Penalty	15	19
Third Down: Made/Att.	86/180	75/201
Fourth Down: Made/Att.	2/7	9/19
Total Net Yards	4716	4413
Avg. Per Game	294.8	275.8
Total Plays	861	924
Avg. Per Play	5.5	4.8
Net Yards Rushing	2028	1716
Avg. Per Game	126.8	107.3
Total Rushes	496	439
Net Yards Passing	2688	2697
Avg. Per Game	168.0	168.6
Sacked/Yards Lost	29/197	48/335
Gross Yards	2885	3032
Att./Completions	336/183	437/246
Completion Pct.	54.5	56.3
Had Intercepted	10	13
Punts/Avg.	62/37.3	64/38.2
Net Punting Avg.	33.6	31.8
Penalties/Yards Lost	97/682	86/710
Fumbles/Ball Lost	24/14	21/9
Touchdowns	42	26
Rushing	20	4
Passing	19	20
Returns	3	2
Avg. Time of Possession	29:28	30:32

1990 INDIVIDUAL STATISTICS

Scoring	TD Run	TD Pass	TD Ret.	PAT	FG	Saf.	Tot.
Jaeger	0	0	0	40/42	15/20	0	85
Allen	12	1	0	0/0	0/0	0	78
Fernandez	0	5	0	0/0	0/0	0	30
Jackson	5	0	0	0/0	0/0	0	30
Smith	2	3	0	0/0	0/0	0	30
Brown	0	3	0	0/0	0/0	0	18
Gault	0	3	0	0/0	0/0	0	18
Horton	0	3	0	0/0	0/0	0	18
Bell	1	0	0	0/0	0/0	0	6
Graddy	0	1	0	0/0	0/0	0	6
McDaniel	0	0	1	0/0	0/0	0	6
Robinson	0	0	1	0/0	0/0	0	6
Townsend	0	0	1	0/0	0/0	0	6
RAIDERS	20	19	3	40/42	15/20	0	337
OPP.	4	20	2	25/26	29/33	0	268

Passing	Att.	Comp.	Yds.	Pct.	TD	Int.	Tkld.	Rate
Schroeder	334	182	2849	54.5	19	9	29/197	90.8
Evans	1	1	36	100.0	0	0	0/0	118.8
Allen	1	0	0	0.0	0	1	0/0	0.0
RAIDERS	336	183	2885	54..5	19	10	29/197	89.7
OPP.	437	246	3032	56.3	20	13	48/335	80.8

Rushing	Att.	Yds.	Avg.	LG	TD
Jackson	125	698	5.6	88	5
Allen	179	682	3.8	28	12
Smith	81	327	4.0	17	2
Bell	47	164	3.5	21	1
Schroeder	37	81	2.2	17	0
Mueller	13	43	3.3	12	0
McCallum	10	25	2.5	6	0
Fernandez	3	10	3.3	9	0
Evans	1	–2	–2.0	–2	0
RAIDERS	496	2028	4.1	88	20
OPP.	439	1716	3.9	41	4

Receiving	No.	Yds.	Avg.	LG	TD
Fernandez	52	839	16.1	66	5
Gault	50	985	19.7	68	3
Horton	33	404	12.2	36	3
Brown	18	265	14.7	51	3
Allen	15	189	12.6	30	1
Jackson	6	68	11.3	18	0
Smith	4	30	7.5	17	3
Dyal	3	51	17.0	29	0
Graddy	1	47	47.0	47	1
Bell	1	7	7.0	7	0
RAIDERS	183	2885	15.8	68	19
OPP.	246	3032	12.3	80	20

Intercepts.	No.	Yds.	Avg.	LG	TD
Anderson	3	49	16.3	31	0
McDaniel	3	20	6.7	15	0
Harden	3	19	6.3	15	0
Ellison	1	7	7.0	7	0
Robinson	1	5	5.0	5	1
Washington	1	2	2.0	2	0
Townsend	1	0	0.0	0	0
RAIDERS	13	102	7.8	31	0
OPP.	10	100	10.0	32	0

Punting	No.	Yds.	Avg.	In 20	LG
Gossett	60	2315	38.6	19	57
RAIDERS	62	2315	37.3	19	57
OPP.	64	2447	38.2	10	59

Punt Returns	No.	FC	Yds.	Avg.	LG	TD
Brown	34	8	295	8.7	39	0
RAIDERS	34	8	295	8.7	39	0
OPP.	24	6	153	6.4	33	0

Kickoff Returns	No.	Yds.	Avg.	LG	TD
Holland	32	655	20.5	87	0
Brown	30	575	19.2	34	0
McCallum	1	7	7.0	7	0
Turk	1	0	0.0	0	0
RAIDERS	64	1237	19.3	87	0
OPP.	49	1026	20.9	90	0

Sacks	No.
Townsend	12.5
Davis	10.0
Wallace	9.0
Long	6.0
Golic	4.0
McDaniel	2.0
Robinson	2.0
Pickel	1.5
Wise	1.0
RAIDERS	48
OPP.	29

L. A. RAMS

1990 TEAM RECORD

REGULAR SEASON (5–11)

Date	Result	Opponent	Att.
9/9	L 24–36	at Green Bay	57,685
9/16	W 35–14	at Tampa Bay	59,705
9/23	L 21–27	Philadelphia	63,644
10/7	L 31–34	Cincinnati	62,619
10/14	L 9–38	at Chicago	59,383
10/21	W 44–24	Atlanta	54,761
10/29	L 10–41	at Pittsburgh	56,466
11/4	W 17–13	Houston	52,628
11/11	L 7–31	N.Y. Giants	64,632
11/18	L 21–24	Dallas	58,589
11/25	W 28–17	at San Francisco	62,633
12/2	W 38–23	at Cleveland	61,981
12/9	L 20–24	New Orleans	56,864
12/17	L 10–26	San Francisco	65,619
12/23	L 13–20	at Atlanta	30,021
12/31	L 17–20	at New Orleans	68,647

1990 TEAM STATISTICS

	RAMS	Opp.
Total First Downs	311	287
Rushing	89	93
Passing	191	176
Penalty	31	18
Third Down: Made/Att.	78/204	86/201
Fourth Down: Made/Att.	6/18	3/10
Total Net Yards	5430	5411
Avg. Per Game	339.4	338.2
Total Plays	1013	949
Avg. Per Play	5.4	5.7
Net Yards Rushing	1612	1649
Avg. Per Game	100.8	103.1
Total Rushes	422	418
Net Yards Passing	3818	3762
Avg. Per Game	238.6	235.1
Sacked/Yards Lost	30/198	30/180
Gross Yards	4016	3942
Att./Completions	561/310	501/296
Completion Pct.	55.3	59.1
Had Intercepted	17	12
Punts/Avg.	69/38.6	66/41.4
Net Punting Avg.	31.9	34.7
Penalties/Yards	87/632	109/968
Fumbles/Ball Lost	25/14	32/19
Touchdowns	43	49
Rushing	17	17
Passing	24	30
Returns	2	2
Avg. Time of Possession	29:59	30:01

1990 INDIVIDUAL STATISTICS

Scoring	TD Run	TD Pass	TD RT	PAT	FG	Saf	TP
Gary	14	1	0	0/0	0/0	0	90
Lansford	0	0	0	42/43	15/24	0	87
McGee	1	4	0	0/0	0/0	0	30
Ellard	0	4	0	0/0	0/0	0	24
Anderson	0	4	0	0/0	0/0	0	24
Delpino	0	4	0	0/0	0/0	0	24
Johnson	0	3	0	0/0	0/0	0	18
Holohan	0	2	0	0/0	0/0	0	12
Green	0	1	1	0/0	0/0	0	12
Everett	1	0	0	0/0	0/0	0	6
Warner	1	0	0	0/0	0/0	0	6
Faison	0	1	0	0/0	0/0	0	6
Humphery	0	0	1	0/0	0/0	0	6
RAMS	17	24	2	42/43	15/24	0	345
OPP.	17	30	2	46/49	24/31	0	412

Passing	Att.	Comp.	Yds.	Pct.	TD	Int.	Tkld.	Rate
Everett	554	307	3989	55.4	23	17	30/198	79.3
Long	5	1	4	20.0	0	0	0/0	39.6
McGee	2	2	23	100.0	1	0	0/0	154.2
RAMS	561	310	4016	55.3	24	17	30/198	79.6
OPP.	501	296	3942	59.1	30	12	30/180	94.1

Rushing	Att.	Yds.	Avg.	LG	TD
Gary	204	808	4.0	48	14
Green	68	261	3.8	31	0
McGee	44	234	5.3	19	1
Warner	49	139	2.8	9	1
Dupree	19	72	3.8	13	0
Delpino	13	52	4.0	13	0
Everett	20	31	1.6	15	1
Ellard	2	21	10.5	13	0
Anderson	1	13	13.0	13	0
English	2	–19	–9.5	–8	0
RAMS	422	1612	3.8	48	17
OPP.	418	1649	3.9	t74	17

Receiving	No.	Yds.	Avg.	LG	TD
Ellard	76	1294	17.0	t50	4
Anderson	51	1097	21.5	t55	4
Holohan	49	475	9.7	28	2
McGee	47	388	8.3	25	4
Gary	30	150	5.0	t22	1
Cox	17	266	15.6	32	0
Delpino	15	172	11.5	t42	4
Johnson	12	66	5.5	11	3
Carter	8	58	7.3	16	0
Faison	3	27	9.0	12	1
Green	2	23	11.5	t16	1
RAMS	310	4016	13.0	t55	24
OPP.	296	3942	13.3	t71	30

Intercepts.	No.	Yds.	Avg.	LG	TD
Humphery	4	52	13.0	t44	1
Newsome	4	47	11.8	22	0
Newman	2	0	0.0	0	0
Terrell	1	6	6.0	6	0
Henley	1	0	0.0	0	0
RAMS	12	105	8.8	t44	1
OPP.	17	204	12.0	t50	2

Punting	No.	Yds.	Avg.	In 20	LG
English	68	2663	39.2	8	58
RAMS	69	2663	38.6	8	58
OPP.	66	2733	41.4	20	57

Punt Returns	No.	FC	Yds.	Avg.	LG	TD
Henley	19	4	195	10.3	26	0
Sutton	14	3	136	9.7	22	0
Ellard	2	0	15	7.5	8	0
RAMS	35	7	346	9.9	26	0
OPP.	46	11	420	9.1	33	0

Kickoff Returns	No.	Yds.	Avg.	LG	TD
Green	25	560	22.4	t99	1
Delpino	20	389	19.5	38	0
Berry	17	315	18.5	29	0
McDonald	1	15	15.0	15	0
RAMS	63	1279	20.3	t99	1
OPP.	68	1406	20.7	50	0

Sacks	No.
Greene	13.0
Piel	5.0
Hawkins	3.0
Reed	3.0
Bethune	2.0
Faryniarz	2.0
Smith	1.0
Wilcher	1.0
Wright	1.0
RAMS	30
OPP.	30

MIAMI

1990 TEAM RECORD

REGULAR SEASON (12-4)

Date	Result	Opponent	Att.
9/9	W 27-24	at New England	45,305
9/16	W 30-7	Buffalo	68,142
9/23	L 3-20	at N.Y. Giants	76,483
9/30	W 28-6	at Pittsburgh	54,691
10/7	W 20-16	N.Y. Jets	69,678
10/18	W 17-10	New England	62,630
10/28	W 27-7	at Indianapolis	59,213
11/4	W 23-3	Phoenix	54,924
11/11	W 17-3	at N.Y. Jets	68,362
11/19	L 10-13	L.A. Raiders	70,553
11/25	W 30-13	at Cleveland	70,225
12/2	L 20-42	at Washington	53,599
12/9	W 23-20	Philadelphia	67,034
12/16	W 24-17	Seattle	57,851
12/23	L 14-24	at Buffalo	80,235
12/30	W 23-17	Indianapolis	59,547
	PLAYOFFS (1-1)		
1/5	W 17-16	Kansas City	67,276
1/12	L 34-44	at Buffalo	77,087

1990 TEAM STATISTICS

	DOLPHINS	Opp.
Total First Downs	303	268
Rushing	90	110
Passing	190	145
Penalty	23	13
Third Down: Made/Att.	88/206	79/207
Fourth Down: Made/Att.	10/13	7/18
Total Net Yards	5047	4547
Avg. Per Game	315.4	284.2
Total Plays	975	968
Avg. Per Play	5.2	4.7
Net Yards Rushing	1535	1831
Avg. Per Game	95.9	114.4
Total Rushes	420	461
Net Yards Passing	3512	2716
Avg. Per Game	219.5	169.8
Sacked/Yards Lost	16/99	45/348
Gross Yards	3611	3064
Att./Completions	539/310	462/257
Completion Pct.	57.5	55.6
Had Intercepted	12	19
Punts/Avg.	72/42.0	75/40.0
Net Punting Avg.	35.6	34.8
Penalties/Yards Lost	64/486	95/759
Fumbles/Ball Lost	33/15	23/8
Touchdowns	39	26
Rushing	13	11
Passing	21	14
Returns	5	1
Avg. Time of Possession	30:10	29:50

1990 INDIVIDUAL STATISTICS

Scoring	TD Run	TD Pass	TD Ret.	PAT	FG	Saf.	Tot.
Stoyanovich	0	0	0	37/37	21/25	0	100
Smith	8	1	0	0/0	0/0	0	54
Paige	2	4	0	0/0	0/0	0	36
Duper	0	5	0	0/0	0/0	0	30
Clayton	0	3	0	0/0	0/0	0	18
Pruitt	0	3	0	0/0	0/0	0	18
Logan	2	0	0	0/0	0/0	0	12
Martin	0	2	0	0/0	0/0	0	12
Edmunds	0	1	0	0/0	0/0	0	6
Glenn	0	0	1	0/0	0/0	0	6
Higgs	0	0	1	0/0	0/0	0	6
Jensen	0	1	0	0/0	0/0	0	6
Odom	0	0	1	0/0	0/0	0	6
Schwedes	0	1	0	0/0	0/0	0	6
Sochia	0	0	1	0/0	0/0	0	6
Stradford	1	0	0	0/0	0/0	0	6
Williams	0	0	1	0/0	0/0	0	6
DOLPHINS	13	21	5	37/39	21/25	1	336
OPP.	11	14	1	26/26	20/29	0	242

Passing	Att.	Comp.	Yds.	Pct.	TD	Int.	Tkld.	Rate
Marino	531	306	3563	57.6	21	11	15/90	82.6
Secules	7	3	17	42.9	0	1	1/9	10.7
Jensen	1	1	31	100.0	0	0	0/0	118.8
DOLPHINS	539	310	3611	57.5	21	12	16/99	81.6
OPP.	462	257	3064	55.6	14	19	45/348	69.0

Rushing	Att.	Yds.	Avg.	LG	TD
Smith	226	831	3.7	33	8
Logan	79	317	4.0	17	2
Stradford	37	138	3.7	15	1
Paige	32	95	3.0	11	2
Higgs	10	67	6.7	27	0
Secules	8	34	4.3	17	0
Marino	16	29	1.8	15	0
Limbrick	5	14	2.8	5	0
Martin	1	8	8.0	8	0
Jensen	4	6	1.5	2	0
Banks	1	3	3.0	3	0
Edmunds	1	-7	-7.0	-7	0
DOLPHINS	420	1535	3.7	33	13
OPP.	461	1831	4.0	39	11

Receiving	No.	Yds.	Avg.	LG	TD
Duper	52	810	15.6	t60	5
Jensen	44	365	8.3	18	1
Paige	35	247	7.1	t17	4
Clayton	32	406	12.7	43	3
Edmunds	31	446	14.4	35	1
Stradford	30	257	8.6	23	0
Martin	29	388	13.4	45	2
Pruitt	13	235	18.1	t35	3
Banks	13	131	10.1	23	0
Smith	11	134	12.2	t58	1
Logan	7	54	7.7	12	0
Schwedes	6	66	11.0	19	1
Limbrick	4	23	5.8	9	0
Brown	3	49	16.3	24	0
DOLPHINS	310	3611	11.6	t69	21
OPP.	257	3064	11.9	t64	14

Intercepts.	No.	Yds.	Avg.	LG	TD
Oliver	5	87	17.4	35	0
Williams	5	82	16.4	t42	1
McKyer	4	40	10.0	21	0
Glenn	2	31	15.5	t31	1
Offerdahl	1	28	28.0	28	0
Hobley	1	15	15.0	15	0
Kumerow	1	5	5.0	5	0
DOLPHINS	19	288	15.2	t42	2
OPP.	12	184	15.3	73	0

Punting	No.	Yds.	Avg.	In 20	LG
Roby	72	3022	42.0	20	62
DOLPHINS	72	3022	42.0	20	62
OPP.	75	3001	50.0	19	63

Punt Returns	No.	FC	Yds.	Avg.	LG	TD
Martin	26	9	140	5.4	35	0
Schwedes	9	2	89	9.9	23	0
Stradford	3	2	4	1.3	4	0
Williams	1	5	0	0.0	0	0
DOLPHINS	39	18	233	6.0	35	0
OPP.	40	15	397	9.9	36	0

Kickoff Returns	No.	Yds.	Avg.	LG	TD
Logan	20	367	18.4	35	0
Higgs	10	210	21.0	30	0
Adams	2	16	8.0	10	0
Stradford	3	56	18.7	21	0
Collins	2	30	15.0	30	0
Schwedes	2	52	26.0	30	0
Graf	1	6	6.0	6	0
Kinchen	1	16	16.0	16	0
Paige	1	18	18.0	18	0
Sims	1	9	9.0	9	0
DOLPHINS	43	780	18.1	35	0
OPP.	53	1092	20.6	38	0

Sacks	No.
Cross	11.5
Junior	6.0
Griggs	5.5
Wilson	4.0
Hobley	3.0
Oglesby	2.5
Green	2.0
Williams	2.0
Lee	1.5
Brown	1.0
Glenn	1.0
Odom	1.0
Offerdahl	1.0
Oliver	1.0
Sochia	1.0
Turner	1.0
DOLPHINS	45.0
OPP.	16.0

MINNESOTA

1990 TEAM RECORD

REGULAR SEASON (6-10)

Date	Result	Opponent	Att.
9/9	L 21-24	at Kansas City	68,363
9/16	W 32-3	New Orleans	56,272
9/23	L 16-19	at Chicago	65,420
9/30	L 20-23	Tampa Bay	54,462
10/7	L 27-34	Detroit	57,586
10/15	L 24-32	at Philadelphia	66,296
10/28	L 10-24	at Green Bay	55,125
11/4	W 27-22	Denver	57,331
11/11	W 17-7	at Detroit	68,264
11/18	W 24-21	at Seattle	59,735
11/25	W 41-13	Chicago	58,866
12/2	W 23-7	Green Bay	62,058
12/9	L 15-23	at N.Y. Giants	76,121
12/16	L 13-26	at Tampa Bay	47,272
12/22	L 24-28	L.A. Raiders	53,899
12/30	L 17-20	San Francisco	51,590

1990 TEAM STATISTICS

	VIKINGS	Opp.
Total First Downs	288	257
Rushing	106	107
Passing	164	136
Penalty	18	14
Third Down: Made/Att.	81/215	71/207
Fourth Down: Made/Att.	6/15	5/11
Total Net Yards	5034	4717
Avg. Per Game	314.6	294.8
Total Plays	1001	972
Avg. Per Play	5.0	4.9
Net Yards Rushing	1867	2074
Avg. Per Game	116.7	129.6
Total Rushes	455	503
Net Yards Passing	3167	2643
Avg. Per Game	197.9	165.2
Sacked/Yards Lost	49/278	47/277
Gross Yards	3445	2920
Att./Completions	497/265	422/218
Completion Pct.	53.5	51.7
Had Intercepted	24	22
Punts/Avg.	79/41.8	77/39.4
Net Punting Avg.	33.2	35.4
Penalties/Yards Lost	83/565	100/767
Fumbles/Ball Lost	30/13	25/11
Touchdowns	39	34
Rushing	10	12
Passing	25	20
Returns	4	2
Avg. Time of Possession	29:34	30:26

1990 INDIVIDUAL STATISTICS

Scoring	TD Run	TD Pass	TD Ret.	PAT	FG	Saf.	Tot.
Reveiz	0	0	0	19/19	11/12	0	52
Igwebuike	0	0	0	19/19	14/16	0	61
Walker	5	4	0	0/0	0/0	0	54
Carter	0	8	0	0/0	0/0	0	48
Jones	0	7	0	0/0	0/0	0	42
Carter	0	3	0	0/0	0/0	0	18
Jordan	0	3	0	0/0	0/0	0	18
Anderson	20	0	0	0/0	0/0	0	12
Fenney	2	0	0	0/0	0/0	0	12
Noga	0	0	2	0/0	0/0	0	12
Browner	0	0	1	0/0	0/0	0	6
Gannon	1	0	0	0/0	0/0	0	6
Merriweather	0	0	1	0/0	0/0	0	6
Doleman	0	0	0	0/0	0/0	1	2
Dusbabek	0	0	0	0/0	0/0	1	2
VIKINGS	10	25	4	38/39	25/28	2	351
OPP.	12	20	2	32/34	30/36	0	326

Passing	Att.	Comp.	Yds.	Pct.	TD	Int.	Tkld.	Rate
Gannon	349	182	2278	52.1	16	16	34/188	68.9
Wilson	146	82	1155	56.2	9	8	15/90	79.6
Walker	2	1	12	50.0	0	0	0/0	68.8
VIKINGS	497	265	3445	53.3	25	24	49/278	72.0
OPP.	472	218	2920	51.7	20	22	47/277	68.0

Rushing	Att.	Yds.	Avg.	LG	TD
Walker	184	770	4.2	t58	5
Fenney	87	376	4.3	27	2
Gannon	52	268	5.2	27	1
Anderson	59	207	3.5	14	2
Wilson	12	79	6.6	24	0
Rice	22	74	3.4	13	0
Clark	16	49	3.1	11	0
Smith	9	19	2.1	7	0
Carter	3	16	5.3	11	0
Bozier	6	12	2.0	4	0
Carter	2	6	3.0	8	0
Newsper	2	-2	-1.0	0	0
Jones	1	-7	-7.0	-7	0
VIKINGS	455	1867	4.1	t58	10
OPP.	503	2074	4.1	t48	12

Receiving	No.	Yds.	Avg.	LG	TD
Carter	70	1008	14.4	t56	8
Jones	51	810	15.9	t75	7
Jordan	45	636	14.1	38	3
Walker	35	315	9.0	32	4
Carter	27	413	15.3	t78	3
Fenney	17	112	6.6	17	0
Anderson	13	80	6.2	17	0
Rice	4	46	11.5	24	0
Bozier	1	12	12.0	12	0
Lewis	1	9	9.0	9	0
Clark	1	4	4.0	4	0
VIKINGS	265	3445	13.0	t78	25
OPP.	218	2920	13.4	61	20

Intercepts.	No.	Yds.	Avg.	LG	TD
Browner	7	103	14.7	31	1
Merriweather	3	108	36.0	73	0
McMillian	3	20	6.7	20	0
Lee	2	29	14.5	25	0
Rutland	2	21	10.5	16	0
Brim	2	11	5.5	11	0
Doleman	1	30	30.0	30	0
Moss	1	26	26.0	t26	1
Fullington	1	10	10.0	10	0
VIKINGS	22	358	16.3	73	2
OPP.	24	260	10.8	37	1

Punting	No.	Yds.	Avg.	In 20	LG
Newsome	78	3299	42.3	19	61
VIKINGS	79	3299	41.8	19	61
OPP.	77	3030	39.4	24	67

Punt Returns	No.	FC	Yds.	Avg.	LG	TD
Lewis	25	15	180	7.2	30	0
Hillary	8	4	45	5.6	12	0
Carter	0	5	0	0.0	0	0
VIKINGS	33	24	225	6.8	30	0
OPP.	44	12	513	11.7	39	0

Kickoff Returns	No.	Yds.	Avg.	LG	TD
Walker	44	966	22.0	64	0
Rice	12	176	14.7	24	0
Anderson	3	44	14.7	24	0
Lewis	3	39	13.0	15	0
Hillary	1	6	6.0	6	0
Jordan	1	-3	-3.0	-3	0
Schreiber	1	5	5.0	5	0
Smith	1	16	16.0	16	0
VIKINGS	66	1249	18.9	64	0
OPP.	62	1350	21.8	63	0

Sacks	No.
Doleman	11.0
Thomas	8.5
Clarke	7.0
Noga	6.0
Strauthers	4.0
Browner	3.0
Merriweather	2.5
Millard	2.0
Fulllington	1.0
Randle	1.0
VIKINGS	47.0
OPP.	49.0

N E W   E N G L A N D

1990 TEAM RECORD

REGULAR SEASON (1–15)

9/9	L..24–27	Miami	45,305
9/16	W 16–14	at Indianapolis	49,256
9/23	L 7–41	at Cincinnati	56,470
9/30	L 13–37	N.Y. Jets	36,724
10/7	L 20–33	Seattle	39,735
10/18	L 10–17	at Miami	62,630
10/28	L 10–27	Buffalo	51,959
11/4	L 20–48	at Philadelphia	65,514
11/11	L 10–13	Indianapolis	28,924
11/18	L 0–14	at Buffalo	74,720
11/25	L 14–34	at Phoenix	30,110
12/2	L 7–37	Kansas City	26,280
12/9	L 3–24	at Pittsburgh	48,354
12/15	L 10–25	Washington	22,286
12/23	L 7–42	at N.Y. Jets	30,250
12/30	L 10–13	N.Y. Giants	60,410

1990 TEAM STATISTICS

	PATRIOTS	Opp.
Total First Downs	239	307
Rushing	65	151
Passing	156	139
Penalty	18	17
Third Down: Made/Att.	86/227	84/192
Fourth Down: Made/Att.	2/12	7/13
Total Net Yards	4163	5697
Avg. Per Game	260.2	356.1
Total Plays	955	972
Avg. Per Play	4.4	5.9
Net Yards Rushing	1398	2676
Avg. Per Game	87.4	167.3
Total Rushes	383	565
Net Yards Passing	2765	3021
Avg. Per Game	172.8	188.8
Sacked/Yards Lost	58/443	33/224
Gross Yards	3208	3245
Att./Completions	514/274	374/218
Completion Pct.	53.3	58.3
Had Intercepted	20	14
Punts/Avg.	92/40.8	56/40.8
Net Punting Avg.	33.6	36.6
Penalties/Yards Lost	99/742	73/488
Fumbles/Ball Lost	33/16	25/18
Touchdowns	19	52
Rushing	4	29
Passing	14	21
Returns	1	2
Avg. Time of Possession	28:21	31:39

1990 INDIVIDUAL STATISTICS

Scoring	TD Run	TD Pass	TD Ret.	PAT	FG	Saf.	Tot.
Staurovsky	0	0	0	19/19	16/22	0	67
Cook	0	5	0	0/0	0/0	0	30
Fryar	0	4	0	0/0	0/0	0	24
Stephens	2	1	0	0/0	0/0	0	18
Dykes	0	2	0	0/0	0/0	0	12
Adams	0	1	0	0/0	0/0	0	6
Allen	1	0	0	0/0	0/0	0	6
Martin	0	1	0	0/0	0/0	0	6
Perryman	1	0	0	0/0	0/0	0	6
Williams	0	0	1	0/0	0/0	0	6
PATRIOTS	4	14	1	19/19	16/22	0	181
OPP.	29	21	2	51/52	27/31	1	446

Passing	Att.	Comp.	Yds.	Pct.	TD	Int.	Tkld.	Rate
Wilson	265	139	1625	52.5	6	11	29/228	61.6
Hodson	156	85	968	54.5	4	5	20/147	68.5
Grogan	92	50	615	54.3	4	3	9/68	76.1
Stephens	1	0	0	0.0	0	1	0/0	0.0
PATRIOTS	514	274	3208	53.3	14	20	58/443	65.4
OPP.	374	218	3245	58.3	21	14	33/224	89.9

Rushing	Att.	Yds.	Avg.	LG	TD
Stephens	212	808	3.8	26	2
Allen	63	237	3.8	29	1
Adams	28	111	4.0	13	0
Perryman	32	97	3.0	13	1
Hodson	12	79	6.6	23	0
Tatupu	16	56	3.5	15	0
Overton	5	8	1.6	6	0
Wilson	5	7	1.4	6	0
Morris	2	4	2.0	3	0
Gannon	1	0	0.0	0	0
Hansen	1	0	0.0	0	0
Fryar	2	–4	–2.0	–1	0
Grogan	4	–5	–1.3	0	0
PATRIOTS	383	1398	3.7	29	4
OPP.	565	2676	4.7	t80	29

Receiving	No.	Yds.	Avg.	LG	TD
Fryar	54	856	15.9	56	4
Cook	51	455	8.9	t35	5
Dykes	34	549	16.1	t35	2
Stephens	28	196	7.0	43	1
McMurtry	22	240	10.9	26	0
Jones	21	301	14.3	26	0
Adams	16	146	9.1	28	1
Perryman	15	88	5.9	15	0
Sievers	8	77	9.6	25	0
Mowatt	6	67	11.2	16	0
Allen	6	48	8.0	19	0
Timpson	5	91	18.2	42	0
Martin	4	65	16.3	t19	1

	No.	Yds.	Avg.	LG	TD
Overton	2	19	16.3	t19	1
Tatupu	2	10	5.0	6	0
PATRIOTS	274	3208	11.7	56	14
OPP.	218	3245	14.9	t86	21

Intercepts.	No.	Yds.	Avg.	LG	TD
Lippett	4	94	23.5	73	0
Hurst	4	61	15.3	36	0
Marion	4	17	4.3	16	0
Rembert	2	22	11.0	11	0
PATRIOTS	14	194	13.9	73	0
OPP.	20	143	7.2	42	0

Punting	No.	Yds.	Avg.	in 20	LG
Hansen	90	3752	41.7	18	69
PATRIOTS	92	3752	40.8	18	69
OPP.	56	2282	40.8	17	70

Punt Returns	No.	FC	Yds.	Avg.	LG	TD
Fryar	28	10	133	4.8	17	0
Martin	1	0	1	1.0	1	0
PATRIOTS	29	10	134	4.6	17	0
OPP.	50	13	503	10.1	34	0

Kickoff Returns	No.	Yds.	Avg.	LG	TD
Martin	25	515	20.6	38	0
Allen	11	168	15.3	34	0
Morris	11	202	18.4	22	0
Robinson	11	211	19.2	27	0
Overton	10	188	18.8	23	0
Timpson	3	62	20.7	26	0
Coleman	2	18	9.0	12	0
Jones	2	24	12.0	13	0
Adams	1	7	7.0	7	0
McSwain	1	0	0.0	0	0
PATRIOTS	77	1395	18.1	38	0
OPP.	38	665	17.5	38	0

Sacks	No.
Williams	6.0
Tippett	3.5
Hobby	3.0
Singleton	3.0
Agnew	2.5
Brown	2.5
Goad	2.5
McSwain	2.5
Veris	2.0
Williams	2.0
Smith	1.5
Rembert	1.0
Reynolds	1.0
Gannon	0.5
PATRIOTS	33.0
OPP.	58.0

N E W   O R L E A N S

1990 TEAM RECORD

REGULAR SEASON (8–8)

Date	Result	Opponent	Att.
9/10	L 12–13	San Francisco	68,629
9/16	L 3–32	at Minnesota	57,272
9/23	W 28–7	Phoenix	61,110
10/7	L 27–28	at Atlanta	57,401
10/14	W 25–20	Cleveland	68,608
10/21	L 10–23	at Houston	57,908
10/28	L 10–27	Detroit	64,368
11/4	W 24–20	at Cincinnati	60,067
11/11	W 35–7	Tampa Bay	67,865
11/18	L 17–31	at Washington	52,573
11/25	W 10–7	Atlanta	68,629
12/2	L 13–17	at Dallas	60,087
12/9	W 24–20	at L.A. Rams	56,864
12/16	L 6–9	Pittsburgh	68,582
12/23	W 13–10	at San Francisco	60,112
12/31	W 20–17	L.A. Rams	68,647

PLAYOFFS (0–1)

1/6	L 6–16	at Chicago	60,767

1990 TEAM STATISTICS

	SAINTS	Opp.
Total First Downs	254	279
Rushing	107	91
Passing	134	167
Penalty	13	21
Third Down: Made/Att.	84/209	85/217
Fourth Down: Made/Att.	5/9	9/17
Total Net Yards	4476	4878
Avg. Per Game	279.8	304.9
Total Plays	931	986
Avg. Per Play	4.8	4.9
Net Yards Rushing	1850	1559
Avg. Per Game	115.6	97.4
Total Rushes	464	410
Net Yards Passing	2626	3319
Avg. Per Game	164.1	207.4
Sacked/Yards Lost	20/131	42/265
Gross Yards	2757	3584
Att./Completions	447/226	534/316
Completion Pct.	50.6	59.2
Had Intercepted	23	8
Punts/Avg.	71/42.1	74/40.9
Net Punting Avg.	36.2	34.9
Penalties/Yards Lost	108/829	87/655
Fumbles/Ball Lost	29/16	35/19
Touchdowns	30	30
Rushing	14	8
Passing	15	21
Returns	1	1
Avg. Time of Possession	29:59	30:01

1990 INDIVIDUAL STATISTICS

Scoring	TD Run	TD Pass	TD Ret.	PAT	FG	Saf.	Tot.
Andersen	0	0	0	29/29	21/27	0	92
Mayes	7	0	0	0/0	0/0	0	42
Martin	0	5	0	0/0	0/0	0	30
Heyward	4	0	0	0/0	0/0	0	24
Turner	0	4	0	0/0	0/0	0	24
Brenner	0	2	0	0/0	0/0	0	12
Fenerty	2	0	0	0/0	0/0	0	12
Perriman	0	2	0	0/0	0/0	0	12
Fourcade	1	0	0	0/0	0/0	0	6
Hilliard	0	1	0	0/0	0/0	0	6
Maxie	0	0	1	0/0	0/0	0	6
Scales	0	1	0	0/0	0/0	0	6
SAINTS	14	15	1	29/30	21/27	1	274
OPP.	8	21	1	30/30	21/35	1	275

Passing	Att.	Comp.	Yds.	Pct.	TD	Int.	Tkld.	Rate
Walsh	327	175	1970	53.5	12	13	10/76	67.5
Fourcade	116	50	785	43.1	3	8	8/44	46.1
Kramer	3	1	2	33.3	0	1	2/11	2.8
Heyward	1	0	0	0.0	0	1	0/0	0.0
SAINTS	447	226	2757	50.6	15	23	20/131	59.7
OPP.	534	316	3584	59.2	21	8	42/265	86.2

Rushing	Att.	Yds.	Avg.	LG	TD
Heyward	129	599	4.6	t47	4
Mayes	138	510	3.7	18	7
Fenerty	73	355	4.9	t60	2
Hilliard	90	284	3.2	17	0
Fourcade	15	77	5.1	12	1
Walsh	19	25	1.3	18	0
SAINTS	464	1850	4.0	t60	14
OPP.	410	1559	3.8	35	8

Receiving	No.	Yds.	Avg.	LG	TD
Martin	63	912	14.5	58	5
Perriman	36	382	10.6	29	2
Turner	21	396	18.9	t68	4
Fenerty	18	209	11.6	28	0
Heyward	18	121	6.7	12	0
Brenner	17	213	12.5	t31	2
Hilliard	14	125	8.9	20	1
Mayes	12	121	10.1	66	0
Tice	11	113	10.3	19	0
Scales	8	64	8.0	20	1
Alphin	4	57	14.3	17	0
Hill	3	35	11.7	13	0
Hilgenberg	1	9	9.0	9	0
SAINTS	226	2757	12.2	t68	15
OPP.	316	3584	11.3	t51	21

Intercepts.	No.	Yds.	Avg.	LG	TD
Maxie	2	88	44.0	t50	1
Cook	2	55	27.5	50	0
Atkins	2	15	7.5	15	0
Thompson	2	0	0.0	0	0
SAINTS	8	158	19.8	t50	1
OPP.	23	283	12.3	73	0

Punting	No.	Yds.	Avg.	In 20	LG
Barnhardt	70	2990	42.7	20	65
SAINTS	71	2990	42.1	20	65
OPP.	74	3024	40.9	18	57

Punt Returns	No.	FC	Yds.	Avg.	LG	TD
Buck	37	8	305	8.2	33	0
Morse	8	1	95	11.9	19	0
SAINTS	45	9	400	8.9	33	0
OPP.	43	12	302	7.0	24	0

Kickoff Returns	No.	Yds.	Avg.	LG	TD
Fenerty	28	572	20.4	58	0
Atkins	19	471	24.8	50	0
Morse	4	56	14.0	18	0
V. Buck	3	38	12.7	17	0
Mayes	2	39	19.5	21	0
Heyward	1	12	12.0	12	0
Mack	1	17	17.0	17	0
SAINTS	58	1205	20.8	58	0
OPP.	36	583	16.2	56	0

Sacks	No.
Swilling	11.0
Turnbull	9.0
Jackson	6.0
Wilks	5.5
W. Martin	4.0
Atkins	3.0
Cook	1.0
Johnson	1.0
Simmons	1.0
Mills	0.5
SAINTS	42.0
OPP.	20.0

N.Y. GIANTS

1990 TEAM RECORD

REGULAR SEASON (13-3)

Date	Result	Opponent	Att.
9/9	W 27-20	Philadelphia	76,202
9/16	W 28-7	at Dallas	61,090
9/23	W 20-3	Miami	76,483
9/30	W 31-17	Dallas	75,923
10/14	W 24-20	at Washington	54,737
10/21	W 20-19	Phoenix	76,518
10/28	W 21-10	Washington	75,321
11/5	W 24-7	at Indianapolis	58,688
11/11	W 31-7	at L.A. Rams	64,632
11/18	W 20-0	Detroit	76,109
11/25	L 13-31	at Philadelphia	66,706
12/3	L 3-7	at San Francisco	66,092
12/9	W 23-15	Minnesota	76,121
12/15	L 13-17	Buffalo	66,893
12/23	W 24-21	at Phoenix	41,212
12/30	W 13-10	at New England	60,410

PLAYOFFS (3-0)

Date	Result	Opponent	Att.
1/13	W 31-3	Chicago	77,025
1/20	W 15-13	at San Francisco	65,750
1/27	W 20-19	Buffalo, at Tampa	73,813

1990 TEAM STATISTICS

	GIANTS	Opp.
Total First Downs	273	245
Rushing	120	90
Passing	135	139
Penalty	18	16
Third Down: Made/Att.	81/209	72/199
Fourth Down: Made/Att.	8/17	7/17
Total Net Yards	4805	4206
Avg. Per Game	300.3	262.9
Total Plays	968	914
Avg. Per Play	5.0	4.6
Net Yards Rushing	2049	1459
Avg. Per Game	128.1	91.2
Total Rushes	541	388
Net Yards Passing	2756	2747
Avg. Per Game	172.3	171.7
Sacked/Yards Lost	29/142	30/186
Gross Yards	2898	2933
Att./Completions	398/231	496/278
Completion Pct.	58.0	56.0
Had Intercepted	5	23
Punts/Avg.	75/44.1	76/41.3
Net Punting Avg.	37.3	34.1
Penalties/Yards Lost	83/655	83/569
Fumbles/Ball Lost	21/9	28/11
Touchdowns	39	23
Rushing	17	9
Passing	18	12
Returns	4	2
Avg. Time of Possession	32:15	27:45

1990 INDIVIDUAL STATISTICS

Scoring	TD Run	TD Pass	TD Ret.	PAT	FG	Saf.	Tot.
Bahr	0	0	0	29/30	17/23	0	80
Anderson	11	0	0	0/0	0/0	0	66
Bavaro	0	5	0	0/0	0/0	0	30
Ingram	0	5	0	0/0	0/0	0	30
Baker	0	4	0	0/0	0/0	0	24
Hampton	2	2	0	0/0	0/0	0	24
Allegre	0	0	0	9/9	4/5	0	21
Hostetler	2	0	0	0/0	0/0	0	12
Meggett	0	1	1	0/0	0/0	0	12
Duerson	0	0	1	0/0	0/0	0	6
Mrosko	0	1	0	0/0	0/0	0	6
Simms	1	0	0	0/0	0/0	0	6
Taylor	0	0	1	0/0	0/0	0	6
Tillman	1	0	0	0/0	0/0	0	6
Walls	0	0	1	0/0	0/0	0	6
GIANTS	17	18	4	38/39	21/28	0	335
OPP.	9	12	2	23/23	16/22	1	211

Passing	Att.	Comp.	Yds.	Pct.	TD	Int.	Tkld.	Rate
Simms	311	184	2284	59.2	15	4	20/104	92.7
Hostetler	87	47	614	54.0	3	1	9/38	83.2
GIANTS	398	231	2898	58.0	18	5	29/142	90.6
OPP.	496	278	2933	56.0	12	23	30/186	62.2

Rushing	Att.	Yds.	Avg.	LG	TD
Anderson	225	784	3.5	28	11
Hampton	109	455	4.2	41	2
Tillman	84	231	2.8	17	1
Hostetler	39	190	4.9	30	2
Meggett	22	164	7.5	51	0
Carthon	36	143	4.0	12	0
Simms	21	61	2.9	20	1
Rouson	3	14	4.7	6	0
Ingram	1	4	4.0	4	0
Baker	1	3	3.0	3	0
GIANTS	541	2049	3.8	51	17
OPP.	388	1459	3.8	31	9

Receiving	No.	Yds.	Avg.	LG	TD
Meggett	39	410	10.5	38	1
Bavaro	33	393	11.9	61	5
Hampton	32	274	8.6	t27	2
Baker	26	541	20.8	t80	4
Ingram	26	499	19.2	t57	5
Anderson	18	139	7.7	18	0
Carthon	14	151	10.8	63	0
Manuel	11	169	13.3	21	0
Cross	8	106	13.3	21	0
Tillman	8	18	2.3	16	0
Turner	6	69	11.5	18	0
Kyles	4	77	19.3	35	0
Mrosko	3	27	9.0	16	1
Robinson	2	13	6.5	7	0
Rouson	1	12	12.0	12	0
GIANTS	231	2898	12..5	t80	18
OPP.	278	2933	10.6	t68	12

Intercepts.	No.	Yds.	Avg.	LG	TD
Walls	6	80	13.3	40	1
Jackson	5	8	1.6	5	0
Reasons	3	13	4.3	10	0
Williams	3	4	1.3	4	0
Collins	2	0	0.0	0	0
Taylor	1	11	11.0	t11	1
Duerson	1	0	0.0	0	0
Guyton	1	0	0.0	0	0
Johnson	1	0	0.0	0	0
GIANTS	23	116	5.0	40	2
OPP.	5	54	10.8	t22	1

Punting	No.	Yds.	Avg.	In 20	LG
Landeta	75	3306	44.1	24	67
GIANTS	75	3306	44.1	24	67
OPP.	76	3140	41.3	12	57

Punt Returns	No.	FC	Yds.	Avg.	LG	TD
Meggett	43	12	467	10.9	t68	1
GIANTS	43	12	467	10.9	t68	1
OPP.	41	6	291	7.1	32	0

Kickoff Returns	No.	Yds.	Avg.	LG	TD
Meggett	21	492	23.4	58	0
Hampton	20	340	17.0	33	0
Ingram	3	42	14.0	26	0
Cross	1	10	10.0	10	0
Whitmore	1	0	0.0	0	0
Guyton	0	0	0.0	0	0
GIANTS	46	884	19.2	58	0
OPP.	65	1245	19.2	t90	1

Sacks	No.
Taylor	10.5
Marshall	4.5
Jackson	4.0
Johnson	3.5
Howard	3.0
Fox	1.5
Banks	1.0
Cooks	1.0
Thompson	1.0
GIANTS	30.0
OPP.	29.0

N.Y. JETS

1990 TEAM RECORD

REGULAR SEASON (6-10)

Date	Result	Opponent	Att.
9/9	L 20-25	at Cincinnati	56,467
9/16	W 24-21	Cleveland	67,354
9/24	L 7-30	Buffalo	69,927
9/30	W 37-13	at New England	36,724
10/7	L 16-20	at Miami	69,678
10/14	L 3-39	San Diego	63,311
10/21	L 27-30	at Buffalo	79,002
10/28	W 17-12	at Houston	56,337
11/4	W 24-9	Dallas	68,086
11/11	L 3-17	Miami	68,362
11/18	L 14-17	at Indianapolis	47,283
11/25	L 7-24	Pittsburgh	57,806
12/2	L 17-38	at San Diego	40,877
12/16	L 21-29	Indianapolis	41,423
12/23	W 42-7	New England	30,250
12/30	W 16-13	at Tampa Bay	46,543

1990 TEAM STATISTICS

	JETS	Opp.
Total First Downs	295	318
Rushing	128	112
Passing	143	186
Penalty	24	20
Third Down: Made/Att.	74/193	88/199
Fourth Down: Made/Att.	5/21	10/14
Total Net Yards	4886	5455
Avg. Per Game	305.4	340.9
Total Plays	967	977
Avg. Per Play	5.1	5.6
Net Yards Rushing	2127	2018
Avg. Per Game	132.9	126.1
Total Rushes	476	423
Net Yards Passing	2759	3437
Avg. Per Game	172.4	214.8
Sacked/Yards Lost	40/300	38/308
Gross Yards	3059	3745
Att./Completions	451/246	516/311
Completion Pct.	54.5	60.3
Had Intercepted	11	18
Punts/Avg.	61/39.3	56/41.4
Net Punting Avg.	33.9	33.6
Penalties/Yards Lost	101/848	106/874
Fumbles/Ball Lost	28/13	29/11
Touchdowns	32	39
Rushing	16	15
Passing	14	23
Returns	2	1
Avg. Time of Possession	30:05	29:55

1990 INDIVIDUAL STATISTICS

Scoring	TD Run	TD Pass	TD Ret.	PAT	FG	Saf.	Tot.
Leahy	0	0	0	32/32	23/26	0	101
Baxter	6	0	0	0/0	0/0	0	36
McNeil	6	0	0	0/0	0/0	0	36
Moore	0	6	0	0/0	0/0	0	36
Toon	0	6	0	0/0	0/0	0	36
Hector	2	0	0	0/0	0/0	0	12
Thomas	1	1	0	0/0	0/0	0	12
Boyer	0	1	0	0/0	0/0	0	6
Davis	0	0	1	0/0	0/0	0	6
Mathis	0	0	1	0/0	0/0	0	6
Taylor	1	0	0	0/0	0/0	0	6
Byrd	0	0	0	0/0	0/0	1	2
JETS	16	14	2	32/32	23/26	1	295
OPP.	15	23	1	35/39	24/32	2	345

Passing	Att.	Comp.	Yds.	Pct.	TD	Int.	Tkld.	Rate
O'Brien	411	226	2855	53.0	13	10	34/262	77.3
Eason	28	13	155	46.4	0	1	4/35	49.0
Taylor	10	7	49	70.0	1	0	2/3	114.2
Toon	2	0	0	0.0	0	0		39.6
JETS	451	246	3059	54.5	14	11	40/300	76.0
OPP.	516	311	3745	60.3	23	18	38/308	82.9

Rushing	Att.	Yds.	Avg.	LG	TD
Thomas	123	620	5.0	41	1
Baxter	124	539	4.3	t28	6
McNeil	99	438	4.6	29	6
Hector	91	377	4.1	22	2
O'Brien	21	72	3.4	15	0
Eason	7	29	4.1	24	0
Taylor	2	20	10.0	15	1
Mathis	2	9	4.5	10	0
Brown	1	8	8.0	8	0
Prokop	3	2	0.7	2	0
Wellstandt	1	-3	-3.0	-3	0
Moore	2	-4	-2.0	4	0
JETS	476	2127	4.5	41	16
OPP.	423	2018	4.8	60	15

Receiving	No.	Yds.	Avg.	LG	TD
Toon	57	757	13.3	t46	6
Moore	44	692	15.7	t69	6
Boyer	40	334	8.4	25	1
Thomas	20	204	10.2	55	1
Mathis	19	245	12.9	23	0
McNeil	16	230	14.4	59	0
Burkett	14	204	14.6	46	0
Baxter	8	73	9.1	22	0
Hector	8	72	9.0	25	0
Dressel	6	66	11.0	21	0
Dawkins	5	68	13.6	31	0
Wellsandt	5	57	11.4	20	0
Townsell	4	57	14.3	18	0
JETS	246	3059	12.4	t69	14
OPP.	311	3745	12.0	t69	23

Intercepts.	No.	Yds.	Avg.	LG	TD
McMillan	5	92	18.4	25	0
Clifton	3	49	16.3	39	0
Washington	3	22	7.3	13	0
Curtis	2	45	22.5	23	0
Hasty	2	0	0.0	0	0
Stargell	2	-3	-1.5	0	0
Mayes	1	0	0.0	0	0
JETS	18	205	11.4	39	0
OPP.	11	186	16..9	36	0

Punting	No.	Yds.	Avg.	In 20	LG
Prokop	59	2363	40.1	18	58
O'Brien	1	23	23.0	0	23
Leahy	1	12	12.0	0	12
JETS	61	2398	39.3	18	58
OPP.	56	2321	41.4	14	69

Punt Returns	No.	FC	Yds.	Avg.	LG	TD
Townsell	17	4	154	9.1	20	0
Mathis	11	7	165	15.0	t98	1
Hasty	1	0	0	0.0	0	0
Odegard	1	0	0	0.0	0	0
JETS	30	11	319	10.6	t98	1
OPP.	33	8	269	7.7	35	0

Kickoff Returns	No.	Yds.	Avg.	LG	TD
Mathis	43	787	18.3	35	0
Townsell	7	158	22.6	38	0
Odegard	5	89	17.8	25	0
Nichols	2	3	1.5	3	0
Boyer	1	14	14.0	14	0
Brown	1	63	63.0	63	0
Dressel	1	7	7.0	7	0
Duffy	1	8	8.0	8	0
JETS	61	1129	18.5	63	0
OPP.	61	1185	19.4	t98	1

Sacks	No.
Byrd	13.0
Davis	5.0
Mersereau	4.5
Washington	4.5
Lageman	4.0
Nichols	3.5
Johnson	1.0
Stallworth	1.0
Washington	1.0
Clifton	0.5
JETS	38.0
OPP.	40.0

PHILADELPHIA

1990 TEAM RECORD

REGULAR SEASON (10-6)

9/9	L 20–27	at N.Y. Giants	76,202
9/16	L 21–23	Phoenix	64,396
9/23	W 27–21	at L.A. Rams	63,644
9/30	L 23–24	Indianapolis	62,067
10/15	W 32–24	Minnesota	66,296
10/21	L 7–13	at Washington	53,567
10/28	W 21–20	at Dallas	62,605
11/4	W 48–20	New England	65,514
11/12	W 28–14	Washington	65,857
11/18	W 24–23	at Atlanta	53,755
11/25	W 31–13	N.Y. Giants	66,706
12/2	L 23–30	at Buffalo	79,320
12/9	L 20–23	at Miami	67,034
12/16	W 31–0	Green Bay	65,627
12/23	W 17–3	Dallas	63,895
12/29	W 23–21	at Phoenix	31,796

PLAYOFFS (0–1)

1/5	L 6–20	Washington	65,287

1990 TEAM STATISTICS

	EAGLES	Opp.
Total First Downs	325	251
Rushing	132	59
Passing	170	169
Penalty	23	23
Third Down: Made/Att.	90/218	68/217
Fourth Down: Made/Att.	9/12	8/18
Total Net Yards	5700	4660
Avg. Per Game	356.3	291.3
Total Plays	1069	948
Avg. Per Play	5.3	4.9
Net Yards Rushing	2556	1172
Avg. Per Game	159.8	73.3
Total Rushes	540	336
Net Yards Passing	3144	3488
Avg. Per Game	196.5	218.0
Sacked/Yards Lost	50/438	46/283
Gross Yards	3582	3771
Att./Completions	479/281	566/273
Completion Pct.	58.7	48.2
Had Intercepted	13	19
Punts/Avg.	74/40.9	86/40.3
Net Punting Avg.	35.5	34.4
Penalties/Yards Lost	120/981	94/706
Fumbles/Ball Lost	32/15	32/11
Touchdowns	48	33
Rushing	10	9
Passing	34	23
Returns	4	1
Avg. Time of Possession	33:19	26:41

1990 INDIVIDUAL STATISTICS

Scoring	TD Run	TD Pass	TD Ret.	PAT	FG	Saf.	Tot.
Ruzek	0	0	0	45/48	21/29	0	108
Williams	0	9	0	0/0	0/0	0	54
Barnett	0	8	0	0/0	0/0	0	48
Jackson	0	6	0	0/0	0/0	0	36
Cunningham	5	0	0	0/0	0/0	0	30
Sherman	1	3	0	0/0	0/0	0	30
Toney	1	3	0	0/0	0/0	0	24
Byars	0	3	0	0/0	0/0	0	18
Allen	0	0	1	0/0	0/0	0	6
Drummond	1	0	0	0/0	0/0	0	6
Evans	0	0	1	0/0	0/0	0	6
Frizzell	0	0	1	0/0	0/0	0	6
Hargrove	0	1	0	0/0	0/0	0	6
Quick	0	1	0	0/0	0/0	0	6
Sanders	1	0	0	0/0	0/0	0	6
Simmons	0	0	1	0/0	0/0	0	6
Vick	1	0	0	0/0	0/0	0	6
EAGLES	10	34	4	45/48	21/29	0	396
OPP.	9	23	1	32/33	23/32	0	299

Passing	Att.	Comp.	Yds.	Pct.	TD	Int.	Tkld.	Rate
Cunningham	465	271	3466	58.3	30	13	49/431	91.6
McMahon	9	6	63	66.7	0	0	1/7	86.8
Byars	4	4	53	100.0	4	0	0/0	158.3
Feagles	1	0	0	0.0	0	0	0/0	39.6
EAGLES	479	281	3582	58.7	34	13	50/438	94.5
OPP.	466	273	3771	48.2	23	19	46/283	69.6

Rushing	Att.	Yds.	Avg.	LG	TD
Cunningham	118	942	8.0	t52	5
Sherman	164	685	4.2	36	1
Toney	132	452	3.4	20	1
Sanders	56	208	3.7	39	1
Byars	37	141	3.8	23	0
Vick	16	58	3.6	17	1
Drummond	8	33	4.1	9	1
Williams	2	20	10.0	18	0
Barnett	2	13	6.5	12	0
Feagles	2	3	1.5	3	0
McMahon	3	3	0.3	3	0
EAGLES	540	2556	4.7	t52	10
OPP.	336	1172	3.5	51	9

Receiving	No.	Yds.	Avg.	LG	TD
Byars	81	819	10.1	54	3
Jackson	50	670	13.4	t37	6
Williams	37	602	16.3	t45	9
Barnett	36	721	20.0	t95	8
Sherman	23	167	7.3	26	3
Shuler	18	190	10.6	25	0
Toney	17	133	7.8	29	3
Quick	9	135	15.0	39	1
Drummond	5	39	7.8	29	0
Sanders	2	20	10.0	12	0
Jackson	1	43	43.0	43	0
Hargrove	1	34	34.0	t34	1

	No.	Yds.	Avg.	LG	TD
LeBel	1	9	9.0	9	0
EAGLES	281	3582	12.7	t95	34
OPP.	273	3771	13.8	t78	23

Intercepts.	No.	Yds.	Avg.	LG	TD
Hopkins	5	45	9.0	21	0
Frizzell	3	91	30.3	37	1
Allen	3	37	12.3	t35	0
Smith	3	1	0.3	1	0
Evans	1	43	43.0	t22	0
White	1	33	33.0	33	0
Golic	1	12	12.0	12	0
Joyner	1	9	9.0	9	0
Hoage	1	0	0.0	0	0
EAGLES	19	271	14.3	42	3
OPP.	13	88	6.8	38	0

Punting	No.	Yds.	Avg.	In 20	LG
Feagles	72	3026	42.0	20	60
EAGLES	74	3026	40.9	20	60
OPP.	86	3470	40.3	22	59

Punt Returns	No.	FC	Yds.	Avg.	LG	TD
Harris	16	2	151	9.4	30	0
Hargrove	12	2	83	6.9	13	0
Edwards	8	7	60	7.5	13	0
Bellamy	2	0	22	11.0	22	0
Williams	2	0	−1	−0.5	1	0
EAGLES	40	11	315	7.9	30	0
OPP.	37	19	338	9.1	t68	1

Kickoff Returns	No.	Yds.	Avg.	LG	TD
Hargrove	19	341	17.9	30	0
Sanders	15	299	19.9	37	0
Jackson	6	125	20.8	30	0
Barnett	4	65	16.3	22	0
Edwards	3	36	12.0	14	0
Harris	1	44	44.0	44	0
Vick	2	22	11.0	13	0
Allen	1	2	2.0	2	0
Bellamy	1	17	17.0	17	0
Hager	1	0	0.0	0	0
Jenkins	1	14	14.0	14	0
EAGLES	54	965	17.9	44	0
OPP.	74	1408	19.0	40	0

Sacks	No.
White	15.0
Joyner	7.5
Simmons	7.5
Small	3.5
Pitts	3.0
Golic	2.0
Hopkins	2.0
Frizzell	1.5
Brown	1.0
Chapura	1.0
Evans	1.0
Hoage	1.0
EAGLES	46.0
OPP.	50.0

PHOENIX

1990 TEAM RECORD

REGULAR SEASON (5-11)

Date	Result	Opponent	Att.
9/9	L 0–31	at Washington	52,649
9/16	W 23–21	at Philadelphia	64,396
9/23	L 7–28	at New Orleans	61,110
9/30	L 10–38	Washington	49,303
10/14	W 20–3	Dallas	45,235
10/21	L 19–20	at N.Y. Giants	76,518
10/28	L 21–31	Chicago	71,233
11/4	L 3–23	at Miami	54,924
11/11	L 14–45	at Buffalo	74,904
11/18	L 21–24	Green Bay	46,878
11/25	W 34–14	New England	30,110
12/2	W 20–17	Indianapolis	31,885
12/9	W 24–13	at Atlanta	36,222
12/16	L 10–41	at Dallas	60,190
12/23	L 21–24	N.Y. Giants	41,212
12/29	L 21–23	Philadelphia	31,796

1990 TEAM STATISTICS

	CARDINALS	Opp.
Total First Downs	270	306
Rushing	115	140
Passing	135	146
Penalty	20	20
Third Down: Made/Att.	77/194	90/198
Fourth Down: Made/Att.	7/16	8/16
Total Net Yards	4742	5216
Avg. Per Game	296.4	326.0
Total Plays	935	959
Avg. Per Play	5.1	5.4
Net Yards Rushing	1912	2318
Avg. Per Game	119.5	144.9
Total Rushes	452	521
Net Yards Passing	2833	2898
Avg. Per Game	177.1	181.1
Sacked/Yards Lost	43/285	36/232
Gross Yards	3118	3130
Att./Completions	439/238	402/233
Completion Pct.	54.2	58.0
Had Intercepted	18	16
Punts/Avg.	67/42.8	63/43.6
Net Punting Avg.	37.4	36.3
Penalties/Yards Lost	96/883	96/834
Fumbles/Ball Lost	25/14	28/11
Touchdowns	31	50
Rushing	13	20
Passing	16	29
Returns	2	1
Avg. Time of Possession	28:38	31:22

1990 INDIVIDUAL STATISTICS

Scoring	TD Run	TD Pass	TD Ret.	PAT	FG	Saf.	Tot.
Del Greco	0	0	0	31/31	17/27	0	82
Johnson	5	0	0	0/0	0/0	0	30
Green	0	4	0	0/0	0/0	0	24
Jones	0	4	0	0/0	0/0	0	24
Proehl	0	4	0	0/0	0/0	0	24
Thompson	4	0	0	0/0	0/0	0	24
Rosenbach	3	0	0	0/0	0/0	0	18
Flagler	1	1	0	0/0	0/0	0	12
Smith	0	2	0	0/0	0/0	0	12
Turner	0	0	2	0/0	0/0	0	12
Sharpe	0	1	0	0/0	0/0	0	6
CARDINALS	13	16	2	31/31	17/27	0	268
OPP.	20	29	1	48/50	16/20	0	396

Passing	Att.	Comp.	Yds.	Pct.	TD	Int.	Tkld.	Rate
Rosenbach	437	237	3098	54.2	16	17	43/285	72.8
Green	1	1	20	100.0	0	0	0/0	118.8
Johnson	1	0	0	0.0	0	1	0/0	0.0
CARDINALS	439	238	3118	54.2	16	18	43/285	71.9
OPP.	402	233	3130	58.0	29	16	36/232	90.3

Rushing	Att.	Yds.	Avg.	LG	TD
Johnson	234	926	4.0	41	5
Rosenbach	86	470	5.5	25	3
Thompson	106	390	3.7	40	4
Flagler	13	85	6.5	t29	1
Jones	4	33	8.3	15	0
Sikahema	3	8	2.7	4	0
Proehl	1	4	4.0	4	0
Smith	1	4	4.0	4	0
Wolfley	2	3	1.5	2	0
Tupa	1	0	0.0	0	0
Camarillo	1	−11	−11.0	−11	0
CARDINALS	452	1912	4.2	41	13
OPP.	521	2318	4.4	43	20

Receiving	No.	Yds.	Avg.	LG	TD
Proehl	56	802	14.3	t45	4
Green	53	797	15.0	54	4
Jones	43	724	16.8	t68	4
Johnson	25	241	9.6	35	0
Smith	18	225	12.5	t45	2
Reeves	18	126	7.0	16	0
Flagler	13	130	10.0	21	1
Sikahema	7	51	7.3	13	0
Thompson	2	11	5.5	6	0
Jorden	2	10	5.0	6	0
Sharpe	1	1	1.0	1	1
CARDINALS	238	3118	13.1	t68	16
OPP.	233	3130	13.4	t67	29

Intercepts.	No.	Yds.	Avg.	LG	TD
McDonald	4	63	15.8	38	0
Taylor	3	50	16.7	34	0
Mack	2	53	26.5	39	0
Young	2	8	4.0	5	0
Jax	2	5	2.5	4	0
Turner	1	70	70.0	t47	2
Zordich	1	25	25.0	25	0
Bell	1	0	0.0	0	0
CARDINALS	16	274	17.1	t47	2
OPP.	18	201	11.2	t57	1

Punting	No.	Yds.	Avg.	In 20	LG
Camarillo	67	2865	42.8	16	63
CARDINALS	67	2865	42.8	16	63
OPP.	63	2747	43.6	16	60

Punt Returns	No.	FC	Yds.	Avg.	LG	TD
Sikahema	36	6	306	8.5	20	0
Smith	3	0	34	11.3	16	0
Proehl	1	1	2	2.0	2	0
CARDINALS	40	7	342	8.6	20	0
OPP.	41	11	258	6.3	27	0

Kickoff Returns	No.	Yds.	Avg.	LG	TD
Sikahema	27	544	20.1	32	0
Centers	16	272	17.0	26	0
Flagler	10	167	16.7	27	0
Proehl	4	53	13.3	15	0
Jax	2	17	8.5	9	0
Green	1	15	15.0	15	0
CARDINALS	60	1068	17.8	32	0
OPP.	56	1060	18.9	39	0

Sacks	No.
Harvey	10.0
Nunn	9.0
Saddler	4.0
Bell	3.0
Jax	3.0
Wahler	2.5
Hill	1.5
Hairston	1.0
Mack	1.0
CARDINALS	36.0
OPP.	43.0

PITTSBURGH

1990 TEAM RECORD

REGULAR SEASON (9-7)

Date	Result	Opponent	Att.
9/9	L 3-13	at Cleveland	78,298
9/16	W 20-9	Houston	54,814
9/23	L 3-20	at L.A. Raiders	50,657
9/30	L 6-28	Miami	54,691
10/7	W 36-14	San Diego	53,486
10/14	W 34-17	at Denver	74,285
10/21	L 7-27	at San Francisco	64,301
10/29	W 41-10	L.A. Rams	56,466
11/4	W 21-9	Atlanta	57,093
11/18	L 3-27	at Cincinnati	60,064
11/25	W 24-7	at N.Y. Jets	57,806
12/2	L 12-16	Cincinnati	58,200
12/9	W 24-3	New England	48,354
12/16	W 9-6	at New Orleans	68,582
12/23	W 35-0	Cleveland	51,665
12/30	L 14-34	at Houston	56,906

1990 TEAM STATISTICS

	STEELERS	Opp.
Total First Downs	263	257
Rushing	93	102
Passing	150	130
Penalty	20	25
Third Down: Made/Att.	74/187	81/205
Fourth Down: Made/Att.	4/10	6/17
Total Net Yards	4525	4115
Avg. Per Game	282.8	257.2
Total Plays	897	940
Avg. Per Play	5.0	4.4
Net Yards Rushing	1880	1615
Avg. Per Game	117.5	100.9
Total Rushes	456	446
Net Yards Passing	2645	2500
Avg. Per Game	165.3	156.3
Sacked/Yards Lost	33/242	34/228
Gross Yards	2887	2728
Att./Completions	408/237	460/236
Completion Pct.	58.1	51.3
Had Intercepted	15	24
Punts/Avg.	66/37.2	64/40.9
Net Punting Avg.	34.1	33.7
Penalties/Yards Lost	110/928	89/719
Fumbles/Ball Lost	40/17	33/18
Touchdowns	33	26
Rushing	11	13
Passing	20	9
Returns	2	4
Avg. Time of Possession	30:06	29:54

1990 INDIVIDUAL STATISTICS

Scoring	TD Run	TD Pass	TD Ret.	PAT	FG	Saf.	Tot.
Anderson	0	0	0	32/32	20/25	0	92
Hoge	7	3	0	0/0	0/0	0	60
Green	0	7	0	0/0	0/0	0	42
Williams	3	1	0	0/0	0/0	0	24
Lipps	0	3	0	0/0	0/0	0	18
Mularkey	0	3	0	0/0	0/0	0	18
Bell	0	1	0	0/0	0/0	0	6
Calloway	0	1	0	0/0	0/0	0	6
Foster	1	0	0	0/0	0/0	0	6
Johnson	0	0	1	0/0	0/0	0	6
Stone	0	1	0	0/0	0/0	0	6
Woodson	0	0	1	0/0	0/0	0	6
Stowe	0	0	0	0/0	0/0	1	2
STEELERS	11	20	2	32/33	20/25	1	292
OPP.	13	9	4	26/26	18/28	2	240

Passing	Att.	Comp.	Yds.	Pct.	TD	Int.	Tkld.	Rate
Brister	387	223	2725	57.6	20	14	28/213	81.6
Strom	21	14	162	66.7	0	1	5/29	69.9
STEELERS	408	237	2887	58.1	20	15	33/242	81.0
OPP.	460	236	2728	51.3	9	24	34/228	54.3

Rushing	Att.	Yds.	Avg.	LG	TD
Hoge	203	772	3.8	t41	7
Worley	109	418	3.8	38	0
Williams	68	389	5.7	t70	3
Foster	36	203	5.6	38	1
Brister	25	64	2.6	11	0
Bell	5	18	3.6	12	0
Stryzinski	3	17	5.7	9	0
Strom	4	10	2.5	10	0
Lipps	1	-5	-5.0	-5	0
Stone	2	-6	-3.0	10	0
STEELERS	456	1880	4.1	t70	11
OPP.	446	1615	3.6	31	13

Receiving	No.	Yds.	Avg.	LG	TD
Lipps	50	682	13.6	37	3
Hoge	40	342	8.6	27	3
Green	34	387	11.4	46	7
Mularkey	32	365	11.4	28	3
Hill	25	391	15.6	66	0
Stone	19	332	17.5	90	1
Bell	12	137	11.4	43	1
Calloway	10	124	12.4	t20	1
Worley	8	70	8.8	27	0
Williams	5	42	8.4	13	1
O'Shea	1	13	13.0	13	0
Foster	1	2	2.0	2	0
STEELERS	237	2887	12.2	90	20
OPP.	236	2728	11.6	t66	9

Intercepts.	No.	Yds.	Avg.	LG	TD
Woodson	5	67	13.4	34	0
Griffin	4	75	18.8	36	0
Woodruff	3	110	36.7	59	0
Everett	3	2	0.7	2	0
Johnson	2	60	30.0	34	1
Little	1	35	35.0	35	0
Hinkle	1	19	19.0	19	0
Lloyd	1	9	9.0	9	0
Willis	1	5	5.0	5	0
Jones	1	3	3.0	3	0
Hall	1	0	0.0	0	0
Lake	1	0	0.0	0	0
STEELERS	24	385	16.0	59	1
OPP.	15	124	8.3	24	0

Punting	No.	Yds.	Avg.	In 20	LG
Stryzinski	65	2454	37.8	18	51
STEELERS	66	2454	37.2	18	51
OPP.	64	2616	40.9	13	62

Punt Returns	No.	FC	Yds.	Avg.	LG	TD
Woodson	38	8	398	10.5	t52	1
Hill	1	0	0	0.0	0	0
STEELERS	39	8	398	10.2	t52	1
OPP.	16	32	105	6i.6	39	0

Kickoff Returns	No.	Yds.	Avg.	LG	TD
Woodson	35	764	21.8	49	0
Stone	5	91	18.2	24	0
Foster	3	29	9.7	13	0
Williams	3	31	10.3	20	0
Griffin	2	16	8.0	14	0
Green	1	16	16.0	16	0
Lipps	1	9	9.0	9	0
Olsavsky	0	0	0.0	0	0
STEELERS	50	956	19.1	49	0
OPP.	56	1245	22.2	t99	1

Sacks	No.
Williams	6.0
Willis	5.0
Lloyd	4.5
Davidson	3.5
Evans	3.0
Freeman	2.0
Hinkle	2.0
Jones	2.0
Jenkins	2.0
Nickerson	2.0
Lake	1.0
Williams	1.0
STEELERS	34.0
OPP.	33.0

SAN DIEGO

1990 TEAM RECORD

REGULAR SEASON (6-10)

Date	Result	Opponent	Att.
9/9	L 14-17	at Dallas	48,063
9/16	L 16-21	Cincinnati	48,098
9/23	W 24-14	at Cleveland	77,429
9/30	L 7-17	Houston	48,762
10/7	L 14-36	at Pittsburgh	53,486
10/14	W 39-3	at N.Y. Jets	63,311
10/21	L 9-24	L.A. Raiders	60,569
10/28	W 41-10	Tampa Bay	40,653
11/4	W 31-14	at Seattle	59,646
11/11	W 19-7	Denver	59,557
11/18	L 10-27	at Kansas City	63,717
11/25	L 10-13	Seattle	50,097
12/2	W 38-17	N.Y. Jets	40,877
12/16	L 10-20	at Denver	64,919
12/23	L 21-24	Kansas City	45,135
12/30	L 12-17	at L.A. Raiders	62,593

1990 TEAM STATISTICS

	CHARGERS	Opp.
Total First Downs	272	268
Rushing	112	92
Passing	142	152
Penalty	18	24
Third Down: Made/Att.	101/223	86/203
Fourth Down: Made/Att.	6/20	6/14
Total Net Yards	4940	4425
Avg. Per Game	308.8	276.6
Total Plays	976	931
Avg. Per Play	5.1	4.8
Net Yards Rushing	2257	1515
Avg. Per Game	141.1	94.7
Total Rushes	484	424
Net Yards Passing	2683	2910
Avg. Per Game	167.7	181.9
Sacked/Yards Lost	20/157	45/345
Gross Yards	2840	3255
Att./Completions	472/246	462/254
Completion Pct.	52.1	55.0
Had Intercepted	19	24
Punts/Avg.	62/39.4	70/41.2
Net Punting Avg.	36.6	35.0
Penalties/Yards Lost	103/886	87/720
Fumbles/Ball Lost	24/13	26/11
Touchdowns	36	33
Rushing	14	14
Passing	18	22
Returns	4	1
Avg. Time of Possession	30:19	29:41

1990 INDIVIDUAL STATISTICS

Scoring	TD Run	TD Pass	TD Ret.	PAT	FG	Saf.	Tot.
Carney	0	0	0	27/28	19/21	0	84
Butts	8	0	0	0/0	0/0	0	48
Miller	0	7	0	0/0	0/0	0	42
Bernstine	4	0	0	0/0	0/0	0	24
Lewis	1	1	1	0/0	0/0	0	18
McEwen	0	3	0	0/0	0/0	0	18
Reveiz	0	0	0	7/8	2/7	0	13
Harmon	0	2	0	0/0	0/0	0	12
Miller	0	0	2	0/0	0/0	0	12
Plummer	1	1	0	0/0	0/0	0	12
Caravello	0	1	0	0/0	0/0	0	6
Cox	0	1	0	0/0	0/0	0	6
Early	0	1	0	0/0	0/0	0	6
Taylor	0	0	1	0/0	0/0	0	6
Walker	0	1	0	0/0	0/0	0	6
Grossman	0	0	0	0/0	0/0	1	2
CHARGERS	14	18	4	34/36	21/28	1	315
OPP.	10	22	1	33/33	16/21	2	281

Passing	Att.	Comp.	Yds.	Pct.	TD	Int.	Tkld.	Rate
Tolliver	410	216	2574	52.7	16	16	19/150	68.9
Vlasic	40	19	168	47.5	1	2	0/0	46.7
Friesz	22	11	98	50.0	1	1	1/7	58.5
CHARGERS	472	246	2840	52.1	18	19	20/157	66.5
OPP.	462	254	3255	55.0	22	19	45/345	76.0

Rushing	Att.	Yds.	Avg.	LG	TD
Butts	265	1225	4.6	52	8
Bernstine	124	589	4.8	t40	4
Harmon	66	363	5.5	41	0
Lewis	4	25	6.3	t10	1
Tolliver	14	22	1.6	14	0
Nelson	3	14	4.7	5	0
Miller	3	13	4.3	10	0
Friesz	1	3	3.0	3	0
Plummer	2	3	1.5	2	1
Vlasic	1	0	0.0	0	0
Wilson	1	0	0.0	0	0
CHARGERS	484	2257	4.7	52	14
OPP.	424	1515	3.6	27	10

Receiving	No.	Yds.	Avg.	LG	TD
Miller	63	933	14.8	t31	7
Harmon	46	511	11.1	t36	2
McEwen	29	325	11.2	32	3
Walker	23	240	10.4	23	1
Butts	16	117	7.3	26	0
Early	15	238	15.9	t45	1
Lewis	14	192	13.7	40	1
Cox	14	93	6.6	12	1
Wilson	10	87	8.7	20	0
Bernstine	8	40	5.0	11	0
Nelson	4	29	7.3	10	0
Caravello	2	21	10.5	t17	1
Hendrickson	1	12	12.0	12	0

Plummer	1	2	2.0	t2		1
CHARGERS	246	2840	11.5	t45		18
OPP.	254	3255	12.8	t90		22

Intercepts.	No.	Yds.	Avg.	LG	TD
Byrd	7	63	9.0	24	0
Seale	2	14	7.0	14	0
Smth	2	12	6.0	12	0
Frank	2	8	4.0	4	0
Rolling	1	67	67.0	67	0
Lyles	1	19	19.0	19	0
Fuller	1	5	5.0	5	0
Bayless	1	0	0.0	0	0
Elder	1	0	0.0	0	0
Glenn	1	0	0.0	0	0
CHARGERS	19	188	9.9	67	0
OPP.	19	310	16.3	t64	1

Punting	No.	Yds.	Avg.	In 20	LG
Kidd	61	2442	40.0	14	59
CHARGERS	62	2442	39.4	14	59
OPP.	70	2886	41.2	15	67

Punt Returns	No.	FC	Yds.	Avg.	LG	TD
Lewis	13	8	117	9.0	t63	1
Mays	7	4	30	4.3	17	0
Taylor	6	3	112	18.7	t55	1
Schwedes	5	1	33	6.6	12	0
Nelson	3	0	44	14.7	33	0
Lyles	1	0	0	0.0	0	0
CHARGERS	35	16	336	9.6	t63	2
OPP.	28	15	131	4.7	18	0

Kickoff Returns	No.	Yds.	Avg.	LG	TD
Elder	24	571	23.8	90	0
Lewis	17	383	22.5	39	0
Frank	8	172	21.5	31	0
Nelson	4	36	9.0	26	0
Miller	1	13	13.0	13	0
Orr	1	13	13.0	13	0
CHARGERS	55	1188	21.6	90	0
OPP.	62	1048	16.9	75	0

Sacks	No.
O'Neal	13.5
Grossman	10.0
Williams	7.5
Rolling	3.5
Bayless	3.0
Robinson	2.0
Miller	1.0
Seau	1.0
Smith	1.0
Elder	0.5
Hinkle	0.5
Phillips	0.5
CHARGERS	45.0
OPP.	20.0

SAN FRANCISCO

1990 TEAM RECORD

REGULAR SEASON (14–2)

Date	Result	Opponent	Att.
9/10	W 13–12	at New Orelans	68,629
9/16	W 26–13	Washington	64,287
9/23	W 19–13	Atlanta	62,858
10/7	W 24–21	at Houston	59,931
10/14	W 45–35	at Atlanta	57,921
10/21	W 27–7	Pittsburgh	64,301
10/28	W 20–17	Cleveland	63,672
11/4	W 24–20	at Green Bay	58,835
11/11	W 24–6	at Dallas	62,966
11/18	W 31–7	Tampa Bay	62,221
11/25	L 17–28	L.A. Rams	62,633
12/3	W 7–3	N.Y. Giants	66,092
12/9	W 20–17	at Cincinnati	60,084
12/17	W 26–10	at L.A. Rams	65,619
12/23	L 10–13	New Orleans	60,112
12/30	W 20–17	at Minnesota	51,590

PLAYOFFS (1–1)

Date	Result	Opponent	Att.
1/12	W 28–10	Washington	65,292
1/20	L 13–15	N.Y. Giants	65,750

1990 TEAM STATISTICS

	49ERS	Opp.
Total First Downs	324	250
Rushing	107	77
Passing	201	157
Penalty	16	16
Third Down: Made/Att.	113/233	71/199
Fourth Down: Made/Att.	7/9	4/15
Total Net Yards	5895	4273
Avg. Per Game	368.4	267.1
Total Plays	1074	919
Avg. Per Play	5.5	4.6
Net Yards Rushing	1718	1258
Avg. Per Game	107.4	78.6
Total Rushes	454	353
Net Yards Passing	4177	3015
Avg. Per Game	261.1	188.4
Sacked/Yards Lost	37/194	44/263
Gross Yards	4371	3278
Att./Completions	583/360	522/265
Completion Pct.	61.7	50.8
Had Intercepted	16	17
Punts/Avg.	70/36.2	82/40.0
Net Punting Avg.	30.9	34.2
Penalties/Yards Lost	104/828	85/641
Fumbles/Ball Lost	24/14	21/14
Touchdowns	40	26
Rushing	12	7
Passing	28	17
Returns	0	2
Avg. Time of Possession	32:49	27:11

1990 INDIVIDUAL STATISTICS

Scoring	TD Run	TD Pass	TD Ret.	PAT	FG	Saf.	Tot.
Cofer	0	0	0	39/39	24/36	0	111
Rice	0	13	0	0/0	0/0	0	78
Rathman	7	0	0	0/0	0/0	0	42
Taylor	0	7	0	0/0	0/0	0	42
Jones	0	5	0	0/0	0/0	0	30
Sydney	2	1	0	0/0	0/0	0	18
Sherrard	0	2	0	0/0	0/0	0	12
Craig	1	0	0	0/0	0/0	0	6
Carter	1	0	0	0/0	0/0	0	6
Montana	1	0	0	0/0	0/0	0	6
Turner	0	0	0	0/0	0/0	1	2
49ERS	12	28	0	39/40	24/36	1	353
OPP.	7	17	2	26/26	19/23	0	239

Passing	Att.	Comp.	Yds.	Pct.	TD	Int.	Tkld.	Rate
Montana	520	321	3944	61.7	26	16	29/153	89.0
Young	62	38	427	61.3	2	0	8/41	92.6
Helton	1	1	0	100.0	0	0	0/0	79.2
49ERS	583	360	4371	61.7	28	16	37/194	89.4
OPP.	522	265	3278	50.8	17	17	44/263	67.8

Rushing	Att.	Yds.	Avg.	LG	TD
Carter	114	460	4.0	t74	1
Craig	141	439	3.1	26	1
Rathman	101	318	3.1	22	7
Sydney	35	166	4.7	19	2
Montana	40	162	4.1	20	1
Young	15	159	10.6	31	0
Henderson	6	14	2.3	9	0
Rice	2	0	0.0	2	0
49ERS	454	1718	3.8	t74	12
OPP.	353	1258	3.6	27	7

Receiving	No.	Yds.	Avg.	LG	TD
Rice	100	1502	15.0	t64	13
Jones	56	747	13.3	t67	5
Taylor	49	748	15.3	t78	7
Rathman	48	327	6.8	23	0
Carter	25	217	8.7	26	0
Craig	25	201	8.0	31	0
Sherrard	17	264	15.5	43	2
Sydney	10	116	11.6	t23	1
Williams	9	54	6.0	9	0
Wilson	7	89	12.7	34	0
Lewis	5	44	8.8	14	0
Walls	5	27	5.4	11	0
Henderson	4	35	8.8	9	0
49ERS	360	4371	12.1	t78	28
OPP.	265	3278	12.4	t75	17

Intercepts.	No.	Yds.	Avg.	LG	TD
Waymer	7	64	9.1	24	0
Griffin	3	32	10.7	23	0
Lott	3	26	8.7	15	0
K. Lewis	1	28	28.0	28	0
Davis	1	13	13.0	13	0
Millen	1	8	8.0	8	0
Pollard	1	0		0	0
49ERS	17	171	10.1	28	0
OPP.	16	176	11.0	t65	0

Punting	No.	Yds.	Avg.	In 20	LG
Helton	69	2537	36.8	15	56
49ERS	70	2537	36.2	15	56
OPP.	82	3280	40.0	15	59

Punt Returns	No.	FC	Yds.	Avg.	LG	TD
Taylor	26	5	212	8.2	30	0
Griffin	16	8	105	6.6	20	0
Davis	5	3	38	7.6	24	0
Wilson	1		1	1.0	1	0
49ERS	48	16	356	7.4	30	0
OPP.	30	13	215	7.2	20	0

Kickoff Returns	No.	Yds.	Avg.	LG	TD
Carter	41	783	19.1	35	0
Tillman	6	111	18.5	30	0
Sydney	2	33	16.5	19	0
Williams	2	7	3.5	7	0
Griffin	1	15	15.0	15	0
Walls	1	16	16.0	16	0
49ERS	53	965	18.2	35	0
OPP.	66	1284	19.5	50	0

Sacks	No.
Haley	16.0
Fagan	9.0
Brown	6.0
Holt	6.0
Burt	2.0
Carter	1.0
Jackson	1.0
Roberts	1.0
Romanowski	1.0
Turner	1.0
49ERS	44.0
OPP.	37.0

SEATTLE

1990 TEAM RECORD

REGULAR SEASON (9–7)

Date	Result	Opponent	Att.
9/9	L 0–17	at Chicago	64,400
9/16	L 13–17	L.A. Raiders	61,889
9/23	L 31–34	at Denver	75,290
10/1	W 31–16	Cincinnati	60,135
10/7	W 33–20	at New England	39,735
10/14	L 17–24	at L.A. Raiders	50,624
10/21	W 19–7	Kansas City	60,358
11/4	L 14–31	San Diego	59,646
11/11	W 17–16	at Kansas City	71,285
11/18	L 21–24	Minnesota	59,735
11/25	W 13–10	at San Diego	50,097
12/2	W 13–10	Houston	57,592
12/9	W 20–14	at Green Bay	52,015
12/16	L 17–24	at Miami	57,851
12/23	W 17–12	Denver	55,845
12/30	W 30–10	Detroit	50,681

1990 TEAM STATISTICS

	SEAHAWKS	Opp.
Total First Downs	284	280
Rushing	111	86
Passing	155	171
Penalty	18	23
Third Down: Made/Att.	87/200	83/207
Fourth Down: Made/Att.	6/7	7/11
Total Net Yards	4583	4609
Avg. Per Game	286.4	288.1
Total Plays	945	950
Avg. Per Play	4.8	4.9
Net Yards Rushing	1749	1605
Avg. Per Game	109.3	100.3
Total Rushes	457	413
Net Yards Passing	2834	3004
Avg. Per Game	177.1	187.8
Sacked/Yards Lost	40/360	33/252
Gross Yards	3194	3256
Att./Completions	448/265	504/300
Completion Pct.	59.2	59.5
Had Intercepted	20	12
Punts/Avg.	67/40.6	77/41.9
Net Punting Avg.	34.4	36.2
Penalties/Yards Lost	89/746	108/766
Fumbles/Ball Lost	32/16	32/18
Touchdowns	34	32
Rushing	18	7
Passing	15	19
Returns	1	6
Avg. Time of Possession	30:47	29:13

1990 INDIVIDUAL STATISTICS

Scoring	TD Run	TD Pass	TD Ret.	PAT	FG	Saf.	Tot.
Johnson	0	0	0	33/34	23/32	0	102
Fenner	14	1	0	0/0	0/0	0	90
Chadwick	0	4	0	0/0	0/0	0	24
Kane	0	4	0	0/0	0/0	0	24
Blades	0	3	0	0/0	0/0	0	18
Williams	3	0	0	0/0	0/0	0	18
Skansi	0	2	0	0/0	0/0	0	12
Heller	0	1	0	0/0	0/0	0	6
Robinson	0	0	1	0/0	0/0	0	6
Warren	1	0	0	0/0	0/0	0	6
SEAHAWKS	18	15	1	33/34	23/32	0	306
OPP.	7	19	6	32/32	20/27	1	286

Passing	Att.	Comp.	Yds.	Pct.	TD	Int.	Tkld.	Rate
Krieg	448	265	3194	59.2	15	20	40/360	73.6
SEAHAWKS	448	265	3194	59.2	15	20	40/360	73.6
OPP.	504	300	3256	59.5	19	12	33/252	81.3

Rushing	Att.	Yds.	Avg.	LG	TD
Fenner	215	859	4.0	36	14
Williams	187	714	3.8	25	3
Krieg	32	115	3.6	25	0
Jones	5	20	4.0	5	0
Blades	3	19	6.3	12	0
Loville	7	12	1.7	4	0
Warren	6	11	1.8	4	1
McNeal	1	2	2.0	2	0
Chadwick	1	–3	–3.0	–3	0
SEAHAWKS	457	1749	3.8	36	18
OPP.	413	1605	3.9	t58	18

Receiving	No.	Yds.	Avg.	LG	TD
Williams	73	699	9.6	60	0
Kane	52	776	14.9	t63	4
Blades	49	525	10.7	24	3
Chadwick	27	478	17.7	t54	4
Skansi	22	257	11.7	t25	2
Fenner	17	143	8.4	50	1
Heller	13	157	12.1	23	1
McNeal	10	143	14.3	30	0
Jones	1	22	22.0	22	0
Krieg	1	–6	–6.0	–6	0
SEAHAWKS	265	3194	12.1	t63	15
OPP.	300	3256	10.9	46	19

Intercepts.	No.	Yds.	Avg.	LG	TD
Robinson	3	89	29.7	39	0
Harper	3	69	23.0	47	0
Wyman	2	24	12.0	22	0
Bolcar	1	0	0.0	0	0
Hunter	1	0	0.0	0	0
Jefferson	1	0	0.0	0	0
Jenkins	1	0	0.0	0	0
SEAHAWKS	12	182	15.2	47	0
OPP.	20	252	12.6	442	0

Punting	No.	Yds.	Avg.	In 20	LG
Donnelly	67	2722	40.6	18	54
SEAHAWKS	67	2722	40.6	18	54
OPP.	77	3225	41.9	22	67

Punt Returns	No.	FC	Yds.	Avg.	LG	TD
Warren	28	16	269	9.6	39	0
Jefferson	8	0	68	8.5	14	0
SEAHAWKS	36	16	337	9.4	39	0
OPP.	29	21	254	8.8	t66	2

Kickoff Returns	No.	Yds.	Avg.	LG	TD
Warren	23	478	20.8	71	0
Loville	18	359	19.9	29	0
Jefferson	4	96	24.0	26	0
Jones	2	21	10.5	13	0
McNeal	2	29	14.5	17	0
Glasgow	1	2	2.0	2	0
Seahawk	50	985	19.7	71	0
OPP.	51	910	17.8	39	0

Sacks	No.
Green	12.5
Bryant	5.5
Porter	5.0
Woods	3.0
Glasgow	2.0
Comeaux	1.0
Kennedy	1.0
McElroy	1.0
Nash	1.0
Wyman	1.0
SEAHAWKS	33.0
OPP.	40.0

TAMPA BAY

1990 TEAM RECORD

REGULAR SEASON (6-10)

9/9	W 38-21	at Detroit	56,692
9/16	L 14-35	L.A. Rams	59,705
9/23	W 23-20	Detroit	55,075
9/30	W 23-20	at Minnesota	54,462
10/7	L 10-14	at Dallas	60,076
10/14	W 26-14	Green Bay	67,472
10/21	L 13-17	Dallas	68,315
10/28	L 10-41	at San Diego	40,653
11/4	L 6-26	Chicago	68,555
11/11	L 7-35	at New Orleans	67,865
11/18	L 7-31	at San Francisco	62,221
11/25	L 10-20	at Green Bay	53,677
12/2	W 23-17	Atlanta	42,839
12/16	W 26-13	Minnesota	47,272
12/23	L 14-27	at Chicago	46,456
12/30	L 14-16	N.Y. Jets	46,543

1990 TEAM STATISTICS

	BUCCANEERS	Opp.
Total First Downs	238	313
Rushing	83	129
Passing	142	168
Penalty	13	16
Third Down: Made/Att.	76/204	93/205
Fourth Down: Made/Att.	9/19	7/13
Total Net Yards	4475	5479
Avg. Per Game	279.7	342.4
Total Plays	911	1001
Avg. Per Play	4.9	5.5
Net Yards Rushing	1626	2223
Avg. Per Game	101.6	138.9
Total Rushes	410	496
Net Yards Passing	2849	3256
Avg. Per Game	178.1	203.5
Sacked/Yards Lost	53.433	34/204
Gross Yards	3282	3460
Att./Completions	448/245	471/263
Completion Pct.	54.7	55.8
Had Intercepted	24	25
Punts/Avg.	72/40.3	55/40.5
Net Punting Avg.	34.0	35.7
Penalties/Yards Lost	77/651	78/617
Fumbles/Ball Lost	38/19	33/17
Touchdowns	28	45
Rushing	7	20
Passing	18	22
Returns	3	3
Avg. Time of Possession	28:11	31:49

1990 INDIVIDUAL STATISTICS

Scoring	TD Run	TD Pass	TD Rt.	PAT	FG	Saf.	Tot.
Christie	0	0	0	27/27	23/27	0	96
Anderson	3	2	0	0/0	0/0	0	30
Hill	0	5	0	0/0	0/0	0	30
Carrier	0	4	0	0/0	0/0	0	24
Haddix	0	0	3	0/0	0/0	0	18
Cobb	2	0	0	0/0	0/0	0	12
Hall	0	2	0	0/0	0/0	0	12
Perkins	0	2	0	0/0	0/0	0	12
Chandler	0	1	0	0/0	0/0	0	6
Drewrey	0	1	0	0/0	0/0	0	6
Harvey	0	1	0	0/0	0/0	0	6
Peebles	0	1	0	0/0	0/0	0	6
Testaverde	1	0	0	0/0	0/0	0	6
BUCCANEERS	7	18	3	27/28	23/27	0	264
OPP.	20	22	3	43/45	18/27	0	367

Passing	Att.	Comp.	Yds.	Pct.	TD	Int.	Tkld.	Rate
Testaverde	365	203	2818	55.6	17	18	38/330	75.6
Chandler	83	42	464	50.6	1	6	15/103	41.4
BUCCANEERS	448	245	3282	54.7	18	24	53/433	69.3
OPP.	471	263	3460	55.8	22	25	34/204	72.7

Rushing	Att.	Yds.	Avg.	LG	TD
Anderson	166	646	3.9	22	3
Cobb	151	480	3.2	17	2
Testaverde	38	280	7.4	t48	1
Harvey	27	113	4.2	14	0
Chandler	13	71	5.5	18	1
Perkins	13	36	2.8	9	0
Carlson	1	0	0.0	0	0
Hill	1	0	0.0	0	0
BUCCANEERS	410	1626	4.0	t48	7
OPP.	496	2223	4.5	t47	20

Receiving	No.	Yds.	Avg.	LG	TD
Carrier	49	813	16.6	t68	4
Hill	42	641	15.3	t48	5
Cobb	39	299	7.7	17	0
Anderson	38	464	12.2	74	2
Hall	31	464	15.0	t54	2
Harvey	11	86	7.8	18	1
Pillow	8	118	14.8	23	0
Perkins	8	85	10.6	34	2
Drewrey	7	182	26.0	t89	1
Peebles	6	50	8.3	18	1
Anderson	5	77	15.4	52	0
Testaverde	1	3	3.0	3	0
BUCCANEERS	245	3282	13.4	t89	18
OPP.	263	3460	13.2	t75	22

Intercepts.	No.	Yds.	Avg.	LG	TD
Haddix	7	231	33.0	65t	3
Hamilton	5	39	7.8	27	0
Robinson	4	81	20.3	27	0
Reynolds	3	70	23.3	46	0
Everett	3	28	9.3	23	0
Rice	2	7	3.5	4	0
Moss	1	31	31.0	31	0
BUCCANEERS	25	487	19.5	t65	3
OPP.	24	346	14.4	t64	2

Punting	No.	Yds.	Avg.	In 20	LG
Royals	72	2902	40.3	8	62
BUCCANEERS	72	2902	40.3	8	62
OPP.	55	2230	40.5	16	54

Punt Returns	No.	FC	Yds.	Avg.	LG	TD
Drewrey	23	15	184	8.0	16	0
BUCCANEERS	23	15	184	8.0	16	0
OPP.	39	16	352	9.0	36	0

Kickoff Returns	No.	Yds.	Avg.	LG	TD
Peebles	18	369	20.5	55	0
Drewrey	14	244	17.4	29	0
Harvey	12	207	17.3	27	0
Cobb	11	223	20.3	45	0
Anderson	6	123	20.5	37	0
Coleman	1	9	9.0	9	0
Hall	1	0	0.0	0	0
BUCCANEERS	63	1175	18.7	55	0
OPP.	43	1036	24.1	65	0

Sacks	No.
Thomas	7.5
Randle	5.5
Murphy	4.0
Moss	3.5
Newton	3.0
White	2.5
Marve	2.0
McCants	2.0
Skow	2.0
Cannon	1.0
Davis	1.0
BUCCANEERS	34.0
OPP.	53.0

WASHINGTON

1990 TEAM RECORD

REGULAR SEASON (10-6)

Date	Result	Opponent	Att.
9/9	W 31-0	Phoenix	52,649
9/16	L 13-26	at San Francisco	64,287
9/23	W 19-15	Dallas	53,804
9/30	W 38-10	at Phoenix	49,303
10/14	L 20-24	N.Y. Giants	54,737
10/21	W 13-7	Philadelphia	53,567
10/28	L 10-21	at N.Y. Giants	75,321
11/4	W 41-38	at Detroit	69,326
11/12	L 14-28	at Philadelphia	65,857
11/18	W 31-17	New Orleans	52,573
11/22	L 17-27	at Dallas	60,355
12/2	W 42-20	Miami	53,599
12/9	W 10-9	Chicago	53,920
12/15	W 25-10	at New England	22,286
12/22	L 28-35	at Indianapolis	58,173
12/30	W 29-14	Buffalo	52,397
PLAYOFFS (1-1)			
1/5	W 20-6	at Philadelphia	65,287
1/12	L 10-28	at San Francisco	65,292

1990 TEAM STATISTICS

	REDSKINS	Opp.
Total First Downs	327	267
Rushing	117	77
Passing	193	166
Penalty	17	24
Third Down: Made/Att.	103/221	77/201
Fourth Down: Made/Att.	6/15	7/16
Total Net Yards	5562	4730
Avg. Per Game	347.6	295.6
Total Plays	1073	941
Avg. Per Play	5.2	5.0
Net Yards Rushing	2083	1587
Avg. Per Game	130.2	99.2
Total Rushes	515	382
Net Yards Passing	3479	3143
Avg. Per Game	217.4	196.4
Sacked/Yards Lost	22/132	45/340
Gross Yards	3611	3483
Att./Completions	536/301	514/281
Completion Pct.	56.2	54.7
Had Intercepted	22	21
Punts/Avg.	55/37.5	76/43.3
Net Punting Avg.	33.4	36.9
Penalties/Yards Lost	102/824	89/712
Fumbles/Ball Lost	14/6	24/12
Touchdowns	41	35
Rushing	16	8
Passing	22	21
Returns	3	6
Avg. Time of Possession	32:19	27:41

1990 INDIVIDUAL STATISTICS

Scoring	TD Run	TD Pass	TD Ret.	PAT	FG	Saf.	Tot.
Lohmiller	0	0	0	41/41	30/40	0	131
Clark	0	8	0	0/0	0/0	0	48
Byner	6	1	0	0/0	0/0	0	42
Riggs	6	0	0	0/0	0/0	0	36
Monk	0	5	0	0/0	0/0	0	30
Sanders	0	3	0	0/0	0/0	0	18
Humphries	2	0	0	0/0	0/0	0	12
Johnson	0	2	0	0/0	0/0	0	12
Bryant	0	1	0	0/0	0/0	0	6
Gouveia	0	0	1	0/0	0/0	0	6
Green	0	0	1	0/0	0/0	0	6
Hobbs	0	1	0	0/0	0/0	0	6
Mitchell	1	0	0	0/0	0/0	0	6
Rutledge	1	0	0	0/0	0/0	0	6
Walton	0	0	1	0/0	0/0	0	6
Warren	0	1	0	0/0	0/0	0	6
REDSKINS	16	22	3	41/41	30/40	2	381
OPP.	8	21	6	35/35	18/23	1	301

Passing	Att.	Comp.	Yds.	Pct.	TD	Int.	Tkld.	Rate
Rypien	304	166	2070	54.6	16	11	6/33	78.4
Humphries	156	91	1015	58.3	3	10	9/62	57.5
Rutledge	68	40	455	58.8	2	1	6/34	82.7
Mitchell	6	3	40	50.0	0	0	1/3	71.5
Byner	2	1	31	50.0	1	0	0/0	135.4
REDSKINS	536	301	3611	56.2	22	22	22/132	73.5
OPP.	514	281	3483	54.7	21	21	45/340	72.5

Rushing	Att.	Yds.	Avg.	LG	TD
Byner	297	1219	4.1	22	6
Riggs	123	475	3.9	20	6
Humphries	23	106	4.6	17	2
Dupard	19	85	4.5	11	0
Mitchell	15	81	5.4	21	1
Monk	7	59	8.4	26	0
Bryant	6	24	4.0	12	0
Sanders	4	17	4.3	12	0
Rutledge	4	12	3.0	t12	1
Rypien	15	4	0.3	8	0
Clark	1	1	1.0	1	0
Mojsiejenko	1	0	0.0	0	0
REDSKINS	515	2083	4.0	26	16
OPP.	382	1587	4.2	t48	8

Receiving	No.	Yds.	Avg.	LG	TD
Clark	75	1112	14.8	t53	8
Monk	68	770	11.3	44	5
Sanders	56	727	13.0	38	3
Byner	31	279	9.0	19	1
Bryant	26	248	9.5	37	1
Johnson	15	218	14.5	35	2
Warren	15	123	8.2	18	1
Riggs	7	60	8.6	18	0
Howard	3	36	12.0	17	0
Stanley	2	15	7.5	12	0
Mitchell	2	5	2.5	5	0
Hobbs	1	18	18.0	t18	1
REDSKINS	301	3611	12.0	t53	22
OPP.	281	3483	12.4	t80	21

Intercepts.	No.	Yds.	Avg.	LG	TD
Mayhew	7	20	2.9	15	0
Green	4	20	5.0	t18	1
Bowles	3	74	24.7	43	0
Walton	2	118	59.0	61	1
Edwards	2	33	16.5	33	0
Marshall	1	6	6.0	6	0
Johnson	1	0	0.0	0	0
Coleman	1	0	0.0	0	0
REDSKINS	21	271	12.9	61	2
OPP.	22	271	12.3	t42	5

Punting	No.	Yds.	Avg.	In 20	LG
Moojsiejenko	43	1687	39.2	17	53
Goodburn	11	377	34.3	6	48
REDSKINS	55	2064	37.5	23	53
OPP.	76	3290	43.3	21	59

Punt Returns	No.	FC	Yds.	Avg.	LG	TD
Stanley	24	8	176	7.3	32	0
Mitchell	12	4	107	8.9	26	0
Howard	10	4	99	9.9	21	0
Green	1	1	6	6.0	6	0
Thomas	1	0	0	0.0	0	0
REDSKINS	48	17	388	8.1	32	0
OPP.	30	10	205	6.8	30	0

Kickoff Returns	No.	Yds.	Avg.	LG	TD
Howard	22	427	19.4	35	0
Mitchell	18	365	20.3	37	0
Stanley	9	177	19.7	37	0
Hobbs	6	92	15.3	21	0
Dupard	2	0	0.0	0	0
Gouveia	2	23	11.5	15	0
Bowles	1	0	0.0	0	0
Middleton	1	7	7.0	7	0
Sanders	1	22	22.0	22	0
REDSKINS	62	1113	18.0	37	0
OPP.	58	1008	17.4	47	0

Sacks	No.
Stokes	7.5
Collins	6.0
Mann	5.5
Marshall	5.0
Coleman	3.0
Geathers	3.0
T. Johnson	3.0
Rocker	3.0
Williams	3.0
Koch	2.0
Bowles	1.0
Caldwell	1.0
Gouveia	1.0
Grant	1.0
REDSKINS	45.0
OPP.	22.0

AFC LEADERS

Passers	Att.	Comp.	Pct. Comp.	Yds.	Avg. Gain	TD	Pct. TD	Long	Int.	Pct. Int.	Rating
Kelly, Buff.	346	219	63.3	2829	8.18	24	6.9	71	9	2.6	101.2
Moon, Hou.	584	362	62.0	4689	8.03	33	5.7	t87	13	2.2	96.8
DeBerg, K.C.	444	258	58.1	3444	7.76	23	5.2	t90	4	0.9	96.3
Schroeder, L.A. Raiders	334	182	54.5	2849	8.53	19	5.7	t68	9	2.7	90.8
Marino, Mia.	531	306	57.6	3563	6.71	21	4.0	t69	11	2.1	82.6
Brister, Pitt.	387	223	57.6	2725	7.04	20	5.2	90	14	3.6	81.6
Elway, Den.	502	294	58.6	3526	7.02	15	3.0	66	14	2.8	78.5
O'Brien, N.Y. Jets	411	226	55.0	2855	6.95	13	3.2	t69	10	2.4	77.3
Esiason, Cin.	402	224	55.7	3031	7.54	24	6.0	53	22	5.5	77.0
George, Ind.	334	181	54.2	2152	6.44	16	4.8	75	13	3.9	73.8

Punters	No.	Yds.	Long	Avg.	TB	Blk.	Ret./Yds.	In 20	Net Avg.
Horan, Den.	58	2575	67	44.4	6	1	22/159	14	38.9
Stark, Ind.	71	3084	61	43.4	3	1	42/334	24	37.4
Johnson, Cin.	64	2705	70	42.3	8	0	36/352	12	34.3
Roby, Mia.	72	3022	62	42.0	3	0	40/397	20	35.6
Hansen, N.E.	90	3752	69	41.7	8	2	50/503	18	33.6
Donnelly, Sea.	67	2722	54	40.6	8	0	29/254	18	34.4
Prokop, Jets	59	2363	58	40.1	3	0	33/257	18	34.7
Kidd, S.D.	61	2442	59	40.0	2	1	28/131	14	36.6
Tuten, Buff.	53	2107	55	39.8	4	0	26/214	12	34.2
Wagner, Cle.	74	2879	65	38.9	2	4	41/425	13	30.9

Rushers	Att.	Yds.	Avg.	Long	TD
Thomas, Buff	271	1297	4.8	t80	11
Butts, S.D.	265	1225	4.6	52	8
Humphrey, Den.	288	1202	4.2	t37	7
Word, K.C.	204	1015	5.0	t53	4
Brooks, Cin.	195	1004	5.1	t56	5
Fenner, Sea.	215	859	4.0	36	14
Smith, Mia.	226	831	3.7	33	8
Stephens, N.E.	212	808	3.8	26	2
Okoye, K.C.	245	805	3.3	32	7
Hoge, Pitt.	203	772	3.8	t41	7

Scorers/TDs	No.	Rush	Rec.	Ret.	Pts.
Fenner, Sea.	15	14	1	0	90
Allen, L.A. Raiders	13	12	1	0	78
Thomas, Buff.	13	11	2	0	78
White, Hou.	12	8	4	0	72
Hoge, Pitt.	10	7	3	0	60
Brooks, Cin.	9	5	4	0	54
Brown, Cin.	9	0	9	0	54
Givins, Hou.	9	0	9	0	54
Smith, Mia.	9	8	1	0	54

Three tied with eight touchdowns.

Scorers/Kicking	PAT	FG	Long	Pts.
Lowery, K.C.	37/38	34/37	48	139
Norwood, Buff.	50/52	20/29	48	110
Treadwell, Den.	34/36	25/34	49	109
Johnson, Sea.	33/34	23/32	51	102
Leahy, Jets	32/32	23/26	47	101
Stoyanovich, Mia.	37/37	21/25	53	100
Anderson, Pitt.	32/32	20/25	48	92
Breech, Cin.	41/44	17/21	46	92
Jaeger, Raiders	40/42	15/20	50	85
Carney, S.D.	27/28	19/21	43	84

Receptions	No.	Yds.	Avg.	Long	TD
Jeffires, Hou.	74	1048	14.2	t87	8
Hill, Hou.	74	1019	13.8	57	8
Williams, Sea.	73	699	9.6	60	0
Givins, Hou.	72	979	13.6	t80	9
Reed, Buff.	71	945	13.3	t56	8
Bentley, Ind.	71	664	9.4	73	2
Duncan, Hou.	66	785	11.9	t37	1
Paige, K.C.	65	1021	15.7	t86	5
Miller, S.D.	63	933	14.8	t31	7
Brooks, Ind.	62	823	13.3	75	5

Punt Returners	No.	Yds.	Avg.	Long	TD
Verdin, Ind.	31	396	12.8	36	0
Woodson, Pitt.	38	398	10.5	t52	1
Warren, Sea.	28	269	9.6	39	0
Brown, L.A.	34	295	8.7	39	0
Price, Cin.	29	251	8.7	t66	1
Clark, Den.	21	159	7.6	32	0
Worthen, K.C.	25	180	7.2	37	0
McNeil, Hou.	30	172	5.7	26	0
Martin, Mia.	26	140	5.4	35	0
Fryar, N.E.	28	133	4.8	17	0

Kickoff Returners	No.	Yds.	Avg.	Long	TD
Clark, Den.	20	505	25.3	75	0
Elder, S.D.	24	571	23.8	90	0
Woodson, Pitt.	35	764	21.8	49	0
Warren, Sea.	23	478	20.8	71	0
Martin, N.E.	25	515	20.6	38	0
Holland, Raiders	32	655	20.5	87	0
McNeil, Hou.	27	551	20.4	64	0
Metcalf, Cle.	52	1052	20.2	t101	2
Jennings, Cin.	29	584	20.1	33	0
D. Smith, Buff.	32	643	20.1	38	0

Sacks	No.
Thomas, K.C.	20.0
B. Smith, Buff.	19.0
O'Neal, S.D.	13.5
Byrd, Jets	13.0
Green, Sea.	12.5
Jones, Hou.	12.5
Townsend, L.A. Raiders	12.5
Cross, Mia.	11.5
Perry, Cle.	11.5
Fletcher, Den.	11.0

Interceptions	No.	Yds.	Long	TD
Johnson, Hou.	8	100	35	1
Byrd, S.D.	7	63	24	0
Ross, K.C.	5	97	40	0
McMillian, Jets	5	92	25	0
Oliver, Mia.	5	87	35	0
Williams, Mia.	5	82	t42	1
Woodson, Pitt.	5	67	34	0

AWARDS

AP:

MVP .... Joe Montana, S.F.
Off. Player of
    the Year .... Warren Moon, Hou.
Def. Player of
    the Year .... Bruce Smith, Buff.
Off. Rookie of
    the Year .... Emmitt Smith, Dall.
Def. Rookie of.
    the Year .... Mark Carrier, Chi.
Coach of
    the Year .... Jimmy Johnson, Dall.

UPI:

AFC Off. Player of
    the Year .... Warren Moon, Hou.
AFC Def. Player of
    the Year .... Bruce Smith, Buff.
AFC Rookie of
    the Year .... Richmond Webb, Mia.
NFC Off. Player of
    the Year ...... Randall Cunningham, Phi.
NFC Def. Player of
    the Year .... Charles Haley, S.F.
NFC Rookie of
    the Year .... Mark Carrier, Chi.
AFC Coach of
    the Year .... Art Shell, Raiders
NFC Coach of
    the Year .... Jimmy Johnson, Dall.

Sporting News

Player of the Year .... Jerry Rice, S.F.
Rookie of the Year .... Richmond Webb, Mia.

Pete Rozelle Trophy

Super Bowl MVP .... Ottis Anderson, Giants

Bert Bell Trophy

Player of the Year ... Randall Cunningham, Phi.
(Maxwell Club)

AP All-Pro Team

Offense:
WR: Jerry Rice, S. F.; Andre Rison, Atl.
TE: Keith Jackson, Phi.
T: Anthony Munoz, Cin.; Jim Lachey, Wash.
G: Randall McDaniel, Minn.; Bruce Matthews, Hou.
C: Kent Hull, Buff.
QB: Joe Montana, S.F.
RB: Barry Sanders, Det.; Thurman Thomas, Buff.
Defense:
DE: Reggie White, Phi.; Bruce Smith, Buff.
DT: Michael Dean Perry, Cle.; Jerome Brown, Phi.
OLB: Derrick Thomas, K.C.; Charles Haley, S.F.
ILB: Pepper Johnson, Giants; John Offerdahl, Mia.
CB: Rod Woodson, Pitt.; Albert Lewis, K.C.
S: Joey Browner, Minn.; Ronnie Lott, S.F.
Specialists
P: Sean Landeta, Giants
K: Nick Lowery, K.C.
KR: Mel Gray, Det.

NFC LEADERS

Passers	Att.	Comp.	Pct. Comp.	Yds.	Avg. Gain	TD	Pct. TD	Long	Int.	Pct. Int.	Rating
Simms, N.Y. Giants	311	184	59.2	2284	7.34	15	4.8	t80	4	1.3	92.7
Cunningham, Phi.	465	271	58.3	3466	7.45	30	6.5	t95	13	2.8	91.6
Montana, S.F.	520	321	61.7	3944	7.58	26	5.0	t78	16	3.1	89.0
Harbaugh, Chi.	312	180	57.7	2178	6.98	10	3.2	t80	6	1.9	81.9
Peete, Det.	271	142	52.4	1974	7.28	13	4.8	t68	8	3.0	79.8
Everett, L.A. Rams	554	307	55.4	3989	7.20	23	4.2	t55	17	3.1	79.3
Miller, Atl.	388	222	57.2	2735	7.05	17	4.4	t75	14	3.6	78.7
Rypien, Wash.	304	166	54.6	2070	6.81	16	5.3	t53	11	3.6	78.4
Testaverde, T.B.	365	203	55.6	2818	7.72	17	4.7	t89	18	4.9	75.6
Majkowski, G.B.	264	150	56.8	1925	7.29	10	3.8	t76	12	4.5	73.5

Punters	No.	Yds.	Long	Avg.	TB	Blk.	Ret./Yds.	In 20	Net Avg.
Landeta, N.Y. Giants	75	3306	67	44.1	11	0	41/291	24	37.3
Saxon, Dall.	79	3413	62	43.2	8	0	43/438	20	35.6
Camarillo, Phoe.	67	2865	63	42.8	5	0	41/258	16	37.4
Barnhardt, N.O.	70	2990	65	42.7	6	1	43/302	20	36.2
Newsome, Minn.	78	3299	61	42.3	8	1	44/513	19	33.2
Feagles, Phil.	72	3026	60	42.0	3	2	37/338	20	35.5
Fulhage, Atl.	70	2913	59	41.6	4	0	39/314	15	36.0
Arnold, Det.	63	2560	59	40.6	5	0	29/233	10	35.3
Buford, Chi.	76	3073	59	40.4	7	2	39/322	22	33.5
Royals, T.B.	72	2902	62	40.3	5	0	39/352	8	34.0

Rushers	Att.	Yds.	Avg.	Long	TD
B. Sanders, Det.	255	1304	5.1	t45	13
Byner, Wash.	297	1219	4.1	22	6
Anderson, Chi.	260	1078	4.1	52	10
Cunningham, Phi.	118	942	8.0	t52	5
E. Smith, Dall.	241	937	3.9	t48	11
Johnson, Phoe.	234	926	4.0	41	5
Gary, Rams	204	808	4.0	48	14
Anderson, Giants	225	784	3.5	28	11
Walker, Minn.	184	770	4.2	t58	5
Rozier, Hou./Atl.	163	717	4.4	67	3

Scorers/TDs	No.	Rush	Rec.	Ret.	Pts.
B. Sanders, Det.	16	13	3	0	96
Gary, Rams	15	14	1	0	90
Anderson, Chi.	13	10	3	0	78
Rice, S.F.	13	0	13	0	78
Anderson, Giants	11	11	0	0	66
E. Smith, Dall.	11	11	0	0	66
Rison, Atl.	10	0	10	0	60
Walker, Minn.	9	5	4	0	54
Williams, Phi.	9	0	9	0	54

Four tied with eight touchdowns.

Scorers/Kicking	PAT	FG	Long	Pts.
Lohmiller, Wash.	41/41	30/40	56	131
Butler, Chi.	36/37	26/37	52	114
Cofer, S.F.	39/39	24/36	56	111
Ruzek, Phi.	45/48	21/29	53	108
Davis, Atl.	40/40	22/33	53	106
Jacke, G.B.	28/29	23/30	53	97
Christie, T.B.	27/27	23/27	54	96
Andersen, N.O.	29/29	21/27	52	92
Lansford, Rams	42/43	15/24	46	87
Del Greco, Phoe.	31/31	17/27	50	82

Receptions	No.	Yds.	Avg.	Long	TD
Rice, S.F.	100	1502	15.0	t64	13
Rison, Atl.	82	1208	14.7	t75	10
Byars, Phi.	81	819	10.1	54	3
Ellard, Rams	76	1294	17.0	t50	4
Clark, Wash.	75	1112	14.8	t53	8
A. Carter, Minn.	70	1008	14.4	t56	8
Monk, Wash.	68	770	11.3	44	5
Sharpe, G.B.	67	1105	16.5	t76	6
Martin, Dall.	64	732	11.4	45	0
Johnson, Det.	64	727	11.4	t44	6

Interceptions	No.	Yds.	Long	TD
Carrier, Chi.	10	39	14	0
Haddix, T.B.	7	231	t65	3
Browner, Minn.	7	103	31	1
Waymer, S.F.	7	64	24	0
Mayhew, Wash.	7	20	15	0
Walls, Giants	6	80	40	1
Stinson, Chi.	6	66	30	0

Punt Returners	No.	Yds.	Avg.	Long	TD
Bailey, Chi.	36	399	11.1	t95	1
Meggett, Giants	43	467	10.9	t68	1
Gray, Det.	34	361	10.6	39	0
Query, G.B.	32	308	9.6	25	0
Sanders, Atl.	29	250	8.6	t79	1
Sikahema, Phoe.	36	306	8.5	20	0
V. Buck, N.O.	37	305	8.2	33	0
Taylor, S.F.	26	212	8.2	30	0
Drewrey, T.B.	23	184	8.0	16	0
R. Harris, Dall./Phi.	28	214	7.6	30	0

Kickoff Returners	No.	Yds.	Avg.	Long	TD
Meggett, Giants	21	492	23.4	58	0
Gray, Det.	41	939	22.9	65	0
Wilson, G.B.	35	798	22.8	36	0
Green, Rams	25	560	22.4	t99	1
Walker, Minn.	44	966	22.0	64	0
Sanders, Atl.	39	851	21.8	50	0
Dixon, Dall.	36	736	20.4	47	0
Fenerty, N.O.	28	572	20.4	58	0
Sikahema, Phoe.	27	544	20.1	32	0
Delpino, Rams	20	389	19.5	38	0

Sacks	No.
Haley, San Francisco	16.0
White, Phi.	14.0
Greene, Rams	13.0
Dent, Chi.	12.0
Doleman, Minn.	11.0
Swilling, N.O.	11.0
Taylor, Giants	10.5
Armstrong, Chi.	10.0
Cofer, Det.	10.0
Harvey, Phoe.	10.0

TEAM RANKINGS	Off. Total	Off. Rush	Off. Pass	Def. Total	Def. Rush	Def. Pass
Atlanta	10	21	6	19	3	28
Buffalo	6	7	10	8	15	7
Chicago	13	2	28	6	7	10
Cincinnati	9	5	15	25	22	26
Cleveland	25	28	12	17	23	15
Dallas	28	23	27	10	18	2
Denver	8	14	7	20	17	21
Detroit	14	11	14	28	27	20
Green Bay	20	26	8	22	20	22
Houston	1	24	1	11	8	14
Indianapolis	27	27	16	26	24	23
Kansas City	7	10	9	16	12	17
L.A. Raiders	19	9	23	4	14	4
L.A. Rams	5	20	3	21	13	27
Miami	11	22	4	7	16	5
Minnesota	12	15	11	13	21	3
New England	26	25	20	27	28	13
New Orleans	23	16	26	15	6	19
N.Y. Giants	17	8	22	2	4	6
N.Y. Jets	16	4	21	23	19	24
Philadelphia	3	1	13	12	1	25
Phoenix	18	12	19	18	26	8
Pittsburgh	22	13	25	1	11	1
San Diego	15	3	24	5	5	9
San Francisco	2	18	2	3	2	12
Seattle	21	17	18	9	10	11
Tampa Bay	24	19	17	24	25	18
Washington	4	6	5	14	9	16

P H O T O G R A P H Y   C R E D I T S

COVER, John Biever

INTRODUCTION
1, John W. McDonough
2–3, John Biever
6, Heinz Kleutmeier
7, John W. McDonough
8, Damian Strohmeyer
9, Richard Mackson

FIRST QUARTER
10–11, John Biever
13, Al Tielemans
14–15, John Biever
16–17, Mitchell Layton
18, John Biever
19, Brian Spurlock
20, John W. McDonough
21 top, John Iacono
bottom, Al Tielemans
22, Peter Read Miller
23, John Biever
24, Al Tielemans
25, Damian Strohmeyer
26, John Biever
27 top, Al Tielemans
bottom, John W. McDonough
28, John Biever
29 top, Jonathon Daniel / Allsport USA
bottom, Tim DeFrisco / Allsport USA

SECOND QUARTER
30–31, John W. McDonough
33, Neil Liefer
34–35, Jim Turner
36–37, Ronald C. Modra
38, Janet Worne / Lexington Herald-Leader
39, Don Larson
40, Al Tielemans
41, John W. McDonough
42, Peter Read Miller
43 top, Andy Hayt
bottom, Kevin Horan
44, Al Tielemans
45 top, John Biever

bottom, Michael S. Green / Detroit News
46, John W. McDonough
47, John Biever
48, John W. McDonough
49 top Bill Baptist
bottom, Al Tielemans
50, John Biever
51 top, Mike Powell / Allsport USA
bottom, Peter Read Miller
52–57, Illustrations by Victor Juhász

THIRD QUARTER
58–59, Mike Powell / Allsport USA
61, John Biever
62, Peter Read Miller
63 top, John Biever
bottom, Heinz Kleutmeier
64, Al Tielemans
65 top, Al Tielemans
bottom, John Biever
66–67, Mickey Pfleger
68, Tony Tomsic
69, Al Tielemans
70, John W. McDonough
71 top, Al Tielemans
bottom, Caryn Levy
72, Peter Red Miller
73 top, John Biever
bottom, John Swart / Allsport USA
74, Mike Scully
75, Joe Traver
76, Al Tielemans
77 top Al Tielemans
bottom, Mitchell Layton / Duomo

FOURTH QUARTER
78–79, John W. McDonough
80–81 John Biever
82 , John Biever
83, Al Tielemans
84, John Biever
85, Robert Rosamilio / New York Daily News
86, Al Tielemans
87, Damian Strohmeyer

89, Peter Read Miller
90–91, Richard Mackson
93, John Biever
94–95, John Iacono
96 top, Damian Strohmeyer
bottom, John Biever
97, John Biever
99, John W. McDonough
100, John W. McDonough
101 top, V.J. Lovero
bottom, Richard Mackson
102–103, Damian Strohmeyer
104, Walter Iooss Jr.
105 top, Damian Strohmeyer
bottom, John Biever
106–107, Illustrations by Victor Juhász

FEATURES
108–109, Heinz Kleutmeier
110, Heinz Kleutmeier
111, Richard Mackson
112–113, Heinz Kleutmeier
114–115, Philip Saltonstall
116, Al Tielemans
117, Andy Hayt
118–119, John W. McDonough
120–121, Brad Trent
123, Michael Zagaris
125, James Schnepf
126–127, V.J. Lovero

OVERTIME
128–129, John W. McDonough
131, John Biever
132–133, John W. McDonough
134–135, John W. McDonough
136, Peter Read Miller
137 top, Al Tielemans
center, Manny Millan
bottom, John W. McDonough

APPENDIX
138–139, John W. McDonough

BACK COVER,
John W. McDonough